# 802.11WLAN Hands-On Analysis

## Unleashing the Network Monitor for Troubleshooting & Optimization

*by*

Byron W. Putman

authorHOUSE™

1663 LIBERTY DRIVE, SUITE 200
BLOOMINGTON, INDIANA 47403
(800) 839-8640
WWW.AUTHORHOUSE.COM

First published by AuthorHouse 11/30/05

ISBN: 1-4259-0735-0 (sc)

Printed in the United States of America
Bloomington, Indiana

This book is printed on acid-free paper.

# Dedication

To my Kris and all the EWGs that grace our existence.
It's a dark and descending path that we'd trod without them.

## The Author

**Byron W. Putman** is an author, lecturer and consultant with a specialty in Windows Server 2003 Active Directory and GPO design, and a passion for WLAN security, troubleshooting and frame-level analysis. He holds professional certifications from Microsoft, Cisco, CompTIA and Planet3 Wireless. Byron has written several college text books on digital and microprocessor design, networking and communications, and has also created nearly a dozen professional networking and security seminars.

# Foreword

This is a phenomenal journey through the operation of wireless networking frame flow that can be understood and used even by a WLAN novice. Having taught networking 20 years, it's refreshing to discover a hands-on book can be embraced by hard-core tech-types and newbies alike.

The synergy of the *802.11WLAN Hands-On Analysis* text coupled with the LinkFerret Network Monitor and bundled capture files lets you "experience" how a real wireless network functions, and more important, what it looks like when it breaks. This is much more revealing than passively perusing the typical sample network monitor output found in most technical analysis books.

Don Johnston
CCSI (Cisco Certified Systems Instructor)

# Preface

I've consulted and lectured in more than a dozen countries and I've developed a sense of how hard-headed, technical pragmatists prefer to learn. Technology blunders forward in an odd, erratic gait and we follow frantically grasping at odds-and-ends in never ending pursuit. Most support professionals are fire fighters, focused on extinguishing daily production blazes, leaving little time, energy and enthusiasm to gird one's loins and tackle the new stuff.

The best case learning scenario is that you and I hang out for a long weekend in a well appointed WLAN lab stocked with a variety of access points, client stations, a rack of Cisco routers, VLAN switches, RADIUS and certificate servers and a multi-tree Server 2003 forest. Throw in a spectrum analyzer and top off the whole mess with a great 802.11 Network Monitor and we'd be set. If you're ever in Palm Springs drop on by. But make sure you bring a cold case of Guinness – it's the desert after all, and this is mighty thirsty work.

The worst case learning scenario is that you purchase one of the dozens of painfully mediocre WLAN trade books that drone on like bad 70s disco music in bleak, unimaginative two-tone. Ripped verbatim from IEEE 802.11 white papers with little interpretation or enhancement, they have the nutritional equivalent of fast food.

*You should demand more.* I respect your time, attention and effort. Every detail of this book has been carefully crafted. I've sifted through dozens of reference manuals, white papers and technical presentations; done hundreds of network captures and analyzed WLAN packets in variety of production environments and I've drawn a few conclusions.

1) Knowing how much is enough is always the toughest choice. An author that buries readers in a pile of trivia is as ineffective as the author that delivers a mile-wide, inch-deep array of generalities. Throw into the mix ridiculous wireless certification exams obsessed with worthless minutia and you've got a no-win situation.
2) Access Points and WLAN client adapters are painfully cheap. Current generation, full featured APs from Cisco, Orinoco and the rest of the big boys can be had for pocket change on eBay. Putting together a solid WLAN test/development lab is easy.
3) You can't perform effective WLAN troubleshooting and performance optimization without a full-featured, promiscuous 802.11 Network Monitor and there's the rub. My first two 802.11 Network monitors had retail prices of $1,200 and $3,500 – well out of the reach of most sane individuals.

Enter the good people from Tuca Software and the LinkFerret Network Monitor. Bundled with this book is a license for a fully functional 90-day version of LinkFerret that supports

Ethernet and 802.11 promiscuous capture and analysis. Also included with the book are two dozen capture files in native LinkFerret format.

Instead of grinding through irrelevant theory and nonsense, I've written this book in a style that parallels you and me hanging out and doing some network captures. Of course it's not quite that simple, structure and theory are needed to support "hands-on" inquiry; but I've cut that to a bare-bone minimum. You'll learn best ripping through capture files, observing the ebb-and-flow of conversation-by-frame and internalizing what makes 802.11 tick and topple.

Afterward I encourage you to set up your own lab that parallels the book's examples so you and LinkFerret can get down to business and perform your own live captures and analysis. There's nothing like taking hard won knowledge out for a spin.

**Why LinkFerret?**
I support four WLAN network monitors: WildPacket's AiroPeek SE, Network Instrument's Observer, AirMagnet's Handheld and LinkFerret. Other than the purchase and maintenance price, the functional difference between WLAN network monitors is their capability to be extended with remote probes to support a large distributed architecture with centralized capture and analysis. With respect to troubleshooting the local WLAN, in the hands of a skilled practitioner all network monitors can do the job.

Most WLAN network monitor evaluation downloads have greatly reduced functionality, are limited to 15 to 30 days and won't load capture files larger than 32 frames. Link Ferret is the most inexpensive, fully featured promiscuous WLAN network monitor on the market. Tuca Software has generously created a fully functional 90-day version of LinkFerret exclusively for the readers of this book – it's not available through any other venue.

When you've mastered one WLAN network monitor learning others is a snap. It's only a matter of finding the correct configuration dialogs. Tuca Software is betting for the price and functionality that you're going to purchase the commercial version of LinkFerret. That decision is yours. However it's a safe bet that once you've experienced the power and precision that a network monitor brings to the table you'll never attempt to manage a WLAN without one.

- Cheers
Byron W. Putman
MCSE NT 3.51, NT 4.0, Windows 200
CCNA, A+, Security + and Planet3 Wireless: CWNA, CWSP, & CWAP

# Table of Contents

# Introduction

## Prerequisites

This book doesn't require any significant WLAN experience. It presumes that you have a working handle on networking fundamentals and TCP/IP. If you understand the OSI layered model and know the difference between an access point, an Ethernet switch and IP router you'll be fine.

## LinkFerret Download Registration

Register your book at http://www.dot11wlan.com/ and you'll be granted a license to download the hands-on course compressed file which includes everything you'll need for a challenging, high-quality educational experience:

1) 90-day fully functional LinkFerret Network Monitor.
2) 24 LinkFerret native-format capture files
3) Import filter file with 24 custom LinkFerret filters
4) Symbolic namespace file
5) Installation and configuration PDF file

*A supported wireless client adapter is not required to analyze capture files. LinkFerret runs under Windows 2000 and Windows XP. See http://linkferret.ws/ for system requirements*

## Take Advantage of the Hands-On Learning Experience

Although this book is great as a standalone text and study guide, coupled with a computer running LinkFerret it becomes an accelerated frame analysis learning machine. Learning 802.11 frame analysis is an intense, frustrating, demanding, minutia-orientated pursuit. But it's worth it - by the end of the book you'll emerge as a swaggering, virtuoso 802.11 frame-chaser looking for any excuse to crank-up your analyzer to tackle the most arcane and demanding challenge.

# Acknowledgements

Thanks to Dave Ebert the Director of Engineering at Tuca Software for the 90-day book edition of LinkFerret. Without it, this book couldn't be hands-on and without hands-on I probably wouldn't have written it.

Thanks to the guys at TechSmith. I can't imagine writing books and creating presentations and support material without Snag-It and Camtasia.

Lastly, thanks to the fine people at Inspiration Software for their flagship product Inspiration. A great thinking, planning and multi-layer diagram creation system. It allowed me to maintain context and consistency in every diagram.

# Chapter 1: Physical Layer Essentials

## *802.11 Concepts*:

- RF Propagation
- BSA, BSS, ESS & STA
- DS & DSS
- Ethernet & CSMA/CD
- Collision Domains
- Access Point Coordination functions: PCF, DCF & HCF
- OSI Model Review
- Ethernet II/802.3 frame formats
- L2: 802.2/LLC & SNAP
- L1: DSSS, HR/DSSS & ERP-OFDM
- PLCP-preamble and header
- Preambles: long, short & ERP
- MPDU, MSDU, PSDU and PPDU
- Spread Spectrum and Barker spreading
- Slot times
- Mixed-mode compatibility issues
- DSSS PBCC
- CCK-ODDM

## *RF Propagation*

Effective 802.11 troubleshooting and optimization requires an awareness of the nature of RF (radio frequency) energy and how it propagates in a standard office environment. A BSS (basic service set) is a logical grouping of an AP (access point) and associated STAs (wireless clients.) A BSS is often called a WLAN (wireless LAN) or simply a "wireless network."

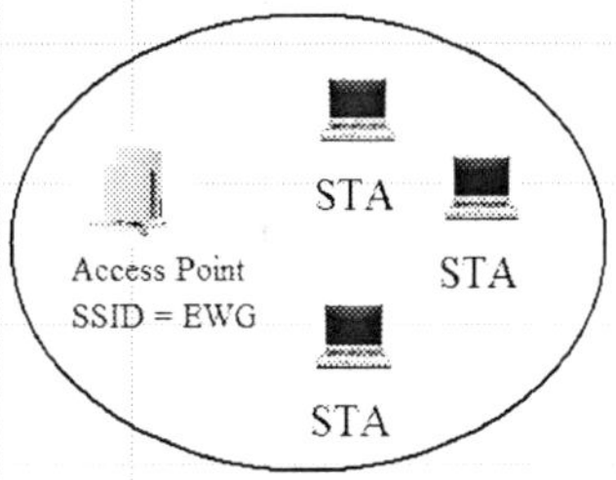

Basic Service Set

The graphic associated with the BSS definition shows an AP and several STAs all enclosed in a circle. Often the circle is interpreted as not only a symbolic boundary specifying the relationship of the STAs to the AP, but also as the signal transmission boundary, as if the circle was an impenetrable RF barrier.

Most APs and wireless client adapters have an omnidirectional antenna typified by the standard 2.2-dBi gain "rubber duck." It radiates (and receives) in a 360-degree horizontal pattern. The antenna gain is a function of compressing the vertical radiation and focusing the RF energy along the horizontal axis. Placing a dipole antenna in a vertical position and dropping a donut over it provides a fair visual representation of the radiation pattern.

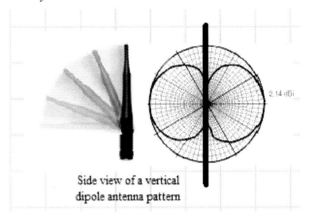

Side view of a vertical dipole antenna pattern

Ethernet signals are constrained by the cable. ***The air surrounding the WLAN is the network medium.*** The propagation of 2.4-GHz RF energy is notoriously difficult to measure and control. This diagram provides a better sense of the radiation patterns of the members of the BSS. The strength of the 2.4-GHz RF energy propagating through air is attenuated by roughly the square of the distance from the transmitter. The boundary of an RF transmission is based on:

- transmit power
- antenna gain and orientation
- physical environment
- receiver sensitivity

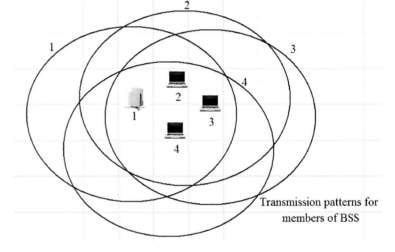

Transmission patterns for members of BSS

Unless otherwise stated, we'll assume an ideal RF environment with two major characteristics:
1. The members of the BSS have exclusive access to the medium.
   a. No other BSSs are located on the same or overlapping channels
   b. No significant RFI (radio frequency interference.)
2. Every member of the BSS ***receives every transmission*** from every other member of the BSS.

The second point is critical. We'll discover in the next chapter that 802.11 media access control (CSMA/CA) is predicated on every member of the BSS receiving every transmission. When this doesn't occur, CSMA/CA effectiveness is diminished, collision rate increases and network throughput is reduced.

## Multipath Interference

Multipath interference occurs when multiple signal paths resulting from RF reflective surfaces produce out of phase components which converge at the antenna. Multipath degrades the received signal quality. Antenna diversity uses multiple antennas to compensate for multipath; the strongest, highest quality signal from one of the antenna's is processed by the receiver. Antenna diversity is supported on many APs and wireless client adapters.

## *BSS and BSA*

The BSA (basic service area) is the air volume surrounding wireless nodes. It's the shared transmission medium for all wireless nodes in the physical area which are configured on the same or overlapping channels. Overlapped channel are addressed at the end of the chapter.

It's easy to confuse the terms BSS and BSA. ***BSS is a logical concept referring to an AP and its relationship to associated STAs. BSA is a physical concept referring to a 22-MHz range of frequencies (one channel) and a localized physical area***.

- Consider two BSSs located in the same small office. One AP is configured for channel 1 and the other for channel 6. These are non-overlapping channels so each BSS resides in a different BSA and has exclusive use of the medium's bandwidth even though there may be a physical overlap of RF signals.
- The diagram illustrates an overlapped BSA. The two APs are configured on the same or overlapping channels. Four STAs reside in the overlapped portion of the BSAs; they receive transmissions from all of the nodes in both BSSs and consequently only have access to 50% of the available bandwidth.

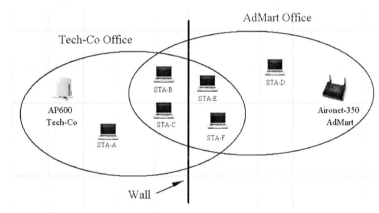

Frame corruption is proportional to the physical area and frequency overlap. ***CSMA/CA media access control is based on the concept of physical BSA, rather than a logical BSS***!

## *DS (distribution system) and DSS (distribution system service)*

A business-class AP typically has three interfaces:
- Ethernet Interface (called the portal) connects the AP to the organization's internal distribution system, the network's backbone.
  - o The Ethernet interface has a unique MAC address and usually is configured with an IP address for remote management capabilities.
- Radio Interface
  - o Enables communication between the AP and STAs
  - o ***The radio interface's MAC address is the BSS's unique hardware identifier; therefore it is called the BSSID (BSS identifier.)***
  - o The radio interface is dedicated to BSS communications so it is not configured with an IP address.
- Serial Interface
  - o The AP is usually managed via an HTTP server or a SSH v2 secure command line interface.
  - o If remote network management is not available, the AP's local serial port provides an alternative command line interface. Cisco APs have the option of employing a simple menu driven interface, or a full Cisco IOS command line environment.

SOHO-class and home-APs are also broadband routers. They usually don't have a serial configuration interface and they have a dedicated Ethernet connection for a cable or DSL-modem.

> **! Terminology Alert**: BSS is the logical name of the wireless network. BSSID is the unique MAC address of the AP's radio interface. The BSSID appears as an address in the majority of 802.11 frames.

This book is concerned with troubleshooting and optimizing 802.11 infrastructure networks.
- Infrastructure 802.11 networks are based on the functionality of an AP
  - o IBSS (independent basic service sets) are ad hoc networks, similar to peer-to-peer networks. The wireless nodes communicate without an AP. They are put-up and torn-down for short periods and can't communicate with an organization's Ethernet backbone.
  - o This book does not address ad-hoc network concepts.

In practical production computing environments ***all server resources*** are hung-off of a high-speed wired Ethernet network. The BSS is just a means by which to connect STAs to the organization's Ethernet backbone.
- Because of security and performance limitations a WLAN is not an appropriate platform from which to share network resources.
- The AP is also a translational bridge.

- o provides standard bridge functions: ***filtering, forwarding and flooding***
- o business-class APs support 802.1d, the STP (spanning tree protocol)
- o translates frame formats between 802.11 and Ethernet/802.3

The DSS (distribution system service) runs on the AP. The To-DS and From-DS bits in the MAC-header and the MAC destination address enable the DSS to determine if and where a frame should be forwarded. We spend the majority of Chapter 3 analyzing the critical function provided by the To-DS and From-DS bits.

The DSS uses a DS (distribution system) to interconnect the BSS with an Ethernet network or another BSS.

- The standard DS connects an AP's Ethernet interface to an internal backbone.
- A WDS (wireless distribution system) connects multiple BSSs via a wireless backbone. ***WDS performance is poor and is usually a solution of last-resort.***

**Terminology Note**: Cisco WDS is not a wireless distribution system. Cisco WDS (wireless domain system) is a proprietary roaming technology with centralized authentication.

## ESS (extended service set)

The ESS is a group of BSSs that share a:

- SSID (service set ID) which is the network name
- distribution system

The ESS facilitates:

- load balancing among BSSs on non-overlapping channels
- automatic fail-over when an AP goes off-line
- physically roaming between BSSs in the same ESS

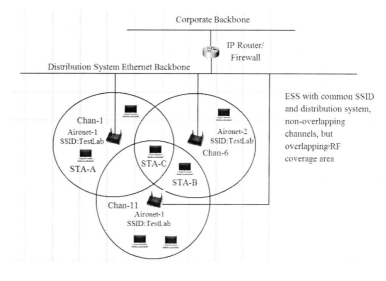

## 802.11 STA (station)

***The IEEE term "STA" (station) formally signifies any node in a WLAN, including an AP.*** In this book, "STA" refers to any computer with a wireless client adapter – an AP is always explicitly specified as an access point or AP.

**Stealth-Mode**: A notebook computer running an 802.11 network monitor application isn't a STA when it operates in stealth-mode promiscuously capturing 802.11 frames because it doesn't associate with the BSS. It's a passive device, invisible to the members of the BSS.

## CSMA/CD

CSMA/CD (carrier sense for multiple access with collision detection) is Ethernet's "listen, wait and transmit" media access control mechanism. If a collision occurs, each transmitting node generates a random back-off. After the node's back-off timer is decremented to zero it retransmits the frame.

Ethernet frame reception is unacknowledged because most lost frames are due to collisions. Ethernet nodes detect collisions, so most corrupted frames are automatically retransmitted. The high overhead of positive frame acknowledgement is not required.

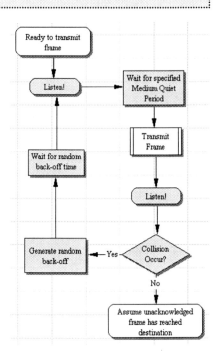

## Collision Domains and Promiscuous Capture

A collision domain is the portion of a network in which the nodes contend for access to a *shared medium*. All of the ports on an Ethernet hub share the same collision domain. All of the computers connected to the hub contend for access to the medium. An Ethernet switch is a multi-port bridge. Each switch port is an individual collision domain.

A network adapter usually processes frames with three types of MAC addresses:
- Unicast, directly addressed to that node
- Broadcast, MAC address of all 1's
- Multicast, directed to nodes that belong to a specific multicast group

Ethernet network monitor applications place the Ethernet client adapter into promiscuous mode. Promiscuous mode captures all of the frames in the collision domain and stores them in a capture buffer for analysis. A network monitor connected to a hub captures:
- All of the unicast traffic sent to every computer connected to the hub
- All of the traffic transmitted from every computer connected to the hub
- All of the broadcast traffic
- Any of the multicast traffic bound for any computer in the subnet

However, if the network monitor is connected to a switch port it captures:
- Only the unicast traffic transmitted to that adapter
- Only the traffic transmitted from that adapter

- All network broadcast traffic
- Any of the multicast traffic bound for any computer in the subnet

That's the great impediment to Ethernet network monitor capturing. Many years ago network hubs were replaced by switches. Although some switches have a virtual capture port which provides access to the aggregate switch traffic, most promiscuous capture for the purposes of troubleshooting and optimization must employ a tap. The tap is placed on the appropriate backbone and captures all of the traffic routed along the backbone. Taps are expensive and physically restrictive.

***A BSA is equivalent to an Ethernet hub*** because the 22-MHz channel and the air volume surrounding the AP and STAs is the shared medium. For 802.11 troubleshooting and optimization that's very good news and also very bad news:
- *Good News* – properly positioned, an 802.11 network monitor captures all of the traffic in the BSA! There's no need for the equivalent of an Ethernet tap.
- *Bad News* – Network monitors configured with a static WEP key decrypt BSS data frame upper-layer protocols and payload. However, most production 802.11 networks employ dynamically keyed encryption which can't be decrypted by any network monitor. To view 802.11 upper-layer protocols and payload data an Ethernet Network monitor must be used to tap the output of the AP's Ethernet portal or the DS backbone.
- *Good News* – The upper-layer protocol information is the only part of the data frame that's encrypted; 802.11 management and control frames are never encrypted; encryption is not an impediment to troubleshooting and optimizing 802.11 L1 (physical) & L2 (data-link) issues.
- *Bad News* – like a hub, the entire BSA shares the same medium and bandwidth! Bandwidth in this sense represents the total amount of information that can be transmitted over a data communications connection. Because there are only three non-overlapping channels (1, 6 and 11) a specific physical area is limited to three BSAs for load balancing.

For these reasons 802.11 network optimization is an extremely important function and the 802.11 promiscuous network monitor is the only device that provides direct access to statistical analysis of BSA traffic.

## Access Point Coordination Function: Myth and Reality

The AP provides the BSS coordination function. Although "Coordination function" implies that the AP controls the STA's access to the medium of the three coordination functions ***only DCF is widely implemented and it has no role in controlling medium access!***

IEEE 802.11 defines two channel access methods (coordination functions) called PCF and DCF. 802.11e QoS (quality of service) introduced the HCF coordination function which is a hybrid of PCF and DCF.

> **Packet versus Frame**: Packet describes any generic unit of protocol information. Usually it specifies an IP datagram used in the context of a "packet-switched network." Frame is the generic designation of an L2 protocol unit, such as an Ethernet frame or 802.11 frame. Network analyzers use the terms packet and frame interchangeably.

## PCF (point coordination function)

- *Optional* 802.11 coordination function
- According to Cisco's *Wireless Quality of Service Deployment Guide*, "**no known vendor claims to support PCF**." Furthermore, it was made obsolete by 802.11e QoS and HCF.
- PCF defines a polling mechanism by which the AP centrally controls access to the network medium during a CF (contention free) period.
- Several 802.11 control and data type frames are exclusive to PCF mode:
- PCF was intended to interoperate with DCF, the 802.11 mandatory coordination
- *The only place you'll see PCF is in certification exams*.

## DCF (distributed coordination function)

- *Mandatory* 802.11 coordination function, all APs and STAs support DCF
- Not centrally managed by the access point
- DCF uses CSMA/CA to provide medium access control
- Attempts to provide "fair access" for all nodes in the BSA.
- The negative performance impacts of DCF and CSMA/CA are the main reasons that 802.11 network optimization is such a critical issue.

## HCF (hybrid control function)

- Supported in the *proposed draft* standard P802.11e Quality of Service HCF.
- Replaces both PCF and DCF functions in QSTAs (QoS-STAs) that implement 802.11e.
- Backwards compatible with DCF legacy, non-QSTAs
- HCF provides prioritized access and full duplex communication including VoIP.

The current generation of 802.11 production networks are based on DCF and CSMA/CA media access control. The future high performance quality of service-based WLANs will usher in HCF and prioritized access.

## *Quick OSI Model Review*

802.11 is an L1/L2 technology. Layers L3 through L7 are encapsulated in the payload of 802.11 data frames. Let's review basic network layer terminology.

This book assumes a TCP/IP environment. The information produced by the upper three layers (L7 – L5) is encapsulated into an L4 TCP segment or UDP datagram. The segment or datagram is passed to L3 where it is further encapsulated into IP datagram with logical addresses. Depending on the context, this unit may be called an IP datagram, the frame's payload, or a packet. Because our focus is L1/L2 functionality, the remainder of the book calls the IP datagram the MSDU (MAC service data unit.) It's an awkward, but standard term, which appears in all IEEE 802.11 documentation and industry whitepapers.

## L2: The Data-Link Layer

The frame is independent of the L1 implementation. Ethernet II and 802.3 are the standard frame types. Ethernet II, aka DIX (Digital Intel Xerox), is the default frame type for most operating systems.

Subsequent to passing the frame to L1, the Data-Link Layer generates a 32-bit CRC (cyclic redundancy check) called the FCS (frame check sequence.) The CRC detects bit-level transmission errors, but doesn't provide an ECC (error correcting code) recovery mechanism.

The L2 frame is also called the MPDU (MAC protocol data unit.)

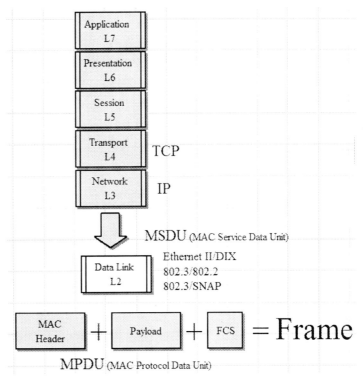

## L2 Sublayers

There are three major L2 implementations used in wired LANS:
- Ethernet II (DIX)
- 802.3 with 802.2 LLC
- 802.3 with 802.2 LLC and SNAP

We'll forego the standard network frame diagrams and use a network monitor capture to examine the details of the L2 implementations.

## Ethernet II Frame

The Ethernet II header has four simple fields:

Destination & Source Address:

48-bits: physical (MAC) address of the destination and source of the frame expressed in hexadecimal notation. If the destination or source node is on a different IP subnet, one of the MAC address is the subnet's default gateway.

Ether Type:

16-bits: Ether Type, often called the next protocol field, usually designates the L3 protocol which will process the packet. IP, (0x0800) is the most common Ether Type.

```
⊞ Physical Frame
⊟ Ethernet II (DIX) Media Access Control
   ⊟ Destination Address
      ⋯Hex Address        00-04-5A-69-9F-DA
      ⋯Group Address Bit off [xxxxxxx0 xxxxxxxx xxxxxxxx xxxxxxxx xxxxxxxx xxxxxxxx]
      ⋯Local Address Bit off [xxxxxx0x xxxxxxxx xxxxxxxx xxxxxxxx xxxxxxxx xxxxxxxx]
      ⋯Vendor Name        Linksys
   ⊟ Source Address
      ⋯Hex Address        00-0C-6E-57-52-25
      ⋯Group Address Bit off [xxxxxxx0 xxxxxxxx xxxxxxxx xxxxxxxx xxxxxxxx xxxxxxxx]
      ⋯Local Address Bit off [xxxxxx0x xxxxxxxx xxxxxxxx xxxxxxxx xxxxxxxx xxxxxxxx]
   ⊟ Ether Type
      ⋯Ether Type         0800  DOD Internet Protocol
⊞ Internet Protocol
⊞ Transmission Control Protocol
⊞ NetBios Session Service Protocol
⊞ Server Message Block Protocol
```

FCS (frame check sequence):

The 32-bit FCS field is used to verify the integrity of the received frame. Network analyzers flag frames received with CRC errors, but most don't display the actual FCS field or value. When you view a captured frame with a strange address or protocol it's usually the result of a CRC error. Network monitors do their best to interpret the information in corrupted frames but it's usually random nonsense.

## 802.3/802.2 LLC Frame

802.3 MAC fields:
Destination & Source address:
Identical to the Ethernet II address fields.

Frame Length:
16-bits: Specifies the number of bytes in the 802.2 LLC subfield and Payload.

802.2 LLC fields:
Destination & Source
SAP (Service Access Points):

```
⊞ Physical Frame
⊟ IEEE 802.3 Media Access Control
   ⊟ Destination Address
      ⋯Hex Address        01-80-C2-00-00-00
      ⋯Group Address Bit on [xxxxxxx1 xxxxxxxx xxxxxxxx xxxxxxxx xxxxxxxx xxxxxxxx]
      ⋯Local Address Bit off [xxxxxx0x xxxxxxxx xxxxxxxx xxxxxxxx xxxxxxxx xxxxxxxx]
      ⋯Logical Name(s)    [[Spanning Tree]]
   ⊟ Source Address
      ⋯Hex Address        00-20-A6-4B-6B-8E
      ⋯Group Address Bit off [xxxxxxx0 xxxxxxxx xxxxxxxx xxxxxxxx xxxxxxxx xxxxxxxx]
      ⋯Local Address Bit off [xxxxxx0x xxxxxxxx xxxxxxxx xxxxxxxx xxxxxxxx xxxxxxxx]
      ⋯Vendor Name        PROXIM
   ⋯Frame Length          38
⊟ IEEE 802.2 Logical Link Control
   ⋯Destination SAP       42 IEEE 802.1
   ⋯Source SAP            42 IEEE 802.1
   ⋯Frame Type            Command
   ⋯Unnumbered Frame      Unnumbered Information
⊞ IEEE 802.1 Spanning Tree Protocol
```

16-bits each, they provide a similar function to the Ethernet II Ether Type field. Usually both SAPs designate the same protocol. This frame specifies protocol 0x42, IEEE 802.1 Spanning Tree. The source is a Proxim AP. Most business-Class APs participate in the STP (spanning tree protocol) multicast group to ensure a loop-free bridging topology.

Control:

16 or 32-bits: Designates Type-1 or Type-2 LLC.

- Specified in this capture as Frame Type field
- Type-1 LLC is a connectionless, unreliable service. Called a UI (Unnumbered Information) with a 0x03 Control field value. ***IP only supports Type-1 LLC***.
- Type-2 LLC is a connection-oriented, reliable service, usually associated with SNA. Type 2 frames require a positive acknowledgement.

**Regarding 802.2 LLC and 802.11:**

It's important to note two points regarding ***802.11's implementation of 802.2 LLC***:

- 802.11 employs LLC Type-1, connectionless, unreliable service, required by IP.
- 802.11 positive frame acknowledgement is accomplished with an 802.11 ACK Control frame, not the 802.2 LLC Type-2 service.

802.11 with 802.2LLC/SNAP is examined in the Chapter 3.

## L1: Physical Layer

The Physical Layer prepares the logical MPDU for transmission on a specific medium by adding the appropriate preamble. L1 and L2 are independent, enabling new L1 technologies to support legacy frame types. This is especially important in the quickly evolving 802.11 standard.

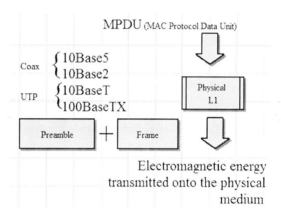

Electromagnetic energy transmitted onto the physical medium

## 802.11 Physical Layer Concepts

Network optimization requires a solid understanding of the PHY (L1) layer(s) implemented by the AP and STAs. ***This is especially critical in a mixed-mode BSS, where the AP concurrently supports 802.11b and 802.11g STAs.*** The information in this section lays the foundation for understanding 802.11 performance bottlenecks and optimization techniques.

The following descriptions specify an input and output data unit for each sublayer. The name of a data unit appears in the context of the current operation. An input operation describes receiving a frame and an output operation transmitting a frame. Receiving a frame involves each sublayer processing the appropriate header, stripping the header from the data unit and passing it up to the next sublayer. Transmitting a frame involves the process of each sublayer encapsulating the current data unit with a header and/or trailer and passing it down to the next sublayer. Understanding the precise terminology is critical for creating a foundation onto which troubleshooting and optimization skills can be bolted.

## The SDU (service data unit) and PDU (protocol data unit)

The easiest way to understand these terms is to *associate SDU with the top of a layer* and *PDU with the bottom of a layer*.

- Preparing for transmission the MAC sublayer receives a MSDU from the 802.2 LLC sublayer. It encapsulates the MSDU with a MAC-Header and FCS-Trailer to create a MPDU. The MPDU is then passed to the PLCP sublayer.
- During reception the reverse happens; the MAC sublayer receives a MPDU from the PLCP sublayer. If the frame is valid (error-free) the MPDU is processed with the information contained in the MAC-header. The MAC-header and MAC-trailer are discarded and the MSDU is passed to the 802.2 LLC-sublayer for processing.

The concept of input and output are relative to the type operation. To minimize confusion the following descriptions of the sublayers use "top" and "bottom" to visually associate the type of data unit with the sublayer. It will probably take a few chapters before you're comfortable with this odd terminology. Although it might seem trivial, consistent and precise use of terminology is critical!

## PLCP (physical layer convergence protocol) Sublayer

Top: PSDU (PLCP service data unit)
Bottom: PPDU (PLCP protocol data unit)

The PLCP sublayer is the interface between the MAC and PMD sublayers. *It appends a PHY specific preamble and header (and sometimes trailer) to the PHY-independent PSDU*.

## PMD (physical media dependent) Sublayer

Top: PPDU (PLCP protocol data unit)
Bottom: Radio Frequency energy

The PMD sublayer is the interface between a unique PHY and the media independent functions provided by 802.11.

## PSDU versus MPDU

You may have noticed that the terms MPDU and PSDU represent the same unit of information. It's all a matter of context, *when considering the MAC sublayer use the term MPDU, in the context of the PLCP sublayer use the term PSDU* – It's that simple.

## *Modulation*

Modulation imposes information onto an RF carrier. Each PHY layer uses one or more types of modulation. PHY specifications are regulated by each country's equivalent of the FCC. Troubleshooting, performance optimization and certification exam prep only require that you know the specifications, speeds and times associated with each type of modulation employed by 802.11. For those with an academic or engineering interest there are many books and whitepapers that describe the grisly details.

## *PLCP-Preamble*

The preamble enables a receiver to:
- acquire the incoming signal
- sense the carrier
- synchronize its demodulator

The PLCP-preamble has two fields:
- Sync field is a string of scrambled ones that the receiver uses to acquire the signal and synchronize the receiver's carrier tracking and timing.
- SFD (start of frame delimiter) flags the start of the PLCP-header with a fixed value of 0xf3a0.

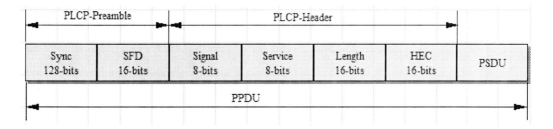

## *PLCP-Header*

The PLCP-header has four fields:
- Signal field specifies the ***type of modulation*** and the ***data rate*** in the PSDU.
  o The bit-rate of the PLCP-preamble and header are often much slower than the bit-rate of PSDU (MPDU.)
- Service field was not implemented in the original 802.11 standard
- Length field specifies the ***number of microseconds required to receive the incoming PSDU at the rate specified in the signal field***. This enables a receiver to determine the end of the frame.
- HEC (header error check, also called CRC field) is a 16-bit CRC error check used to verify the integrity of the PLCP-header.

**PHY Layer Terminology**: "Preamble" implies both the PLCP-preamble and the PLCP-header. In the next section we'll review the specifications of the long and short preambles which include both a PLCP-preamble and PLCP-header. An 802.11 frame only has one preamble, but each layer has its own header encapsulated in the frame.

## 802.11 Clause 15: DSSS PHY

***Defined in Clause 15 of the IEEE specifications, DSSS (direct sequence, spread spectrum) is the original 1- and 2-Mpbs PHY DSSS technology.***
- PLCP-Preamble and Header are transmitted at
    - 1-Mbps with DBSK (differential binary phase shift keying) modulation.
- PSDU is transmitted at
    - 1-Mbps with DBSK modulation or
    - 2-Mbps with DQPSK (differential quadrature phase shift keying) modulation.

Although it's been many years since DSSS client adapters have resided in production networks the format and speed of the 802.11b (HR/DSSS) long-preamble is identical to the original 802.11 DSSS PLCP-preamble and header.

## 802.11b Clause 18: HR/DSSS PHY

***Defined in Clause 18 of the IEEE specifications, HR (high rate) DSSS PHY is an extension of the 802.11 DSSS:***
- Supports additional PSDU bit-rates of 5.5- and 11-Mbps using CCK (complementary code keying) modulation/spreading code
- Automatically falls-back to DSSS 1- and 2-Mbps bit-rates
- Supports native HR/DSSS short preamble and DSSS long preamble
- Frequency Agility enables APs to seek the least congested channel
    - Because channel selection is a critical factor in designing overlapped BSAs for extended coverage, most APs are configured on a fixed channel.

## Barker Spreading Method

Spread spectrum transmissions spread a baseband signal (narrow band) over a large bandwidth by injecting a high-frequency signal. The transmitter uses a pseudorandom spread spectrum code to spread the transmission bandwidth. The same code is used by the receiver to remove the spread spectrum signal and reconstitute the original narrow band signal. ***Spread spectrum is resistant to many sources of RFI because the extraneous signal doesn't contain the spread spectrum key.*** The spread spectrum code is not encryption, it doesn't provide data confidentiality. It's only a means by which the true signal can be differentiated from RFI.

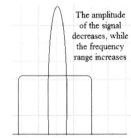

The amplitude of the signal decreases, while the frequency range increases

***Barker is the DSSS PHY spreading method which converts a narrow band signal into a 22-MHz wide spread spectrum transmission.***
- Spread spectrum signals are more resistant to RFI corruption
- Both the DSSS and HR/DSSS PHY employ the barker spreading method to transmit the Preamble and PLCP-Header.
- HR/DSSS uses CCK spreading to transmit the PSDU at 5.5- and 11-Mpbs rates.

## 802.11b Bit-Rate Support

HR/DSSS supports three classes of bit rates:
- **Basic Rate:** The DSSS *1-Mbps* rate employing DBSK (differential binary phase shift keying) modulation and Barker spreading code.
- **Extended Rate:** The DSSS *2-Mbps* rate employing DQPSK (differential quadrature phase shift keying) modulation and Barker spreading code.
- **Enhanced Rates:** The HS-DSSS *5.5- and 11-Mbps* rates supported with CCK (complementary code keying) or optional PBCC coding.

Often there is confusion between the terminology of the DSSS Basic Rate of 1-Mbps and an AP's Basic Rate Set. ***The AP's basic rates define mandatory rates that must be supported by all STAs***. This important performance configuration issue is discussed in detail in Chapter 4.

Certification exams love to twist words, so it's best to memorize the terms: basic, extended and enhanced as they relate to HR/DSSS bit-rate support.

## The Long Preamble

Long preamble is the mandatory DSSS preamble which provides backwards compatibility.
- PLCP-preamble is 144-μs
- PLCP-header is 48-μs
- Total duration is 192-μs.
- Transmitted at 1-Mbps with DBPSK modulation and Barker spreading.
- The PSDU may be transmitted at 1-, 2-, 5.5- or 11-Mpbs as specified in the signal field

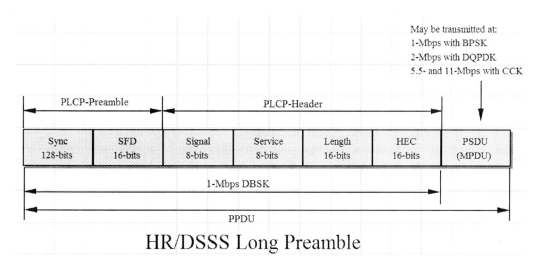

### HR/DSSS Long Preamble

## The Short Preamble

Short preamble support is optional:

- Short PLCP-preamble is 72-μs because the Sync field is reduced to 56-bits
- Short PLCP-preamble is ***transmitted at the same bit rate as the long PLCP-preamble***.
- Short PLCP-header is only 24-μs because it's ***transmitted at twice the bit rate as the long PLCP-header***; 2-Mbps with DQPSK modulation and Barker spreading.
- The total time is 96-μs, ***half the time of the long preamble***.
- Because a significant percentage of 802.11 frames are very short management and control frames, short preamble dramatically improves BSA throughput.
- The "lowest common denominator" rule applies. Any associated STA that doesn't support short preamble forces the entire BSS to fall-back to long preamble.
- Generally speaking, ***APs should be configured to prohibit long preamble support. The rare 802.11b client adapter that doesn't support short preamble needs to be upgraded – it's well worth the performance gain***.

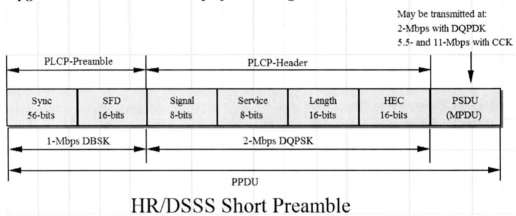

### HR/DSSS Short Preamble

## DSSS PBCC (packet binary convolutional code)

*This information is for certification exam preparation only. APs and client adapters that support DSSS PBCC are rare.*

- ***PBCC is an 802.11b optional coding scheme***
- Extends data rates to 22- and 33-Mbps
- Often associated with Texas Instruments chip sets, it never enjoyed wide adoption and was made obsolete by 802.11g.

## Slot Time

Slot time is a basic time interval that supports media access control mechanisms. It's unique to every PHY implementation. A familiar example is Ethernet's slot time which defines the round-trip transmission time of the electro-magnetic energy between nodes at the end of a maximum length cable segment. A 100BaseT network has a slot tie of approximately 512 bit times or 5.12-μs. A node defers transmission until one slot time of inactivity is sensed. The maximum length of a cable segment and CSMA/CD specifications are based on the Ethernet slot time.

Slot time is a bit trickier to define when the medium isn't bound by the constraints of a cable. The 802.11 slot time is the time required for a STA to detect the transmission from any other STA in the BSA. It's calculated by factoring in the bit-rate, maximum power transmitted from an omnidirectional antenna, a typical receiver's sensitivity and RF energy attenuation.

> **Receiver sensitivity** (rated in dBms) specifies the amount of power required for the detector to achieve a reasonable BER (bit error rate.) You'll also hear the term signal-to-noise ratio which specifies a receiver's minimum input level relative to the noise floor.

## 802.11 Slot Times:
- ***One of two basic PHY time intervals***
- Slot time and SIFS (short interframe space) are used to calculate the other interframe space intervals.
- 20-µs standard slot time is supported in DSSS and HR/DSSS (802.11b.)
- 9-µs short slot time is used in an ERP-OFDM (802.11g) native mode BSS

In the next chapter we'll see how slot times are used to determine the basic timing parameters in a WLAN and how these time intervals are applied to CSMA/CA.

## 802.11g Clause 19: ERP PHY

***Defined in Clause 19 of the IEEE specifications*** ERP (extended rate PHY) is a further extension of DSS Clause 15 and HR/DSSS Clause 18 PHYs in the 2.4 GHz ISM band.

802.11a and 802.11g support the OFDM (orthogonal frequency division multiplexing) PHY. ***Since the brilliant, but largely ignored 802.11a standard has sadly become the Beta-Max technology of the WLAN world, we'll only examine 802.11g in this book***. The best approach to 802.11g is to consider that:
- ERP describes the format of the preamble and PLCP-header
- OFDM describes the PSDU modulation/coding method.

## OFDM Modulation and Bit Rates
- BPSK (binary phase shift keying) 6- and 9-Mbps
- QPSK (quadrature phase shift keying) 12- and 18-Mbps
- 16-QAM (quadrature amplitude modulation) 24- and 36-Mbps
- 64-QAM (quadrature amplitude modulation) 48- and 54-Mbps

## IEEE and WiFi

Many people confuse the IEEE and WiFi standards. IEEE is the international standards organization responsible for 802.11. Many of the 802.11 implementation details are optional, or rather sketchy and open to interpretation. The WiFi Alliance is an international industry association of WLAN component manufacturers whose products are based on the

IEEE 802.11 specification. WiFi components are certified to interoperate. *WiFi certification is based on a superset of 802.11 specifications*.

## 802.11g ERP-OFDM PHY Features

- Data rates to 54-Mbps
- Supports three preambles:
    - DSSS long preamble
    - HR/DSSS short preamble
    - Native ERP preamble
- Backwards compatible with DSSS and HR/DSSS PHY
- Mandatory rates are 6-, 12- and 24-Mbps.
- Optional rates are 9-, 18-, 36-, 48- and 54-Mbps.
- *54-Mbps support is mandatory for WiFi certification*.

## 802.11g Short Slot Time Support

- 20-μs slot time for backwards compatibility
- 9-μs short slot time

## ERP Preamble and PLCP-Header

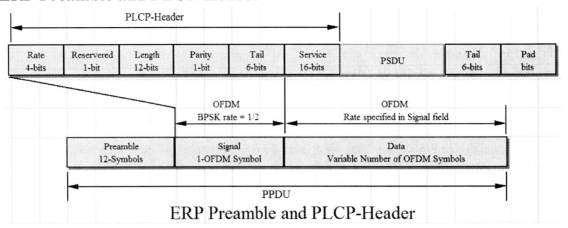

ERP Preamble and PLCP-Header

## 802.11g Preamble and PLCP-Header Transmission Rates

- The preamble is 16-μs and transmitted at 6-Mbps
- The PLCP-header is 4-μs and transmitted at 6-Mbps with BPSK-OFDM modulation
- The PSDU may be transmitted at 6- to 54-Mbps

## Mixed mode compatibility Issues

An 802.11g STA has backward support for the DSSS and HR/DSSS PHYs:

- Non-ERP STAs interpret the ERP preamble and header as wide-band noise, not as a busy channel!
- Without additional methods of reserving the medium, non-ERP STAs simultaneously transmit with ERP nodes and the resulting collisions corrupt the transmissions of all parties.

***802.11a was never widely implemented because it uses a different frequency range than 802.11b and is not backwards compatible with DSSS and HR/DSSS PHYs.*** 802.11g uses the same ISM channels as 802.11b and is capable of falling back and emulating an 802.11b STA. To an 802.11b AP an 802.11g client adapter appears to be a standard 802.11b STA.

The important issue is, "how does an 802.11bg mixed-mode BSS enable 802.11g STAs to operate in ERP-OFDM mode without having transmissions constantly corrupted by 802.11b STAs?" Several HR/DSSS and ERP-OFDM coexistence methods have been proposed.

Two performance issues arise in a mixed mode BSS:
- An 802.11b STA transmitting one 1,500 byte frame with a short-preamble at 11-Mbps takes roughly ***five times the bandwidth*** of an 802.11g STA transmitting in native ERP-OFDM mode at 54-Mbps. Because of preamble length and bit-rate limitations, 802.11b STAs consume a disproportional percentage of the BSA bandwidth.
- At the cost of overhead and efficiency 802.11g STAs may modify their native ERP-OFDM transmissions to be recognized by 802.11b STAs.
- While not always practical, ***technically the best solution is to upgrade 802.11b STAs and configure the BSS to only operate in ERP-OFDM only-mode with a high basic rate set***.

## DSSS-OFDM Transmission (also called CCK-OFDM)

The strategy behind DSSS-OFDM is simple, use a PLCP-preamble/header that's recognized by non-ERP STAs and then transmit the PSDU with OFDM modulation at standard 802.11g rates:
- DSSS-OFDM is an ***optional feature*** that supports 802.11 b & g coexistence by transmitting the PLCP-preamble/header with DSSS, and the PSDU with OFDM.
- Enables 802.11b STAs to read the length field in the CCK PLCP-Header and defer the medium to minimize collisions.
- The PSDU is transmitted with OFDM. ***802.11b STAs can't read the MAC header and implement all of the features of CSMA/CA.*** This topic is examined in the next chapter.
- Has significant technical issues regarding the transition from the single carrier DSSS mode to the multi-carrier OFDM mode.
- Protects the current frame, but not the subsequent acknowledgement.
- Supports long and short preambles as specified in 802.11b.
- ***Currently CCK-OFDM (DSSS-OFDM) is not supported on any commercial AP or wireless client adapter.***
- CTS-to-Self is a much simpler mechanism that provides the same throughput as CCK-OFDM, with more comprehensive protection and is supported on all 802.11g APs. CTS-to-Self is examined in the next chapter.

| Sync 128-bits | SFD 16-bits | Signal 8-bits | Service 8-bits | Length 16-bits | HEC 16-bits |
|---|---|---|---|---|---|

PLCP-Preamble / PLCP-Header

1-Mbps DBSK

HR/DSSS Long Preamble

| Sync 56-bits | SFD 16-bits | Signal 8-bits | Service 8-bits | Length 16-bits | HEC 16-bits |
|---|---|---|---|---|---|

PLCP-Preamble / PLCP-Header

1-Mbps DBSK / 2-Mbps DQPSK

HR/DSSS Short Preamble

PSDU - OFDM Modulation

| Long-Sync 8-μs | Signal Field 4-μs | Data | Signal Ext 6-μs |
|---|---|---|---|

6-Mbps / 6 - 54-Mbps

**DSSS-OFDM PPDU with Long and Short preamble/PLCP-Headers
(also called CCK-OFDM)**

## The Index and Chapter Reviews

The index is a combination index and glossary. Instead of presenting typical sterile technical glossary definitions, the index points the reader to a location where the term may be viewed in a representative context.

Each chapter has an intense, highly compressed chapter review. The chapter reviews are not indexed because that might result in terms not appearing in the richest context. The best way to find a topic which appears in a chapter review is to refer to the table of contents where each review topic is listed at a major subheading.

# Chapter 1 Review

## RF Propagation

The typical BSS diagram uses a circle as a symbolic boundary to specify the relationship of the STAs to the AP. The physical boundary of RF transmissions from each AP and STA is a function of:

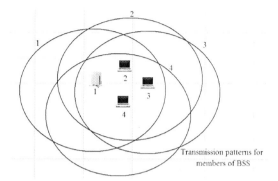

Transmission patterns for members of BSS

- configured transmit power
- antenna gain and orientation
- physical environment
- receiver sensitivity

Also remember that RF energy is attenuated by the square of the distance from the transmitter.

## The Ideal BSS

- The members of the BSS have exclusive access to the medium and bandwidth.
- Every member of the BSS receives every transmission in the BSS

## BSS and BSA

- BSS is a *logical concept* referring to an AP and its relationship to associated STAs.
- BSA is a *physical concept* referring to a specific channel and a localized physical area.
- *CSMA/CA is based on the concept of physical BSA!*

## Server Resources

- Server resources are hung-off of a high-speed wired Ethernet network
  - Security and performance issues prohibit sharing WLAN-based resources

## DS (distribution system)

- The DSS (distribution system service) runs on the AP and uses a DS (distribution system) to interconnect a BSS with an Ethernet network or another BSS.
  - A conventional DS connects an AP's portal to the Ethernet backbone.
  - WDS (Wireless Distribution System) connects BSSs via a wireless backbone.

## ESS (extended service set)

- Have a common SSID and distribution system
- Facilitates: load balancing on non-overlapping channels, automatic failure-over when an AP goes off-line, roaming between BSSs in the same ESS

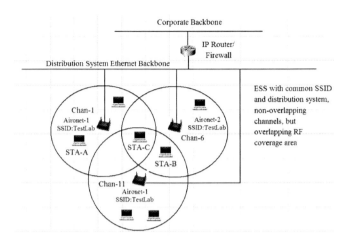

## 802.11 STA (station)

- Formally signifies every node in a WLAN, including an AP. In common usage STA usually designates a computer with a wireless adapter that is associated with a BSS.

## CSMA/CD

- Ethernet's "listen, wait and transmit and listen for collisions" media access control. If a collision occurs, each node generates a random back-off.
- Ethernet frame reception is unacknowledged.
  - Nodes detect collisions and corrupted frames are automatically retransmitted.
  - TCP at L4 provides a reliable delivery service

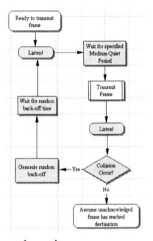

## Collision Domains

- The portion of a network in which the nodes contend for access to a **shared medium**.
  - All of the ports on an Ethernet hub are a single collision domain.
  - Each switch port is its own collision domain.

## Ethernet Network Monitor Promiscuous Capture

- Captures all frames in the collision domain
- Connected to a switch port captures only the unicast traffic transmitted to that adapter and all the network broadcast traffic
- Requires an Ethernet tap placed on the appropriate backbone
  - Taps are expensive and restrictive.

## WLAN Promiscuous Capture

- The BSA is a single collision domain!
- **Good News:** an 802.11 network monitor captures all of the BSA traffic!
- **Bad News:** WPA/802.11i encryption can't be decrypted by any network monitor.

- **Good News:** 802.11 management and control frames are never encrypted
- **Bad News:** the entire BSA shares the same medium and same shared bandwidth!

## Access Point Coordination Function

- *PCF (point coordination function)*
  - **Optional** 802.11 coordination function which **has never been implemented** in a production AP.
  - Defines a polling mechanism by which the AP centrally controls access to the network medium during a CF (contention free) period
- *DCF (distributed coordination function)*
  - **Mandatory** 802.11 coordination function, all APs and STAs support DCF
  - Uses CSMA/CA to provide medium access to provide "fair access" for all nodes in the BSA
- *HCF (Hybrid control function)*
  - Supported in P802.11e Quality of Service draft proposal.
  - Replaces PCF and DCF functions in QSTAs (QoS-STAs)
  - Backwards compatible with DCF legacy, non-QSTAs
  - Provides prioritized access and full duplex communication, including voice.

## Packet versus Frame

- "Packet" formally it specifies an L3 IP datagram
- "Frame" is an L2 protocol unit which contains an upper-layer payload
  - 802.11 management and control don't have an upper-layer protocol
  - There are two context sensitive terms used to describe 802.11 frames

## L2: The Data-Link Layer

- Independent of the L1 physical implementation.
- The FCS (frame check sequence) detects bit-level transmission errors
- An 802.11 frame is also called a MPDU

## L2 Sublayers

- Wired LANS have three major L2 implementations:
  - Ethernet II (DIX)
  - 802.3 with 802.2 LLC
    - 802.3 with 802.2 LLC and SNAP

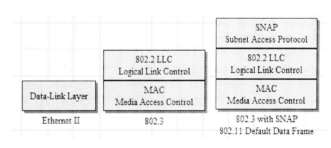

## Ethernet II Frame

- <u>Destination &
Source Address</u> 48-
bits: physical
(MAC) address
expressed in
hexadecimal
notation.

```
⊞ Physical Frame
⊟ Ethernet II (DIX) Media Access Control
   ⊟ Destination Address
      ⊢ Hex Address        00-04-5A-69-9F-DA
      ├ Group Address Bit off [XXXXXXX0 XXXXXXXX XXXXXXXX XXXXXXXX XXXXXXXX XXXXXXXX]
      ├ Local Address Bit off [XXXXXX0X XXXXXXXX XXXXXXXX XXXXXXXX XXXXXXXX XXXXXXXX]
      └ Vendor Name         Linksys
   ⊟ Source Address
      ⊢ Hex Address        00-0C-6E-57-52-25
      ├ Group Address Bit off [XXXXXXX0 XXXXXXXX XXXXXXXX XXXXXXXX XXXXXXXX XXXXXXXX]
      └ Local Address Bit off [XXXXXX0X XXXXXXXX XXXXXXXX XXXXXXXX XXXXXXXX XXXXXXXX]
   ⊟ Ether Type
      └ Ether Type          0800   DOD Internet Protocol
⊞ Internet Protocol
⊞ Transmission Control Protocol
⊞ NetBios Session Service Protocol
⊞ Server Message Block Protocol
```

- <u>Ether Type</u> is the
next protocol field
- <u>FCS (frame check sequence)</u> used to verify the integrity of the received frame.

## 802.3/802.2 LLC Frame

- <u>Destination & Source
address</u> are identical
to the Ethernet II
address fields.

```
⊞ Physical Frame
⊟ IEEE 802.3 Media Access Control
   ⊟ Destination Address
      ⊢ Hex Address        01-80-C2-00-00-00
      ├ Group Address Bit on  [XXXXXXX1 XXXXXXXX XXXXXXXX XXXXXXXX XXXXXXXX XXXXXXXX]
      ├ Local Address Bit off [XXXXXX0X XXXXXXXX XXXXXXXX XXXXXXXX XXXXXXXX XXXXXXXX]
      └ Logical Name(s)    [[Spanning Tree]]
   ⊟ Source Address
      ⊢ Hex Address        00-20-A6-4B-6B-8E
      ├ Group Address Bit off [XXXXXXX0 XXXXXXXX XXXXXXXX XXXXXXXX XXXXXXXX XXXXXXXX]
      ├ Local Address Bit off [XXXXXX0X XXXXXXXX XXXXXXXX XXXXXXXX XXXXXXXX XXXXXXXX]
      └ Vendor Name         PROXIM
   └ Frame Length        38
⊟ IEEE 802.2 Logical Link Control
   ⊢ Destination SAP     42 IEEE 802.1
   ├ Source SAP          42 IEEE 802.1
   ├ Frame Type          Command
   └ Unnumbered Frame    Unnumbered Information
⊞ IEEE 802.1 Spanning Tree Protocol
```

- <u>Frame Length</u> the
number of bytes in
the 802.2 LLC
subfield and Payload.
- 802.2 LLC fields:
  - <u>Destination &
Source SAP (Service Access Points)</u> provide a similar function to the Ethernet
II Ether Type field.
  - <u>Control</u> designates Type-1 or Type-2 LLC.
    - Specified in this capture as Frame Type field
    - Type-1 LLC is a connectionless, unreliable service. Called a UI
(Unnumbered Information) only LLC type supported by IP.
    - Type-2 LLC is a connection-oriented, reliable service, associated with
SNA. Type 2 frames must be acknowledged by the receiver.

## L1: Physical Layer

- Prepares the logical MPDU for transmission.
  - independent from L2 frame format
  - enables new L1 technologies to support legacy frame types

## The SDU (service data unit) and PDU (protocol data unit)

- SDU associated with the top of a layer
- PDU with the bottom of a layer:
  - <u>Example</u>: during a transmit operation, the input of the L2 MAC-sublayer is
a MSDU and the output is the MDPU.

# PLCP (physical layer convergence protocol) Sublayer

- <u>Top</u>: PSDU (PLCP service data unit)
- <u>Bottom</u>: PPDU (PLCP protocol data unit)
- The PLCP sublayer is the interface between the MAC and PMD sublayers.
    - Appends PHY specific preamble and header to the physical-independent PSDU.

# PMD (physical media dependent) Sublayer

- <u>Top</u>: PPDU (PLCP protocol data unit)
- <u>Bottom</u>: RF energy
- Interface between a unique PHY and the media independent PLCP functions

# PSDU versus MPDU

- MPDU and PSDU represent the same unit
    - when considering the MAC sublayer use MPDU
    - in the context of the PLCP sublayer use PSDU

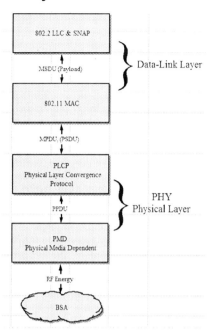

# PLCP-Preamble

- The preamble enables a receiver to acquire the incoming signal, sense the carrier and synchronize its demodulator.
- Sync field is a string of scrambled ones that the receiver uses to acquire the signal, and synchronize the receiver's carrier tracking and timing.
- SFD (start of frame delimiter) flags the start of the PPDU with a fixed value 0xf3a0.

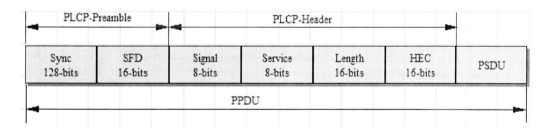

# PLCP-Header

- Signal field specifies the type of modulation in the PSDU and the data rate.
- Service field is not implemented in the original 802.11 standard
- Length field specifies the number of microseconds required to receive the incoming PSDU which enables the receiver to determine when the end of frame.
- HEC (header error check, also called CRC field) is 16-bit CRC error check that verifies the integrity of the PLCP-header.

## 802.11 DSSS PHY

- DSSS (direction sequence, spread spectrum) is the original 1- and 2-Mpbs DSSS technology.
- PLCP-Preamble and Header are transmitted at
    - 1-Mbps with DBSK (differential binary phase shift keying) modulation.
- PSDU is transmitted at
    - 1-Mbps with DBSK modulation
    - 2-Mbps with DQPSK (differential quadrature phase shift keying) modulation.

## Slot Time

- 802.11 slot time is the time to detect the transmission from any other STA in the BSA.
    - 20-μs standard slot time
    - 9-μs short slot time supported in 802.11g native mode
    - if one associated STA doesn't support short slot time, BSS falls back to long slot time

## 802.11b HR/DSSS PHY

- HS (high speed) DSSS is a PHY layer extension of 802.11:
    - Supports PSDU bit rates of 5.5- and 11-Mbps with CCK (complementary code keying) modulation/spreading code.
    - Provides ARS (automatic rate shifting) to fall-back to 1- and 2-Mbps data rates
    - Supports long and short preambles.
    - Frequency agility enables APs to seek the least congested channel.

## Barker Spreading and Spread Spectrum Transmissions

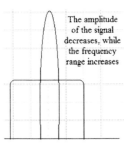

The amplitude of the signal decreases, while the frequency range increases

- Spread spectrum transmissions spread a baseband signal (narrow band) over a large bandwidth
- Employs a pseudorandom spread spectrum code to spread the transmission bandwidth.
- Resistant to many sources of RFI.
- Barker is the DSSS PHY spreading method
- Both the DSSS and HS-DSSS PHY layers employ the barker spreading method to transmit the Preamble and PLCP-Header.
- CCK is the HS-DSSS at 5.5- and 11-Mpbs spreading method.

## 802.11b Bit Rate Support

- **Basic Rate:** The DSSS 1-Mbps rate employing DBSK (differential binary phase shift keying) modulation and Barker spreading code.
- **Extended Rate:** The DSSS 2-Mbps rate employing DQPSK (differential quadrature phase shift keying) modulation and Barker spreading code.

- **Enhanced Rates:** The HS-DSSS 5.5- and 11-Mbps rates supported with CCK (complementary code keying) or optional PBCC coding.

## The Long Preamble

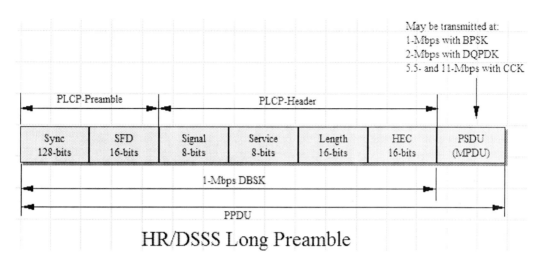

HR/DSSS Long Preamble

- Mandatory preamble provides backwards compatibility with DSSS.
    - PLCP-preamble is 144-μs
    - PLCP-header is 48-μs
    - Total duration is 192-μs.
- Transmitted at 1-Mbps with DBPSK modulation and Barker spreading.
- The PSDU may be transmitted at 1-, 2-, 5.5- or 11-Mpbs as specified in the header's signal field.

## The Short Preamble

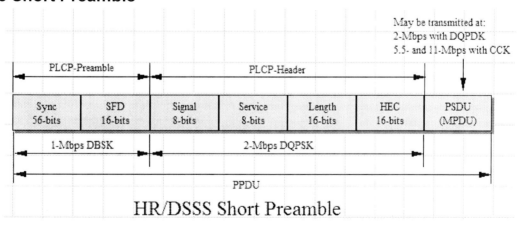

HR/DSSS Short Preamble

- 802.11b Optional preamble
    - PLCP-preamble is 72-μs (transmitted at the same bit-rate as the long preamble.)
    - PLCP-header is 24-μs (2-Mbps with DQPSK modulation and Barker spreading.)
    - The total time is 96-μs (half the duration of long preamble.)

- If a STA without short preamble support associates, the entire BSS falls-back to long preamble.

## DSSS PBCC (packet binary convolutional code)

- ***Optional*** 802.11b coding scheme, rarely supported on APs or client adapters
- Supports 22- and 33-Mbps data rates
- Made obsolete with the introduction of 802.11g.

## ERP-OFDM

- ERP-OFDM (extended rate physical – orthogonal frequency division multiplexing)
  - supported by 802.11a and 802.11g
  - ERP describes the format of the preamble and PLCP-header
  - OFDM describes the PSDU modulation/coding method.
- Modulation and Bit Rates
  - BPSK (binary phase shift keying) at 6- and 9-Mbps
  - QPSK (quadrature phase shift keying) at 12- and 18-Mbps
  - 16-QAM (quadrature amplitude modulation) at 24- and 36-Mbps
  - 64-QAM (quadrature amplitude modulation) at 48- and 54-Mbps

## Short Slot Time

- 802.11g Support supports two slot times:
  - 20-µs slot time for backwards compatibility
  - 9-µs short slot time in native 802.11g BSS-only

## ERP Preamble and PLCP-Header

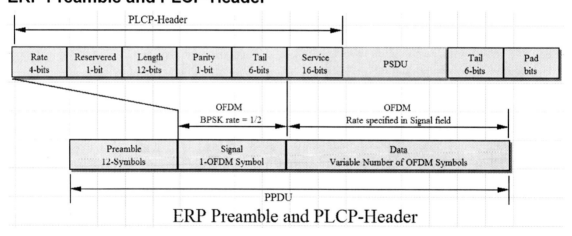

ERP Preamble and PLCP-Header

- Native mode ERP Preamble and PLCP-Header
- The PLCP-preamble is 16-µs and transmitted at 6-Mbps
- The PLCP-header is 4-µs and transmitted at 6-Mbps with BPSK-OFDM modulation
- The PSDU may be transmitted at 6- to 54-Mbps

## Mixed mode compatibility Issues

- Non-ERP STAs interpret the ERP preamble and PLCP-header as wide-band noise
- To minimize 802.11b and 802.11g collisions, mixed mode BSSs require additional methods of medium reservation,

## Mixed Mode Performance Issues

- An 802.11b STA transmitting a 1,500 byte frame with short-preamble at 11-Mbps takes roughly *eight times the bandwidth* of an 802.11g STA transmitting in native ERP-OFDM mode at 54-Mbps.
- 802.11g STAs modify ERP-OFDM transmissions to be recognized by 802.11b STAs.
- Technically the best solution is to upgrade all 802.11b STAs and configure:
    - the BSS to operate in ERP-OFDM native mode only
    - the highest BSS basic rates

## CCK-OFDM Transmission

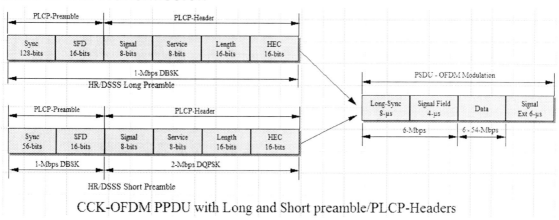

CCK-OFDM PPDU with Long and Short preamble/PLCP-Headers

- optional feature of 802.11g
- also called DSSS-OFDM
- Has a PLCP-preamble/header which is recognized by non-ERP STAs
    - the PSDU is transmitted with OFDM modulation at standard 802.11g rates
- Non-ERP STAs read the length field in the CCK PLCP-Header and defer the medium
    - protects the current frame, but not acknowledgement
- Supports long and short preambles
- **CCK-OFDM (DSSS-OFDM) is not currently supported on any commercial AP**

# Chapter 2: Sharing the Air with CSMA/CA

## *802.11 Concepts:*

- CSMA/CA and the need for acknowledgements
- Interframe Spaces: SIFS, PIFS, DIFS & EIFS
- Case #1: CSMA: Medium is free, listen for one DIFS and then transmit
- Physical Carrier Sense and CCA
- Case #2: Collision Avoidance: Medium is busy, back-off timer is implemented
- Contention Window & Back-off Timer
- Case #3: The successful reception of an ACK
- Case #4: CRC error or unacknowledged transmission
- Case #5: Virtual carrier
- Duration field and the NAV
- ACK duration and fragmented frames exception
- CTS-to-Self and 802.11bg mixed-mode
- ERP Information Element
- RTS/CTS
- 802.11 PPDU Overview
- Frame Control Byte-0 and Frame Types/Subtypes
- Bit positions and filter issues
- ISM overlap and network monitor capture confusion

## *Sharing the Air*

As specified in the last chapter, 802.11 PCF mode has never been implemented in any commercial product. Until 802.11e and HCF usher in a new generation of QoS-based functionality, ***DCF and CSMA/CA is the only game in town***.

Ethernet's CSMA/CD is simple because the nodes detect collisions, generate random back-offs and retransmit the corrupted frames. The electro-magnetic energy is constrained to a well-controlled, consistent medium with an easily controlled length.

Wireless adapters use the same antenna for transmission and reception. They're half-duplex devices because they can't simultaneously transmit and receive. Imagine that you're shouting at the top of your lungs and while someone access the room is whispering. That describes the relative signal strengths that simultaneously exist in the STA's antenna. ***Because half-duplex radios can't sense other nodes simultaneously transmitting, they don't detect collisions***. 802.11 compensates for a wireless client adapter's inability to detect collisions with CSMA/CA medium access control and positive acknowledgements.

## CSMA/CA

- CSMA/CA (carrier sense for multiple access with collision avoidance) is much more complex than CSMA/CD
- Provides three mechanisms:
    1) physical carrier sense
    2) dynamically CW (contention window) with exponential back-off algorithm
    3) virtual carrier sense

## Received Frame Acknowledgment

An ACK is a positive acknowledgement that signifies the reception of a valid frame.

- Unicast frames must be acknowledged by the receiver with an ACK frame.
- Broadcast frames transmitted by a STA are acknowledged by the AP and then processed by the DSS.
- If an ACK isn't received within the ACK Timeout interval, then the original frame must be retransmitted.

## The Need for Frame Prioritization

There are many reasons why a transmitted frame may not be successfully received and acknowledged. The most obvious is when frame corruption occurs because multiple simultaneous nodes transmit:

1) Properly observing CSMA/CA procedures a STA transmits a frame with the expectation of receiving a timely acknowledgement.
2) Without the ability to detect collisions, the absence of an ACK implies that the frame was corrupted by a collision.
    a. Although RFI or multipath issues may be the true cause of the frame loss, *the transmitter always assumes an unacknowledged frame is due to a collision*.
3) After the ACK Timeout is exceeded each transmitter contends for the medium and retransmits the original frame with the frame's Retry-bit set.

*Perhaps the BSA is so saturated that the receiver's ACK was corrupted in a collision with another STA's transmission and each retransmission only fuels the collision chain-reaction!* This would eventually culminate in a transmission storm in which every frame is retransmitted because either the transmitter's original frame, subsequent retransmissions, or every acknowledgement is corrupted by a collision.

**Three CSMA/CA techniques reduce the possibility of that scenario**:

- The collision avoidance mechanism is dynamically modified after each retransmission.
    o An exponentially increasing CW (contention window) reduces the probability of collisions.
- A physical carrier independent, virtual carrier mechanism by which the original frame reserves the medium for the subsequent ACK.
    o That's the function of the duration field in the MAC-header and the NAV (network allocation vector) timer which we examine in the next section.

- **ACK frames have priority over all other traffic!** The receiver circumvents the normal CSMA/CA mechanism and immediately transmits an ACK.
  - IFS (InterFrame Spaces) provide a simple 802.11 frame prioritization mechanism.

## 802.11 IFS (InterFrame Spaces)

CSMA/CA is a "best effort" or 'fair access" media access control protocol. However, certain frames must be given priority over all other traffic. **Interframe spaces are sometimes called arbitration interframe spaces because they provide a frame prioritization mechanism.**

In the introductory chapter we examined the concept of slot time. Slot time is specific to a PHY implementation. HR/DSSS has a slot time of 20-µs and the native-mode ERP-OFDM slot time is 9-µs. Slot time roughly corresponds to the sum of:

- CCA (clear channel assessment) time - the time to acquire the carrier
- Receiver to transmitter turnaround time
- RF energy propagation delay

### SIFS (Short InterFrame space)

**ACK and CTS control frames are high-priority frames.** The node waits only one SIFS before transmitting the ACK or CTS response. The SIFS provides time for the receiver to:

- Verify the frame's integrity
- Turn-around the receiver to transmitter mode
- Create an ACK or CTS PPDU

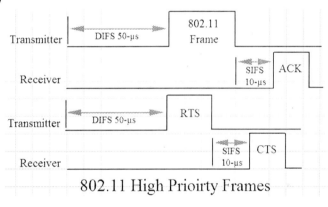

802.11 High Priority Frames

**The SIFS is 10-µs and independent of the BSS's slot time.**

### PIFS (Point coordination function InterFrame space)

In spoken conversation they're called "priority interface spaces."
The PIFS is associated with the mythical CF (contention free) PCF mode.

- **PIFS** = SIFS + Slot Time = **30-µs (standard slot time)**
- **PIFS** = SIFS + Slot Time = **19-µs (short slot time)**

## DIFS (Distributed coordination function InterFrame Space)

In spoken conversation they're called "distributed interface spaces." *The DIFS is associated with the mandatory DCF.* With the exception of ACK and CTS frames, CSMA/CA mandates that the medium must be idle for a minimum of one DIFS before transmission.

- DIFS = SIFS + (2 * slot time) = 10-µs + (2 * 20-µs) = *50-µs (standard slot time)*
- DIFS = SIFS + (2 * slot time) = 10-µs + (2 * 9-µs) = *28-µs (short slot time)*

## EIFS (Extended InterFrame Space)

This is the most misunderstood and least documented IFS. EIFS is *employed when a frame is not acknowledged.* In the absence of an ACK, the medium must be free for one EIFS. *The EIFS prevents STAs from colliding with a frame that is associated with the current incomplete dialog – either a retransmission of the original frame or its subsequent ACK:*

- If a transmitter doesn't receive an ACK within the ACK Timeout interval, the collision avoidance CW is doubled
- The non-transmitting nodes defer the medium for an entire EIFS or until a valid frame is received that concludes the dialog.

The EIFS is equivalent to the time it takes to transmit eight ACK frames, a SIFS and a DIFS:

$$EIFS = (8 *ACK) + PLCP\text{-}Preamble + PLCP\text{-}Header + DIFS$$

This is why lost or corrupted frames have such an impact on BSA throughput. In the next section we'll see how the DIFS and EIFS are employed by CSMA/CA.

> **! Exam Alert**: When you see EIFS think CSMA/CA *Error Recovery Mode.*

## Physical CS (carrier sense) and CCA (clear channel assessment)

CCA describes the physical sensing of the medium's state:

- Physical CS senses uses a combination of RF carrier detect and ED (energy detect) to enable a receiver to acquire the PLCP-preamble and synchronize its demodulator.
- When a node has a PPDU queued for transmission CCA determines if the medium is idle or busy.

## CSMA/CA

This section's goal is to understand how CSMA/CA affects the throughput of a congested, mixed-mode BSS. The book subdivides the process into five logical elements. Here are two standard terms used with media access control:

- "Defer the medium" means to wait to transmit because CSMA/CA procedures indicate the medium is currently in-use or reserved.
- A node that is "contending" for access is observing CSMA/CA rules to determine when it may transmit a frame with the least probability of collision.

## CSMA/CA Case #1: Medium is Idle

With a PPDU in the transmit queue, a node invokes CCA. *If the medium is idle, and stays idle for an entire DIFS, the node transmits the PPDU.*

In an idealized environment, every node in the BSA receives and processes every frame. The timing diagram on page 43 depicts a node waiting one DIFS before transmitting. *In this simple case the time it takes to complete a frame dialog is:*

$$DIFS + Frame + SIFS + ACK$$

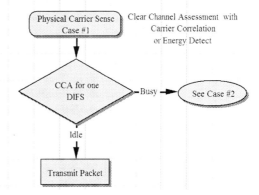

**Case #1: Medium is free, listen for for one DIFS and then transmit**

## CSMA/CA Case #2: Collision Avoidance and the Back-Off Timer

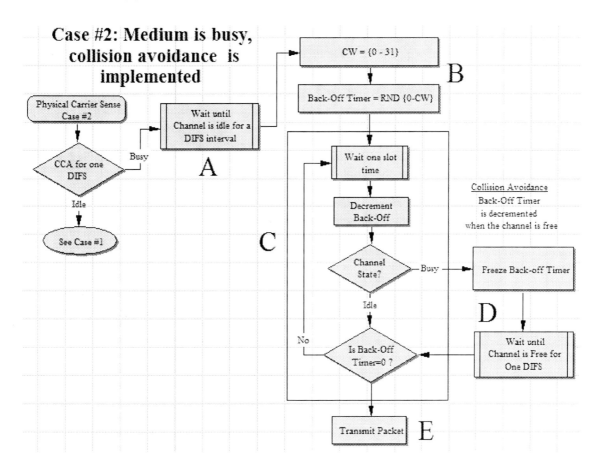

A. Although a node may have a PPDU ready to transmit, the medium is busy and every node in the BSA is in receiver mode, processing the incoming frame. The channel must be idle for a complete DIFS before nodes start to contend for the medium.

B. ***Because the medium was busy there's a greater probability that multiple nodes are waiting to transmit. The random back-off timer is one of two collision avoidance mechanisms implemented in CSMA/CA.*** Each "tick" of the back-off timer represents one slot time. The initial CW (contention window) has a range of 0 to 31. A random integer back-off value from within the range of the CW is generated.

C. ***While the medium continues to be idle the back-off timer is decremented for each slot time deferred.***

D. If the back-off timer of another node reaches zero first, it transmits a frame. ***Without the random back-off timer mechanism, all deferring nodes would have transmitted at the end of the DIFS at Point A in the flowchart, and a collision would have occurred!***

- Nodes waiting to transmit freeze their back-off timers
- Every node in the BSA receives and processes the frame
- After the medium is idle for one DIFS, those nodes waiting to transmit return to the back-off timer loop at Point C in the flow chart.

E. ***When the node's back-off timer finally reaches zero, it transmits a frame. With any luck, no other deferring node generated the same random back-off at Point B.***

## CSMA/CA Case #3: Receiving the ACK

A node successfully contends for the medium and transmits a frame. Every node in the BSA senses the carrier and synchronizes its demodulator.

***If a valid frame is received, all nodes assume that an ACK will be transmitted by the destination node in one SIFS. The reception of the ACK ends the two-frame dialog.*** All deferring nodes return to the back-off timer loop.

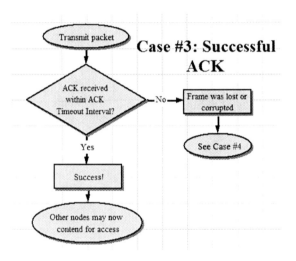

**Case #3: Successful ACK**

## CSMA/CA Case #4: CRC Error or No ACK

A. A CRC mismatch or absence of an ACK indicates that a transmission error occurred.

B. Non-Transmitting Nodes Response: The nodes that received the frame are aware that an expected ACK wasn't received or that a corrupted frame was received. If waiting to transmit, a node freezes its back-off timer and defers the medium for *one EIFS or until a reception of an error-free frame is received*.

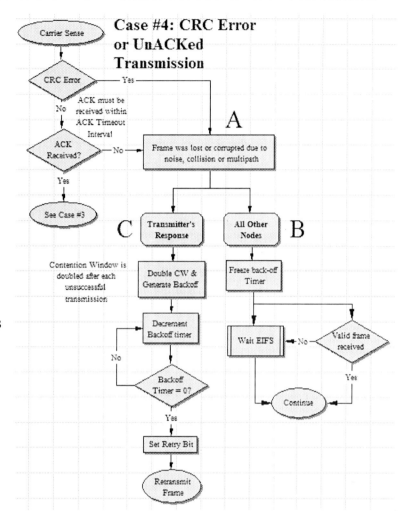

**Case #4: CRC Error or UnACKed Transmission**

C. Transmitting Nodes Response: Because a collision involves multiple frames, there is a higher probability of subsequent collisions with the retransmissions. *In response to each consecutive collision, the transmitter doubles its CW to further reduce the probability of another collision.*
*The maximum CW is 0-1,023 slot times.* A new random back-off is generated from the current CW and the standard back-off mechanism is followed. When the frame is successfully transmitted, the node reinitializes its CW to the initial value of $0 - 31$.

## CSMA/CA Case #5: Virtual Carrier and Medium Reservation

*Virtual carrier is based on the value of the duration field of a received frame; it specifies the time that the medium will be occupied with the current frame sequence dialog.*

- Every node in the BSA receives every transmission.
- The integrity of the frame is verified.
- The frame's destination address specifies the receiver's MAC address. The designated receiver processes the frame and prepares to transmit an ACK.
- The rest of the nodes read the frame's duration field which specifies the number of microseconds that virtual carrier has reserved the medium.
- Every node in the BSA initializes its NAV (network allocation vector) timer to the duration value of the received frame.
- When the NAV timers decrement to zero, virtual carrier is released and the nodes continue with the physical CCA and back-off timer mechanisms.

Physical carrier sense depends on the presence of an RF carrier which can be demodulated by a receiver. Virtual carrier is based on the value of the duration field contained in a received frame. ***Regardless of the physical state of the medium, virtual carrier forces a node to defer the medium until its NAV timer has been decremented to zero!***

## The Duration/ID field

The Duration/ID field in the MAC header appears in every 802.11 frame.

- With the exception of the PS-Poll frame, it specifies the duration of the virtual carrier in microseconds.
- In the PS-Poll control frame it specifies the AID (association ID) of the STA. PS-Poll retrieves data buffered by the AP during PS (power save) mode. See Chapter 7 for PS operation details.

```
⊞·Physical Frame
⊟·IEEE 802.11 MAC Protocol
 ┊ ··Function                    Data
 ┊ ⊞·PLCP Header
 ┊ ⊞·Frame Control Byte 0
 ┊ ⊞·Frame Control Byte 1
 ┊ ⊞·WEP Information
 ┊ ▐Duration ID            117 ▌
 ┊ ⊞·BSSID
 ┊ ⊞·Source Address
 ┊ ⊞·Destination Address
 ┊ ··Fragment          [xxxxxxxx xxxx0000]  0
 ┊ ··Sequence          [00010111 1010xxxx]  378
 ⊞·IEEE 802.2 Logical Link Control
 ⊞·IEEE Sub-Network Access Protocol
 ⊞·Address Resolution Protocol
```

```
00000    08 41 75 00 00 09 B7 7E E9 AA 00 40 96 A2 F4 34
00016    FF FF FF FF FF FF A0 17 AA AA 03 00 00 00 08 06
00032    00 01 08 00 06 04 00 01 00 40 96 A2 F4 34 C0 A8
00048    00 42 00 00 00 00 00 00 C0 A8 00 49
```

The value of the duration field ***represents the transmitter's estimate of how much time is needed to complete the current frame sequence.*** In this example the frame was transmitted by an HR/DSSS STA with short preamble with an 11-Mbps PSDU bit-rate. ***The data frame is reserving an additional 117-µs of medium time to accommodate the subsequent ACK!***

**SIFS (10-µs) + PLCP-preamble (72-µs) + PLCP-header (24-µs) + ACK (11-µs)**

Chapter 7 details the simple calculations used to determine theoretical maximum throughputs, typical BSS overhead and duration values.

## ACK Frame Duration Field Value

That begs the question, "what's the value of an ACK frame's duration field?" It's zero, as illustrated in this capture fragment, because the ACK frame completes the dialog. *After the reception of an ACK, the NAV timers should have decremented to zero, releasing virtual carrier so nodes may return to physical CCA and the back-off timer loop.*

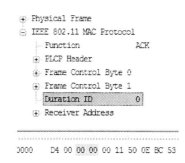

```
⊞ Physical Frame
⊟ IEEE 802.11 MAC Protocol
    Function           ACK
  ⊞ PLCP Header
  ⊞ Frame Control Byte 0
  ⊞ Frame Control Byte 1
    Duration ID         0
  ⊞ Receiver Address
.........................................
0000    D4 00 00 00 00 11 50 0E BC 53
```

> **NAV Update Note** When a STA receives a valid frame its NAV timer is updated only if the frame's duration field value is greater than the STA's current NAV timer value.

802.11 Fragmentation is the exception to the ACK Zero Duration Rule. In Chapter 6 we analyze fragmented data frame captures in detail. For now remember this, the duration value of *all but the last ACK* in a sequential burst of 802.11 data fragment frames *provides virtual carrier protection for the next data fragment and its subsequent ACK.*

## Case #5: Virtual Carrier, Duration field and the NAV Timer

A. Back-Off timers of nodes waiting to transmit are frozen when physical carrier is sensed.
B. When a corrupted frame is received or an expected ACK isn't transmitted the BSA enters error recovery mode.
C. Set the NAV timer with the value of the duration field of the received frame.
D. The receiver processes the frame, waits one SIFS and transmits an ACK.
E. All nodes enter the virtual carrier mode counting down the NAV timer
F. When a valid ACK is received with a duration value of zero, all nodes reset their NAV timers and return to CCA.

**Case #5: Virtual Carrier**

Carrier Sense → Freeze Back-Off Timer **A** → Read Frame → CRC OK? — No → See Case #4 **B**

Notes: When destination address = broadcast address, the frame is not acknowledged

CRC OK? — Yes **C** → Set NAV = Duration Field Value → Destination Address? — All Others **E** → All nodes decrement NAV to zero → Was ACK Received? **B** — No (loops to See Case #4)

Was ACK Received? — Yes → Return to CCA

Destination Address? — Receiver **D** → Wait SIFS → Transmit ACK

## NAV Timer versus Back-Off Timer

Although both the *NAV and Back-Off timers support collision avoidance*, they perform very different functions. *A non-zero NAV timer indicates that virtual carrier has allocated the medium. A non-zero back-off timer identifies a node in a randomly ordered queue waiting to transmit.*

- **Every node** in the BSA sets its NAV to the same value, the number of microseconds specified in the duration field of the last received frame.
- **Individual nodes** contending to access a busy medium generate a random back-off time from within the range of their current CW.

## RTS/CTS Medium Reservation Frames

802.11 RTS and CTS control frames carry duration values that reserve the medium for a subsequent data frame and ACK. They enhance the functionality of CSMA/CA In the ideal WLAN every node receives every transmission and sets its NAV timer properly. In many production networks because of distance, poorly placed antennas or obstructions, not all STAs receive all frames. Collisions increase when NAV timers aren't set and virtual carrier isn't properly implemented. In Chapter 6 we'll investigate how RTS/CTS control frames compensate for this "hidden node," aka "hidden terminal" issue.

## CTS-to-Self

Physical carrier sense and virtual carrier mechanisms are predicated on a node's ability to demodulate a carrier. HR/DSSS STAs can't demodulate ERP-OFDM carriers. When an 802.11g STA transmits in native mode both physical and virtual carrier mechanisms of HR/DSSS STAs fail and they simultaneously transmit causing collisions and corruption.

RTS/CTS is a stateless protocol - a STA sets its NAV timer from the duration value of a CTS frame regardless of whether a preceding RTS frame was transmitted. A CTS-to-Self frame is simply a CTS frame transmitted without a preceding RTS frame. It is always transmitted with HR/DSSS modulation at a basic rate to ensure that all STAs in the BSA properly set their NAV timers. With virtual carrier medium reservation, the ERP STA may transmit an ERP-OFDM data frame and receive the subsequent ERP-OFDM ACK.

*The value of the duration field of a CTS-to-Self frame specifies the number of microseconds required to transmit the subsequent ERP-OFDM data frame and ACK.*

CTS-to-Self protection is used in mixed-mode BSSs supporting 802.11b and 802.11g STAs. It "protects" ERP-OFDM transmissions from being corrupted by HR/DSSS STAs. CTS-to-Self protection imposes a 21% overhead on maximum-sized 802.11 data frames. Percentage of overhead increases as the size of the data frame decreases.

Unfortunately, CTS-to-Self configuration on business-class APs is rare. General guidelines for APs that support mixed-mode protection configuration are:

- A BSS with a high-ratio of ERP to HR/DSSS STAs should have protection disabled. The resulting collisions and retransmissions consume less bandwidth than the CTS-to-Self overhead.
- If HR/DSSS STAs outnumber ERP STAs, protection should be enabled.

"Rules of thumb" are fine for those who without the training or tools to confront the beast in its lair. The only accurate way to determine whether mixed-mode protection should be enabled is with a network monitor. ***Run baseline captures and analyze frame error rates with an 802.11 network monitor. Use a retry filter and timestamps to determine the percentage of errors that are attributable to collisions between HR/DSSS and ERP/OFDM STAs.*** That may sound like a huge effort now, but by the end of the book it should seem like a routine task.

## ERP Information Element

Here's a fragment of a beacon frame from a mixed-mode AP. Basic and Extended (not in Basic Rate Set) Rates are supported.

- **Non-ERP Present** is set to indicate that an 802.11b STA is associated to the BSS.
- **Use Protection** is set to instruct ERP STAs to precede ERP-OFDM transmissions with a basic rate HR/DSSS CTS-to-Self frame.

```
Information Element
   Identity            Supported Rates
   Length              8
   Rate                1.0 MB    [1xxxxxxx]  In Basic Rate Set
   Rate                2.0 MB    [1xxxxxxx]  In Basic Rate Set
   Rate                5.5 MB    [1xxxxxxx]  In Basic Rate Set
   Rate                11.0 MB   [1xxxxxxx]  In Basic Rate Set
   Rate                18.0 MB   [0xxxxxxx]  Not in Basic Rate Set
   Rate                24.0 MB   [0xxxxxxx]  Not in Basic Rate Set
   Rate                36.0 MB   [0xxxxxxx]  Not in Basic Rate Set
   Rate                54.0 MB   [0xxxxxxx]  Not in Basic Rate Set
Information Element
   Identity            DS Parameter Set
   Length              1
   Current Channel     11
Information Element
Information Element
   Identity            ERP
   Length              1
   Non-ERP Present     [xxxx xxx1]  On
   Use Protection      [xxxx xx1x]  On
   Barker Preamble     [xxxx x1xx]  On
```

- **Barker Preamble Mode** Specifies which DSSS preamble to use with the HR/DSSS CTS-to-Self frame; set specifies long preamble and reset specifies short preamble.

Think about the meaning of the Non-ERP Present and Use Protection bits – don't they seem redundant? In a troubleshooting mini-case study in Chapter 4 we'll examine an AP beacon with "Non-ERP Present" "Off", but Use Protection "On." The clue is that this mechanism protects the physical BSA, not just the logical BSS.

## CSMA/CA Review: The Simplified Big Picture

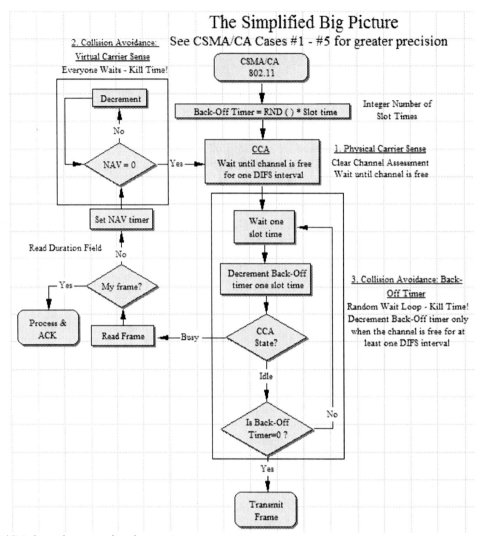

CSMA/CA has three main elements:

1. <u>Physical Carrier Sense</u>
   a. CCA/CS
   b. Node must be able to demodulate carrier
2. <u>Virtual Carrier sense</u>
   a. Based on microseconds
   b. Duration field and NAV timer
   c. Enhanced by CTS-to-Self in mixed-mode

> ❗ **Exam Alert**: Collision avoidance is supported by both virtual carrier and back-off timer.

3. <u>Back-Off Timer</u>
   a. Based on slot times
   b. Exponentially increasing CW is doubled with each consecutive collision

## *802.11 PPDU Overview*

All Ethernet frames are data frames in the sense that the only purpose of an Ethernet frame is to have an upper-layer data payload. In a typical WLAN over 70% of the frames don't have an upper-layer payload, they carry 802.11 management or control information.

The 802.11 PPDU has four major components:

- PHY Preamble and Header
- Data-Link Headers
- Payload (data frames only)
- FCS, 32-bit CRC

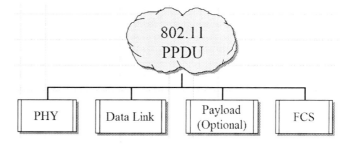

### PLCP-Header

802.11 network monitors don't display the values of PLCP-header fields. However they derive the following from the PLCP-header and the wireless client adapter's driver:

- Frame size in bytes
- Timestamp (Network monitors support several timestamp formats.)
- Signal strength and quality (driver and client adapter specific.)
- Bit-rate and ISM channel

### 802.11 MAC-Header Fields

The Ethernet MAC-header that we examined in Chapter 1 was very simple. It has three fields: destination address, source address and ether-type. The number of fields in the 802.11 MAC-header reflects the inherent complexity of WLAN communication.

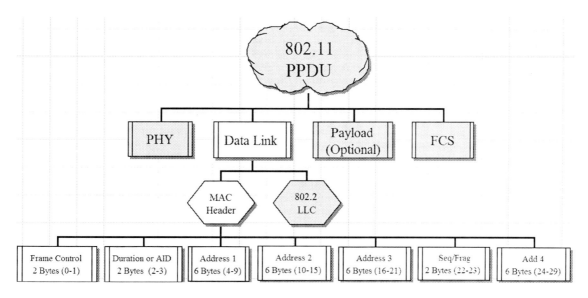

***By the end of the book you'll be expert on the features and functions of every field and bit of the 802.11 MAC-header.*** Each topic is introduced in a functional context. Using the capture files you'll review every aspect of the 802.11 frame at the bit-level as revealed by the network monitor.

## Frame Control Byte-0 and 802.11 Frame Types and Subtypes

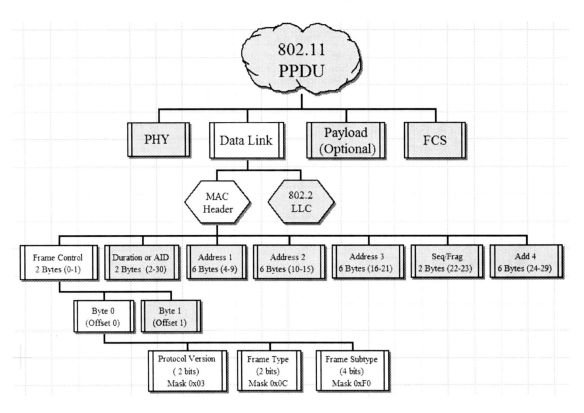

Frame Control Byte-0 has three fields: ***Protocol Version, Frame Type and Frame Subtype***. By definition, the first byte in the MAC header has an offset of 0 bytes. The offset and mask included in the following diagrams and tables must be specified when creating custom network monitor capture and display filters. We'll build and employ filers as needed throughout the book. ***Once you learn to write LinkFerret filters, writing filters for any network monitor will be a snap!***

| Mac Header Control | | | |
|---|---|---|---|
| Field | Offset | Bits | Mask |
| Protocol Version | 0 | 2 | 0x03 |
| Frame Type | 0 | 2 | 0x0c |
| Frame Subtype | 0 | 4 | 0xf0 |

MAC Header, Control Byte-0

| $V_0$ | $V_1$ | $T_0$ | $T_1$ | $S_0$ | $S_1$ | $S_2$ | $S_3$ |
|---|---|---|---|---|---|---|---|

$B_0$    Version      Frame Type          Frame Subtype     B7

**Protocol Version**: $(V_0 - V_1)$ isn't currently implemented and has a value of zero.
**Frame Type field**: $(T_0 - T_1)$ 802.11 has three frame types: Management, Control and Data.
**Frame Subtype field**: $(S_0 - S_3)$ 11 Management, 4 Control and 2 Data frames subtypes may be used during DCF, the mandatory coordination function.

<u>Note</u>: There are several PCF-specific frames that aren't covered in the text because PCF has never been implemented in a production network.

**Terminology Note**: Sometimes to emphasize a frame's function both the frame subtype and type are cited, e.g. "Beacon *Management* frame" or a "CTS *Control* frame." It's purely a matter of style, rather than a technical distinction. Your ability to contextualize a frame reinforces its function and relationship to other 802.11 frames. Use the "subtype-type" form until you have internalized each frame and its function.

## Type: (00) - Management Frame

There are 11 Management frames defined by the subtype field. This capture fragment shows a beacon frame.

```
⊟ Frame Control Byte 0
  ⊢ Protocol Level    [xxxxxx00]  0
  ⊢ Type              [xxxx00xx]  Management
  ⊢ Sub-Type          [1000xxxx]  Beacon
```

The 802.11 association mechanism is the equivalent of "plugging" a STA into an AP. Management frames support the relationship between a STA and the AP:

- Determine the presence of APs
- Initiate authentication and association
- Roam between APs in the same ESS
- Terminate the association

| 00 | Management |
|------|-----------|
| | Subtype |
| 0000 | Association Request |
| 0001 | Association Response |
| 0010 | Reassociation Request |
| 0011 | Reassociation Response |
| 0100 | Probe Request |
| 0101 | Probe Response |
| 1000 | Beacon |
| 1001 | ATIM |
| 1010 | Disassociation |
| 1011 | Authentication |
| 1100 | Deauthentication |

Ethernet doesn't require the equivalent of management frames because Ethernet nodes are connected to a switch/hub with a physical cable and are stationary (non-roaming.)

## Type: (01) - Control Frame

802.11 defines four DCF Control frames. This capture fragment shows an ACK.

```
⊟ Frame Control Byte 0
  ⊢ Protocol Level    [xxxxxx00]  0
  ⊢ Type              [xxxx01xx]  Control
  ⊢ Sub-Type          [1101xxxx]  ACK
```

Control frames coordination the movement of data frames:

- Acknowledge the receipt of a valid frame
- Read PS-mode (power save) buffered data
- Support mixed-mode virtual carrier medium reservation
- Support RTS/CTS medium reservation to compensate for "hidden nodes."

| 01 | Control |
|------|---------|
| | Subtype |
| 1010 | PS-Poll |
| 1011 | RTS |
| 1100 | CTS |
| 1101 | ACK |

## Type: (10) - Data Frame

802.11 defines two data frames. This capture fragment shows a null data frame.

```
⊟ Frame Control Byte 0
  ⊢ Protocol Level    [xxxxxx00]  0
  ⊢ Type              [xxxx10xx]  Data
  ⊢ Sub-Type          [0100xxxx]  Null
```

- Standard data frames have an 802.2 LLC field and carry an upper-layer payload.
- Null-Data frames don't have an 802.2 LLC field or payload; they are typically used to communicate the STA's power management state to the AP.

| 10 | Data |
|------|------|
| | Subtype |
| 0000 | Data (payload) |
| 0100 | Data (null) |

## Reading Bit Positions

For those new to network monitors a huge confusion factor, especially for filter novices, is the reversal in visual bit position representation. Conventional diagrams depict bit-0 is on the left and bit-7 on the right. While the network monitor shows the true position of the bits with bit-0 is on the right and bit-7 on the left.

| MAC Header, Control Byte-0 | | | | | | | |
|---|---|---|---|---|---|---|---|
| $V_0$ | $V_1$ | $T_0$ | $T_1$ | $S_0$ | $S_1$ | $S_2$ | $S_3$ |

$B_0$  Version   Frame Type   Frame Subtype   $B7$

```
⊟ Frame Control Byte 0
    Protocol Level    [xxxxxx00]   0
    Type              [xxxx00xx]   Management
    Sub-Type          [1000xxxx]   Beacon
```

Many people are confused by the way that frame formats are represented in print and contradictions of bit-masks associated with the fields. English reads left to right. If a byte starts with bit-0 we expect to see it on the left, with bit-1 listed to its right, and so on.

With numbers the least significant bit is on the right. We interpret numbers by starting with the most significant bit and working left-to-right, such as: 3,952 or $7.95.

Here's a typical illustration of Control Byte-0. Bit-0 is on the left, where we would expect it. *However, this illustration can't be used to create the bit-mask for each field; it's the reverse of how the bits appear in the capture.*

| Protocol Version | | Frame Type | | | Frame Subtype | | |
|---|---|---|---|---|---|---|---|
| 0 | 1 | 2 | 3 | 4 | 5 | 6 | 7 |

Normal Illustration
Reading Left to Right

Here's the same byte in a technically correct format. The hexadecimal value for each bit position is listed inside each box. *This drawing can be used to create the correct bit-masks and is consistent with network capture details.*

| Frame Subtype | | | | Frame Type | | Protocol Version | |
|---|---|---|---|---|---|---|---|
| 8 | 4 | 2 | 1 | 8 | 4 | 2 | 1 |
| 7 | 6 | 5 | 4 | 3 | 2 | 1 | 0 |

Bit Masking Illustration
Math reads LSB to the right

This may appear obscure or pedantic, but if you've ever tried to write custom, bit-level filters using field and bit position information taken from normal WLAN books, the bit-masks are backwards and the filters didn't work! It's a very frustrating experience. We'll get plenty of experience using bit masks writing simple filters throughout the book. Writing quick, precise and highly illuminating on-the-fly filters is what separates WLAN gurus from the pack of wannabes.

## 2.4-GHz ISM Channel Overlap

In Chapter 1 we examined the concept of spread spectrum signals and the reason that they're more resistant to RFI corruption. The downside to spread spectrum is the channel overlap and resultant interference that occurs when 11, 22-MHz wide channels are jammed into an 85-MHz wide band! Most WLAN administrators are oblivious to this issue, but promiscuous WLAN network monitor capture brings channel overlap to the forefront.

Any RF energy that degrades the quality of 802.11 signals is considered interference. The amount of interference that a receiver can tolerate is a function of:
- Physical location
- Receiver Sensitivity – specified minimum S/N (signal to noise ratio)
- The RSSI (received or radio signal strength indicator), which is the ***average received power over the channel's 22-MHz bandwidth***.

The interference induced by overlapping channels is a function of:
- Physical location
- Channel separation
- Transmit power
- Antenna gain and directionality

The U.S.A. 2.4-GHz ISM (industrial, scientific and medical) band is subdivided into 11 overlapped, staggered channels. It's commonly accepted that BSSs configured on Channels 1, 6 and 11 can be physically co-located without significant interference. Here's the numbers in a nutshell:
- ISM channels have a 22-MHz bandwidth
- 5-MHz separates the channel center frequencies
- A five channel separation provides 25-MHz (5 x 5-MHz) of isolation

This produces a 3-MHz guard band between the energy radiation on Channels 1, 6 and 11. However, the IEEE specifications tell a much different story. The spectrum mask must only be attenuated from the channel's center frequency by a minimum of:

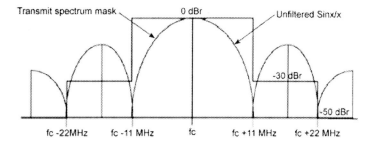

- 30-dB at 11-MHz from center freq.
- 50-dB at 22-MHz from center freq.

This shows that there's significant energy overlap between the three "non-overlapping" channels.

The spectrum mask specifications for 802.11g provides even less isolation.

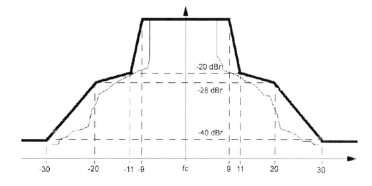

Consider the specifications of Cisco APs and wireless client adapters:
- Maximum transmit power of 100-mW, or +20-dBm.
- Receiver sensitivity of -85-dBm.

Assume that HR/DSSS is in use. The overlap between Channel -6 with Channels -1 and -11 begins about 12.5-MHz from center frequency. The signal transmitted from a Cisco AP configured at maximum power is approximately -13 -dBm, well within the range of the Cisco receiver specifications. Moving out to 22-MHz off center frequency and the power is attenuated by 50-dB or about -30-dBm – still well within the sensitivity of a Cisco receiver! *These "non-overlapping" channels in the same physical area may still have quite an overlap. However, the amount of corruption due to this overlap is not significant unless the three APs on Channels-1, -6 and -11 are placed in very close physical proximity.*

## Channel Overlap and the Network Monitor Confusion Factor

There are specialized occasions, such as searching for rogue APs, when a network monitor is configured to scan the entire range of ISM channels. However, for troubleshooting and performance optimization network monitors are configured to capture a single channel:
- Although APs can be configured to automatically seek the least congested channel, they are assigned usually assigned a fixed channel.
- In preparation for roaming or to maintain a list of available APs to facilitate failover, STAs periodically go off-channel to scan for APs on other channels.
- An environment designed to support roaming has a 20% to 30% BSA overlap.

Depending on several factors, including the physical location and antenna orientation of your network monitor, you may receive beacons from APs configured on other channels, or probe requests transmitted by STAs tuned to other channels.

**Troubleshooting Tip:** What may appear to be meaningless bursts of probe request frames are often transmitted by STAs as they sequentially step through the channels. Don't assume that the STA is malfunctioning. If the signal level decreases with each pair of probe request frames, the network monitor is simply capturing off-channel frames.

*Although the network monitor is configured to capture traffic on a fixed channel, frames such as beacons and probe requests may be received on other channels, with no distinguishing feature other than a lower RSSI and a higher CRC error rate.*

The remainder of this book focuses on analyzing LinkFerret capture files. Theory is minimized and hands-on capture file analysis is maximized. You'll develop a sense of the routine frame flow that occurs in a properly functioning BSS. We'll also examine many mini-case studies that demonstrate common 802.11 faults.

# Chapter 2 Review

## 802.11 Lack of Collision Detection

- Wireless adapters use the same antenna to transmit and receive.
    - half-duplex devices, can transmit or receive but not simultaneously
    - 802.11 compensates for a wireless adapter's inability to detect collisions with CSMA/CA and acknowledgements.
- **CSMA/CA**
    - Provides three mechanisms - physical carrier sense, dynamically adjusted back-off timer and virtual carrier sense

## 802.11 Acknowledgments

- All unicast 802.11 frames must be acknowledged.
- Broadcast frames transmitted by a STA are acknowledged by the AP and processed by the distribution system service
- If an ACK is not received within the ACK Timeout interval the node recontends for transmit access and retransmits the original frame with the Retry bit set.

## Frame Prioritization and the SIFS (short interframe space)

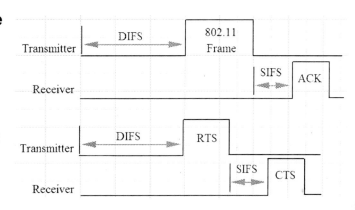

- ACK and CTS are high-priority response frames. The receiver may bypasses CSMA/CA and simply wait one SIFS before transmitting the ACK or CTS.
- *The SIFS is always 10-μs*

## PIFS (PCF InterFrame space)

- Associated with CF (contention free) PCF mode.
    - standard slot time PIFS = SIFS + 20-μs = *30-μs*
    - short slot time PIFS = SIFS + 9-μs = *19-μs*
- *PCF, CF mode and PIFS are not supported on any commercial AP or wireless client adapter*

### DIFS (DCF InterFrame Space)

- ***DIFS is associated with the mandatory DCF mode***. CSMA/CA specifies that the medium must be idle for one DIFS before it is available for transmission.
- ***DIFS = SIFS + (2 \* slot time)***
  - DIFS (standard slot time) = SIFS + (2 \* 20-µs) = ***50-µs***
    - 802.11b and mixed mode
  - DIFS (short slot time) = SIFS + (2 \* 9-µs) = ***28-µs***
    - 802.11g native mode only

### EIFS (Extended InterFrame Space)

- Employed when a frame is not acknowledged. In the absence of an ACK, the medium must be deferred for one EIFS.
- The EIFS ***prevents STAs from colliding with a future frame associated with the current dialog***
  - If a transmitter doesn't receive an ACK within the ACK Timeout, the collision avoidance CW (contention window) is doubled
  - The non-transmitting nodes defer the medium for an entire EIFS or until a valid frame is received.
- ***The EIFS is equivalent to the time it takes to transmit eight ACK frames, one SIFS and one DIFS.***

### Physical CS (carrier sense) & CCA (clear channel assessment)

- <u>Reception:</u> Physical ***CS*** senses an RF carrier enabling the receiver to acquire the PLCP-preamble and synchronize its demodulator in preparation for reception.
- <u>Transmission:</u> ***CCA*** is employed when a node has a PPDU queued for transmission to determine the current state of the medium.

### CSMA/CA Case #1: Medium is Idle

- A node invokes CCA when it has a PPDU in the transmit queue.
  - If the medium is idle, and stays idle for an entire DIFS, the node transmits the PPDU.
- ***The CS of every node in the BSA detects the transmission, and receives and processes this frame.***

### Case #1: Medium is free, listen for for one DIFS and then transmit

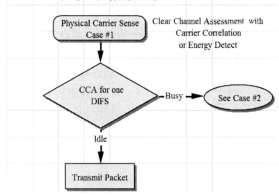

## CSMA/CA Case #2: Collision Avoidance and the Back-Off Timer

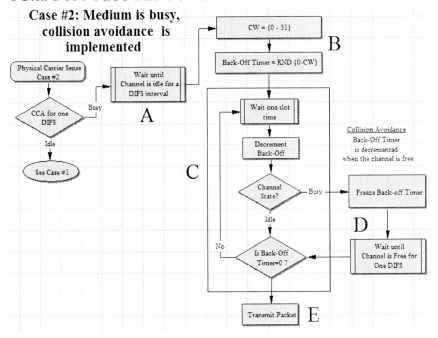

A. The medium is busy. The node is in receiver mode and processing the incoming frame.
   - The channel must be idle for *one DIFS* before the node contends for the medium.
B. There is a greater probability that other nodes are also waiting to transmit. The random back-off timer provides collision avoidance.
   - The initial CW (contention window) range is 0 to 31 slot times.
   - A random delay is generated and the back-off timer is initialized.
C. While the medium remains idle, the back-off timer is decremented
D. If back-off timer of another node reaches zero first, it transmits
   - Nodes waiting to transmit freeze their back-off timers
   - Every node in the BSA receives and processes the frame
   - After the medium is idle for one DIFS, those nodes waiting to transmit return to the back-off timer loop at point C.
E. When a node's back-off reaches zero, it transmits a frame.

## CSMA/CA Case #3: Receiving the ACK

- A node successfully contends for the medium and transmits a frame.
  - Every node in the BSA senses the carrier and synchronizes its demodulator.
- If a valid frame is received all nodes assume that an ACK will be transmitted in one SIFS.
  - The reception of the ACK ends the two-frame dialog.

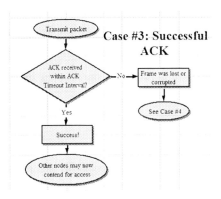

## CSMA/CA Case #4: CRC Error or No ACK

A. A CRC error or no ACK indicates that a transmission error occurred.

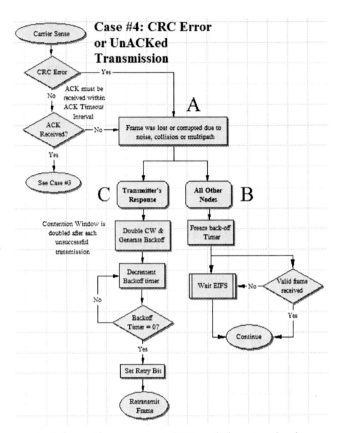

B. <u>Non-Transmitting Nodes Response</u>: An expected ACK wasn't received or that a frame was corrupted. If waiting to transmit, a node freezes its back-off timer and defers the medium for *one EIFS or until a reception of an error-free frame is received*.

C. <u>Transmitting Nodes Response</u>: There is a higher probability of subsequent collisions with the retransmissions.

- In response to each consecutive transmissions attempt and collision, the transmitter doubles its CW to further reduce the probability of another collision.

- A new random back-off is generated from the *current CW* and the standard back-off is followed.

- *The maximum CW is 0-1,023 slot times.*

## The Duration/ID field

- Usually specifies the duration of the virtual carrier expressed in microseconds.
- In the PS-Poll frame it specifies the AID (association ID) of the STA.
- Represents how much time, *after the frame containing the duration field is complete*, is needed to complete the current frame sequence.
- Associate the duration field with the NAV timer and virtual carrier.

## ACK Frame Duration Field Value

- The duration value of an ACK is zero, because completes the dialog.
- *At that point the NAV timers have decremented to zero, virtual carrier is released and nodes return to physical CS and back-off timer loop.*

## NAV Timer Update

- When a frame is received and verified, the value of its duration field always replaces the current NAV timer value!
- ***The receipt of an ACK with a duration value of 0 resets every NAV timer in the BSA.***

## Exception to the ACK Zero Duration Rule

- 802.11 L2 frame fragmentation is the exception to the ACK zero duration rule
- The duration field value of ***all but the last ACK*** in a sequential burst of 802.11 data fragment frames ***provides virtual carrier for the next data fragment and its subsequent ACK.***

## Case #5: Virtual Carrier, Duration field and the NAV Timer

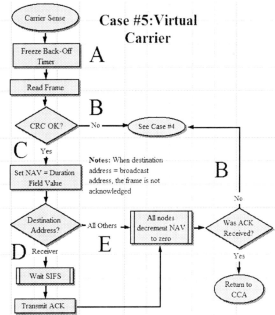

A. When physical carrier is sensed back-off timers of nodes waiting to transmit are frozen.
B. When a corrupted frame is received or an expected ACK is not transmitted the BSA enters error recovery mode.
C. Set the NAV with the value of the duration field of the received frame.
D. The receiver processes the frame, waits one SIFS and transmits an ACK.
E. All nodes enter the virtual carrier mode counting down the NAV timer
F. When a valid ACK is received with a duration value of zero, all nodes reset their NAV timers and return to CCA.

## NAV Timer versus Back-Off Timer

- The ***NAV and Back-Off timers both support collision avoidance***
  - A non-zero NAV timer indicates that virtual carrier has allocated the medium.
  - A non-zero back-off timer establishes a randomly ordered queue of nodes waiting to transmit.
- **Every node** in the BSA sets its NAV to the **same value,** the number of **microseconds** specified in the duration field of the **last received frame**.
- **Individual nodes** contending to access a busy medium generate a **random back-off time** from within the range of their own CW.

## RTS/CTS Medium Reservation

- RTS and CTS frames carry duration values that reserve the medium for a subsequent data frame and ACK.
- Distance, poorly placed antennas and obstructions are common reasons that STAs may not receive all frames in the BSS.
- Collisions increase when NAV timers aren't set and virtual carrier isn't implemented.
- The "hidden node" issue and RTS/CTS are addressed in Chapter 6.

## CTS-to-Self Mixed Mode Protection

- HR/DSSS STAs can't demodulate ERP-OFDM carriers so they "step-on" on ERP-OFDM transmissions
- The CTS-to-Self frame is transmitted with HR/DSSS modulation at a basic rate

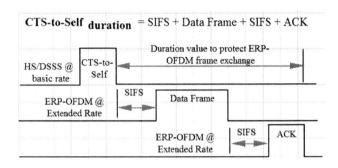

CTS-to-Self duration = SIFS + Data Frame + SIFS + ACK

- It reserves the medium for an ERP-OFDM transmission to follow.
- ***The duration field specifies the number of microseconds required to transmit the subsequent ERP-OFDM frame and ACK.***

## CTS-to-Self Configuration

- Enabling CTS-to-Self protection on business-class APs is optional.
- A BSS with a high ratio of ERP to HR/DSSS STAs should have protection disabled. The collisions/retransmissions consume less bandwidth than the CTS-to-Self overhead.
- If the HR/DSSS STAs outnumber ERP STAs protection should be enabled.
- The only accurate way to determine whether mixed-mode protection should be enabled on your network is to ***run baseline captures and analyze frame error rates with an 802.11 network monitor.***
- Chapter 7 analyzes the maximum throughput of 802.11g with CTS-to-Self enabled

## ERP Information Element

- Appears in Beacon and Probe Response frames
- **Non-ERP Present = On** indicates that an 802.11b STA is associated with the BSS.
- **Use Protection = On** instructs ERP STAs to precede ERP-OFDM transmissions with a basic rate HS-DSSS CTS-to-Self frame.
- **Barker Preamble Mode = On** specifies that the CTS-to-Self frame should use a long DSSS preamble; reset specifies the use of a short preamble.

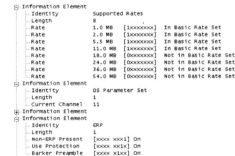

## CSMA/CA: The Simplified Big Picture

- Physical Carrier Sense
  - CCA/CS
  - Node must be able to demodulate carrier
- Virtual Carrier sense
  - Based on microseconds
  - Duration field and NAV timer
  - Enhances CTS-to-Self in mixed mode
- Back-Off Timer
  - Based on slot times
  - Exponentially increasing CW is doubled with each consecutive collision
- Collision avoidance is provided by both virtual carrier sense and back-off timer.

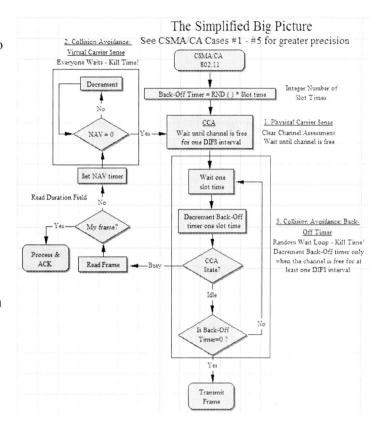

## 802.11 PPDU Overview

- The 802.11 PPDU has four major components:
  - **PHY Preamble and Header**
  - **Data-Link Headers**
  - **Payload (data frames only)**
  - **FCS, 32-bit CRC**

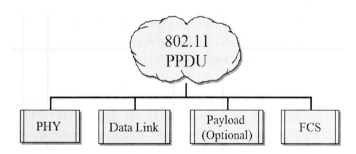

## 802.11 Frame Types and Subtypes

### Byte-0 Fields

- **Protocol Version**: (V0 – V1)
    - not implemented
- **Frame Type field**: (T0 – T1)
    - 802.11 defines three frame types: Management, Control and Data.
- **Frame Subtype field**: (S0 – S3)
    - DCF supports 11 Management, 4 Control and 2 Data frames subtypes

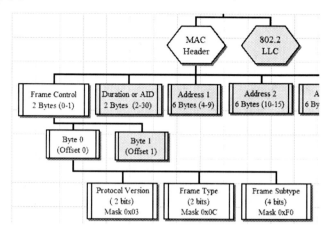

| | | | | MAC Header, Control Byte-0 | | | |
|---|---|---|---|---|---|---|---|
| $V_0$ | $V_1$ | $T_0$ | $T_1$ | $S_0$ | $S_1$ | $S_2$ | $S_3$ |

B0      Version      Frame Type      Frame Subtype      B7

### Type: (00) - Management Frame

- There are 11 DCF-supported Management frames.
- Management frames support the relationship between a STA and AP:
    - determine the presence of APs
    - initiate authentication and association
    - roam between APs in the same ESS
    - terminate the association
- Ethernet doesn't require the equivalent of management frames because its nodes are connected to a switch/hub with a physical cable.

```
Frame Control Byte 0
 Protocol Level   [xxxxxx00]   0
 Type             [xxxx00xx]   Management
 Sub-Type         [1000xxxx]   Beacon
```

| 00 | Management |
|---|---|
| | Subtype |
| 0000 | Association Request |
| 0001 | Association Response |
| 0010 | Reassociation Request |
| 0011 | Reassociation Response |
| 0100 | Probe Request |
| 0101 | Probe Response |
| 1000 | Beacon |
| 1001 | ATIM |
| 1010 | Disassociation |
| 1011 | Authentication |
| 1100 | Deauthentication |

### Type: (01) - Control Frame

- There are four DCF-supported Control frames.
- Control frames coordination the movement of data frames:
    - Provide frame reception acknowledgement
    - Read data which was buffered at an AP during PS (power save) mode
    - Support virtual carrier medium reservation in mixed mode
    - Support RTS/CTS medium reservation to compensate for "hidden nodes."
- ***The 802.11 ACK Control frame is not related to the TCP ACK or LLC Type-2 frames.***

```
Frame Control Byte 0
 Protocol Level   [xxxxxx00]   0
 Type             [xxxx01xx]   Control
 Sub-Type         [1101xxxx]   ACK
```

| 01 | Control |
|---|---|
| | Subtype |
| 1010 | PS-Poll |
| 1011 | RTS |
| 1100 | CTS |
| 1101 | ACK |

## Type: (10) - Data Frame

- 802.11 defines two DCF-supported data frames.
- Standard data frames have an 802.2 LLC field and carry an upper-layer payload.
- Null-Data frames don't have an 802.2 LLC field or payload
  - in combination with the PwrMgmt bit in the Mac header they communicate the STAs PS status.

```
⊟ Frame Control Byte 0
   Protocol Level   [xxxxxx00]  0
   Type             [xxxx10xx]  Data
   Sub-Type         [0100xxxx]  Null
```

| 10 | Data |
|----|------|
| Subtype | |
| 0000 | Data (payload) |
| 0100 | Data (null) |

## 2.4-GHz ISM Channel Overlap

- The amount of interference that a receiver can tolerate is a function of physical location, receiver sensitivity and minimum S/N (signal to noise ratio)
  - The RSSI (received or radio signal strength indicator), the ***average received power over the channel's 22-MHz bandwidth***.
- The interference induced by overlapping channels is a function of physical location, channel separation, transmit power and antenna gain and directionality

## ISM Channel Spectrum Mask

- The U.S. 2.4-GHz ISM band has 11 overlapped, staggered channels. Channels 1, 6 and 11 can be physically co-located without significant interference.
- ISM channels have a 22-MHz bandwidth; 5-MHz separates the channel center frequencies and five channels of separation provide 25-MHz of isolation.
- The FCC specifies that the spectrum mask must be attenuated from the channel's center frequency by a minimum of:
  - 30-dB at 11-MHz from center freq.
  - 50-dB at 22-MHz from center freq.
- There is a still a significant amount of energy overlap between the three "non-overlapping" channels
- The spectrum mask specifications for 802.11g provides even less isolation.

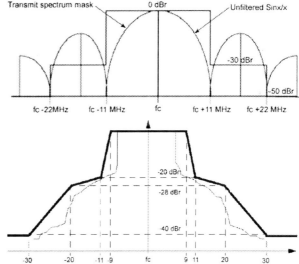

## Channel Overlap and Network Monitor Confusion

Although the network monitor is configured to capture traffic on a fixed channel, frames such as beacons and probe requests may be received on other channels, with no distinguishing feature other than a lower RSSI and a higher CRC error rate.

# Chapter 3: Unleashing the 802.11 Network Monitor

## *802.11 Concepts*

- Distribution System
- 802.11 Addresses
- Frame Control, Byte-1 To- and From-DS Bits
- Error Checking, FCS and Frame Control, Byte-1 Retry Bit
- Intra-BSS Communications
- Inter-BSS Communications
- 802.11 to Ethernet Communications
- 802.1lg Protection and CTS-to-Self
- 802.2 LLC and SNAP

The first two chapters were about as enjoyable as a root canal. They were written last, after I had determined precisely what PHY layer concepts are needed to support L2 frame analysis. As you progress through the next five chapters you'll see PHY concepts frequently cited to reinforce the subtle and detailed issues of real-world 802.11 frame analysis, and that's the foundation of synergistic learning

This chapter is dedicated to understanding the WLAN troubleshooter's most fundamental skill, which is BSS/Ethernet frame flow. It also provides the perspective that why, beyond the usual security issues, network resource sharing between wireless nodes stresses the AP's DSS and the BSA bandwidth. By the end of the first capture file analysis you'll be so outraged that you'll agree that ***the first law of WLAN performance optimization is to ensure that all shared resources are hung off of the wired Ethernet***.

The chapter is best read in the close company of a computer running LinkFerret. Although the relevant portions of each capture are reproduced in the text, one always learns best from the driver's seat. I encourage you to expand the nodes, scour the fields, contemplate the frame sequencing in the brief decode windows. Feel the pulse of the BSS as made manifest through network monitor capture files.

## *Quantifying CSMA/CA Parameters*

In the last chapter we did a detailed analysis of CSMA/CA. From an optimization perspective unless an 802.11 node has a significantly high retry rate (i.e. retransmitting corrupted frames due to collisions) we must assume that the physical CS/CAA mechanisms are functioning properly

### Collision Avoidance with the CW and Back-Off Timer

The collision avoidance provided by the variable CW and back-off timer is unique to every node in the BSS and can't be directly measured by a network monitor. A poorly written driver may not implement the back-off timer mechanism correctly, which increases collisions and retransmissions. Bad drivers are identified by symptoms revealed in network monitor captures rather than objective measurement.

## Collision Avoidance with the Duration Field and NAV Timers

The only part of CSMA/CA that can be objectively measured with a network monitor is a frame's duration field value. We're still making the assumption that every node in the BSA receives every transmission and sets its NAV timer appropriately. Chapter 6 investigates what happens when the virtual carrier mechanism fails because some STAs don't receive transmissions from other STAs in the BSA. The maximum throughput calculations in Chapter 7 provide all the material that you need to verify duration field calculations.

## *Distribution System (DS)*

The AP's DSS (distribution system service) may:

- ***Forward*** the frame to another STA in the BSS
- ***Forward*** the frame to another AP in the ESS. Along a wired backbone or a WDS (wireless distribution system.)
- ***Convert*** the frame to Ethernet and ***forward*** it to its Ethernet portal interface.

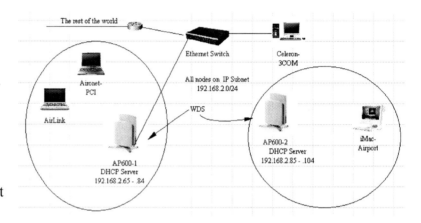

- ***Consume*** the frame if the AP itself is the frame's ultimate destination. That's what happens when an AP's http management services are accessed or the AP is pinged.

The AP maintains several management tables:
- Association table with MAC addresses and capabilities of associated STAs
- ESS table, with information about every AP in the ESS
- Dynamic bridging table that has the MAC addresses of nodes currently residing on of its radio and Ethernet interfaces

## 802.11 Fields Examined in This Chapter

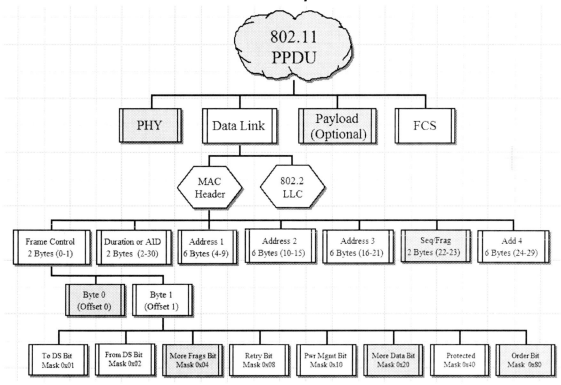

- *Frame Control Byte-1*: To/From DS bits, Retry bit, PwrMgmt bit and Protected bit.
- *Duration field* providing virtual carrier to protect the subsequent ACK
- *Addresses fields*: We'll examine frames that use one to four addresses.
- **802.2 LLC and SNAP**
- **FCS:** 32-bit CRC used to valid the integrity of the received frame

## To/From DS Bits

The number of address fields in an 802.11 frame is variable. The meaning of each address field changes as the frame is processed and forwarded by the DSS.

*Address-1 is the key address, it may specify*:
- the destination STA
- the local AP
- another AP in the ESS

It depends on the bridged-path which the frame travels. *The To-DS and From-DS bits provide the context to interpret the meaning of the address fields in the current frame.*

> **LinkFerret Fact:** The Destination and Source addresses are displayed in the Brief Decode window. They designate the frame's **originator** and **final recipient**. The To/From DS bits and other addresses are viewed in the Detail Decode Window.

| To-DS | From-DS | Address-1 | Address-2 | Address-3 | Address-4 |
|-------|---------|-----------|-----------|-----------|-----------|
| 0 | 0 | Destination | Source | BSSID | None |
| 0 | 1 | Destination | BSSID | Source | None |
| 1 | 0 | BSSID | Source | Destination | None |
| 1 | 1 | Receiver | Transmitter | Destination | Source |

***Don't memorize this table!*** Let the network monitor show you the function of these bits. The meaning of each combination of the To/From bits and the associated addresses will be obvious after we've completed the analysis of three Ping capture files.

Do memorize this key concept! *Address-1 <u>always</u> designates the next node to receive and process the frame, even though it may not be the final destination.*

## Error Checking and the Retry Bit

### 802.11 FCS Field

A 32-bit CRC is generated from the data in the frame and compared to the value of the received FCS field. If they don't match, the frame is silently discarded and the node enters CSMA/CA EIFS error recovery mode.

If the calculated and received CRC match, the receiver waits one SIFS and sends an ACK. On receipt of the ACK with a zero value duration field, the medium is available for contention.

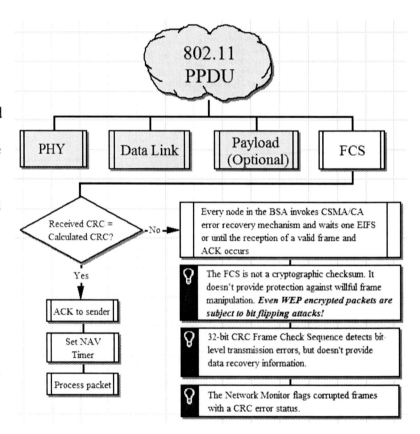

The sender keeps of a copy of the frame in a transmit buffer. If a timely ACK is received the frame is deleted; if the ACK Time-out interval occurs, the sender sets the frame's Retry-bit and resends the frame within the EIFS recovery interval.

## The Retry Bit

Frame Control Byte-1 consists of 8 single-bit flags. Bit and byte numbering always starts zero, so the Retry bit is specified as bit-3 and has a filter mask of 0x08.

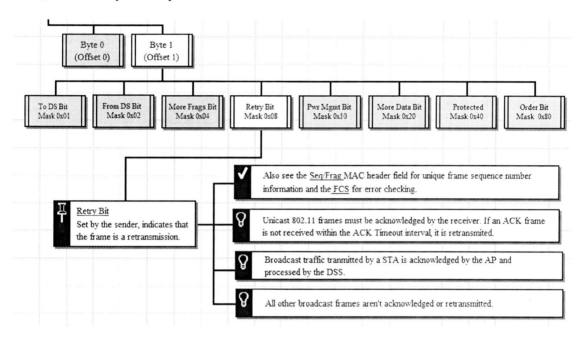

Retry frames have the same 12-bit sequence and 4-bit fragment number as the original frame. When analyzing frame flow try to match each unicast frame with its associated ACK. *Although theoretically it should always be the next frame in a promiscuous capture, the receiver's response time is based on many factors which are independent of the network load.* The errors and retries rates for live capture and capture files are accessed in the LinkFerret Statistics Window, Error Rate Tab.

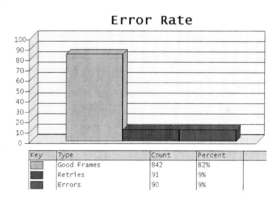

**Error Rate**

| Key | Type | Count | Percent |
|---|---|---|---|
| | Good Frames | 842 | 82% |
| | Retries | 91 | 9% |
| | Errors | 90 | 9% |

**Troubleshooting Tip** It's best practice to determine the PER and Retries Rate before starting a complex analysis. Captures with a high PER and associated retry frames produce strange, unanticipated frame sequencing. A frame received by the network monitor with a CRC error is counted as an Error. A frame received with the Retry bit set is counted as a Retry. Frames are retransmitted because an ACK was not received. A missing ACK may be due to a corrupted frame (collision or RFI), the ACK itself was corrupted, or simply that the receiver was off-line, off-channel or dropped the frame. These statistics provide frame analysis context.

## Intra-BSS Communication

The primary function of an AP is to provide translational bridge services enabling 802.11 STAs to access Ethernet and WAN based resources. SOHO (small-office, home-office) networks and 802.11 enabled-peripherals (e.g. wireless printers) may utilize the BSS as a peer-to-peer LAN, but because of performance and security issues wireless resource sharing should be discouraged.

An AP performs translation between:
- 802.11and Ethernet frames which bridges the WLAN and wired network
- HR/DSSS and ERP-OFDM translation in a mixed-mode BSS

## How do the frames flow when <u>Aironet-PCI pings iMac-Airport?</u>

That's a simple question. Everyone knows how an ICMP Echo Request works.
- Does Belkin-AP function like a transparent Ethernet bridge and passively relay the Echo Request frame to iMac-Airport?
- Aironet-PCI is an 802.11g STA connected at 54-Mbps and iMac-Airport is an 802.11b STA connected at 11-Mbps. How do the different PHY layers communicate?
- At what bit-rate is the Ping transmitted? Does the Aironet-PCI need to fall-back to 11-Mbps because the target is an 802.11b STA?
- How is CSMA/CA affected? If Belkin-AP creates a new HR/DSSS frame, does it have to contend for the medium? That definitely would slow the ping process.
- How much of the BSA's bandwidth is consumed? Counting ACKs and other control frame overhead, how many frames are transmitted to exchange one Echo Request/Echo Reply sequence?

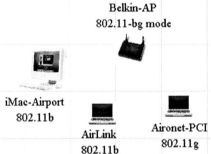

*Think about it - It should be straight-forward. Frame-level analysis is an intense, hands-on, down-and-dirty, bit-level obsession. Jot down some notes on your musings. This may seem like a lot of silly questions for a simple Ping, but that's the whole point.*

## Ten Frames per Ping, Surely, you must be joking?

It's time to get your hands dirty. Execute LinkFerret, open the PSP-SRV namespace and then the capture file Ping-54-to-11-Final. The original raw capture was saved to file and several iterations of link filters were applied to remove extraneous frames. The rest of the capture files won't be so squeaky clean.

> **LinkFerret Fact:** LinkFerret doesn't automatically reset the display filter. Unless specified otherwise, always ensure that the No Filter is applied.

> **LinkFerret Fact:** A name table maps a MAC or IP address to a symbolic name. Each mapping can also be assigned a different display color when used as a source or destination address. If the namespace is loaded after the capture file is opened, refresh the display (F5) and MAC addresses are replaced with symbolic names. All of the captures in this book use the PSP-SRV namespace.

## The Ping Scenario

- HR/DSSS STAs are associated to the BSS
- "Non-ERP Present" and "Use Protection" bits are set in Belkin-AP's beacon
- 802.11g STAs precede ERP-OFDM transmissions with an HR/DSSS CTS-to-Self frame enabling 802.11b STAs to set their NAV timers.

Here's the Brief Decode display of the first Echo Request & Reply. The simple task that takes two Ethernet frames to accomplish requires 10 frames between two different PHY layer STAs in a mixed-mode BSS!

| Number | Destination | Source | Function | Protocol |
|---|---|---|---|---|
| [0-11]-5 | Aironet-PCI | | CTS | IEEE 802.11 |
| [0-11]-6 | iMac-Airport | Aironet-PCI | Echo Request | ICMP |
| [0-11]-7 | Aironet-PCI | | ACK | IEEE 802.11 |
| [0-11]-8 | iMac-Airport | Aironet-PCI | Echo Request | ICMP |
| [0-11]-9 | Belkin-AP | | ACK | IEEE 802.11 |
| [0-11]-10 | Aironet-PCI | iMac-Airport | Echo Reply | ICMP |
| [0-11]-11 | iMac-Airport | | ACK | IEEE 802.11 |
| [0-11]-12 | Belkin-AP | | CTS | IEEE 802.11 |
| [0-11]-13 | Aironet-PCI | iMac-Airport | Echo Reply | ICMP |
| [0-11]-14 | Belkin-AP | | ACK | IEEE 802.11 |

The "Number" column indicates that channel 11 was captured. If you're following along with LinkFerret and want your brief decode display to be like the one above, ***configure column order in LinkFerret Preferences, Brief Display***.

Frame 5: CTS-to-Self
HR/DSSS PHY Layer, transmitted at 11-Mbps.

| Number | Destination | Source | Function | Protocol |
|---|---|---|---|---|
| [0-11]-5 | Aironet-PCI | | CTS | IEEE 802.11 |

To DS=0, From DS=0
The frame isn't processed by the DSS

**Address** (self-addressed frame)
Receiver: CTS-to-Self is a variation of the RTS/CTS protocol. Aironet-PCI sends itself this frame to make it appear to the rest of the BSS that a traditional RTS/CTS handshake occurred.

Duration: 96-µs is the time required to transmit an Echo Request frame and subsequent ACK with ERP-OFDM modulation at 54-Mbps.

```
⊕ Physical Frame
⊟ IEEE 802.11 MAC Protocol
  ├ Function              CTS
  ⊕ PLCP Header
  ⊕ Frame Control Byte 0
  ⊟ Frame Control Byte 1
    ├ Order            [0xxxxxxx]   off
    ├ WEP              [x0xxxxxx]   off
    ├ More Data        [xx0xxxxx]   off
    ├ Power Mgmt       [xxx0xxxx]   off
    ├ Retry            [xxxx0xxx]   off
    ├ More Fragments   [xxxxx0xx]   off
    ├ From DS          [xxxxxx0x]   off
    └ To DS            [xxxxxxx0]   off
  ├ Duration ID          96
  ⊟ Receiver Address
    ├ Hex Address       00-40-96-A2-F4-34
    ├ Group Bit         [xxxxxxx0 xxxxxxx:
    ├ Local Bit         [xxxxxx0x xxxxxxx:
    ├ Logical Names     [[Aironet-PCI]]
    └ Vendor Name       Aironet
```

> ***Bit Terminology***: A bit that's equal to <u>1</u> is also <u>set</u> or <u>true</u>; a bit that's equal to <u>0</u> is also <u>reset</u> or <u>false</u>. It's a matter of context and taste. I prefer the set/reset terminology.

<u>Frame 6: Echo Request</u>

| Number | Destination | Source | Function | Protocol |
|--------|-------------|--------|----------|----------|
| [0-11]-6 | iMac-Airport | Aironet-PCI | Echo Request | ICMP |

**Physical frame header:**
Now that it controls the medium, Aironet-PCI shifts to ERP-OFDM mode at 54-Mbps.

```
⊟ Physical Frame
   ├ Status              No Errors
   ├ Interface Number    0
   ├ Frame Number        6
   ├ Frame size          92
   ├ Bytes Captured      92
   ├ Frame Media Type    IEEE 802.11
   ├ Frame Captured      April  9, 2005  2
   ├ Frame Captured      April  9, 2005  1
   ├ Trace Delta         00:00:02:662:740
   ├ Packet Delta        00:00:00:000:151
   ├ Channel             11
   ├ Speed               54MBS
   ├ Signal              82
   └ Quality             0
```

**MAC Header:**
The Echo Request is encapsulated in an 802.11 data frame.

<u>To-DS=1, From-DS=0</u>
This indicates that the frame was transmitted by a STA and must be processed by the DSS.

<u>Duration</u> = 44-µs. Of the original 96-µs reserved by the CTS-to-Self frame 44-µs remains to protect the subsequent ACK.

**Addresses**
BSSID: Belkin-AP's Radio card is the ***first address***. Although it's not the final destination, this frame must be processed by the BSS's DSS which runs on Belkin-AP.
<u>Source</u>: Aironet-PCI transmitted the frame
<u>Destination</u>: iMac-Airport. This is the frame's final destination. iMac-Airport may be in the same BSS, in another BSS in the ESS or perhaps a wired node on the Ethernet network. This is determined by the DSS accessing the AP's bridging table.

```
⊞ Physical Frame
⊟ IEEE 802.11 MAC Protocol
   ├ Function                 Data
 ⊞ PLCP Header
 ⊞ Frame Control Byte 0
 ⊟ Frame Control Byte 1
   │  ├ Order          [0xxxxxxx]  off
   │  ├ WEP            [x1xxxxxx]  on
   │  ├ More Data      [xx0xxxxx]  off
   │  ├ Power Mgmt     [xxx0xxxx]  off
   │  ├ Retry          [xxxx0xxx]  off
   │  ├ More Fragments [xxxxx0xx]  off
   │  ├ From DS        [xxxxxx0x]  off
   │  └ To DS          [xxxxxxx1]  on
 ⊞ WEP Information
   ├ Duration ID              44
 ⊟ BSSID
   │  ├ Hex Address    00-11-50-0E-BC-53
   │  ├ Group Bit      [xxxxxxx0 xxxxxxxx xxxxxxx
   │  ├ Local Bit      [xxxxxx0x xxxxxxxx xxxxxxx
   │  └ Logical Names  [[Belkin-AP]]
 ⊟ Source Address
   │  ├ Hex Address    00-40-96-A2-F4-34
   │  ├ Group Bit      [xxxxxxx0 xxxxxxxx xxxxxxx
   │  ├ Local Bit      [xxxxxx0x xxxxxxxx xxxxxxx
   │  ├ Logical Names  [[Aironet-PCI]]
   │  └ Vendor Name    Aironet
 ⊟ Destination Address
   │  ├ Hex Address    00-30 65-2B-48-3C
   │  ├ Group Bit      [xxxxxxx0 xxxxxxxx xxxxxxx
   │  ├ Local Bit      [xxxxxx0x xxxxxxxx xxxxxxx
   │  ├ Logical Names  [[iMac-Airport]]
   │  └ Vendor Name    APPLE Computer
   ├ Fragment          [xxxxxxxx xxxx0000]  0
   └ Sequence          [11111011 1111xxxx]  4031
```

> **Important Addressing Note**: As in a conventional Ethernet environment, if the destination node is on a different IP Subnet, the frame's Destination MAC address is the MAC address of the subnet's default gateway and is determined by the STA broadcasting an ARP request prior to constructing the data frame.

Frame 7: ACK

| Number | Destination | Source | Function | Protocol |
|--------|-------------|--------|----------|----------|
| [0-11]-7 | Aironet-PCI | | ACK | IEEE 802.11 |

Which node acknowledges the receipt of the Echo Request? The frame's speed is 24-Mbps; it can't be iMac-Airport. This ACK was transmitted by Belkin-AP the receiver of frame 6.

To/From DS=0
Like CTS, an ACK is a control frame. Control frames are valid only in the BSS where they are generated. They are never processed by the DSS

Duration = 0 With the exception of 802.11 fragmentation, ACK duration is zero. The frame dialog is complete, virtual carrier is released and nodes may decrement their back-off timers.

**Address**
Receiver: Aironet-PCI. ***The address of the sender isn't in the frame.*** It's inferred by scanning the capture and locating the last frame sent by the recipient of the ACK. ***A node doesn't transmit additional frames until the ACK is received or the ACK Timeout interval expires.***

```
⊟ Physical Frame
   - Status                 No Errors
   - Interface Number       0
   - Frame Number           7
   - Frame size             10
   - Bytes Captured         10
   - Frame Media Type       IEEE 802.11
   - Frame Captured         April  9, 2005  2
   - Frame Captured         April  9, 2005  1
   - Trace Delta            00:00:02:662:833
   - Packet Delta           00:00:00:000:093
   - Channel                11
   - Speed                  24MBS
   - Signal                 87
   - Quality                0
⊟ IEEE 802.11 MAC Protocol
   - Function               ACK
⊞ PLCP Header
⊞ Frame Control Byte 0
⊟ Frame Control Byte 1
   - Order          [0xxxxxxx]   off
   - WEP            [x0xxxxxx]   off
   - More Data      [xx0xxxxx]   off
   - Power Mgmt     [xxx0xxxx]   off
   - Retry          [xxxx0xxx]   off
   - More Fragments [xxxxx0xx]   off
   - From DS        [xxxxxx0x]   off
   - To DS          [xxxxxxx0]   off
   - Duration ID            0
⊟ Receiver Address
   - Hex Address            00-40-96-A2-F4-34
   - Group Bit      [xxxxxxx0 xxxxxxx)
   - Local Bit      [xxxxxx0x xxxxxxx)
   - Logical Names          [[Aironet-PCI]]
   - Vendor Name            Aironet
```

| Number | Destination | Source | Function | Protocol |
|--------|-------------|--------|----------|----------|
| [0-11]-8 | iMac-Airport | Aironet-PCI | Echo Request | ICMP |

Frame 8: Echo Request
The brief decode Window entries for frames 6 & 8 are identical! This frame is transmitted with HR/DSSS at 11-Mbps because an 802.11b STA is the recipient.

To-DS=0, From-DS=1
The frame is sourced by the DSS

**Addresses**
Destination: iMac-Airport.
BSSID: Belkin-AP, The DSS created the HS-DSSS frame.
Source: Aironet-PCI, the frame's originator.

Frames 6 and 8 have the same three addresses, but in different orders and with different meanings as specified by the To/From-DS bits. In this frame, From-DS=1 specifies that iMac-Airport, the final destination, is the first address.

```
⊞ Physical Frame
⊟ IEEE 802.11 MAC Protocol
   - Function               Data
⊞ PLCP Header
⊞ Frame Control Byte 0
⊟ Frame Control Byte 1
   - Order          [0xxxxxxx]   off
   - WEP            [x1xxxxxx]   on
   - More Data      [xx0xxxxx]   off
   - Power Mgmt     [xxx0xxxx]   off
   - Retry          [xxxx0xxx]   off
   - More Fragments [xxxxx0xx]   off
   - From DS        [xxxxxx1x]   on
   - To DS          [xxxxxxx0]   off
⊞ WEP Information
   - Duration ID            213
⊟ Destination Address
   - Hex Address            00-30-65-2B-48-3C
   - Group Bit      [xxxxxxx0 xxxxxxxx xxxxxxx:
   - Local Bit      [xxxxxx0x xxxxxxxx xxxxxxx:
   - Logical Names          [[iMac-Airport]]
   - Vendor Name            APPLE Computer
⊟ BSSID
   - Hex Address            00-11-50-0E-BC-53
   - Group Bit      [xxxxxxx0 xxxxxxxx xxxxxxx:
   - Local Bit      [xxxxxx0x xxxxxxxx xxxxxxx:
   - Logical Names          [[Belkin-AP]]
⊟ Source Address
   - Hex Address            00-40-96-A2-F4-34
   - Group Bit      [xxxxxxx0 xxxxxxxx xxxxxxx:
   - Local Bit      [xxxxxx0x xxxxxxxx xxxxxxx:
   - Logical Names          [[Aironet-PCI]]
   - Vendor Name            Aironet
   - Fragment       [xxxxxxxx xxxx0000]   0
   - Sequence       [10101000 1100xxxx]   2700
```

### Duration value comparison

Frame 6 was transmitted at 54-Mbps with a duration field value of 44-µs, the time required to transmit an ERP-OFDM ACK at 54-Mbps. Frame 6 was transmitted with at 11-Mbps with a duration field value of 213, the time required to transmit an HR/DSSS ACK with a long preamble at 11-Mbps. Each Echo Request frame protects its subsequent ACK.

Frame 9: ACK

The HR/DSSS PHY-layer bit rate of 11-Mbps reinforces that iMac-Airport is acknowledging the receipt of the Echo Request.

To-DS=0, From-DS=0:
ACK is not processed by the DSS.

Duration = 0, Virtual carrier is released and nodes may start to decrement their back-off timers.

**Address**
Receiver: Belkin-AP.

Wow! It took five frames to get there, and iMac-Airport is now ready to respond with an Echo Reply.

| Number | Destination | Source | Function | Protocol |
|---|---|---|---|---|
| [0-11]-9 | Belkin-AP | | ACK | IEEE 802.11 |

```
Physical Frame
   Status                No Errors
   Interface Number      0
   Frame Number          9
   Frame size            10
   Bytes Captured        10
   Frame Media Type      IEEE 802.11
   Frame Captured        April  9, 2005  :
   Frame Captured        April  9, 2005  :
   Trace Delta           00:00:02:663:329
   Packet Delta          00:00:00:000:208
   Channel               11
   Speed                 11MBS
   Signal                84
   Quality               0
IEEE 802.11 MAC Protocol
   Function              ACK
   PLCP Header
   Frame Control Byte 0
   Frame Control Byte 1
      Order              [0xxxxxxx]   off
      WEP                [x0xxxxxx]   off
      More Data          [xx0xxxxx]   off
      Power Mgmt         [xxx0xxxx]   off
      Retry              [xxxx0xxx]   off
      More Fragments     [xxxxx0xx]   off
      From DS            [xxxxxx0x]   off
      To DS              [xxxxxxx0]   off
   Duration ID           0
   Receiver Address
      Hex Address        00-11-50-0E-BC-53
      Group Bit          [xxxxxxx0 xxxxxxx:
      Local Bit          [xxxxxx0x xxxxxxx:
      Logical Names      [[Belkin-AP]]
```

## Frame 10: Echo Reply

As you might imagine the return trip also takes five frames.

To-DS=1, From-DS=0:
The frame will be processed by the DSS.

Duration: 213-µs, like in frame 8, protects an ACK transmitted at 11-Mbps with long PLCP-preamble/header.

**Addresses**
BSSID: Belkin-AP is the intermediate recipient and provides the DSS.
Source: iMac-Airport
Destination: Aironet-PCI, the final receiver

*ERP-OFDM STAs can demodulate HS-DSSS transmissions. 802.11b STAs never use CTS-to-Self medium reservation.*

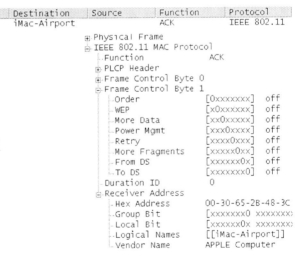

| Number | Destination | Source | Function | Protocol |
|---|---|---|---|---|
| [0-11]-10 | Aironet-PCI | iMac-Airport | Echo Reply | ICMP |

```
⊞ Physical Frame
⊟ IEEE 802.11 MAC Protocol
   ├Function              Data
   ⊞ PLCP Header
   ⊞ Frame Control Byte 0
   ⊟ Frame Control Byte 1
      ├Order            [0xxxxxxx]   off
      ├WEP              [x1xxxxxx]   on
      ├More Data        [xx0xxxxx]   off
      ├Power Mgmt       [xxx0xxxx]   off
      ├Retry            [xxxx0xxx]   off
      ├More Fragments   [xxxxx0xx]   off
      ├From DS          [xxxxxx0x]   off
      └To DS            [xxxxxxx1]   on
   ⊞ WEP Information
   ├Duration ID          213
   ⊟ BSSID
      ├Hex Address      00-11-50-0E-BC-53
      ├Group Bit        [xxxxxxx0 xxxxxxxx xxxxxx:
      ├Local Bit        [xxxxxx0x xxxxxxxx xxxxxx:
      └Logical Names    [[Belkin-AP]]
   ⊟ Source Address
      ├Hex Address      00-30-65-2B-48-3C
      ├Group Bit        [xxxxxxx0 xxxxxxxx xxxxxx:
      ├Local Bit        [xxxxxx0x xxxxxxxx xxxxxx:
      ├Logical Names    [[iMac-Airport]]
      └Vendor Name      APPLE Computer
   ⊟ Destination Address
      ├Hex Address      00-40-96-A2-F4-34
      ├Group Bit        [xxxxxxx0 xxxxxxxx xxxxxx:
      ├Local Bit        [xxxxxx0x xxxxxxxx xxxxxx:
      ├Logical Names    [[Aironet-PCI]]
      └Vendor Name      Aironet
   ├Fragment             [xxxxxxxx xxxx0000]   0
   └Sequence             [00000111 1011xxxx]   123
```

## Frame 11: ACK

Belkin-AP acknowledges the receipt of the Echo Reply frame.

To-DS=0, From-DS=0:
ACK is not processed by the DSS.

Duration: 0-µs, the virtual carrier is released

**Address**
Receiver: iMac-Airport.

| Number | Destination | Source | Function | Protocol |
|---|---|---|---|---|
| [0-11]-11 | iMac-Airport | | ACK | IEEE 802.11 |

```
⊞ Physical Frame
⊟ IEEE 802.11 MAC Protocol
   ├Function             ACK
   ⊞ PLCP Header
   ⊞ Frame Control Byte 0
   ⊟ Frame Control Byte 1
      ├Order           [0xxxxxxx]   off
      ├WEP             [x0xxxxxx]   off
      ├More Data       [xx0xxxxx]   off
      ├Power Mgmt      [xxx0xxxx]   off
      ├Retry           [xxxx0xxx]   off
      ├More Fragments  [xxxxx0xx]   off
      ├From DS         [xxxxxx0x]   off
      └To DS           [xxxxxxx0]   off
   ├Duration ID         0
   ⊟ Receiver Address
      ├Hex Address     00-30-65-2B-48-3C
      ├Group Bit       [xxxxxxx0 xxxxxxx:
      ├Local Bit       [xxxxxx0x xxxxxxx:
      ├Logical Names   [[iMac-Airport]]
      └Vendor Name     APPLE Computer
```

## Frame 12: CTS-to-Self

Belkin-AP's association table specifies that Aironet-PCI is an ERP-OFDM STA.

**To-DS=0, From-DS=0:**
CTS is a control frame and not processed by the DSS.

Duration: 96-µs, just like frame 5, protects the ERP-OFDM Echo Reply and subsequent ACK.

**Address**
Receiver: "Self-addressed" to Belkin-AP

| Number | Destination | Source | Function | Protocol |
|---|---|---|---|---|
| [0-11]-12 | Belkin-AP | | CTS | IEEE 802.11 |

```
⊞ Physical Frame
⊟ IEEE 802.11 MAC Protocol
    Function                CTS
  ⊞ PLCP Header
  ⊞ Frame Control Byte 0
  ⊟ Frame Control Byte 1
      Order           [0xxxxxxx]  off
      WEP             [x0xxxxxx]  off
      More Data       [xx0xxxxx]  off
      Power Mgmt      [xxx0xxxx]  off
      Retry           [xxxx0xxx]  off
      More Fragments  [xxxxx0xx]  off
      From DS         [xxxxxx0x]  off
      To DS           [xxxxxxx0]  off
    Duration ID             96
  ⊟ Receiver Address
      Hex Address     00-11-50-0E-BC-53
      Group Bit       [xxxxxxx0 xxxxxxx>
      Local Bit       [xxxxxx0x xxxxxxx>
      Logical Names   [[Belkin-AP]]
```

## Frame 13: Echo Reply

Like the two Echo Request frames, the two Echo Reply frames are identical in the Brief Decode Window.

**To-DS=0, From-DS=1:**
Sourced by the DSS and bound to a STA in the BSS

Duration: 44-µs, which protects the ERP-OFDM ACK to follow.

**Addresses**
Destination: Aironet-PCI finally receives the Echo Response.
BSSID: Belkin-AP
Source: iMac-Airport

| Number | Destination | Source | Function | Protocol |
|---|---|---|---|---|
| [0-11]-13 | Aironet-PCI | iMac-Airport | Echo Reply | ICMP |

```
⊞ Physical Frame
⊟ IEEE 802.11 MAC Protocol
    Function                Data
  ⊞ PLCP Header
  ⊞ Frame Control Byte 0
  ⊟ Frame Control Byte 1
      Order           [0xxxxxxx]  off
      WEP             [x1xxxxxx]  on
      More Data       [xx0xxxxx]  off
      Power Mgmt      [xxx0xxxx]  off
      Retry           [xxxx0xxx]  off
      More Fragments  [xxxxx0xx]  off
      From DS         [xxxxxx1x]  on
      To DS           [xxxxxxx0]  off
  ⊞ WEP Information
    Duration ID             44
  ⊟ Destination Address
      Hex Address     00-40-96-A2-F4-34
      Group Bit       [xxxxxxx0 xxxxxxxx xxxxxxx:
      Local Bit       [xxxxxx0x xxxxxxxx xxxxxxx:
      Logical Names   [[Aironet-PCI]]
      Vendor Name     Aironet
  ⊟ BSSID
      Hex Address     00-11-50-0E-BC-53
      Group Bit       [xxxxxxx0 xxxxxxxx xxxxxxx:
      Local Bit       [xxxxxx0x xxxxxxxx xxxxxxx:
      Logical Names   [[Belkin-AP]]
  ⊟ Source Address
      Hex Address     00-30-65-2B-48-3C
      Group Bit       [xxxxxxx0 xxxxxxxx xxxxxxx:
      Local Bit       [xxxxxx0x xxxxxxxx xxxxxxx:
      Logical Names   [[iMac-Airport]]
      Vendor Name     APPLE Computer
    Fragment          [xxxxxxxx xxxx0000]  0
    Sequence          [10101000 1101xxxx]  2701
```

## Frame 14: ACK

| Number | Destination | Source | Function | Protocol |
|--------|-------------|--------|----------|----------|
| [0-11]-14 | Belkin-AP | | ACK | IEEE 802.11 |

Aironet-PCI acknowledges the receipt of the Echo Response frame.

```
⊞ Physical Frame
⊟ IEEE 802.11 MAC Protocol
   ├─Function              ACK
   ⊞ PLCP Header
   ⊞ Frame Control Byte 0
   ⊟ Frame Control Byte 1
   │  ├─Order              [0xxxxxxx]   off
   │  ├─WEP                [x0xxxxxx]   off
   │  ├─More Data          [xx0xxxxx]   off
   │  ├─Power Mgmt         [xxx0xxxx]   off
   │  ├─Retry              [xxxx0xxx]   off
   │  ├─More Fragments     [xxxxx0xx]   off
   │  ├─From DS            [xxxxxx0x]   off
   │  └─To DS              [xxxxxxx0]   off
   ├─Duration ID           0
   ⊟ Receiver Address
      ├─Hex Address        00-11-50-0E-BC-53
      ├─Group Bit          [xxxxxxx0 xxxxxxx
      ├─Local Bit          [xxxxx0x xxxxxxx
      └─Logical Names      [[Belkin-AP]]
```

### To/From DS=0
Not processed by the DSS

<u>Duration</u>: 0-μs, the virtual carrier is released and STAs may start to decrement their back-off timers

**Address**
<u>Receiver</u>: Belkin-AP

That's it! If you have LinkFerret running analyze each of the three remaining Echo Request/Reply sequences in the capture. Look through the nooks and crannies and become comfortable with the Brief and Detailed Decode Windows.

## *Where did that Netware Server come from?*

Strange things happen when a network monitor parses a

| Number | Destination | Source | Function | Protocol |
|--------|-------------|--------|----------|----------|
| [0-11]-15 | Netware Server | | ACK | IEEE 802.11 |

corrupted frame. The Brief Decode windows list an ACK with the destination as a Netware Server. That's perplexing because they're aren't any Netware servers on the monitored network.

The first piece of information in the Physical Frame specifies that frame-15 has a CRC Error.

```
⊟ Physical Frame
   └─Status              Frame Error [CRC Error]
```

The interpretation of a corrupted frame is meaningless, but their presence is always meaningful as described at the beginning of the chapter.

## *Pinging between 802.11b STAs*

In the previous analysis the intra-BSS communication was between STAs with different PHY layers. What about communications between STAs with the same PHY layer? Since there's no frame conversion required does the DSS still have to recreate and redistribute every frame, thereby doubling the BSA traffic?

Let's examine the raw (unfiltered) capture of an Echo Request/Response between two 802.11b STAs in which ***AirLink pings iMac-Airport***.

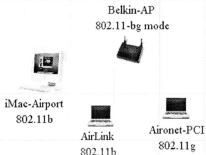

Belkin-AP
802.11-bg mode

iMac-Airport
802.11b

AirLink
802.11b

Aironet-PCI
802.11g

## The Ping 802.11b Brief Display

Open the capture file Ping-11-to-11-Raw. The LinkFerret Capture Rate and Error Rate statistics indicate that this is a typical capture with no dropped frames. But the important issue to notice is that the retry rate is 11%, about twice the error rate of 5%.

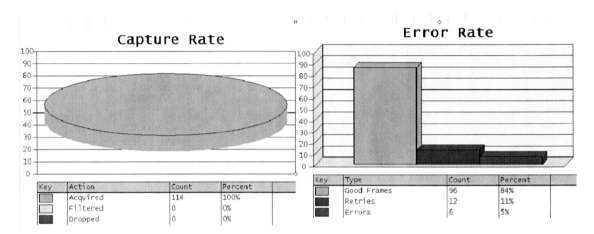

| Key | Action | Count | Percent |
|---|---|---|---|
| | Acquired | 114 | 100% |
| | Filtered | 0 | 0% |
| | Dropped | 0 | 0% |

| Key | Type | Count | Percent |
|---|---|---|---|
| | Good Frames | 96 | 84% |
| | Retries | 12 | 11% |
| | Errors | 6 | 5% |

| Number | Destination | Source | Function | Protocol | Time |
|---|---|---|---|---|---|
| [0-11]-16 | iMac-Airport | AirLink | Echo Request | ICMP | 00:00:02:910:154 |
| [0-11]-17 | AirLink | | ACK | IEEE 802.11 | 00:00:02:910:353 |
| [0-11]-18 | iMac-Airport | AirLink | Echo Request | ICMP | 00:00:02:910:708 |
| [0-11]-19 | Belkin-AP | | ACK | IEEE 802.11 | 00:00:02:910:926 |
| [0-11]-20 | AirLink | iMac-Airport | Echo Reply | ICMP | 00:00:02:911:843 |
| [0-11]-21 | iMac-Airport | | ACK | IEEE 802.11 | 00:00:02:912:030 |

| Number | Destination | Source | Function | Protocol | Time |
|---|---|---|---|---|---|
| [0-11]-62 | AirLink | iMac-Airport | Echo Reply | ICMP | 00:00:03:709:268 |
| [0-11]-63 | Belkin-AP | | ACK | IEEE 802.11 | 00:00:03:709:475 |

AirLink initiates the sequence with an Echo Request frame to iMac-Airport in frame-16. Note the absence of CTS-to-Self frames. The Time column is configured in Preferences, Brief Display as Start Relative time. All times are relative to the start of the capture. The time at frame-16 is 2 seconds, 910ms and 154μs. Another very useful time configuration is packet-delta, which displays the approximate time interval between consecutive captured frames.

It takes four frames to get the Echo Request to iMac-Airport. One would expect four frames to return the Echo Reply. Other than the absence of CTS-to-Self, the frame sequence is identical to the previous Ping example.

When the frame is send by a STA it has the To-DS bit set and the BSSID is the first address. When the frame is sent by the AP it has the From-DS bit set and the destination STA is the first address. The ACKs have To/From-DS=0 and are not processed by the DSS.

In frame 21, iMac-Airport receives the ACK from Belkin-AP for the Echo Reply. ***Why does it take almost 800ms and 41 frames before Belkin-AP relays the Echo Reply to AirLink?***

| Number | Destination | Source | Function | Protocol | Time |
|--------|-------------|--------|----------|----------|------|
| [0-11]-22 | Broadcast | AirLink | Probe Request | IEEE 802.11 | 00:00:02:970:649 |
| [0-11]-23 | AirLink | Belkin-AP | Probe Response | IEEE 802.11 | 00:00:02:971:526 |
| [0-11]-24 | Broadcast | AirLink | Probe Request | IEEE 802.11 | 00:00:02:972:438 |
| [0-11]-25 | AirLink | Belkin-AP | Probe Response | IEEE 802.11 | 00:00:02:973:548 |
| [0-11]-26 | Belkin-AP | | ACK | IEEE 802.11 | 00:00:02:973:854 |
| [0-11]-27 | Broadcast | AirLink | Probe Request | IEEE 802.11 | 00:00:02:974:309 |
| [0-11]-28 | AirLink | Belkin-AP | Probe Response | IEEE 802.11 | 00:00:02:974:999 |
| [0-11]-29 | Belkin-AP | | ACK | IEEE 802.11 | 00:00:02:975:265 |
| [0-11]-30 | Broadcast | AirLink | Probe Request | IEEE 802.11 | 00:00:03:091:727 |
| [0-11]-31 | Broadcast | AirLink | Probe Request | IEEE 802.11 | 00:00:03:092:307 |
| [0-11]-32 | Broadcast | AirLink | Probe Request | IEEE 802.11 | 00:00:03:092:720 |
| [0-11]-33 | AirLink | Belkin-AP | Probe Response | IEEE 802.11 | 00:00:03:093:656 |
| [0-11]-34 | Broadcast | AirLink | Probe Request | IEEE 802.11 | 00:00:03:094:579 |
| [0-11]-35 | AirLink | Belkin-AP | Probe Response | IEEE 802.11 | 00:00:03:095:572 |
| [0-11]-36 | AirLink | Belkin-AP | Probe Response | IEEE 802.11 | 00:00:03:097:754 |
| [0-11]-37 | AirLink | Belkin-AP | Probe Response | IEEE 802.11 | 00:00:03:101:214 |
| [0-11]-38 | AirLink | Belkin-AP | Probe Response | IEEE 802.11 | 00:00:03:103:689 |
| [0-11]-39 | Belkin-AP | | ACK | IEEE 802.11 | 00:00:03:104:001 |
| [0-11]-40 | AirLink | Belkin-AP | Probe Response | IEEE 802.11 | 00:00:03:452:001 |
| [0-11]-41 | AirLink | Belkin-AP | Probe Response | IEEE 802.11 | 00:00:03:455:511 |
| [0-11]-42 | AirLink | Belkin-AP | Probe Response | IEEE 802.11 | 00:00:03:457:475 |
| [0-11]-43 | AirLink | Belkin-AP | Probe Response | IEEE 802.11 | 00:00:03:459:692 |
| [0-11]-44 | AirLink | Belkin-AP | Probe Response | IEEE 802.11 | 00:00:03:462:272 |
| [0-11]-45 | AirLink | Belkin-AP | Probe Response | IEEE 802.11 | 00:00:03:463:554 |
| [0-11]-46 | Belkin-AP | | ACK | IEEE 802.11 | 00:00:03:463:859 |
| [0-11]-47 | Broadcast | AirLink | Probe Request | IEEE 802.11 | 00:00:03:571:295 |
| [0-11]-48 | Broadcast | AirLink | Probe Request | IEEE 802.11 | 00:00:03:571:944 |
| [0-11]-49 | Broadcast | AirLink | Probe Request | IEEE 802.11 | 00:00:03:572:555 |
| [0-11]-50 | Broadcast | AirLink | Probe Request | IEEE 802.11 | 00:00:03:573:202 |
| [0-11]-51 | FF02::2 | iMac-Airport | Router Solicitation | ICMPv6 | 00:00:03:639:931 |
| [0-11]-52 | iMac-Airport | | ACK | IEEE 802.11 | 00:00:03:640:099 |
| [0-11]-53 | Broadcast | AirLink | Probe Request | IEEE 802.11 | 00:00:03:691:504 |
| [0-11]-54 | Broadcast | AirLink | Probe Request | IEEE 802.11 | 00:00:03:692:465 |
| [0-11]-55 | Broadcast | AirLink | Probe Request | IEEE 802.11 | 00:00:03:693:416 |
| [0-11]-56 | Broadcast | AirLink | Probe Request | IEEE 802.11 | 00:00:03:693:925 |
| [0-11]-57 | FF02::2 | iMac-Airport | Router Solicitation | ICMPv6 | 00:00:03:706:631 |
| [0-11]-58 | AirLink | Belkin-AP | Probe Response | IEEE 802.11 | 00:00:03:707:616 |
| [0-11]-59 | Belkin-AP | | ACK | IEEE 802.11 | 00:00:03:707:918 |
| [0-11]-60 | Belkin-AP | AirLink | PS-Poll | IEEE 802.11 | 00:00:03:708:421 |
| [0-11]-61 | AirLink | | ACK | IEEE 802.11 | 00:00:03:708:720 |

The brief capture shows frames 22 -61 of the capture. These frames represent the missing 800-ms that occurred between the two Echo Reply frames.

> **Troubleshooting Tip** A STA transmits a probe request frame to actively scan for APs. The probe request isn't acknowledged because it has a broadcast destination address and the To/From DS bits reset. *But the probe response is a unicast frame that must be acknowledged by the recipient or it will be retransmitted as a retry.*

Remember the high rate of retries in the LinkFerret statistics window? The majority of the traffic is Probe Request frames sent by AirLink and Probe Response frames sent by Belkin-AP. What the capture doesn't directly show is that AirLink isn't just probing for APs on channel 11, but it is also actively probing all of the other channels.

Although this started out as a standard 802.11b ping analysis, let's divert our attention to determine why this additional traffic is being generated and whether it indicates a malfunction or performance issue.

## Applying a Retires Filter

The LinkFerret Error Rate statistics window specified that of the 114 frames captured, 12 frames were retries. Let's filter the frames in the capture buffer by applying a retries filter.

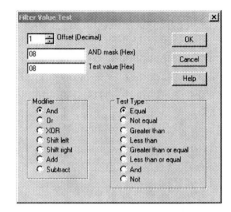

- Offset: 1
- AND mask: 0x08
- Test value: 0x08
- Modifier: AND
- Test type: Equal

This filter says, "Look in the second byte of the MAC-header. If bit-3 is set, display the frame, otherwise, hide it"

Select the **Retries** filter from the jump-up window at the bottom of the LinkFerret display and press **F5** to refresh the display.

| Number | Destination | Source | Function | Protocol | Time |
|---|---|---|---|---|---|
| [0-11]-1 | AirLink | Belkin-AP | Probe Response | IEEE 802.11 | 00:00:02:732:592 |
| [0-11]-2 | AirLink | Belkin-AP | Probe Response | IEEE 802.11 | 00:00:02:733:925 |
| [0-11]-3 | AirLink | Belkin-AP | Probe Response | IEEE 802.11 | 00:00:02:973:548 |
| [0-11]-4 | AirLink | Belkin-AP | Probe Response | IEEE 802.11 | 00:00:03:095:572 |
| [0-11]-5 | AirLink | Belkin-AP | Probe Response | IEEE 802.11 | 00:00:03:097:754 |
| [0-11]-6 | AirLink | Belkin-AP | Probe Response | IEEE 802.11 | 00:00:03:101:214 |
| [0-11]-7 | AirLink | Belkin-AP | Probe Response | IEEE 802.11 | 00:00:03:103:689 |
| [0-11]-8 | AirLink | Belkin-AP | Probe Response | IEEE 802.11 | 00:00:03:455:511 |
| [0-11]-9 | AirLink | Belkin-AP | Probe Response | IEEE 802.11 | 00:00:03:457:475 |
| [0-11]-10 | AirLink | Belkin-AP | Probe Response | IEEE 802.11 | 00:00:03:459:692 |
| [0-11]-11 | AirLink | Belkin-AP | Probe Response | IEEE 802.11 | 00:00:03:462:272 |
| [0-11]-12 | AirLink | Belkin-AP | Probe Response | IEEE 802.11 | 00:00:03:463:554 |

All 12 retries are probe response frames sent by Belkin-AP to AirLink. Inspecting the physical frame parameters in LinkFerret shows that these frames are valid; they were received by the network monitor without a CRC error. ***We can assume that the retries occurred because AirLink did not transmit a timely ACK to Belkin-AP***. Examine the previous unfiltered Brief Decode Window and you'll notice a flurry of six Probe Response frames before Belkin-AP finally receives AirLink's ACK.

***Why didn't AirLink send the ACK? Collisions aren't an issue***. In the next Chapter we'll discuss active probing, going off-channel and communicating a STA status to the AP but here's the overview of what's occurring:

AirLink is out probing for APs on other channels so it's missing Belkin-AP's Probe Response frames to its original Probe Request. A STA only receives frames on the channel to which its radio is tuned. Properly-written drivers set the PwrMgmt bit in Frame Control Byte-1 to inform the AP that the STA will be temporarily unavailable; either entering Power Save sleep mode or going off-channel. The AP buffers data for the STA until it returns to full-power mode or is back on-channel.

We have to determine:

- Is AirLink staying on-channel long enough to allow an AP to transmit a probe response?
- Is AirLink correctly notifying the AP that it's going off-channel?
- If so, is the AP buffering AirLink's frames until it is back on-channel?
- Is AirLink properly informing the AP when it is back on-channel and ready to read the buffered data?
- How do ACKs work when the data is being buffered by the AP?

You're starting to get the idea that an 802.11 network monitor and some well-developed skills will forever change the way that you troubleshoot and maintain WLANs. We'll revisit the Ping-11-to-11-Raw capture when we learn a bit more about the Beacon TIM, PS-Poll frames and power management bit flipping.

## Yet Another Ping – STA to Wired Ethernet

One always learned best by studying variations on a theme. Each variation teaches you something new, while reinforcing the original concept. The concept that we're hammering on here is the function of the AP's DSS. We've seen intra-BSS pings between STAs with the same and different PHY layers.

Let's see what happens when AirLink pings iMac-Ethernet. To get the complete picture we'd have to monitor the 802.11 and wired Ethernet networks. The Ethernet side is routine, so we'll focus on the 802.11 frames.

**LinkFerret Fact** LinkFerret is also an Ethernet monitor. As an alternative to an expensive Ethernet tap to capture iMac-Ethernet's traffic you could simply plug a cheap 100-Mbps hub into one of the Ethernet Switch's ports. Then plug iMac-Ethernet into one hub port and the LinkFerret capture appliance into another hub port. Since the hub is a shared collision domain you'll capture all frames bound to/from iMac-Ethernet. It's low tech and low performance but it's flexible and it works!

Open the capture file Ping-WLAN-Ethernet-Raw, apply No Filter and press **F5**. Frames 1 through 17 contain the Echo Request/Reply of AirLink's first ping exchange with iMac-Ethernet.

| Number | Destination | Source | Function | Protocol | Time |
|--------|-------------|--------|----------|----------|------|
| [0-11]-1 | Broadcast | AirLink | Request-192.168.0.69 | ARP | 00:00:02:140:311 |
| [0-11]-2 | AirLink | | ACK | IEEE 802.11 | 00:00:02:140:520 |
| [0-11]-3 | Belkin-AP | AirLink | PS-Poll | IEEE 802.11 | 00:00:02:157:413 |
| [0-11]-4 | AirLink | | ACK | IEEE 802.11 | 00:00:02:157:720 |
| [0-11]-5 | AirLink | iMac-Ethernet | Response-192.168.0.69 | ARP | 00:00:02:158:138 |
| [0-11]-6 | Belkin-AP | | ACK | IEEE 802.11 | 00:00:02:158:340 |
| [0-11]-7 | Belkin-AP | AirLink | PS-Poll | IEEE 802.11 | 00:00:02:158:950 |
| [0-11]-8 | AirLink | | ACK | IEEE 802.11 | 00:00:02:159:249 |
| [0-11]-9 | AirLink | Belkin-AP | Null | IEEE 802.11 | 00:00:02:159:731 |
| [0-11]-10 | Belkin-AP | | ACK | IEEE 802.11 | 00:00:02:159:956 |
| [0-11]-11 | iMac-Ethernet | AirLink | Echo Request | ICMP | 00:00:02:160:641 |
| [0-11]-12 | AirLink | | ACK | IEEE 802.11 | 00:00:02:160:837 |
| [0-11]-13 | Broadcast | AirLink | Request-192.168.0.69 | ARP | 00:00:02:260:225 |
| [0-11]-14 | Belkin-AP | AirLink | PS-Poll | IEEE 802.11 | 00:00:02:260:666 |
| [0-11]-15 | AirLink | | ACK | IEEE 802.11 | 00:00:02:260:979 |
| [0-11]-16 | AirLink | iMac-Ethernet | Echo Reply | ICMP | 00:00:02:261:546 |
| [0-11]-17 | Belkin-AP | | ACK | IEEE 802.11 | 00:00:02:261:748 |

Overview:

- <u>Frames 1 & 2</u>: ARP to target IP address 192.168.0.69
- <u>Frames 5 & 6</u>: ARP response from iMac-Ethernet
- <u>Frames 11&12</u>: Echo Request and ACK
- <u>Frames 16 & 17</u>: Echo Reply and ACK

| Number | Destination | Source | Function | Protocol | Time |
|--------|-------------|--------|----------|----------|------|
| [0-11]-1 | Broadcast | AirLink | Request-192.168.0.69 | ARP | 00:00:02:140:311 |

<u>Frame 1</u>: ARP Request

<u>To-DS=1</u>: the frame is processed by the DSS

**Addresses**
BSSID: Belkin-AP
<u>Source</u>: AirLink
<u>Destination</u>: Broadcast. A MAC address of all one's designates network broadcast. The AP's bridging service translates the 802.11 ARP frame to an Ethernet format and broadcasts it out the AP's Ethernet portal.

<u>802.2 LLC and Upper-Layer Payload</u>
This is the first frame that we've seen with the LLC and payload fields exposed. LinkFerret is configured with the BSS's static WEP key so the 802.2 LLC and data payload are automatically decrypted. As discussed in Chapter 1, Ethernet II is the most common frame type and uses the Ether Type field. 802.11 employs LLC 802.2. SNAP supports standard Ether Type designations. The SNAP Ether-Type 0x0806

```
⊞-Physical Frame
⊟-IEEE 802.11 MAC Protocol
   ├─Function              Data
   ⊞-PLCP Header
   ⊞-Frame Control Byte 0
   ⊞-Frame Control Byte 1
   ⊞-WEP Information
   ├─Duration ID           213
   ⊟-BSSID
   │  ├─Hex Address        00-11-50-0E-BC-53
   │  ├─Group Bit          [xxxxxxx0 xxxxxxxx xxxxxxxx
   │  ├─Local Bit          [xxxxxx0x xxxxxxxx xxxxxxxx
   │  └─Logical Names      [[Belkin-AP]]
   ⊟-Source Address
   │  ├─Hex Address        00-0D-88-E5-D3-2A
   │  ├─Group Bit          [xxxxxxx0 xxxxxxxx xxxxxxxx
   │  ├─Local Bit          [xxxxxx0x xxxxxxxx xxxxxxxx
   │  └─Logical Names      [[AirLink]]
   ⊟-Destination Address
   │  ├─Hex Address        FF-FF-FF-FF-FF-FF
   │  ├─Group Bit          [xxxxxxx1 xxxxxxxx xxxxxxxx
   │  ├─Local Bit          [xxxxxx1x xxxxxxxx xxxxxxxx
   │  └─Logical Names      [[Broadcast]]
   ├─Fragment              [xxxxxxxx xxxx0000]  0
   └─Sequence              [00001011 0010xxxx]  178
⊟-IEEE 802.2 Logical Link Control
   ├─Destination SAP       AA SNAP
   ├─Source SAP            AA SNAP
   ├─Frame Type            Command
   └─Unnumbered Frame      Unnumbered Information
⊟-IEEE Sub-Network Access Protocol
   ├─Authority             000000    Xerox
   └─EtherType             0806       IP Address Resolut
⊟-Address Resolution Protocol
   ├─Hardware Type         Ethernet (10Mb)
   ├─Protocol Type         0800   IP
   ├─Hardware Addr Size    6
   ├─Protocol Addr Size    4
   ├─ARP Function          Address Resolution Request
   ├─Sender HW Address     00-0D-88-E5-D3-2A
   ├─Sender Prot Address   192.168.0.68
   ├─Target HW Address     00-00-00-00-00-00
   └─Target Prot Address   192.168.0.69
```

specifies "IP Resolution" i.e. an ARP request. The ARP field indicates that the desired information is the "Target HW address."

Frame-5 is the ARP response.

| Number | Destination | Source | Function | Protocol | Time |
|---|---|---|---|---|---|
| [0-11]-5 | AirLink | iMac-Ethernet | Response-192.168.0.69 | ARP | 00:00:02:158:138 |

## Broadcast Frames and Acknowledgement

| Number | Destination | Source | Function | Protocol | Time |
|---|---|---|---|---|---|
| [0-11]-2 | AirLink | | ACK | IEEE 802.11 | 00:00:02:140:520 |

*Most books and whitepapers incorrectly state that "802.11 only ACKs unicast traffic, never broadcast or multicast traffic." Frame 2 clearly shows the Belkin-AP acknowledging AirLink's broadcast ARP request.*

Why the contradiction? I divide fames into two types, those with To-DS=1 and those with From-DS=1. Broadcast and multicast frames distributed to the BSS via the AP's DSS (From-DS=1) are not acknowledged because the target is any and all active STAs. *However, broadcast frames headed to the AP's DSS (To-DS=1) must be acknowledged because the immediate target is the AP!* How else can the STA know that the broadcast frame was received, processed by the DSS and forwarded to the Ethernet network?

*! Exam Alert*: Those of you with Microsoft and Cisco certifications know all too well that roughly 20% of "correct" certification exam answers are incorrect – both technically and practically. When I'm confronted with the broadcast/ACK question on a certification exam (twice so far) I respond with the least technically correct but *most dogmatically obvious answer*, "Of course not, broadcast frames aren't ACKed."

## Frame 13: Why the second ARP request?

Those of you with eagle eyes may have noticed a second ARP request for 192.168.0.69. Frames 1 and 13 appear to be duplicates.

| Number | Destination | Source | Function | Protocol | Time |
|---|---|---|---|---|---|
| [0-11]-13 | Broadcast | AirLink | Request-192.168.0.69 | ARP | 00:00:02:260:225 |

XP's ARP cache is dynamically aged. The default ARP Lifetime is 2 minutes. An ARP entry is deleted if it is not used in 2 minutes. The Echo Request in Frame-11 proves that AirLink has the correct MAC address for iMac-Ethernet. The second ARP request happened about 120-ms after the first ARP response, that's only 5% of the ARP Lifetime.

The details appear in Chapter 7. Here's a quick explanation. If even one STA is in PS (power save) mode then all broadcasts are buffered by the AP and transmitted by the AP after a special beacon called a DTIM beacon. *When a broadcast is sourced by one of the STAs in the BSS and at least one STA is in PS-mode, then the broadcast gets retransmitted after the DTIM beacon and is essentially duplicated!*

Mindset: *Great packet-chasers get obsessed with things that need explaining!*

## *802.2 LLC and SNAP*

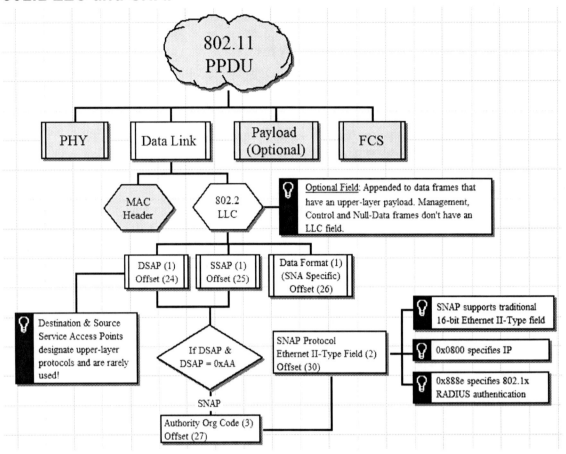

802.2 LLC is the interface between the Data-Link layer and upper-layer protocols. It supports the SAP and SNAP methods of specifying the next service or protocol.

| Number | Destination | Source | Function | Protocol |
|---|---|---|---|---|
| [0-06]-16 | Spanning Tree | AP-600-1(802.3) | BPDU | IEEE 802.1 |

## 802.1 DSAP & SSAP

The Destination and Source SAP (service access points) 42 designate IEEE 802.1 STP (spanning tree protocol) carried in a BPDU (bridge protocol data unit.) This BPDU was multicast between Orinoco APs on the WDS to ensure that a loop-free bridging environment is maintained.

```
Physical Frame
IEEE 802.11 MAC Protocol
IEEE 802.2 Logical Link Control
   Destination SAP        42 IEEE 802.1
   Source SAP             42 IEEE 802.1
   Frame Type             Command
   Unnumbered Frame       Unnumbered Information
IEEE 802.1 Spanning Tree Protocol
   Protocol ID            0
   Version                0
   Type                   0
   Flags                  0
   Root                   80-00   00-20-A6-4B-6B-8E
   Path Cost              0
   Bridge ID              80-00   00-20-A6-4B-6B-8E
   Port ID                32771
   Age                    0
   Maximum Age            34049
   Hello Time             31327
   Forward Delay          13926
```

## 802.2 LLC with SNAP

ICMP runs on top of IP. In this example the destination and source SAPs are "AA" which designate SNAP. The SNAP subfield specifies the EtherType as IP, 0x0800.

```
Number       Destination    Source        Function        Protocol
[0-11]-6     iMac-Airport   Aironet-PCI   Echo Request    ICMP

⊞ Physical Frame
⊞ IEEE 802.11 MAC Protocol
⊟ IEEE 802.2 Logical Link Control
    Destination SAP         AA SNAP
    Source SAP              AA SNAP
    Frame Type              Command
    Unnumbered Frame        Unnumbered Information
⊟ IEEE Sub-Network Access Protocol
    Authority               000000    Xerox
    EtherType               0800      DOD Internet Protocol
⊞ Internet Protocol
⊞ Internet Control Message Protocol
```

A last example is an ARP frame. ARP doesn't use IP. The EtherType designation for ARP is 0x0806.

As Chapter 1 indicated, most 802.11 analysis occurs at L2. The MAC header is always transmitted in clear text.

```
Number       Destination    Source        Function              Protocol
[0-11]-1     Broadcast      AirLink       Request-192.168.0.69  ARP

⊞ Physical Frame
⊞ IEEE 802.11 MAC Protocol
⊟ IEEE 802.2 Logical Link Control
    Destination SAP         AA SNAP
    Source SAP              AA SNAP
    Frame Type              Command
    Unnumbered Frame        Unnumbered Information
⊟ IEEE Sub-Network Access Protocol
    Authority               000000    Xerox
    EtherType               0806      IP Address Resolution Protocol (ARP)
⊞ Address Resolution Protocol
```

However all forms of 802.11 encryption encrypt both the 802.2 LLC subfield and the data payload.

---

**Troubleshooting Tip:** A WLAN network monitor can decrypt static WEP, but not 802.1x dynamically keyed WEP, WPA or 802.11i encryption. In a modern business-class WLAN, *if upper-layer protocol analysis is your goal you're only going to find it by tapping the AP's Ethernet portal!*

---

## *Intra-ESS Frame Addressing*

We've spent quite of a bit time analyzing the relationship between the To/From DS bits and the addresses in the Mac Header. The 802.11 data frames that we've analyzed in this chapter have three addresses Source, Destination and BSSID

- Source and Destination are MAC addresses of STAs or Ethernet node on the IP subnet, including the MAC address of the default gateway.
- *BSSID is always the MAC address of the AP's radio card.*

In the tradition of managed bridges and switches *the AP's radio card, which is the bridging interface, is not assigned an IP address*. For management purposes the AP's portal, the Ethernet interface, is assigned an IP address.

## AP Management Interface

This data frame is transmitted from the AP's integrated web server management interface to a STA running a web browser.

<u>To-DS= 0, From-DS=1</u>
The frame is sourced from the DSS.

### Addresses
<u>Destination</u>: Aironet-PCI
<u>BSSID</u>: AP-600-1
<u>Source</u>: AP-600-1-Ethernet

<u>802.2 LLC</u>: SSAP & DSSAP = AA

<u>SNAP</u>: Ether Type IP, 0x0800

As far as the AP is concerned, its own Ethernet interface is just another interface to which it forwards packets.

```
⊞ Physical Frame
⊟ IEEE 802.11 MAC Protocol
   ┊ Function          Data
   ⊞ PLCP Header
   ⊞ Frame Control Byte 0
   ⊟ Frame Control Byte 1
   ┊  Order           [0xxxxxxx]  off
   ┊  WEP             [x1xxxxxx]  on
   ┊  More Data       [xx0xxxxx]  off
   ┊  Power Mgmt      [xxx0xxxx]  off
   ┊  Retry           [xxxx0xxx]  off
   ┊  More Fragments  [xxxxx0xx]  off
   ┊  From DS         [xxxxxx1x]  on
   ┊  To DS           [xxxxxxx0]  off
   ⊞ WEP Information
   ┊ Duration ID      11264
   ⊟ Destination Address
   ┊  Hex Address     00-40-96-A2-F4-34
   ┊  Group Bit       [xxxxxxx0 xxxxxxxx xxxxxxxx xxx
   ┊  Local Bit       [xxxxxx0x xxxxxxxx xxxxxxxx xxx
   ┊  Logical Names   [[Aironet-PCI]]
   ┊  Vendor Name     Aironet
   ⊟ BSSID
   ┊  Hex Address     00-20-A6-4F-1F-94
   ┊  Group Bit       [xxxxxxx0 xxxxxxxx xxxxxxxx xxx
   ┊  Local Bit       [xxxxxx0x xxxxxxxx xxxxxxxx xxx
   ┊  Logical Names   [[AP600-1]]
   ┊  Vendor Name     PROXIM
   ⊟ Source Address
   ┊  Hex Address     00-20-A6-4B-6B-8E
   ┊  Group Bit       [xxxxxxx0 xxxxxxxx xxxxxxxx xxx
   ┊  Local Bit       [xxxxxx0x xxxxxxxx xxxxxxxx xxx
   ┊  Logical Names   [[AP-600-1-Ethernet]]
   ┊  Vendor Name     PROXIM
   ┊ Fragment         [xxxxxxxx xxxx0000]  0
   ┊ Sequence         [00010011 1000xxxx]  312
⊟ IEEE 802.2 Logical Link Control
   ┊ Destination SAP  AA SNAP
   ┊ Source SAP       AA SNAP
   ┊ Frame Type       Command
   ┊ Unnumbered Frame Unnumbered Information
⊟ IEEE Sub-Network Access Protocol
   ┊ Authority        000000   Xerox
   ┊ EtherType        0800     DOD Internet Protocol
```

## The ESS (extended service set)

As discussed in Chapter 1, An ESS is two or more APs that share the same SSID and DS. The DS may be a wired Ethernet or WDS.

In review the typical reasons to create an ESS are:
- Wireless STAs can be consistently configured throughout an organization. Such as through Server 2003 Group Policy Objects.
- APs can be configured with multiple SSIDs, each assigned to a specific VLAN. Each VLAN represents an IP subnet and broadcast domain. VLAN are configured to optimize performance and security. An ESS enables STAs associated with different APs to be assigned to the same VLAN.
- Enable seamless L2 and L3 "live" roaming between BSSs in the ESS. This is usually associated with handheld devices and IP-phones. The IEEE's 802.11 efforts to provide a universal roaming specification haven't yielded much success. Most roaming is supported with vendor specific, proprietary technologies.

## MAC Addresses in an ESS

TestLab is a single IP subnet ESS with two APs: AP600-1 and AP600-2 connected via a WDS. The WDS link uses the ERP-OFDM PHY. All WDS communications are preceded by a CTS-to-Self frame.

AirLink is associated to AP600-1 and iMac-Airport is associated to AP600-2 – and, you guessed it, AirLink pings iMac-Airport.

How many MAC-header addresses are needed to support this intra-ESS operation? *There are four nodes involved: two STAs and two APs.*

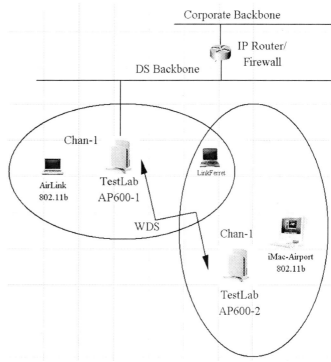

## ESS Network Monitor Setup

*To reliably capture all of the frames in the exchange, both APs are configured for Channel 1 and the notebook computer running LinkFerret is positioned in the BSA overlap.*

In an <u>intra-BSS ping</u> each Echo Request and Echo Reply is <u>repeated twice</u>, with different variations of the To/From DS bits:
- To-DS = 1, From-DS = 0
- From-DS = 0, To-DS = 1

This reflects the AP's DSS role as the "middle-man" relaying the intra-BSS communication.

As you may have guessed, in an <u>intra-ESS ping</u> each Echo Request and Echo Reply is <u>repeated three times</u>:
- To-DS = 1, From-DS = 0
- <u>To-DS = 1, From-DS = 1</u>
- From-DS = 0, To-DS = 1

*In the second combination, when To-DS and From-DS are both set, the MAC-header has four addresses. This enables the frame to transverse the WDS*

Open capture file Ping-WDS-Raw and ensure that No Filter is applied. Focus on frames 218-237. Use the LinkFerret Go-To frame function by pressing **Ctrl-G** and entering 218. Resize the Brief Display number column as needed.

| Number | Destination | Source | Function | Protocol | Time |
|--------|-------------|--------|----------|----------|------|
| [0-01]-218 | iMac-Airport | AirLink | Echo Request | ICMP | 00:00:08:155:491 |
| [0-01]-219 | AirLink | | ACK | IEEE 802.11 | 00:00:08:155:672 |
| [0-01]-220 | AP600-1 | | CTS | IEEE 802.11 | 00:00:08:156:049 |
| [0-01]-221 | iMac-Airport | AirLink | Echo Request | ICMP | 00:00:08:156:308 |
| [0-01]-222 | AP600-1 | | ACK | IEEE 802.11 | 00:00:08:156:311 |
| [0-01]-223 | iMac-Airport | AirLink | Echo Request | ICMP | 00:00:08:156:841 |
| [0-01]-224 | AP600-2 | | ACK | IEEE 802.11 | 00:00:08:157:020 |
| [0-01]-225 | AirLink | iMac-Airport | Echo Reply | ICMP | 00:00:08:158:446 |
| [0-01]-226 | iMac-Airport | | ACK | IEEE 802.11 | 00:00:08:158:642 |
| [0-01]-227 | AP600-2 | | CTS | IEEE 802.11 | 00:00:08:159:096 |
| [0-01]-228 | AirLink | iMac-Airport | Echo Reply | ICMP | 00:00:08:159:336 |
| [0-01]-229 | AP600-2 | | CTS | IEEE 802.11 | 00:00:08:159:784 |
| [0-01]-230 | AirLink | iMac-Airport | Echo Reply | ICMP | 00:00:08:160:108 |
| [0-01]-231 | AP600-2 | | ACK | IEEE 802.11 | 00:00:08:160:111 |
| [0-01]-232 | Broadcast | AP600-2 | Beacon | IEEE 802.11 | 00:00:08:174:901 |
| [0-01]-233 | Broadcast | AP600-1 | Beacon | IEEE 802.11 | 00:00:08:254:682 |
| [0-01]-234 | AP600-1 | AirLink | PS-Poll | IEEE 802.11 | 00:00:08:255:155 |
| [0-01]-235 | AirLink | | ACK | IEEE 802.11 | 00:00:08:255:465 |
| [0-01]-236 | AirLink | iMac-Airport | Echo Reply | ICMP | 00:00:08:256:118 |
| [0-01]-237 | AP600-1 | | ACK | IEEE 802.11 | 00:00:08:256:296 |

To/From DS are both set when the frame is traversing the WDS and the MAC Header has four addresses. But the original address rule still applies: *the first address in the Mac Header always represents the next node to process the frame*. Frame 221 specifies that AP600-2's DSS will process the frame. Frame 223 is the delivery of the Echo Request frame to the ultimate receiver, iMac-Airport.

| Frame | Type | To-From | Address-1 | Address-2 | Address-3 | Address-4 |
|-------|------|---------|-----------|-----------|-----------|-----------|
| 218 | Echo Request | 1,0 | AP600-1 | AirLink | iMac-Airport | |
| 219 | ACK | 0,0 | AirLink | | | |
| 220 | CTS | 0,0 | AP600-1 | | | |
| 221 | Echo Request | 1,1 | AP600-2 | AP600-1 | iMac-Airport | AirLink |
| 222 | ACK | 0,0 | AP-600-1 | | | |
| 223 | Echo Request | 0,1 | iMac-Airport | AP600-2 | AirLink | |
| 224 | ACK | 0,0 | AP600-2 | | | |
| 225 | Echo Reply | 1,0 | AP600-2 | iMac-Airport | AirLink | |
| 226 | ACK | 0,0 | iMac-Airport | | | |
| 227 | CTS | 0,0 | AP600-2 | | | |
| 228 | Echo Reply | 1,1 | AP600-1 | AP600-2 | AirLink | iMac-Airport |
| 229 | CTS | 0,0 | AP600-2 | | | |
| 230 | Echo Reply | 1,1 | AP600-1 | AP600-2 | AirLink | iMac-Airport |
| 231 | ACK | 0,0 | AP600-2 | | | |
| 236 | Echo Reply | 0,1 | AirLink | AP600-1 | iMac-Airport | |
| 237 | ACK | 0,0 | AP600-1 | | | |

You may have noticed an extra pair of CTS/Echo Reply Frames (229,230). *This is the retransmission of the Echo Reply in frame 228 which was never ACKed by AP600-1*. Go ahead; verify the retry bit state in frame 230 with LinkFerret. You more you poke around the details, the better grasp you'll have of the big picture. Contrary to the old saying, "that the devil's in the details", the epiphany that reveals the big concept is often triggered with the tweak of a single bit.

# Chapter 3: Review

## The Distribution System (DS)

- After processing a frame the DSS may:
  - Forward it to another STA in the same BSS
  - Forward it to another AP in the ESS via a wired backbone or a WDS
  - Convert the format to Ethernet and forward the frame to its Ethernet port.
- If the AP itself is the destination of the frame, it's not processed by the DSS.

## 802.11 Frame Review

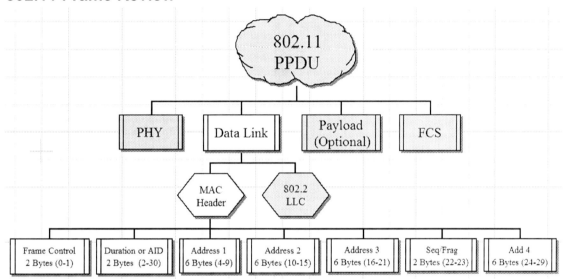

- Frame Control Byte-0 defines frame type and subtype.
- Frame Control Byte-1 has seven subfields.
- Each frame has one to four addresses
- The Sequence/Fragment field has a 12-bit frame sequence identifier and 4-bit fragment fields.

## To/From Bits Summary

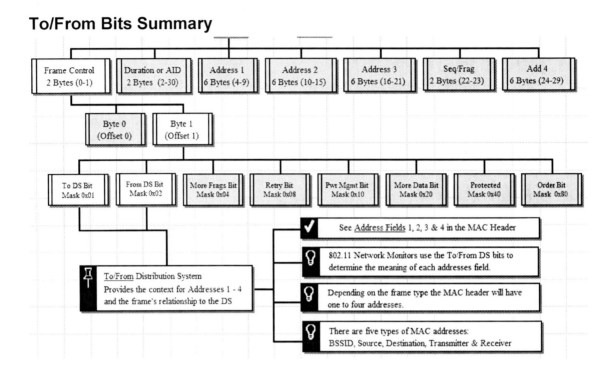

## CRC Error Checking

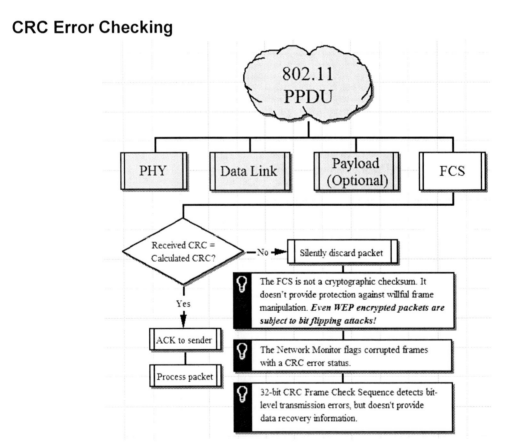

# The Retry Bit

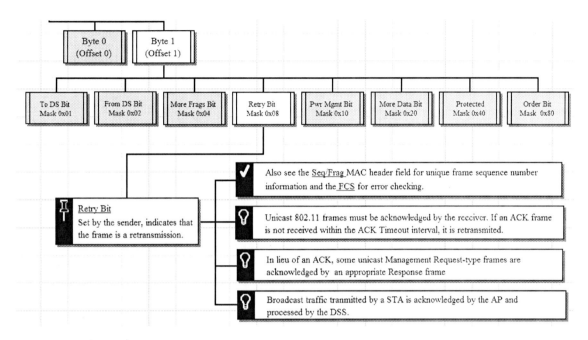

## Error Rate

- Determine the PER (packet error rate) before a starting a complex analysis.
- Captures with a high PER and the associated retry frames produce strange, unanticipated frame sequencing.

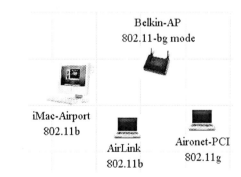

**Error Rate**

| Key | Type | Count | Percent |
|---|---|---|---|
| | Good Frames | 842 | 82% |
| | Retries | 91 | 9% |
| | Errors | 90 | 9% |

## Ping Operation:

The following ping operation is between:

- Aironet-PCI – 802.11g and
- iMac-Airport – 802.11b

## Ten Frames per Ping?

- Assume Beacon specifies "Use Protection" and CTS-to-Self is implemented
- After reserving the medium Aironet-PCI switches to ERP-OFDM mode and transmits at 54-mbps.

| Number | Destination | Source | Function | Protocol |
|--------|-------------|--------|----------|----------|
| [0-11]-5 | Aironet-PCI | | CTS | IEEE 802.11 |
| [0-11]-6 | iMac-Airport | Aironet-PCI | Echo Request | ICMP |
| [0-11]-7 | Aironet-PCI | | ACK | IEEE 802.11 |
| [0-11]-8 | iMac-Airport | Aironet-PCI | Echo Request | ICMP |
| [0-11]-9 | Belkin-AP | | ACK | IEEE 802.11 |
| [0-11]-10 | Aironet-PCI | iMac-Airport | Echo Reply | ICMP |
| [0-11]-11 | iMac-Airport | | ACK | IEEE 802.11 |
| [0-11]-12 | Belkin-AP | | CTS | IEEE 802.11 |
| [0-11]-13 | Aironet-PCI | iMac-Airport | Echo Reply | ICMP |
| [0-11]-14 | Belkin-AP | | ACK | IEEE 802.11 |

| Frame | Type | To DS | From DS | 1st Address in Mac-Header | Description |
|-------|------|-------|---------|---------------------------|-------------|
| 5 | CTS-to-Self | 0 | 0 | Aironet-PCI | Self addressed HR/DSSS frame not processed by DSS |
| 6 | Echo Request | 1 | 0 | Belkin-AP | Echo Request directed to DSS |
| 7 | ACK | 0 | 0 | Aironet-PCI | Belkin-AP ACKs Aironet-PCI ACKs are not processed by DSS |
| 8 | Echo Request | 0 | 1 | iMac-Airport | Echo Request processed by DSS and forwarded to iMac-Airport |
| 9 | ACK | 0 | 0 | Belkin-AP | iMac-Airport ACKs Belkin-AP ACKs are not processed by DSS |
| 10 | Echo Reply | 1 | 0 | Belkin-AP | Echo Reply directed to DSS |
| 11 | ACK | 0 | 0 | iMac-Airport | Belkin-AP ACKs iMac-Airport ACKs are not processed by DSS |
| 12 | CTS-to-Self | 0 | 0 | Belkin-AP | Self addressed HR/DSSS frame not processed by DSS |
| 13 | Echo Reply | 0 | 1 | Aironet-PCI | Echo Reply processed by DSS and forwarded to Aironet-PCI |
| 14 | ACK | 0 | 0 | Belkin-AP | Aironet-PCI ACKs Belkin AP ACKs are not processed by DSS |

Notes:

- ***The first address in the MAC-header specifies the next node to process the frame***
- When To-DS=1 the first address is the BSSID of the AP
- When From-DS=1 the first address is the destination STA
- When both To & From DS =0, the first address (and sometimes only address) specifies the ultimate destination for the frame

## Pinging between 802.11b STAs

- AirLink initiates the sequence with an Echo Request frame to iMac-Airport in frame-16
- In frame 21, iMac-Airport receives the ACK from Belkin-AP for the Echo Reply.

| Number | Destination | Source | Function | Protocol | Time |
|---|---|---|---|---|---|
| [0-11]-16 | iMac-Airport | AirLink | Echo Request | ICMP | 00:00:02:910:154 |
| [0-11]-17 | AirLink | | ACK | IEEE 802.11 | 00:00:02:910:353 |
| [0-11]-18 | iMac-Airport | AirLink | Echo Request | ICMP | 00:00:02:910:708 |
| [0-11]-19 | Belkin-AP | | ACK | IEEE 802.11 | 00:00:02:910:926 |
| [0-11]-20 | AirLink | iMac-Airport | Echo Reply | ICMP | 00:00:02:911:843 |
| [0-11]-21 | iMac-Airport | | ACK | IEEE 802.11 | 00:00:02:912:030 |

| Number | Destination | Source | Function | Protocol | Time |
|---|---|---|---|---|---|
| [0-11]-62 | AirLink | iMac-Airport | Echo Reply | ICMP | 00:00:03:709:268 |
| [0-11]-63 | Belkin-AP | | ACK | IEEE 802.11 | 00:00:03:709:475 |

This Echo Request and Response only takes eight frames because the two CTS-to-Self are not required with 802.11b STAs.

## Use a Retries Filter

| Number | Destination | Source | Function | Protocol | Time |
|---|---|---|---|---|---|
| [0-11]-1 | AirLink | Belkin-AP | Probe Response | IEEE 802.11 | 00:00:02:732:592 |
| [0-11]-2 | AirLink | Belkin-AP | Probe Response | IEEE 802.11 | 00:00:02:733:925 |
| [0-11]-3 | AirLink | Belkin-AP | Probe Response | IEEE 802.11 | 00:00:02:973:548 |
| [0-11]-4 | AirLink | Belkin-AP | Probe Response | IEEE 802.11 | 00:00:03:095:572 |
| [0-11]-5 | AirLink | Belkin-AP | Probe Response | IEEE 802.11 | 00:00:03:097:754 |
| [0-11]-6 | AirLink | Belkin-AP | Probe Response | IEEE 802.11 | 00:00:03:101:214 |
| [0-11]-7 | AirLink | Belkin-AP | Probe Response | IEEE 802.11 | 00:00:03:103:689 |
| [0-11]-8 | AirLink | Belkin-AP | Probe Response | IEEE 802.11 | 00:00:03:455:511 |
| [0-11]-9 | AirLink | Belkin-AP | Probe Response | IEEE 802.11 | 00:00:03:457:475 |
| [0-11]-10 | AirLink | Belkin-AP | Probe Response | IEEE 802.11 | 00:00:03:459:692 |
| [0-11]-11 | AirLink | Belkin-AP | Probe Response | IEEE 802.11 | 00:00:03:462:272 |
| [0-11]-12 | AirLink | Belkin-AP | Probe Response | IEEE 802.11 | 00:00:03:463:554 |

Applying a Retry filter reveals, dialog failures, collision/contention issues and questionable driver behavior as illustrated with the infamous AirLink XP driver.

## STA to Wired Ethernet Ping

AirLink pings iMac-Ethernet

- <u>Frames 1 & 2</u>: ARP to target IP address 192.168.0.69
- <u>Frames 5 & 6</u>: ARP response from iMac-Ethernet
- <u>Frames 11&12</u>: Echo Request and ACK
- <u>Frames 16 & 17</u>: Echo Reply and ACK

| Number | Destination | Source | Function | Protocol | Time |
|---|---|---|---|---|---|
| [0-11]-1 | Broadcast | AirLink | Request-192.168.0.69 | ARP | 00:00:02:140:311 |
| [0-11]-2 | AirLink | | ACK | IEEE 802.11 | 00:00:02:140:520 |
| [0-11]-3 | Belkin-AP | AirLink | PS-Poll | IEEE 802.11 | 00:00:02:157:413 |
| [0-11]-4 | AirLink | | ACK | IEEE 802.11 | 00:00:02:157:720 |
| [0-11]-5 | AirLink | iMac-Ethernet | Response-192.168.0.69 | ARP | 00:00:02:158:138 |
| [0-11]-6 | Belkin-AP | | ACK | IEEE 802.11 | 00:00:02:158:340 |
| [0-11]-7 | Belkin-AP | AirLink | PS-Poll | IEEE 802.11 | 00:00:02:158:950 |
| [0-11]-8 | AirLink | | ACK | IEEE 802.11 | 00:00:02:159:249 |
| [0-11]-9 | AirLink | Belkin-AP | Null | IEEE 802.11 | 00:00:02:159:731 |
| [0-11]-10 | Belkin-AP | | ACK | IEEE 802.11 | 00:00:02:159:956 |
| [0-11]-11 | iMac-Ethernet | AirLink | Echo Request | ICMP | 00:00:02:160:641 |
| [0-11]-12 | AirLink | | ACK | IEEE 802.11 | 00:00:02:160:837 |
| [0-11]-13 | Broadcast | AirLink | Request-192.168.0.69 | ARP | 00:00:02:260:225 |
| [0-11]-14 | Belkin-AP | AirLink | PS-Poll | IEEE 802.11 | 00:00:02:260:666 |
| [0-11]-15 | AirLink | | ACK | IEEE 802.11 | 00:00:02:260:979 |
| [0-11]-16 | AirLink | iMac-Ethernet | Echo Reply | ICMP | 00:00:02:261:546 |
| [0-11]-17 | Belkin-AP | | ACK | IEEE 802.11 | 00:00:02:261:748 |

Notes:

- The broadcast ARP in Frame #1 from AirLink is acknowledged by the AP. Broadcast frames are only ACKed when To-DS=1. The DSS translates the frame to Ethernet and broadcasts it onto the DS backbone.
- The only way to capture The Ethernet dialog between the AP's portal interface and iMac-Ethernet the actual frames is to tap the DS backbone.

## 802.2 LLC and SNAP

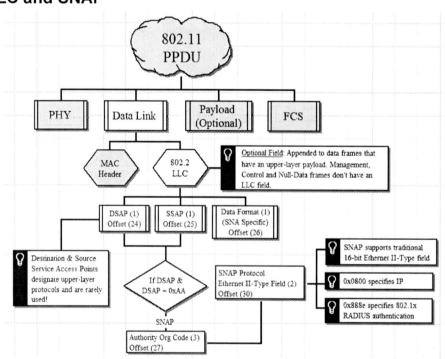

## 802.1 DSAP & SSAP

- The Destination and Source SAP (service access points) 42 designate the 802.1 STP (spanning tree protocol) carried in a BPDU (bridge protocol data unit.)
- This BPDU was send between two Orinoco APs to ensure that a loop-free bridging environment is maintained

```
⊞ Physical Frame
⊞ IEEE 802.11 MAC Protocol
⊟ IEEE 802.2 Logical Link Control
   Destination SAP      42 IEEE 802.1
   Source SAP           42 IEEE 802.1
   Frame Type           Command
   Unnumbered Frame     Unnumbered Information
⊟ IEEE 802.1 Spanning Tree Protocol
   Protocol ID          0
   Version              0
   Type                 0
   Flags                0
   Root                 80-00  00-20-A6-4B-6B-8E
   Path Cost            0
   Bridge ID            80-00  00-20-A6-4B-6B-8E
   Port ID              32771
   Age                  0
   Maximum Age          34049
   Hello Time           31327
   Forward Delay        13926
```

## 802.2 LLC with SNAP

- In this example Destination and Source SAP are "AA" which designate that SNAP (subnet access protocol) is in use.
- The SNAP subfield specifies the Ether Type as 0x0800 which is IP.

```
⊞ Physical Frame
⊞ IEEE 802.11 MAC Protocol
⊟ IEEE 802.2 Logical Link Control
   Destination SAP      AA SNAP
   Source SAP           AA SNAP
   Frame Type           Command
   Unnumbered Frame     Unnumbered Information
⊟ IEEE Sub-Network Access Protocol
   Authority            000000   Xerox
   EtherType            0800     DOD Internet Protocol
⊞ Internet Protocol
⊞ Internet Control Message Protocol
```

## AP Interfaces & Addresses

- APs usually have two MAC Addresses: an 802.11 radio interface & Ethernet interface
- ***The Ethernet interface is configured with the AP's IP Address***
- In this frame Aironet-PCI is performing browser-based AP configuration.
    - The source MAC address is the AP's Ethernet interface
    - The BSSID is the AP's radio interface
    - The destination address is Aironet-PCI, the STA from which remote administration is being performed.

```
Duration ID          11264
Destination Address
  Hex Address        00-40-96-A2-F4-34
  Group Bit          [xxxxxxx0 xxxxxxxx xxxxxxxx xxx
  Local Bit          [xxxxxx0x xxxxxxxx xxxxxxxx xxx
  Logical Names      [[Aironet-PCI]]
  Vendor Name        Aironet
BSSID
  Hex Address        00-20-A6-4F-1F-94
  Group Bit          [xxxxxxx0 xxxxxxxx xxxxxxxx xxx
  Local Bit          [xxxxxx0x xxxxxxxx xxxxxxxx xxx
  Logical Names      [[AP600-1]]
  Vendor Name        PROXIM
Source Address
  Hex Address        00-20-A6-4B-6B-8E
  Group Bit          [xxxxxxx0 xxxxxxxx xxxxxxxx xxx
  Local Bit          [xxxxxx0x xxxxxxxx xxxxxxxx xxx
  Logical Names      [[AP-600-1-Ethernet]]
  Vendor Name        PROXIM
Fragment             [xxxxxxxx xxxx0000]   0
Sequence             [00010011 1000xxxx]   312
```

## Reasons to create an ESS

- Wireless STAs can be consistently configured throughout an organization. Such as through Microsoft Server 2003 Group Policy Objects.
- VLAN Configuration for administration and security
    - An AP can be configured with multiple SSIDs, each assigned to a specific VLAN.
    - Each VLAN represents a physical IP subnet and broadcast domain.
    - An ESS enables STAs associated with different APs to be assigned to the same VLAN.
- Enable seamless layer-2 and layer-3 "live" roaming between BSS in the ESS. However, most successful roaming is supported on a vendor proprietary basis.

## The Fourth Address: MAC Addresses in an ESS

- When AirLink pings iMac-Airport there are *four nodes* involved: the two STAs and the two APs
- As frames 221, 228, and 230 indicate, four addresses are only used when the frame is traversing the WDS

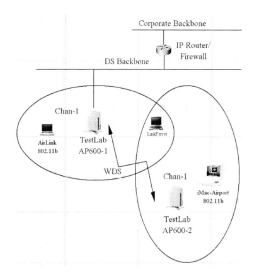

| Number | Destination | Source | Function | Protocol | Time |
|---|---|---|---|---|---|
| [0-01]-218 | iMac-Airport | AirLink | Echo Request | ICMP | 00:00:08:155:491 |
| [0-01]-219 | AirLink | | ACK | IEEE 802.11 | 00:00:08:155:672 |
| [0-01]-220 | AP600-1 | | CTS | IEEE 802.11 | 00:00:08:156:049 |
| [0-01]-221 | iMac-Airport | AirLink | Echo Request | ICMP | 00:00:08:156:308 |
| [0-01]-222 | AP600-1 | | ACK | IEEE 802.11 | 00:00:08:156:311 |
| [0-01]-223 | iMac-Airport | AirLink | Echo Request | ICMP | 00:00:08:156:841 |
| [0-01]-224 | AP600-2 | | ACK | IEEE 802.11 | 00:00:08:157:020 |
| [0-01]-225 | AirLink | iMac-Airport | Echo Reply | ICMP | 00:00:08:158:446 |
| [0-01]-226 | iMac-Airport | | ACK | IEEE 802.11 | 00:00:08:158:642 |
| [0-01]-227 | AP600-2 | | CTS | IEEE 802.11 | 00:00:08:159:096 |
| [0-01]-228 | AirLink | iMac-Airport | Echo Reply | ICMP | 00:00:08:159:336 |
| [0-01]-229 | AP600-2 | | CTS | IEEE 802.11 | 00:00:08:159:784 |
| [0-01]-230 | AirLink | iMac-Airport | Echo Reply | ICMP | 00:00:08:160:108 |
| [0-01]-231 | AP600-2 | | ACK | IEEE 802.11 | 00:00:08:160:111 |
| [0-01]-232 | Broadcast | AP600-2 | Beacon | IEEE 802.11 | 00:00:08:174:901 |
| [0-01]-233 | Broadcast | AP600-1 | Beacon | IEEE 802.11 | 00:00:08:254:682 |
| [0-01]-234 | AP600-1 | AirLink | PS-Poll | IEEE 802.11 | 00:00:08:255:155 |
| [0-01]-235 | AirLink | | ACK | IEEE 802.11 | 00:00:08:255:465 |
| [0-01]-236 | AirLink | iMac-Airport | Echo Reply | ICMP | 00:00:08:256:118 |
| [0-01]-237 | AP600-1 | | ACK | IEEE 802.11 | 00:00:08:256:296 |

| Frame | Type | To-From | Address-1 | Address-2 | Address-3 | Address-4 |
|---|---|---|---|---|---|---|
| 218 | Echo Request | 1,0 | AP600-1 | AirLink | iMac-Airport | |
| 219 | ACK | 0,0 | AirLink | | | |
| 220 | CTS | 0,0 | AP600-1 | | | |
| 221 | Echo Request | 1,1 | AP600-2 | AP600-1 | iMac-Airport | AirLink |
| 222 | ACK | 0,0 | AP-600-1 | | | |
| 223 | Echo Request | 0,1 | iMac-Airport | AP600-2 | AirLink | |
| 224 | ACK | 0,0 | AP600-2 | | | |
| 225 | Echo Reply | 1,0 | AP600-2 | iMac-Airport | AirLink | |
| 226 | ACK | 0,0 | iMac-Airport | | | |
| 227 | CTS | 0,0 | AP600-2 | | | |
| 228 | Echo Reply | 1,1 | AP600-1 | AP600-2 | AirLink | iMac-Airport |
| 229 | CTS | 0,0 | AP600-2 | | | |
| 230 | Echo Reply | 1,1 | AP600-1 | AP600-2 | AirLink | iMac-Airport |
| 231 | ACK | 0,0 | AP600-2 | | | |
| 236 | Echo Reply | 0,1 | AirLink | AP600-1 | iMac-Airport | |
| 237 | ACK | 0,0 | AP600-1 | | | |

## 802.11 Addressing Summary

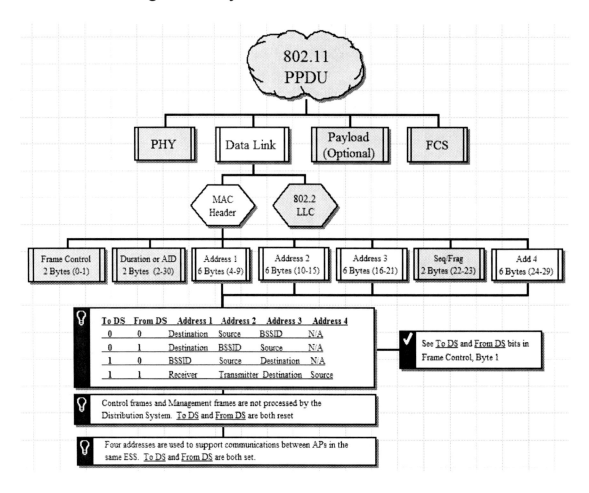

# Chapter 4: Finding the Access Point

## *802.11 Management Commands Analyzed:*

- Beacon Management
- Probe Request and Probe Response

## *802.11 Concepts:*

- Passive and Active Scanning
- Going off-channel and the PwrMgmt bit
- Beacon and Probe frame IEs (information elements)
- SSIDs and VLANs
- SSID Security Concerns
- TIM and DTIM traffic buffering
- Basic and Extended Rates
- XP's WZCSVC and vendor client adapter utilities
- SSID Broadcasting Issues

## *The MMPDU (MAC management protocol data unit)*

Do 802.11management frames carry data? It depends on how we define data. If the question is, "what type of 802.11 frames carry upper-layer protocol data" then the only correct answer is the data frame.

In this chapter we discover that management frames carry a wealth of 802.11 information used to advertise and discover APs, determine a STA's compatibility with a BSS, and initiate authentication and association. These frames are used exclusively by L2 802.11 management processes and don't have any upper-layer information.

The IEEE describes frames that have an upper-layer protocol payload as MPDUs. *Frames that only carry management information are called MMPDUs (MAC management protocol data units.)*

## MMPDU (MAC Management Protocol Data Unit

Beacon, Probe Request, Probe Response, Authentication, Association Request, Association Response,
Reassociation Request, Reassociation Response, Disassociation and Deauthentication

| Frame Control | Duration | Destination Address | Source Address | BSSID Address | Frag/Seq Control | Variable Management Information | FCS |
|---|---|---|---|---|---|---|---|
| 2 bytes | 2 bytes | 6 bytes | 6 bytes | 6 bytes | 2 bytes | | 2 bytes |

———————————— MAC Header 24 Bytes ————————————

- The MMPDU header is always 24 bytes.
- The management information ranges from a few bytes to over 175 bytes in complex beacon frames.
- The information field structure is unique to each management frame type.
- The To/From DS bits are always 0; MMPDUs are never processed by the DSS.
- All MMPDUs are ACKed, except for those with a broadcast destination address such as a standard probe request or beacon frame.
- The AP's MAC address often appears twice in a MMPDU, as either the destination or source address, and as the BSSID address.
- In a standard probe request both the destination and BSSID addresses are the broadcast address.

For example, if a STA transmits an association request frame to an AP it expects the AP to return an association response. ***However, the original association request is always ACKed by the AP prior to transmitting the association response.*** After waiting a SIFS the AP responds with an ACK and then contends for the medium before transmitting the association response. It's very important to get the feel of the ebb-and-flow of frame transmission. It allows you to develop a gut feel to differentiate between normal frame flow and frame flow that signifies BSS failures or performance issues.

## Finding the AP

A STA must authenticate and associate with an AP before its frames are processed by the DSS. Consider a typical situation:

- A wireless client adapter is configured to automatically connect to any AP in a specified ESS. Remember that all BSSs in an ESS have the SSID.
- ***The AP's channel is unknown.*** It may be configured on any of the 11 FCC supported channels.
- The AP is operating in 802.11 mixed-mode.

## Passive Scanning

A STA passively scans for available BSSs by listening for AP beacons on each ISM channel for a brief interval. A beacon's destination address is network broadcast and the To/From DS bits are reset. A STA periodically performs a passive scan by tuning its radio to a different channel and listening for a beacon frame for approximately 125 milliseconds and repeats the process on the remaining channels.

**LinkFerret Fact:** LinkFerret specifies the signal strength and quality of each frame in the Physical Frames attribute in the detail decode window. The AP Discovery Tab in the Statistics Window lists the APs that have been discovered on the monitored channels, and their signal strength and quality. But remember, this is the signal strength measured at the LinkFerret network monitor device.

The information carried in a beacon frame enables a STA to determine if it's compatibility with the AP. Compatibility is based on several factors. MMPDU beacon information has three fixed length fields and several mandatory, optional and proprietary IEs (information elements.)

- Time Stamp
- Beacon Interval
- Capability Information
- Several IEs

```
Time Stamp              40307317312323584000
Beacon Interval         100
Capability Information
Information Element
Information Element
Information Element
Information Element
Information Element
Information Element
```

## Time Stamp

The AP provides the TSF (timing synchronization function) for the BSS. The time stamp is a 64-bit field contains the current value of the AP's synchronized microsecond count-based clock. All STAs synchronize to the beacon's time stamp.

## Why Synchronize Time for DCF Operation?

The theoretical PCF mode requires a common clock as did the original FH (frequency hopping) WLANs. CSMA/CA is asynchronous; no CSMA/CA operation is coordinated with a common clock. DCF medium access is based on asynchronous timing intervals: slot time, SIFS and DIFS. *The great majority of DCF operation is not synchronized to a common clock*. The primary reason for a synchronized BSS clock is to facilitate PS (power save) mode. Beacon transmission is scheduled at regular intervals. In PS-mode a STA wakes up at the specified beacon transmission time to receive the beacon frame and determine if it has buffered data at the AP.

## Beacon Interval

(Also called the Beacon Period.) The Beacon Interval is specified TUs (time units). Each TU is equal to one K-µs (kilo-microsecond) or 1,024-µs. *The default Beacon Interval is 100-TUs or approximately 9.75 beacons per second.* Although the beacon interval is configurable it's rarely modified. *Arbitrarily modifying the beacon interval negatively impacts BSS throughput and the effectiveness of PS-mode.*

**LinkFerret Fact:** To conserve packet buffer space and simplify the brief display window, beacon frames are usually filtered from network captures. Chapter 7 demonstrates several cases where beacon capture is vital to the analysis. Beacon capture is enabled by removing the beacon filter.

## TBTT (target beacon transmission time)

At the TBTT the AP queues the beacon frame for transmission. Since the contention period is variable the TBTT is only an estimate. The beacon has a broadcast destination address with To/From-DS =0, so it's not ACKed or rebroadcast. *The percentage of missed beacons, logged by many wireless client adapter utilities, is a useful indication of the overall heath of the STA and BSS.*

## Capability Information

The Beacon's Capability Information field is 16-bits. All of the features described in the first 8-bits have been available since the introduction of HR/DSSS. With exception of short slot time, the second 8-bits specify features that are yet to be implemented in production networks. Currently LinkFerret only decodes the first 8-bits of capability information. We examine the capability information starting with B7 and working backwards.

| $B_0$ | $B_1$ | $B_2$ | $B_3$ | $B_4$ | $B_5$ | $B_6$ | $B_7$ |
|-------|-------|-------|-------|-------|-------|-------|-------|
| ESS | IBSS | CF Pollable | CF-Poll Request | Privacy | Short Preamble | PBCC | Channel Agility |

Capability Information Field Bits 0 - 7

- Channel Agility Channel agility is an optional HR/DSSS feature. It's set to indicate that the AP automatically changes channels when interference is detected. ***This flag is rarely supported.*** Channel Agility is configured on Cisco APs with use "least congested frequency" or Orinoco APs with "enable auto channel select" but ***neither AP sets the Channel Agility bit!***

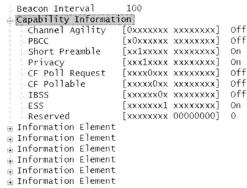

- PBCC An HR/DSSS ***optional and rarely supported coding scheme.*** 802.11g made PBCC obsolete. The only place you're see PBCC is on certification exams or in the Trivial Pursuit Wireless Geeks Edition.

- Short Preamble is set to indicate that the BSS ***is currently using short preamble.*** It's reset when a client adapter without short preamble support associates to the BSS. Best practice is to reconfigure or replace the STA's client adapter and disable long preamble support at the AP.

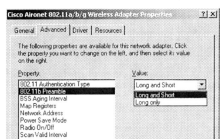

- Privacy is set to signify that the BSS requires WEP or WPA data frame encryption. STAs without encryption support won't be allowed to associate with the BSS. APs that support WPA have a WPA IE which specifies supported encryption algorithms and options.

- CF Poll Request and CF Pollable These two bits are used together to provide four possible PCF compatibility settings.

- IBSS and ESS These bits are compliments – one is set and the other reset. IBSS is set for ad hoc, peer-to-peer networks. ESS is set in AP beacons to specify infrastructure mode.

| B$_8$ | B$_9$ | B$_{10}$ | B$_{11}$ | B$_{12}$ | B$_{13}$ | B$_{14}$ | B$_{15}$ |
|---|---|---|---|---|---|---|---|
| Spectrum Management | QoS | Short Slot Time | APSD | Reserved | DSSS-OFDM | Delayed Block ACK | Immediate Block ACK |

Capability Information Field Bits 8 - 15

Here's a capture fragment from the Network Instruments Observer network monitor. Currently it only decodes two bits in second byte of the capabilities field.

<u>Short Slot Time</u> (9-µs) is the length of the slot time that is currently in use by the BSS. In this example the bit is reset which indicates that the BSS is using the standard 20-µs slot time.

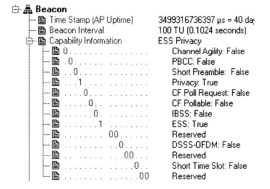

DIFS is calculated from the SIFS and slot time. With long slot time DIFS is 50-µs and the short slot time DIFS is only 28-µs - about a 45% reduction! ***CTS-to-Self and standard slot time are heavy performance penalties in mixed mode BSSs.*** See Chapter 7 for performance calculation details.

<u>DSSS-OFDM</u> (also called CCK-OFDM) Set specifies that ERP transmissions may use a DSSS preamble to provide mixed mode compatibility. HR/DSSS STAs can read the length field in the PLCP-header and defer the medium, but it's not as affective as CTS-to-Self. At the writing of this book ***no current commercially available AP supports DSSS-OFDM.***

<u>The following summaries are for test preparation purposes only.</u>

**802.11a and the 5-GHz Band Only**
<u>Spectrum Management </u> is a feature of the 802.11h specification which defines DFS (dynamic frequency selection) and TPC (transmit power control). Spectrum management provides mechanisms to avoid co-channel operation between 802.11a BSSs and civil/military radar.

**Proposed P802.11e Quality of Service Specification**
<u>QoS </u> indicates that the BSS supports P802.11e quality of service extensions. 802.11e QoS will probably become a standard feature of business-class APs during the middle part of 2006.
<u>APSD</u> (automatic power save delivery) specifies that the BSS supports P802.11e QoS power management mode operation.
<u>Delay Block Acknowledgement and Immediate Block Acknowledgement</u> P802.11e QoS data acknowledgement mechanisms.

## *The Information Elements:*

Flexibility enables growth and IEs provide beacon flexibility. IEs are added to support new modes and vendor-proprietary information. The following table is a snap-shot of the typical IEs found in the current generation of APs. **Appendix D: Information Elements** lists the currently documented non-proprietary IEs.

| Information Element | ID | Comment |
|---|---|---|
| SSID | 0x00 | Main SSID or null |
| Supported Rates | 0x01 | Limited to 8 rates (see Extended Rates IE) |
| FH Parameters | 0x02 | Archaic - Frequency Hoping devices |
| DS Parameters | 0x03 | Direct Sequence - Current AP Channel |
| CF Parameters | 0x04 | Mythical - PCF has never been implemented |
| TIM | 0x05 | Traffic Indication Map for AP buffered traffic |
| ATIM | 0x06 | Announcement Traffic Indication Map (IBSS Only) |
| Shared-Key Challenge | 0x10 | Not in Beacon or Probe frames. See shared key authentication |
| ERP (extended rate physical) | 0x2a | Extended Rate PHY protection parameters. 802.11g APs only |
| Extended Rates | 0x32 | Used when an AP has more than 8 supported rates |
| WPA Parameters | 0xDD | WPA & WPA-PSK encryption and data integrity support |

**LinkFerret Fact:** LinkFerret's decoder converts standard IE information into text, but proprietary or recently released IEs may not be decoded.

## SSID IE

```
Information Element
  Identity      SSID
  Length        5
  SSID          Site2
```
Consider a STA that passively scans for SSID "Site2." Its radio is tuned to Channel-1 and it listens for beacon frames for about 1.25 TUs and it repeats the process on each of the 11 FCC supported channels and builds a table with the Channel, BSSID and RSSI of APs in the "Site2" ESS.

```
Information Element
  Identity      SSID
  Length        0
  SSID
```
A null (0 length) SSID IE indicates that the AP has been configured to suppress SSID advertisement in its beacon.

The SSID IE supports one SSID. Business-Class APs typically support 16 VLANs per AP, and each VLAN may be configured with a different SSID. VLAN SSIDs aren't advertised in beacons. STAs configured with a VLAN SSID can't locate APs from beacons; they employ active scanning with probe request frames as described later in this chapter.

## Basic Rates

Basic Rates are mandatory. *A STA must support every Basic Rate specified in the beacon*. Optional rates described as "not in basic rate set" may be used if supported by both the AP and STA. However, *frames essential to the proper functioning of the BSS are transmitted at basic rates. This includes beacons, CTS and ACK frames.*

## Supported/Extended Rates IEs

The Supported Rates IE supports a maximum of eight rates. APs with more than eight rates have an additional variable length Extended Rates IE.

```
Information Element
  Identity          Supported Rates
  Length            8
  Rate              1.0 MB    [1xxxxxxx]   In Basic Rate Set
  Rate              2.0 MB    [1xxxxxxx]   In Basic Rate Set
  Rate              5.5 MB    [1xxxxxxx]   In Basic Rate Set
  Rate              11.0 MB   [1xxxxxxx]   In Basic Rate Set
  Rate              6.0 MB    [0xxxxxxx]   Not in Basic Rate Set
  Rate              12.0 MB   [0xxxxxxx]   Not in Basic Rate Set
  Rate              24.0 MB   [0xxxxxxx]   Not in Basic Rate Set
  Rate              36.0 MB   [0xxxxxxx]   Not in Basic Rate Set
```

These two IEs illustrate the Supported Rates and Extended Rates IEs of a typical 802.11g mixed mode AP.

```
Information Element
  Identity          Extended Rates
  Length            4
  Rate              9.0 MB    [0xxxxxxx]   Not in Basic Rate Set
  Rate              18.0 MB   [0xxxxxxx]   Not in Basic Rate Set
  Rate              48.0 MB   [0xxxxxxx]   Not in Basic Rate Set
  Rate              54.0 MB   [0xxxxxxx]   Not in Basic Rate Set
```

**LinkFerret Fact:** Basic Rates may appear in either the Supported Rates or Extended Rates IEs. Two rate IEs are needed because the original Supported Rates IE has been traditionally limited to advertising a maximum of eight rates.

The third Supported Rates IE example is from a Business-Class AP in *802.11g-only mode*. The lowest basic rate is 6-Mbps and beacon frames default to the highest basic rate which is 24-Mbps.

```
Information Element
  Identity          Supported Rates
  Length            8
  Rate              6.0 MB    [1xxxxxxx]   In Basic Rate Set
  Rate              12.0 MB   [1xxxxxxx]   In Basic Rate Set
  Rate              24.0 MB   [1xxxxxxx]   In Basic Rate Set
  Rate              36.0 MB   [0xxxxxxx]   Not in Basic Rate Set
  Rate              9.0 MB    [0xxxxxxx]   Not in Basic Rate Set
  Rate              18.0 MB   [0xxxxxxx]   Not in Basic Rate Set
  Rate              48.0 MB   [0xxxxxxx]   Not in Basic Rate Set
  Rate              54.0 MB   [0xxxxxxx]   Not in Basic Rate Set
```

The last Supported Rates IE is from an 802.11g SOHO AP operating in 802.11g-only mode. There are two interesting points:

```
Information Element
  Identity          Supported Rates
  Length            12
  Rate              1.0 MB    [1xxxxxxx]   In Basic Rate Set
  Rate              2.0 MB    [1xxxxxxx]   In Basic Rate Set
  Rate              5.5 MB    [1xxxxxxx]   In Basic Rate Set
  Rate              6.0 MB    [1xxxxxxx]   In Basic Rate Set
  Rate              9.0 MB    [0xxxxxxx]   Not in Basic Rate Set
  Rate              11.0 MB   [1xxxxxxx]   In Basic Rate Set
  Rate              12.0 MB   [1xxxxxxx]   In Basic Rate Set
  Rate              18.0 MB   [0xxxxxxx]   Not in Basic Rate Set
  Rate              24.0 MB   [1xxxxxxx]   In Basic Rate Set
  Rate              36.0 MB   [0xxxxxxx]   Not in Basic Rate Set
  Rate              48.0 MB   [0xxxxxxx]   Not in Basic Rate Set
  Rate              54.0 MB   [0xxxxxxx]   Not in Basic Rate Set
```

- *Contrary to the original 802.11 standard, the Supported Rates IE is expanded to 12 rates*.
- The standard basic rate set for 802.11g is 6-, 12- and 24-Mbps. This AP also requires the basic rate set for 802.11b: 1-, 2-, 5.5- and 11-Mbps even though it is operating in g-only mode. *I assume that it's a firmware bug because the 802.11b basic rates are not employed in a g-only environment*!

*!* *Exam Alert*: Exams assume that that the Supported Rates IE supports a maximum of eight rates. For exam purposes consider the previous example an aberration.

## How bit rates are selected

STAs default to ARS (automatic rate selection). The bit rate between the STA and AP is based on the RSSI and PER. As the RSSI drops by the square of the distance from the AP, the signal-to-noise ratio falls, the PER increases, and the STA falls-back to the next lower supported speed.

**Troubleshooting Tip:** Bit rate falls-back in the presence increased PER due to RFI. However, the longer transmission times of slower bit rates only exacerbate the interference issues! If several STAs physically close to the AP aren't communicating at the highest bit rates use a spectrum analyzer to test for RFI.

## Configuring the AP's Basic Data Rates and Transmit Power

The requirements of the BSA coverage area should be determined by a site survey and the transmit power of the AP configured appropriately. Some SOHO- and all business-class APs enable the configuration of basic rates and transmitter power. This is an example of a Cisco Aironet-350 AP. Setting the required data rate is a trade-off between range and throughput.

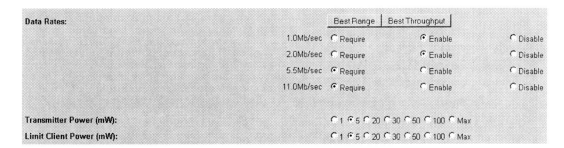

In this example 5.5- and 11-Mbps are basic rates and 1- and 2- are optional (not in basic rate set) rates. The beacon is transmitted at 5.5-Mbps, the lowest basic rate. Security considerations dictate that the BSA should extend only to the required coverage area.

- On the other hand, *what bit rate is acceptable to your users*? 1- or 2- Mbps rates are insufficient to support most network access.
- ***Enabling the lowest basic rates may provide access to the BSA from well beyond the required physical area – perhaps even your parking lot***!
- Setting a reasonable minimum basic rate and transmit power level ensures that legitimate STAs connect at acceptable rates but the signal doesn't propagate to uncontrolled areas and induce uninvited guests.

## DS Parameter Set IE

An 8-bit field specifies the AP's current channel. At first this IE may seems redundant, after all, if a STA receives a beacon while tuned to Channel-3, the STA already knows the AP's channel. Why does the DS Parameter Set IE have to identify the AP's channel?

- We've already discussed the issues of channel overlap and receiving signals transmitted on other channels.
- Also consider Channel Agility, if an AP changes channels due to interference it's important to have the new channel designated in the beacon.

## TIM (traffic indication map) IE

How can a battery-powered STA that periodically enters PS (power save) mode ensure that it doesn't miss frames?

- STA informs the AP that it's entering PS-mode.
- AP buffers frames bound for the STA until it returns to AM (active mode.)
- While asleep the STA's TSF timer continues to run.
- The STA wakes at specified multiples of the TBTT and receives a beacon.
- If the TIM's Virtual Bitmap Control field bit assigned to the STA's AID (association ID) is set, then the STA changes to AM or issues PS-Poll Control frames to read the buffered data.

The PS operation involves several 802.11 elements:

- The beacon's TIM IE
- Frame Control Byte-1
  - PwrMgmt bit to toggles between PS and AM
  - More Data bit indicates that the AP has additional buffered data
- Null-Data frames
  - conveys the state of the PwrMgmt bit and often used as a precursor to passive scanning
- PS-Poll Control frame
  - Polls the AP for buffered data
  - AP responses with data frame and STA checks More Data bit
- Duration/ID field.
  - In the PS-Poll frame the field specifies the STA's AID (association ID)

### *Buffered Multicast Traffic*

Every beacon has a TIM for buffered unicast frames. The DTIM (delivery traffic indication map) only appears in specified beacon frames. It indicates buffered broadcast or multicast traffic which is automatically transmitted following the a DTIM beacon.

**DTIM Count Field** indicates how many more beacons (including the current beacon) will be transmitted before the next DTIM. *A DTIM beacon has a DTIM Count of 0.* In this example the DTIM Count is 1, so the next beacon is a DTIM beacon.

```
⊟ Information Element
  ├ Identity          DS Parameter Set
  ├ Length            1
  └ Current Channel   11
⊟ Information Element
  ├ Identity          TIM
  ├ Length            4
  ├ DTIM Count        1
  ├ DTIM Period       3
  └ Bitmap Control    0
⊟ Information Element
  ├ Identity          ERP
  ├ Length            1
  ├ Non-ERP Present   [xxxx xxx0] Off
  ├ Use Protection    [xxxx xx0x] Off
  └ Barker Preamble   [xxxx x0xx] Off
```

**DTIM Period Field** specifies the number of beacons between DTIMs. *A DTIM Period of 1 means that every beacon has a DTIM*. In this example the DTIM Period is 3, indicating that every third beacon has a DTIM. The DTIM Period has traditionally defaulted to a value of 3. If the DTIM period is reduced, power savings are lowered because deep sleep STAs must wake more often to receive DTIM beacons. See Chapter 7 for a detailed analysis of PS-mode operation.

 **Troubleshooting Tip:** Disable PS-mode on A.C. powered STAs. Buffering unicast and multicast frames for non-battery powered STAs only consumes limited AP CPU cycles and resources, and creates additional traffic BSA traffic.

## ERP IE

We've discussed the ERP IE and protection in 802.11bg networks as it relates to CSMA/CA and virtual carrier. In review:

- Non-ERP Present indicates that an 802.11b STA is associated to the AP.
- Use Protection commands ERP STAs to precede ERP-OFDM transmissions with a DSSS CTS-to-Self frame with a duration field value which reserves the medium for the time required to send the ERP-OFDM data frame and subsequent ACK.
- Barker Preamble Mode specifics which DSSS preamble to use with the CTS-to-Self frame. Set specifies long preamble, reset short preamble.

## Mini-Case Study: ***Phantom Protection:***

During capacity planning baseline captures it's discovered that every data transmission is preceded by a CTS frame.

| Destination | Source | Function | Protocol |
|---|---|---|---|
| Aironet-PCI | | CTS | IEEE 802.11 |
| AP600-1-Ethernet | Aironet-PCI | Ack Fin | TCP |
| Aironet-PCI | | ACK | IEEE 802.11 |
| AP600-1 | | CTS | IEEE 802.11 |
| Aironet-PCI | AP600-1-Ethernet | Ack | TCP |
| AP600-1 | | ACK | IEEE 802.11 |
| Aironet-PCI | . | CTS | IEEE 802.11 |

The BSA is operating in protection mode although the AP's association table only lists 802.11g STAs. LinkFerret captures the following beacon frame from AP600-1.

```
Time Stamp              4008359833370624000
Beacon Interval         100
Capability Information
  Channel Agility   [0xxxxxxx xxxxxxxx]  Off
  PBCC              [x0xxxxxx xxxxxxxx]  Off
  Short Preamble    [xx1xxxxx xxxxxxxx]  On
  Privacy           [xxx1xxxx xxxxxxxx]  On
  CF Poll Request   [xxxx0xxx xxxxxxxx]  Off
  CF Pollable       [xxxxx0xx xxxxxxxx]  Off
  IBSS              [xxxxxx0x xxxxxxxx]  Off
  ESS               [xxxxxxx1 xxxxxxxx]  On
  Reserved          [xxxxxxxx 00000100]  4
Information Element
Information Element
  Identity          Supported Rates
  Length            8
  Rate              1.0 MB    [1xxxxxxx]  In Basic Rate Set
  Rate              2.0 MB    [1xxxxxxx]  In Basic Rate Set
  Rate              5.5 MB    [1xxxxxxx]  In Basic Rate Set
  Rate              11.0 MB   [1xxxxxxx]  In Basic Rate Set
  Rate              6.0 MB    [0xxxxxxx]  Not in Basic Rate Set
  Rate              12.0 MB   [0xxxxxxx]  Not in Basic Rate Set
  Rate              24.0 MB   [0xxxxxxx]  Not in Basic Rate Set
  Rate              36.0 MB   [0xxxxxxx]  Not in Basic Rate Set
Information Element
Information Element
Information Element
  Identity          ERP
  Length            1
  Non-ERP Present   [xxxx xxx0]  Off
  Use Protection    [xxxx xx1x]  On
  Barker Preamble   [xxxx x0xx]  Off
```

This is a standard 802.11 mixed mode beacon, with an interesting twist, although the ***Non-ERP Present bit is reset***, the ***Use Protection bit is set***. That explains why STAs have implemented CTS-to-Self protection, but not why the AP set Protection bit in the absence of HR/DSSS STAs!

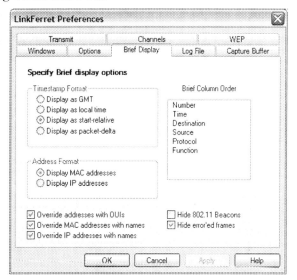

**LinkFerret Fact:** The Hide 802.11 Beacons checkbox in LinkFerret Preferences, Brief Display tab is a built-in beacon filter. It must be cleared to capture beacon frames or display beacon frames in capture files. *Ensure that this checkbox is checked and beacon display is suppressed unless otherwise specified.*

If we need to observe beacon frames in a capture file analysis you will be instructed to clear the check-box and press **F5** to refresh the display.

## AP Discovery

An AP sets Use Protection for two reasons:

- An 802.11b (non-ERP) STA associates to the AP
- The AP receives beacon or probe response frame from another AP on the same or overlapping channels with the Use Protection bit set.

**LinkFerret Fact:** LinkFerret AP discovery is accessed through the Statistics Windows. To perform AP discovery configure LinkFerret Preferences to scan all 11 FCC supported channels with a 3-second hover time.

As we've discussed, ISM channel overlap produces odd and inconsistent behavior. Let's determine if other WLANs are operating in the same BSA. Walking through the BSA area running LinkFerret AP Discovery detected APs on overlapped channels 11 and 9.

| BSSID | ESSID | Channel | Signal Strength |
|---|---|---|---|
| 00-11-50-0E-BC-53 | EWG | 11 | 69 |
| PROXIM-4F-1F-94 | Site2 | 9 | 74 |

**Explanation** The EWG AP is running in 802.11bg mode and has 802.11b associated STAs. It has enabled Use Protection in its beacon. Because of the overlap in physical areas and channel frequencies, the Site2 AP (AP600-1) received EWG beacons with Use Protection set on and reacted by setting Use Protection in its own beacon. This "chain-reaction" is intended to protect the entire shared medium of the BSA.

### Does Phantom Protection Increase or Reduce Network Throughput?

The only way to know is to perform a baseline capture and determine the nominal PER and network throughput. Disable CTS-to-Self protection on the Site2 AP and run another capture to determine the current PER. If the PER goes up and the data throughput goes down, then the Phantom Protection is increasing overall BSA throughput.

**Solutions** The best solution is to perform another site survey and determine why Channel-9 was selected. In the meantime simply moving the AP away from the other BSA may be enough to keep it from receiving Use Protection in beacons and probe response frames.

**Protection and Performance** According to the maximum throughput calculations in Chapter 7, the maximum 802.11g native mode maximum data throughput with TCP/IP is approximately 27.6-Mbps or 52% of the 54-Mbps raw rate. Implementing protection with CTS-to-Self reduces the maximum theoretical throughput to approximately 16.7-Mbps or 31% of the 54-Mbps raw rate.

## *SSIDs, VLANS and Security by Obscurity*

Common wisdom maintains that suppressing the SSID in the beacon improves security.

- If the SSID isn't in the beacon, how does the STA locate an AP?
- When would an AP be configured with multiple SSIDs? How many SSIDs can be advertised a beacon?

Suppressing the beacon's SSID is an example of "security by obscurity." We'll address the security and performance ramifications of SSID suppression in a few pages.

A VLAN (virtual LAN):

- Behaves like a physical IP subnet
- Inter-VLAN communications requires an IP address and VLAN aware router and switches
- Defines a broadcast domain
- Often assigned to the STA by a RADIUS server
- Enables STA physical location independence
- Enhances security and performance

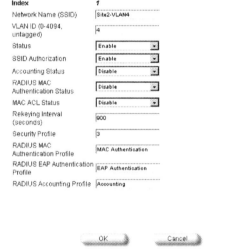

SSID, VLAN, and Security Table - Wireless A - Edit Entries.

This page is used to configure additional SSIDs, VLANs, and their associated security profiles and RADIUS server profiles. Each table entry requires a unique SSID and VLAN ID.

Security Profiles are used to configure the allowed security modes. If RADIUS MAC, 802.1x, WPA or RADIUS accounting is enabled in the SSID's security profile then the respective RADIUS server profiles should be configured and assigned to this SSID.

*Note: Changes to these parameters require access point reboot in order to take effect.*

| Index | 1 |
|---|---|
| Network Name (SSID) | Site2-VLAN4 |
| VLAN ID (0-4094, untagged) | 4 |
| Status | Enable |
| SSID Authorization | Enable |
| Accounting Status | Disable |
| RADIUS MAC Authentication Status | Disable |
| MAC ACL Status | Disable |
| Rekeying Interval (seconds) | 900 |
| Security Profile | 3 |
| RADIUS MAC Authentication Profile | MAC Authentication |
| RADIUS EAP Authentication Profile | EAP Authentication |
| RADIUS Accounting Profile | Accounting |

OK          Cancel

Each VLAN may be assigned a different VLAN ID, SSID, maximum number of associated STAs, security policy, configuration profile and QoS parameters.

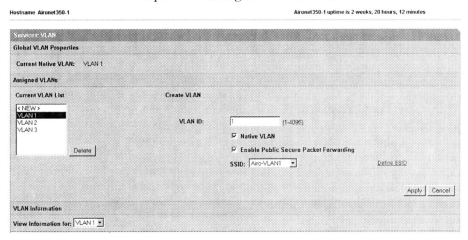

## Active Scanning

STAs transmit Probe Request frames to:

- Actively discover APs prior to initiating authentication and association.
- Maintain a list of the SSID and BSSID (MAC addresses) of every currently available AP which enable a STA to immediately fail-over when the RSSI or transmit rate threshold falls below specified levels.

A changing RF environment is usually associated with mobile STAs. However, RF conditions for a fixed STA in a marginal location, perhaps on the edge of multiple overlapping BSAs, may change with the movement of doors, metallic window coverings or even people walking through the area.

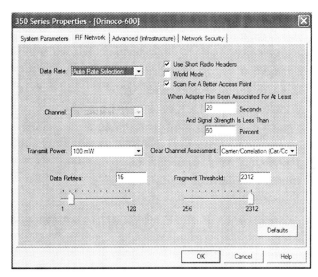

The Cisco Aironet-350 is a popular 802.11b client adapter. By default it "scans for a better access point" when it has been associated for at least 20 seconds and the signal strength is less than 50%. *Enforcing a minimum association period prevents a STA from "bouncing" between APs with the same marginal signal strength.*

**Client Utilities**: Throughput the book Cisco's 802.11b ACU (Aironet client utility) and 802.11a/b/g ADU (Aironet desktop utility) are used to examine adapter-specific settings. XP's adapter-independent WZC (wirelesses zero configuration) Service is used to examine SSID preferences, association and 802.1x authentication configuration.

The probe request rate of an associated STA is client adapter specific. Under control of the WZC Service client adapters typically probe all 11 ISM channels at 60 second intervals. However, drivers can override this default behavior and mobile devices actively scan very aggressively as they move between BSAs.

## 802.11b Probe Request for a specific SSID

<u>Frame Type</u>: Probe Request

<u>Power Mgmt bit</u>: Set
The PwrMgmt bit indicates that it's going off channel and that the AP should buffer its unicast frames.

<u>To/From DS = 0</u> Management frames aren't processed by the DSS.

<u>Duration = 0</u> The Probe Request isn't acknowledged so it doesn't reserve virtual carrier. An AP responding with a probe response frame must contend for the medium.

**Addresses:**
<u>Destination & BSSID</u>: Network Broadcast. Some client adapter utilities support preferred AP configuration which replaces the broadcast address with the MAC address of the preferred AP.
***Preferred AP Configuration provides manual load balancing across co-located APs configured on non-overlapping channels which are members of the same ESS.***

| Number | Destination | Source | Function | Protocol |
|--------|-------------|--------|----------|----------|
| [0-11]-56 | Broadcast | AirLink | Probe Request | IEEE 802.11 |

```
⊞ Physical Frame
⊟ IEEE 802.11 MAC Protocol
   └─Function              Probe Request
   ⊞ PLCP Header
   ⊟ Frame Control Byte 0
     ├─Protocol Level    [xxxxxx00]  0
     ├─Type              [xxxx00xx]  Management
     └─Sub-Type          [0100xxxx]  Probe Request
   ⊟ Frame Control Byte 1
     ├─Order             [0xxxxxxx]  off
     ├─WEP               [x0xxxxxx]  off
     ├─More Data         [xx0xxxxx]  off
     ├─Power Mgmt        [xxx1xxxx]  on
     ├─Retry             [xxxx0xxx]  off
     ├─More Fragments    [xxxxx0xx]  off
     ├─From DS           [xxxxxx0x]  off
     └─To DS             [xxxxxxx0]  off
   ├─Duration ID           0
   ⊟ Destination Address
     ├─Hex Address       FF-FF-FF-FF-FF-FF
     ├─Group Bit         [xxxxxxx1 xxxxxxxx xxxxxxxx xxxxxxxx xx
     ├─Local Bit         [xxxxxx1x xxxxxxxx xxxxxxxx xxxxxxxx xx
     └─Logical Names      [[Broadcast]]
   ⊟ Source Address
     ├─Hex Address       00-0D-88-E5-D3-2A
     ├─Group Bit         [xxxxxxx0 xxxxxxxx xxxxxxxx xxxxxxxx xx
     ├─Local Bit         [xxxxxx0x xxxxxxxx xxxxxxxx xxxxxxxx xx
     └─Logical Names      [[AirLink]]
   ⊟ BSSID
     ├─Hex Address       FF-FF-FF-FF-FF-FF
     ├─Group Bit         [xxxxxxx1 xxxxxxxx xxxxxxxx xxxxxxxx xx
     ├─Local Bit         [xxxxxx1x xxxxxxxx xxxxxxxx xxxxxxxx xx
     └─Logical Names      [[Broadcast]]
   ├─Fragment            [xxxxxxxx xxxx0000]  0
   ├─Sequence            [01110011 0101xxxx]  1845
   ⊟ Information Element
     ├─Identity           SSID
     ├─Length             3
     └─SSID               EWG
   ⊟ Information Element
     ├─Identity           Supported Rates
     ├─Length             4
     ├─Rate              1.0 MB   [1xxxxxxx]  In Basic Rate Set
     ├─Rate              2.0 MB   [1xxxxxxx]  In Basic Rate Set
     ├─Rate              5.5 MB   [1xxxxxxx]  In Basic Rate Set
     └─Rate              11.0 MB  [1xxxxxxx]  In Basic Rate Set
```

<u>SSID IE = EWG</u>
Only APs in the EWG ESS respond to this probe request.

<u>Supported Rates IE</u>:
***APs ignore the supported rates IE in the probe request frame***. The BSS rate requirements are determined from the supported rates IE in the STA's association request frame.

> **Gone Fishing**: The typical probe request has a broadcast destination address and the To/From DS bits are reset - ***it's not acknowledged, retransmitted as a retry or processed by the DSS***. Think of the probe request as a STA that's out fishing for APs and receiving a probe response as the equivalent of getting a "bite" or is that a "byte?"

## Probe Request with a null SSID IE

Not to be mistaken with a broadcast address, *a broadcast Probe Request has a null (empty) SSID IE.*
- Elicits a Probe Response from all APs that are not configured for SSID suppression.
- Originally the SSID "any" was used instead of a null. You may see references to the "any" SSID in older documentation but *in modern usage the terms: null, empty or broadcast SSID are used. Remember all four terms for certification exams*.
- STAs controlled by the WZC Service alternate probe request targets between the SSID of the current associated BSS and the null SSID. *The WZC Service keeps two lists: one with the available APs in the current ESS and a second of "other" APs sorted by preferred network configuration.*

## System Startup Probe Requests

Often network analyzers capture traffic that is more misleading than illuminating. Knowing what's relevant is more art than science. Weird, random or nonsensical SSIDs in probe requests aren't necessarily a symptom of misconfiguration or malfunction. The initial SSID in the probe request of a system during boot or after the wireless adapter is reset varies by operating system and vendor. However, after the client adapter is initialized it should probe for its currently configured preferred network.

## Probe Response Frame

Here's the first half of a probe response frame.

To/From DS = 0 Like the probe request, a probe response is a management frame and not processed by the DSS.

WEP = Off Even though this BSS is configured for encryption, the WEP bit is off for all types of frames except a data frame with an upper-layer payload.

Addresses:
**Source & BSSID** AP600-1
**Destination**: AirLink, an 802.11b STA

| Number | Time | Destination | Source | Protocol | Function |
|---|---|---|---|---|---|
| [0-01]-1 | 00:00:58:709:482 | AirLink | AP600-1 | IEEE 802.11 | Probe Response |

```
Physical Frame
IEEE 802.11 MAC Protocol
   Function              Probe Response
   PLCP Header
   Frame Control Byte 0
      Protocol Level   [xxxxxx00]   0
      Type             [xxxx00xx]   Management
      Sub-Type         [0101xxxx]   Probe Response
   Frame Control Byte 1
      Order            [0xxxxxxx]   off
      WEP              [x0xxxxxx]   off
      More Data        [xx0xxxxx]   off
      Power Mgmt       [xxx0xxxx]   off
      Retry            [xxxx0xxx]   off
      More Fragments   [xxxxx0xx]   off
      From DS          [xxxxxx0x]   off
      To DS            [xxxxxxx0]   off
   Duration ID          314
   Destination Address
   Source Address
   BSSID
   Fragment         [xxxxxxx xxxx0000]  0
   Sequence         [01011001 0011xxxx] 1427
```

Duration = 314-µs, the time required to transmit an ACK @ 1-Mbps with a long preamble. We'll discover in the next chapter that the AP and STA often communicate at very low basic rates until the association process is complete. For now remember: *A probe response is a unicast frame that requires an ACK*.

## Probe Response Frame, Part 2

Here's the second half of a probe response, which should look familiar.

*The beacon and probe response have identical information fields except that the probe response doesn't have a TIM IE. A STA can determine all it needs to know to start the association process from either a beacon or probe response frame!*

> **! Exam Alert**: the last two statements are prime exam fodder.

- A beacon is periodically broadcast as specified in the beacon interval field.
- It has a broadcast destination address and isn't ACKed or retransmitted as a retry.
- A probe response is transmitted in response to a probe request. It has a unicast destination address and must be ACKed or it's retransmitted with the retry bit set.
- An AP can be configured to suppress (hide) the SSID by transmitting a null SSID IE.
- An AP configured for SSID suppression only responds to probe requests with the correct (hidden) SSID in the SSID IE.

### Beacon vs. Probe Response

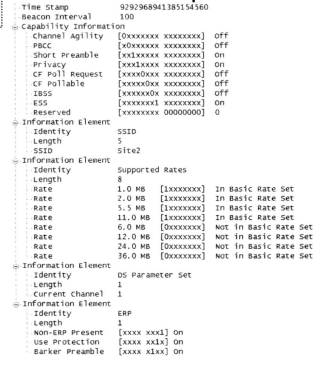

## Passive versus Active Scanning

- Passive scanning listens for a specific interval on each channel for beacon frames.
- Active scanning transmits probe requests on each channel with a specific SSID or a broadcast (null) SSID.
- Passive scanning takes very little power and doesn't consume BSA bandwidth because the STA isn't transmitting.
- Active scanning consumes power and BSA bandwidth.
- Passive scanning is slow because the STA must listen on each channel for about 1.25 TUs to ensure that it doesn't miss a beacon.
- Active scanning is fast. A STA should reasonably expect a probe response within 10-ms, or about 10% of the default beacon interval! But remember, the STA must stay on-channel long enough to receive the probe response and ACK it. Otherwise the AP retransmits the probe response several times creating a fury of extraneous frames

## *A Tale of Two Utilities*

The great majority of businesses computing WLAN STAs are Windows XP-based. The WZC Service uses the client adapter's driver and provides a limited, generic, non-adapter specific set of configuration capabilities. Selecting "**Use Windows to configure my wireless network settings**" seizes control of the adapter from the vendor's client adapter utility.

WZC Service enables one to:
- View available networks
- Manually specify and prioritize preferred networks.
- Set authentication and association configuration.

"Network" in the context of WLANs is the SSID of an ESS. The WZC Service enables preferred networks to be configured, but not the BSSID of specific APs.

Executing the ADU when the client adapter is controlled by the WZC Service produces a warning dialog.

Configuration settings that are only accessible through the vendor's client adapter utility or the wireless adapter's properties typically include:
- Specifying the BSSID of preferred APs for manual load balancing or STA segregation.
- RTS/CTS and Fragmentation thresholds
- Transmit Power levels
- Power Save Mode (also configured in the client adapter's drivers advanced properties tab.)
- Detailed current status information
- Advanced diagnostics
- Accumulated statistics windows
- And a host of other adapter specific information

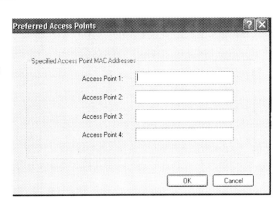

> **! Caution**: Wireless client adapter utilities and the WZC Service often have unforeseen interactions. For example, if the WZC Service configuration is selected, but the vendor's client utility is automatically running through a Run registry entry or the Startup Folder, the WZC Service may not display all of the available authentication types. Configurations made through the wireless adapters properties setting may be overridden by specific profiles. Interactions are vendor-specific and inconsistent. Be cautious when you toggle between these two configuration methods.

## Know the Vendor's Utility Limitations

We've all provided telephone support to a client attempting to connect to a wireless network in a hotel, office building or other unknown location. It's instructive and revealing to see how different utilities determine available APs.

In the AP discovery class of utilities, the current version of NetStumbler is the "big mouth." It transmits an unending stream of null probe requests, but doesn't listen for beacons. The other extreme are promiscuous WLAN analyzers which listen for beacons, but never transmit probe requests.

***The WZC Service and client adapter utilities operate in a hybrid fashion. They listen to beacons and use null and specific-SSID probe requests to build a BSSID scan list.***

## Scan with no configured networks

A LinkFerret capture of the network discovery operation of the WZC Service and the ACU "scan for networks" function is identical. LinkFerret captures a flurry of probe requests on each channel. In this example the WZC Service displays three networks with:

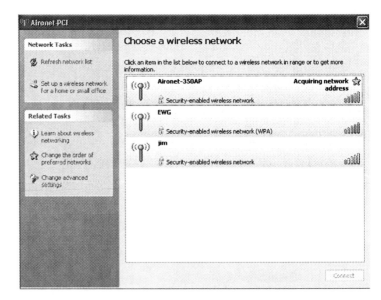

- Network Name (SSID)
- WEP/WPA encryption type
- Signal Strength in bars

The Cisco ADU displays slightly different information. The key icon symbolizes an encrypted network, but the encryption type isn't specified. Signal Strength display is configurable in "%" of maximum or dBm. Most important channel information is specified.

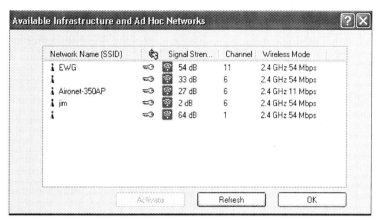

*It's very important to note that the Cisco ADU found two additional unnamed networks on channels 6 and 1. They represent beacons received with suppressed SSIDs!*

## Mini Case Study **SSID Broadcasting:**

The two unknown networks discovered by the Cisco ADU in the previous graphic are actually APs in the Site2 which are configured for SSID suppression. One might think that if Site2 was configured as a preferred network in a client adapter utility that the utility would actively probe for Site2 and it would be listed in the available networks.

*Network captures confirm that both utilities only actively probe with the null SSID and the SSID of the currently connected network, not the SSIDs of every configured preferred network.* This is a very important limitation of client adapter utilities. This means that although one may associate with a preferred network whose beacon SSID advertisement is suppressed, that network won't appear as an "available network" which complicates providing remote support.

**LinkFerret Fact:** LinkFerret builds a list of APs in the Statistics Window, AP Discovery tab by examing the SSID IE of beacon frames. While scanning multiple channels, LinkFerret may receive the same beacon on several adjacent channels. To determine the AP's actual channel open a beacon frame and examine the DS Parameter Set IE.

Five frames types <u>may</u> carry a SSID:
- **Beacon** configurable, but VLANs SSIDs are never advertised.
- **Probe Request** the hidden SSID is in the probe request of STAs preparing for association and periodic probe requests thereafter.
- **Probe Response** the SSID is never suppressed in a probe response frame.
- **Association Request and Reassociation Request** the target SSID always appears in Association Request and Reassociation Request frames. We examine association and reassociation requests in the next chapter.

> **! Exam Alert**: Remember the five frame types that may carry a SSID. It's more than exam question, it's fundamentally information that you should have on your fingertips.

Many whitepapers describe the process of spoofing a Disassociation or Deauthentication frame from an associated STA, which forces the STA to automatically reassociate, thus exposing the "hidden" SSID. ***That's a lot of work and usually not required.*** The WZC Service reveals the hidden SSID to a promiscuous WLAN network monitor within one minute because of its periodic probe requests to the currently associated SSID.

With this background in mind let's use LinkFerret to reveal the hidden SSID of the two APs discovered, but not identified by the Cisco ADU on the previous page.

The LinkFerret AP Discovery function determines that Proxim APs on

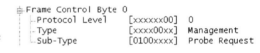

| BSSID | ESSID | Channel | Signal Strength | Signal Quality | Privacy | Last Contact |
|---|---|---|---|---|---|---|
| Netgear-ED-28-90 | jim | 6 | 71 | 0 | Yes | 16:49:52:633 |
| 00-11-50-0E-BC-53 | EWG | 11 | 85 | 0 | Yes | 16:50:22:629 |
| PROXIM-4F-1F-79 | | 6 | 73 | 0 | Yes | 16:50:41:728 |
| PROXIM-4F-1F-94 | | 1 | 80 | 0 | Yes | 16:50:41:743 |
| Cisco-7E-E9-AA | Aironet-350AP | 6 | 69 | 0 | Yes | 16:50:41:756 |

Channels 1 & 6 have suppressed SSID broadcast.

A capture of Channel-1 confirms that the SSID is suppressed in the Beacon, note the Null SSID field.

## Configuring a Probe Request and Response Filter

### Test One – Probe Request
Since we're only interested in Probe Request frames let's configure LinkFerret to capture on Channel 1 with a Probe Request capture filter. The capture fragment of a probe request frame provides us with everything we need to know to construct the filter. ***It's important that you take the time and effort to match the information in the capture fragment of the probe request frame to the construction of the filter.***

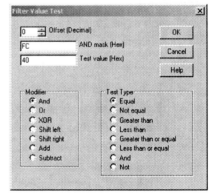

- Offset 0 specifies to test the first byte in the MAC header which is Frame Control Byte-0.
- AND mask 0xFC (1111 1100 binary) means that the filter will examine the six most significant bits and ignore the protocol version bits.
- Test value 0x40 specifies that the value of the frame that we want to match is 0100 00xx, which specifies a Probe Request Management frame – all other frames are discarded. The letters "xx" traditionally signify "don't care" bits – i.e. bits that aren't tested.

**Test 2: Probe Response**
Notice how easy it is to write filter value tests.

```
⊟-Frame Control Byte 0
   ·Protocol Level   [xxxxxx00]   0
   ·Type            [xxxx00xx]   Management
   └·Sub-Type        [0101xxxx]   Probe Response
```

- Examine Frame Control, Byte-0 of an example frame type that you want to filter.
- Convert the binary values in the Detail Decode Window into hex values to create the filter.

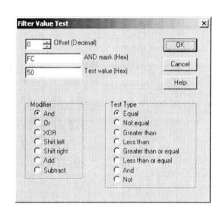

***Take a moment to ensure that you understand how the information from the probe response capture fragment is represented in the Filter Value Test.***

The filter has two include statements. Probe Request and Probe Response frames are saved to the capture buffer – all other packets are discarded.

**Viewing the Filtered Capture**
The capture was performed with only one STA associated to the AP to minimize the amount of active probing for this analysis. Open the capture file SSID-ProbeReqRes and ensure No Filter is selected. LinkFerret was configured to capture with the Probe Request/Probe Response filter on Channel-1.

***The capture yielded 38 frames in about 94 seconds from a single STA.*** But it's difficult to directly determine how many Probe Requests are sent on each of the 11 channels. Because of channel overlap, many of these Probe Requests were probably sent on channels 2, 3 or even 4.

The capture time format is configured as start relative. At just over 22 seconds the

| Number | Time | Destination | Source | Function |
|---|---|---|---|---|
| [0-01]-1 | 00:00:22:226:002 | Broadcast | Aironet-A2-F4-34 | Probe Request |
| [0-01]-2 | 00:00:22:226:620 | Broadcast | Aironet-A2-F4-34 | Probe Request |
| [0-01]-3 | 00:00:22:227:486 | Aironet-A2-F4-34 | PROXIM-4F-1F-94 | Probe Response |
| [0-01]-4 | 00:00:22:677:249 | Aironet-A2-F4-34 | PROXIM-4F-1F-94 | Probe Response |
| [0-01]-5 | 00:00:22:678:612 | Aironet-A2-F4-34 | PROXIM-4F-1F-94 | Probe Response |
| [0-01]-6 | 00:00:23:077:802 | Aironet-A2-F4-34 | PROXIM-4F-1F-94 | Probe Response |
| [0-01]-7 | 00:00:23:078:673 | Aironet-A2-F4-34 | PROXIM-4F-1F-94 | Probe Response |
| [0-01]-8 | 00:00:23:478:266 | Aironet-A2-F4-34 | PROXIM-4F-1F-94 | Probe Response |
| [0-01]-9 | 00:00:23:479:222 | Aironet-A2-F4-34 | PROXIM-4F-1F-94 | Probe Response |
| [0-01]-10 | 00:00:27:081:687 | Broadcast | Aironet-A2-F4-34 | Probe Request |
| [0-01]-11 | 00:00:27:082:380 | Broadcast | Aironet-A2-F4-34 | Probe Request |
| [0-01]-12 | 00:00:27:482:426 | Broadcast | Aironet-A2-F4-34 | Probe Request |
| [0-01]-13 | 00:00:27:483:025 | Broadcast | Aironet-A2-F4-34 | Probe Request |
| [0-01]-14 | 00:00:27:484:817 | Aironet-A2-F4-34 | PROXIM-4F-1F-94 | Probe Response |
| [0-01]-15 | 00:00:27:485:751 | Aironet-A2-F4-34 | PROXIM-4F-1F-94 | Probe Response |
| [0-01]-16 | 00:00:27:882:752 | Broadcast | Aironet-A2-F4-34 | Probe Request |
| [0-01]-17 | 00:00:27:883:387 | Broadcast | Aironet-A2-F4-34 | Probe Request |
| [0-01]-18 | 00:00:28:283:323 | Broadcast | Aironet-A2-F4-34 | Probe Request |
| [0-01]-19 | 00:00:28:284:007 | Broadcast | Aironet-A2-F4-34 | Probe Request |
| [0-01]-20 | 00:00:31:886:982 | Broadcast | Aironet-A2-F4-34 | Probe Request |
| [0-01]-21 | 00:00:31:887:991 | Aironet-A2-F4-34 | PROXIM-4F-1F-94 | Probe Response |
| [0-01]-22 | 00:00:31:889:011 | Broadcast | Aironet-A2-F4-34 | Probe Request |
| [0-01]-23 | 00:01:25:240:404 | Broadcast | Aironet-A2-F4-34 | Probe Request |
| [0-01]-24 | 00:01:25:241:090 | Broadcast | Aironet-A2-F4-34 | Probe Request |
| [0-01]-25 | 00:01:25:242:100 | Aironet-A2-F4-34 | PROXIM-4F-1F-94 | Probe Response |
| [0-01]-26 | 00:01:26:061:593 | Aironet-A2-F4-34 | PROXIM-4F-1F-94 | Probe Response |
| [0-01]-27 | 00:01:26:062:438 | Aironet-A2-F4-34 | PROXIM-4F-1F-94 | Probe Response |
| [0-01]-28 | 00:01:30:467:193 | Broadcast | Aironet-A2-F4-34 | Probe Request |
| [0-01]-29 | 00:01:30:468:064 | Aironet-A2-F4-34 | PROXIM-4F-1F-94 | Probe Response |
| [0-01]-30 | 00:01:30:468:912 | Aironet-A2-F4-34 | PROXIM-4F-1F-94 | Probe Response |
| [0-01]-31 | 00:01:30:469:865 | Broadcast | Aironet-A2-F4-34 | Probe Request |
| [0-01]-32 | 00:01:30:867:155 | Broadcast | Aironet-A2-F4-34 | Probe Request |
| [0-01]-33 | 00:01:30:867:798 | Broadcast | Aironet-A2-F4-34 | Probe Request |
| [0-01]-34 | 00:01:31:267:813 | Broadcast | Aironet-A2-F4-34 | Probe Request |
| [0-01]-35 | 00:01:31:268:467 | Broadcast | Aironet-A2-F4-34 | Probe Request |
| [0-01]-36 | 00:01:34:871:343 | Broadcast | Aironet-A2-F4-34 | Probe Request |
| [0-01]-37 | 00:01:34:872:013 | Broadcast | Aironet-A2-F4-34 | Probe Request |
| [0-01]-38 | 00:01:34:873:278 | Aironet-A2-F4-34 | PROXIM-4F-1F-94 | Probe Response |

first burst of active probing occurs. At about 85 seconds the second burst of active probing occurs. This verifies the WZC Service default 60-second active probe interval.

The BSSID specified in the Packet #3, Proxim-4F-1F-94 matches the AP with the suppressed SSID beacon as recorded in the LinkFerret AP Discovery.

| Number | Time | Destination | Source | Function |
|---|---|---|---|---|
| [0-01]-1 | 00:00:22:226:002 | Broadcast | Aironet-A2-F4-34 | Probe Request |

```
⊞ Physical Frame
⊟ IEEE 802.11 MAC Protocol
    Function                 Probe Request
  ⊞ PLCP Header
  ⊟ Frame Control Byte 0
     Protocol Level     [xxxxxx00]  0
     Type               [xxxx00xx]  Management
     Sub-Type           [0100xxxx]  Probe Request
  ⊞ Frame Control Byte 1
     Duration ID        0
  ⊟ Destination Address
     Hex Address        FF-FF-FF-FF-FF-FF
     Group Bit          [xxxxxxx1 xxxxxxxx xxxxxx)
     Local Bit          [xxxxxx1x xxxxxxxx xxxxxx)
     Logical Names      [[Broadcast]]
  ⊟ Source Address
     Hex Address        00-40-96-A2-F4-34
     Group Bit          [xxxxxxx0 xxxxxxxx xxxxxx)
     Local Bit          [xxxxxx0x xxxxxxxx xxxxxx)
     Vendor Name        Aironet
  ⊟ BSSID
     Hex Address        FF-FF-FF-FF-FF-FF
     Group Bit          [xxxxxxx1 xxxxxxxx xxxxxx)
     Local Bit          [xxxxxx1x xxxxxxxx xxxxxx)
     Logical Names      [[Broadcast]]
    Fragment            [xxxxxxxx xxxx0000]  0
    Sequence            [00110000 0101xxxx]  773
  ⊟ Information Element
     Identity           SSID
     Length             5
     SSID               Site2
  ⊞ Information Element
```

Probe Request from an Associated STA:

**Addresses**
Destination and BSSID Network broadcast
Source Because the "hidden" SSID is exposed, it must have been sent by an associated STA or a STA manually configured with the Site2 SSID.

**SSID IE:** Site2, the suppressed SSID.

This probe request is intended to determine the signal strength and quality of all available APs in the Site2 ESS. The results are stored in the STA's BSSID scan list.

Let's examine just the Probe Request frames in the **SSID-ProbeReqRes** capture. Remember to open the PSP-SRV namespace. Apply the **ProbeReq** filter and press **F5** to refresh the display.

| Number | Time | Destination | Source | Function |
|---|---|---|---|---|
| [0-01]-1 | 00:00:22:226:002 | Broadcast | Aironet-PCI | Probe Request |
| [0-01]-2 | 00:00:22:226:620 | Broadcast | Aironet-PCI | Probe Request |
| [0-01]-3 | 00:00:27:081:687 | Broadcast | Aironet-PCI | Probe Request |
| [0-01]-4 | 00:00:27:082:380 | Broadcast | Aironet-PCI | Probe Request |
| [0-01]-5 | 00:00:27:482:426 | Broadcast | Aironet-PCI | Probe Request |
| [0-01]-6 | 00:00:27:483:025 | Broadcast | Aironet-PCI | Probe Request |
| [0-01]-7 | 00:00:27:882:752 | Broadcast | Aironet-PCI | Probe Request |
| [0-01]-8 | 00:00:27:883:387 | Broadcast | Aironet-PCI | Probe Request |
| [0-01]-9 | 00:00:28:283:323 | Broadcast | Aironet-PCI | Probe Request |
| [0-01]-10 | 00:00:28:284:007 | Broadcast | Aironet-PCI | Probe Request |
| [0-01]-11 | 00:00:31:886:982 | Broadcast | Aironet-PCI | Probe Request |
| [0-01]-12 | 00:00:31:889:011 | Broadcast | Aironet-PCI | Probe Request |

| Frame | Signal |
|---|---|
| 1 | 84 |
| 2 | 84 |
| 3 | 79 |
| 4 | 80 |
| 5 | 78 |
| 6 | 78 |
| 7 | 74 |
| 8 | 74 |
| 9 | 69 |
| 10 | 69 |
| 11 | 84 |
| 12 | 84 |

The STA in these captures is an Aironet-a/b/g client adapter with an external antenna and configured at the maximum transmit power of 100-mw. The LinkFerret capture appliance is within 3 feet of the STA.

***In a nine second interval the Aironet-PCI STA sent a flurry of 12 Probe Request frames on Channel-1 alternating between probing for Site2 and a null SSID – or did it?*** The table specifies the signal strength of each of the 12 frames as recorded in the physical field in the detail decode window. Each pair of frames is associated with a specific signal level. Possible explanations for this flurry of probe requests are:
- ISM channel overlap
- The LinkFerret capture appliance was sitting too close to the Aironet external antenna which was transmitting at 100-mw!

It appears that LinkFerret is capturing traffic on Channel-1 and several other adjacent channels; the further off Channel-1, the lower the signal strength. The flurry of 12 probe requests occurred in pairs on channels 1 through 5. Active probing doesn't generate nearly as much traffic as may be indicated in many network monitor captures.

***The only time that an associated STA goes off-channel is to scan for other APs.*** Since passive scanning is undetectable, the network monitor only captures a STA's active scanning the AP's probe response. A well-behaved STA precedes passive scanning by transmitting a null-data frame with the PwrMgmt bit set. This ensures that the AP buffers it frames while off-channel. ***So, the network monitor can capture an indirect indication of passive scanning!*** As the example in this chapter illustrated, PS-mode toggling is often also integrated into the probe request frame by setting the PwrMgmt bit.

Open capture file **ProbeRequest-Channel-14**, apply **No Filter** and press **F5**. In this capture LinkFerret is configured on Channel 14, a channel not supported by the FCC, and still captures probe request frames from channels 8 through 11.

## Suppressing the SSID, a final Word?

Many high-end WLAN analyzers, such as AirMagnet's Handheld, automatically build a list of all APs and associated clients, deriving the SSID from probe request and probe response frames.

Many consultants argue that suppressing the SSID in the beacon causes STAs to increase their rate of active probing. The whitepaper, "*Debunking the Myth of SSID Hiding*" by Robert Moskowitz of the highly-respected TruSecure's ICALabs contends that the rate of active probing increases for associated STAs with the SSID suppressed in the beacons. He states,

> "A station preparing to roam in a WLAN whose Beacons do not carry the SSID must actively scan to discover APs. The station sends out Probe Requests sequentially on all channels with its SSID and listens for Probe Responses. They may do this channel scanning every 50msec (20 times a second!) as it attempts to discover a stronger signal."

It appears that the author didn't to take into account the ISM channel overlap and that in the presence of strong signals and directional antennas network monitors capture traffic on many adjacent channels. While it is likely that a roaming client on the edge of the BSA may generate a flurry of probe requests, as we saw at the beginning of the active scanning section, ***Cisco and other vendors use a hysteresis value to ensure that a STA doesn't "flap" between APs with a default value of 20-seconds.***

Monitoring production environments under the control of the WZC Service or Cisco's ACU indicate that an associated STA actively probes at a 60 second or 30 second interval with a pair of Probe Requests frames alternating between specifying the currently associated SSID and a null SSID. An associated OS-X Tiger STA with an AirPort adapter doesn't appear actively periodically probe, even in a network with a suppressed SSID beacon. It only probes during start-up or when the RSSI falls below the specific threshold.

The frequency of probe requests is a function of the:
- STA's mobility
- manufacturer of the wireless client adapter
- driver version
- operating system
- environmental conditions

The Bottom Line
Suppressing the SSID in beacon frames:
- ***Doesn't enhance security***
- ***Doesn't create significant additional probe request traffic***
- ***May increase user support issues***

## Going Off Channel and the PwrMgmt Bit

The number of probe response frames transmitted for each pair of probe requests is a function of:
- Whether an AP is configured to response to a null SSID probe request
- The design of overlapping and co-located BSAs
- The number of APs in the ESS
- How well the STA communicates its off-channel status and minimizes retransmissions of probe response frames.

Power Mgmt, bit-5 of Frame Control Byte-1, is set to notify the AP that a STA is:
- Entering (or remaining in) PS-mode
- Or going off-channel to scan for APs

For either reason the AP buffers frames for the STA until it sends a frame with the PwrMgmt bit reset. The status of the PwrMgmt bit can be sent in any frame. The Null-Data frame is used to convey the status of the PwrMgmt bit when the STA has no other information to convey. Open the PSP-SRV namespace and capture file PwrMgmt-NullData, apply No Filter and press F5.

```
Number      Time              Destination   Source        Function
[0-01]-1    00:00:10:529:065  AP600-1       Aironet-PCI   Null

Physical Frame
IEEE 802.11 MAC Protocol
  Function            Null
  PLCP Header
  Frame Control Byte 0
    Protocol Level    [xxxxxx00]  0
    Type              [xxxx10xx]  Data
    Sub-Type          [0100xxxx]  Null
  Frame Control Byte 1
    Order             [0xxxxxxx]  off
    WEP               [x0xxxxxx]  off
    More Data         [xx0xxxxx]  off
    Power Mgmt        [xxx1xxxx]  on
    Retry             [xxxx0xxx]  off
    More Fragments    [xxxxx0xx]  off
    From DS           [xxxxxx0x]  off
    To DS             [xxxxxxx1]  on
  Duration ID         44
  BSSID
  Source Address
  Destination Address
  Fragment            [xxxxxxxx xxxx0000]  0
  Sequence            [00001010 0000xxxx]  160
```

```
[0-01]-3   00:00:45:070:979  AP600-1         Aironet-PCI     Null
[0-01]-4   00:00:45:071:105  Aironet-PCI                     ACK
[0-01]-5   00:00:45:072:139  Broadcast       Aironet-PCI     Probe Request
[0-01]-6   00:00:45:073:023  Aironet-PCI     AP600-1         Probe Response
[0-01]-7   00:00:45:073:320  AP600-1                         ACK
[0-01]-8   00:00:45:073:908  Broadcast       Aironet-PCI     Probe Request
[0-01]-9   00:00:45:114:348  AP600-1         Aironet-PCI     Null
[0-01]-10  00:00:45:114:453  Aironet-PCI                     ACK
[0-01]-11  00:00:45:483:753  AP600-1         Aironet-PCI     Null
[0-01]-12  00:00:45:483:887  Aironet-PCI                     ACK
[0-01]-13  00:00:45:489:610  Aironet-350AP                   ACK
[0-01]-14  00:00:45:534:932  AP600-1         Aironet-PCI     Null
[0-01]-15  00:00:45:535:033  Aironet-PCI                     ACK
[0-01]-16  00:00:45:884:272  AP600-1         Aironet-PCI     Null
```

Feel free to investigate the fine points, but the gist of capture is that Aironet-PCI is currently associated to AP600-1 in Site2. About every 60 seconds it transmits a pair of probe requests specifying Site2 and a null SSID.

Apply the **Data-Null** filter, which displays only Null Data Frames, and press **F5**. Expand Frame Control, Byte-1 in the Detail Decode window. Walk through the Null Data frames and note that the PwrMgmt bit toggles state with each frame. When probing off-channel AP600-1 buffers unicast frames with Aironet-PCI as the destination address. When Aironet-PCI is back on-channel, it sends a Null Data frame with the power management bit reset.

# Chapter 4 Review

## Passive Scanning

- A STA passively scans by listening for AP Beacons on each channel for a brief interval.
- The destination address of a Beacon is network broadcast and it's not ACKed
- Listens for the SSID in Beacon frames for a specified interval
- Repeats the process on every channel.
- If multiple APs in the ESS are detected, the STA associates with the AP that has the RSSI and lowest PER.

## Beacon Frame Information

- Three fixed length fields
    - Time Stamp
    - Beacon Interval
    - Capability Information
- Mandatory, feature specific and proprietary IEs

## Time Stamp

- The AP provides the BSS TSF (timing synchronization function)
    - The time stamp is a 64-bit field, the AP's synchronized μs count-based clock.
    - All STAs synchronize to the Beacon's time stamp
- The primary reason for a synchronized BSS clock is to facilitate PS (power save) mode.

## Beacon Interval (Also called the Beacon Period)
- Specified in TUs (time units), where each TU = 1 K-μs
- ***The default Beacon Interval is 100-TUs** (about 9.75 beacons per second)*
- Configurable it's rarely modified.

## TBTT (target beacon transmission time)
- At the TBTT the beacon is queued for transmission
    - the TBTT is only an estimate
    - the AP contends for the medium so the contention period is variable
- The beacon is a broadcast frame and isn't ACKed or rebroadcast.
    - The percentage of missed beacons is a helpful indication of the overall heath of the STA and BSS.

## Capability Information (first 8-bits)

| B₀ | B₁ | B₂ | B₃ | B₄ | B₅ | B₆ | B₇ |
|---|---|---|---|---|---|---|---|
| ESS | IBSS | CF Pollable | CF-Poll Request | Privacy | Short Preamble | PBCC | Channel Agility |

Capability Information Field Bits 0 - 7

- **Channel Agility**
  - optional feature of HR/DSSS
  - set to indicate that the AP automatically changes channels when interference is detected
  - *This flag is rarely supported*.

- **PBCC**
  - *optional, rarely supported coding scheme* introduced with HR/DSSS
  - made obsolete with the introduction of 802.11g

- **Short Preamble**
  - Set to indicate that the BSS currently supports short preamble
  - reset to indicate that a client adapter without short preamble support has associated to the BSS

- **Privacy**
  - Set to signify that the BSS requires WEP or WPA data frame encryption.
  - When set, STAs without encryption support aren't allowed to associate with the BSS.
  - APs that support WPA have a WPA IE which specifies supported encryption algorithms and options.

- **CF Poll Request and CF Pollable**
  - These two bits are used together to provide four possible PCF compatibility settings.
  - PCF has never been implemented in production APs

- **IBSS and ESS**
  - Complimentary bits – one is set while the other reset.
  - IBSS is set for ad hoc, peer-to-peer networks.
  - ESS is set in AP beacons to specify infrastructure mode.

```
-Beacon Interval        100
⊟ Capability Information
    Channel Agility    [0xxxxxxx xxxxxxxx]   Off
    PBCC               [x0xxxxxx xxxxxxxx]   Off
    Short Preamble     [xx1xxxxx xxxxxxxx]   On
    Privacy            [xxx1xxxx xxxxxxxx]   On
    CF Poll Request    [xxxx0xxx xxxxxxxx]   Off
    CF Pollable        [xxxxx0xx xxxxxxxx]   Off
    IBSS               [xxxxxx0x xxxxxxxx]   Off
    ESS                [xxxxxxx1 xxxxxxxx]   On
    Reserved           [xxxxxxxx 00000000]   0
⊞ Information Element
⊞ Information Element
⊞ Information Element
⊞ Information Element
⊞ Information Element
⊞ Information Element
```

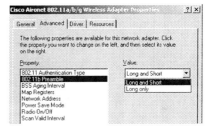

## Capability Information (second 8-bits)

| B8 | B9 | B10 | B11 | B12 | B13 | B14 | B15 |
|---|---|---|---|---|---|---|---|
| Spectrum Management | QoS | Short Slot Time | APSD | Reserved | DSSS-OFDM | Delayed Block ACK | Immediate Block ACK |

Capability Information Field Bits 8 - 15

- Short Slot Time (9-μs)
  - Set to indicate short slot time is in use
  - *Not all 802.11g APs support short slot time!*
- DSSS-OFDM (CCK-OFDM)
  - Set specifies that ERP transmissions may use a short or long DSSS preamble to provide mixed mode compatibility.
  - *To the best of my knowledge no current commercially available AP supports DSSS-OFDM.*

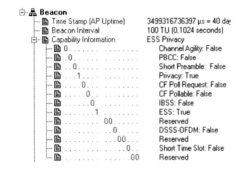

The following summaries are for test preparation purposes only.

- Spectrum Management
  - **802.11a and the 5-GHz Band Only**
  - a feature of the 802.11h specification which provides mechanisms to avoid co-channel operation between 802.11a BSSs and civil/military radar.
- **Proposed P802.11e Quality of Service Specification**
  - QoS indicates that the BSS supports P802.11e quality of service extensions.
    - 802.11e QoS will become a standard feature of business-class APs during the middle part of 2006.
  - APSD (automatic power save delivery) specifies that the BSS supports P802.11e QoS power management mode operation.
  - Delay Block ACK & Immediate Block ACK
    - P802.11e QoS data acknowledgement mechanisms.

## The IEs (Information Elements)

Note: Highlighted IE don't appear in standard beacons

| Information Element | ID | Comment |
|---|---|---|
| SSID | 0x00 | Main SSID or null |
| Supported Rates | 0x01 | 8 rates in 802.11b/bg APs – extendable in g-only APs |
| FH Parameters | 0x02 | Archaic - Frequency Hoping devices |
| DS Parameters | 0x03 | Direct Sequence - Current AP Channel |
| CF Parameters | 0x04 | Mythical - PCF has never been implemented |
| TIM | 0x05 | Traffic Indication Map for AP buffered traffic |
| ATIM | 0x06 | Announcement Traffic Indication Map (IBSS Only) |
| Shared-Key Challenge | 0x10 | Not in Beacon or Probe frames. See shared key authentication |
| ERP (extended rate physical) | 0x2a | Extended Rate PHY protection parameters. 802.11g APs only |
| Extended Rates | 0x32 | Used when an AP has more than 8 supported rates |
| WPA Parameters | 0xDD | WPA & WPA-PSK encryption and data integrity support |

## Standard Beacon SSID IE

```
⊟ Information Element
  ├ Identity          SSID
  ├ Length            5
  └ SSID              Site2
```

## Beacon with a Suppressed SSID IE

Also called a Null SSID

```
⊟ Information Element
  ├ Identity          SSID
  ├ Length            0
  └ SSID
```

## Basic Rates

* Basic Rates are mandatory.
  - *A STA must support every Basic Rate to currently specified in the BSS.*
  - "not in basic rate set" rates are optional
* *Communications that are essential to the proper functioning of the BSS must be transmitted at a basic rate which is supported by all associated STAs.*
  - This includes beacon, CTS and ACK frames.

## Supported & Extended Rates IEs

* The Supported Rates IE supports a maximum of eight rates.
* APs which support more than eight rates have a variable length Extended Rates IE.
* These two IEs illustrate the rates in a typical 802.11g mixed mode AP.

```
⊟ Information Element
  ├ Identity          Extended Rates
  ├ Length            4
  ├ Rate              9.0 MB    [0xxxxxxx]   Not in Basic Rate Set
  ├ Rate              18.0 MB   [0xxxxxxx]   Not in Basic Rate Set
  ├ Rate              48.0 MB   [0xxxxxxx]   Not in Basic Rate Set
  └ Rate              54.0 MB   [0xxxxxxx]   Not in Basic Rate Set
```

```
⊟ Information Element
  ┊ ⋯ Identity          Supported Rates
  ┊ ⋯ Length            8
  ┊ ⋯ Rate              1.0 MB    [1xxxxxxx]   In Basic Rate Set
  ┊ ⋯ Rate              2.0 MB    [1xxxxxxx]   In Basic Rate Set
  ┊ ⋯ Rate              5.5 MB    [1xxxxxxx]   In Basic Rate Set
  ┊ ⋯ Rate              11.0 MB   [1xxxxxxx]   In Basic Rate Set
  ┊ ⋯ Rate              6.0 MB    [0xxxxxxx]   Not in Basic Rate Set
  ┊ ⋯ Rate              12.0 MB   [0xxxxxxx]   Not in Basic Rate Set
  ┊ ⋯ Rate              24.0 MB   [0xxxxxxx]   Not in Basic Rate Set
  ┊ ⋯ Rate              36.0 MB   [0xxxxxxx]   Not in Basic Rate Set
```

## 802.11g Only Mode AP

- HS-DSSS bit rates aren't supported.
- This AP is configured to support 6, 12 & 24-Mbps as basic (mandatory) rates

```
⊟ Information Element
  ┊ ⋯ Identity          Supported Rates
  ┊ ⋯ Length            8
  ┊ ⋯ Rate              6.0 MB    [1xxxxxxx]   In Basic Rate Set
  ┊ ⋯ Rate              12.0 MB   [1xxxxxxx]   In Basic Rate Set
  ┊ ⋯ Rate              24.0 MB   [1xxxxxxx]   In Basic Rate Set
  ┊ ⋯ Rate              36.0 MB   [0xxxxxxx]   Not in Basic Rate Set
  ┊ ⋯ Rate              9.0 MB    [0xxxxxxx]   Not in Basic Rate Set
  ┊ ⋯ Rate              18.0 MB   [0xxxxxxx]   Not in Basic Rate Set
  ┊ ⋯ Rate              48.0 MB   [0xxxxxxx]   Not in Basic Rate Set
  ┊ ⋯ Rate              54.0 MB   [0xxxxxxx]   Not in Basic Rate Set
```

- The Beacon bit rate defaults to the highest basic rate of 24-Mbps with fallback capabilities to 6-Mbps.

## ARS (automatic rate selection)

- A STA's bit rate is a function of the RSSI and PER.
- RF energy is attenuated by the square of the distance from the AP. As RSSI decreases and PER increases the STA falls-back to the next lower supported speed.

## BSA Cell Size and Bit Rates

- The BSA cell should be the absolute minimal size.
  - But what bit rate is acceptable to your users?
- Enabling the lowest basic rates has two downsides:
  - May provide bit rates which are simply too low to support practical applications
    - You must determine the absolute lowest acceptable bit rate which is acceptable to your clients
  - may provide access to the BSA from well beyond the required physical area
- ***Setting a reasonable minimum bit-rate and transmit power level ensures that legitimate clients connect at acceptable rates but the signal doesn't propagate to uncontrolled areas.***

## DS Parameter Set IE

The DS Parameter Set IE specifies the AP's Current Channel.

- ISM channel overlap results in receiving signals that were actually transmitted on other channels.
- When an AP supporting Channel Agility changes channels due to interference the new channel designated in an IE.

```
⊟ Information Element
  ┊ ⋯ Identity          DS Parameter Set
  ┊ ⋯ Length            1
  ┊ ⋯ Current Channel   1
```

## TIM (traffic indication map) IE and PS Mode

How does a battery-powered STA periodically enter PS (power save) mode and not drop packets?

```
⊟ Information Element
    Identity          TIM
    Length            4
    DTIM Count        0
    DTIM Period       1
    Bitmap Control    0
```

- STA informs the AP that it's entering PS mode.
- AP buffers frames bound for the STA
- While asleep the STA's TSF timer continues to run
- The STA wakes at multiples of the TBTT and receives a beacon
- If the TIM bitmap control field bit assigned to the STA's AID (association ID) is set then the STA changes to AM and issues PS-Poll Control frames to read the buffered data.

## PS Operation Components

- The beacon's TIM IE
- Frame Control Byte-1
    - PwrMgmt bit to toggles between PS and AM
    - More Data bit indicates that the AP has additional buffered data
- Null-Data frames
    - convey the state of the PwrMgmt bit when no other information needs to be exchanged
- PS-Poll Control frame
    - Polls the AP for buffered data
    - AP responses with data frame and STA checks More Data bit
- Duration/ID field.
    - In the PS-Poll frame doesn't function as a duration field but specifies the STA's AID (association ID)

## The DTIM & Multicast Traffic

- Every beacon has a TIM.
- The DTIM (delivery traffic indication map) only appears in specified beacons.
    - It indicates the presence of buffered multicast traffic.
    - Individual STAs do not request to read buffered broadcast and multicast frames.
    - They are automatically transmitted following the DTIM beacon transmission.

## DTIM Count and Period

```
⊟ Information Element
    ├ Identity           DS Parameter Set
    ├ Length             1
    └ Current Channel    11
⊟ Information Element
    └ Identity           TIM
    ├ Length             4
    └ DTIM Count         1
    └ DTIM Period        3
    └ Bitmap Control     0
⊟ Information Element
    ├ Identity           ERP
    ├ Length             1
    └ Non-ERP Present    [xxxx xxx0] Off
    └ Use Protection     [xxxx xx0x] Off
    └ Barker Preamble    [xxxx x0xx] Off
```

- DTIM Count
    - indicates how many more beacons (including the current beacon) will be transmitted before the next DTIM
    - *A beacon that contains a DTIM has a DTIM Count of 0.*
    - In this example the DTIM Count is 1, indicating that the next beacon is a DTIM
- DTIM Period
    - indicates the number of beacons between DTIMs
    - *If the DTIM Period is 1, every beacon has a DTIM.*
    - In this example the DTIM Period is 3; every third beacon has a DTIM.
    - The DTIM Period has traditionally defaulted to a value of 3.
    - If the DTIM period is reduced, the power saving in PS-Mode is lowered

## ERP IE Review

- Non-ERP Present
    - set to indicate that an 802.11b STA is associated to the AP
- Use Protection
    - commands ERP-OFDM STAs to precede transmissions with an DSSS CTS-to-Self with a duration field value to protect following ERP-OFDM data frame and subsequent ACK

```
⊟ Information Element
    ├ Identity           ERP
    └ Length             1
    └ Non-ERP Present    [xxxx xxx1] On
    └ Use Protection     [xxxx xx1x] On
    └ Barker Preamble    [xxxx x1xx] On
```

- Barker Preamble (long DSSS Preamble)
    - set when a STA without short preamble support is associated to the AP
    - What's this have to do with ERP?
        - Tells the ERP STA which PLCP-Preamble/Header to use with the DSSS CTS-to-Self frame

## Phantom Protection: Use Protection without Non-ERP Present

- Non-ERP Present reset, but Use Protection is set
- Because of the of BSA overlap in physical areas and channel frequencies, an AP may that receives other beacons with Use Protection set will react by setting Use Protection in its own beacon.
- This "chain-reaction" is intended to protect the entire shared medium of the BSA.
- The best solution is to perform another site survey and determine why the AP's current channels was selected
    - moving the AP away from the other BSA may be enough to keep it from receiving Use Protection beacons
    - continue to perform baseline captures and ensure that the packet error rate doesn't significantly increase

## Protection and Performance:

According to our maximum throughput calculations in Chapter 7:
- the maximum 802.11g native mode maximum data throughput with TCP/IP is approximately ***27.6-Mbps or 52% of the 54-Mbps raw rate***
- Implementing protection ***with CTS-to-Self with short preamble @ 11-Mbps*** reduces the maximum theoretical throughput to approximately ***16.7-Mbps or 31% of the 54-Mbps raw rate.***

## VLAN Overview

- Behaves like a physical IP subnet
- Inter-VLAN communications requires an IP address and VLAN aware router
- Defines a broadcast domain
- Often assigned by a RADIUS server
- Enables STA physical location independence
- Enhances security and performance

## Active Scanning

- Probe Request frames are transmitted to actively discover APs
- The STA Maintain a list of the SSID and BSSID (MAC addresses) of every passively or actively detected AP.
  - enables a STA to quickly failover to another AP when the signal strength or transmit bit rate thresholds fall below specified levels

## Probe Requests and XP

- The probe request rate of an associated STA is client adapter specific. Under control of the WZC Service STAs typically probe all 11 channels at 60 second intervals. However, this is driver specific.

## 802.11b Probe Request for a specific SSID

- <u>Power Mgmt bit</u>: This frame does double duty. It's a probe request that uses the PwrMgmt bit to indicate that the STA is going off channel.
- <u>To/From DS = 0</u> Management frames aren't processed by the DSS.
- <u>Duration = 0</u> A Probe Request isn't ACKed. An AP responding with a probe response frame must contend for the medium.
- **Addresses:**
- <u>Destination & BSSID</u>: Network Broadcast.
- <u>SSID IE = EWG</u> Only APs in the EWG ESS respond to this probe request.
- <u>Supported Rates IE</u> in a probe request is only meaningful in IBSS networks

## Probe Request with a Null SSID IE

- Not to be mistaken with a broadcast address, *a broadcast Probe Request has a null (empty) SSID IE.*
    - Elicits a response from APs that aren't configured for SSID suppression.
    - Originally the SSID "any" was used instead of a null
    - *the terms null, empty or broadcast SSID are synonymous*
- STAs controlled by the WZC Service alternate the probe request target between the current associated SSID and the null SSID.
    - XP keeps two lists: one with the available APs in the current ESS and a second list of the "other" APs.

```
⊞ Physical Frame
⊟ IEEE 802.11 MAC Protocol
   ├ Function          Probe Request
   ⊞ PLCP Header
   ⊟ Frame Control Byte 0
   │  ├ Protocol Level  [xxxxxx00]  0
   │  ├ Type            [xxxx00xx]  Management
   │  └ Sub-Type        [0100xxxx]  Probe Request
   ⊟ Frame Control Byte 1
   │  ├ Order           [0xxxxxxx]  off
   │  ├ WEP             [x0xxxxxx]  off
   │  ├ More Data       [xx0xxxxx]  off
   │  ├ Power Mgmt      [xxx1xxxx]  on
   │  ├ Retry           [xxxx0xxx]  off
   │  ├ More Fragments  [xxxxx0xx]  off
   │  ├ From DS         [xxxxxx0x]  off
   │  └ To DS           [xxxxxxx0]  off
   ├ Duration ID       0
   ⊟ Destination Address
   │  ├ Hex Address     FF-FF-FF-FF-FF-FF
   │  ├ Group Bit       [xxxxxxx1 xxxxxxxx xxxxxxxx xxxxxxxx xx
   │  ├ Local Bit       [xxxxxx1x xxxxxxxx xxxxxxxx xxxxxxxx xx
   │  └ Logical Names   [[Broadcast]]
   ⊟ Source Address
   │  ├ Hex Address     00-0D-88-E5-D3-2A
   │  ├ Group Bit       [xxxxxxx0 xxxxxxxx xxxxxxxx xxxxxxxx xx
   │  ├ Local Bit       [xxxxxx0x xxxxxxxx xxxxxxxx xxxxxxxx xx
   │  └ Logical Names   [[AirLink]]
   ⊟ BSSID
   │  ├ Hex Address     FF-FF-FF-FF-FF-FF
   │  ├ Group Bit       [xxxxxxx1 xxxxxxxx xxxxxxxx xxxxxxxx xx
   │  ├ Local Bit       [xxxxxx1x xxxxxxxx xxxxxxxx xxxxxxxx xx
   │  └ Logical Names   [[Broadcast]]
   ├ Fragment          [xxxxxxxx xxxx0000]  0
   ├ Sequence          [01110011 0101xxxx]  1845
   ⊟ Information Element
   │  ├ Identity        SSID
   │  ├ Length          3
   │  └ SSID            EWG
   ⊟ Information Element
      ├ Identity        Supported Rates
      ├ Length          4
      ├ Rate    1.0 MB  [1xxxxxxx]  In Basic Rate Set
      ├ Rate    2.0 MB  [1xxxxxxx]  In Basic Rate Set
      ├ Rate    5.5 MB  [1xxxxxxx]  In Basic Rate Set
      └ Rate   11.0 MB  [1xxxxxxx]  In Basic Rate Set
```

## Probe Response, Part 1

```
Number   Time                Destination  Source   Protocol     Function
[0-01]-1 00:00:58:709:482    AirLink      AP600-1  IEEE 802.11  Probe Response
```

- <u>To/From DS = 0</u> Like the probe request, a probe response is a management frame and not processed by the DSS.
- <u>WEP = Off</u> When BSS encryption is enabled, the WEP bit is only set on data frames with upper-layer payload.
- <u>Addresses</u>:
- **Source & BSSID** AP600-1
- <u>Destination</u>: AirLink, an 802.11b STA
- <u>Duration</u> = 314-μs, the time required to transmit an ACK @ 1-Mbps with a long preamble.
- *Remember: A probe response is a unicast frame that requires an ACK*.

```
⊕ Physical Frame
⊖ IEEE 802.11 MAC Protocol
    Function              Probe Response
  ⊕ PLCP Header
  ⊖ Frame Control Byte 0
      Protocol Level   [xxxxxx00]  0
      Type             [xxxx00xx]  Management
      Sub-Type         [0101xxxx]  Probe Response
  ⊖ Frame Control Byte 1
      Order            [0xxxxxxx]  off
      WEP              [x0xxxxxx]  off
      More Data        [xx0xxxxx]  off
      Power Mgmt       [xxx0xxxx]  off
      Retry            [xxxx0xxx]  off
      More Fragments   [xxxxx0xx]  off
      From DS          [xxxxxx0x]  off
      To DS            [xxxxxxx0]  off
    Duration ID          314
  ⊕ Destination Address
  ⊕ Source Address
  ⊕ BSSID
    Fragment           [xxxxxxx xxxx0000]  0
    Sequence           [01011001 0011xxxx]  1427
```

## Probe Response, Part 2

- *The informational contents of a beacon and probe response are identical exception that the probe response doesn't have a TIM IE.*
  - A STA searching for APs can determine all it needs to know to start the association process from either a beacon or probe response frame!

## Beacon vs. Probe Response

- A beacon is periodically broadcasted at the specified beacon interval.
  - It has a broadcast destination address and isn't ACKed or retransmitted as a retry.
- A probe response is transmitted in response to a probe request.
  - It has a unicast destination address and must be ACKed. In the absence of an ACK it will be retransmitted just like any other unicast frame.
- An AP can be configured to suppress (hide) the SSID by transmitting a null SSID IE.
  - An AP configured to suppress its SSID only responds to probe requests that have the correct (hidden) SSID in the SSID IE.

## Passive versus Active Scanning

- Listening versus Talking
    - Passive scanning listens for a specified interval on each channel for beacon frames.
    - Active scanning transmits probe requests on every channel with either a specific SSID or a broadcast (null) SSID.
- Power Consumption
    - Passive scanning takes little power and doesn't consume BSA bandwidth.
    - Active scanning consumes power and BSA bandwidth.
- Scan Speed and Extraneous Traffic
    - Passive scanning is slow
        - the STA must listen on each channel for about 1.25 TUs to ensure that it doesn't miss a beacon
    - Active scanning is fast.
        - A STA should expect a probe response within 10-ms
        - However, the STA must stay on-channel long enough to receive the probe response and ACK it. Otherwise the AP retransmits the probe response several times creating a fury of extraneous frames.

## XP's WZC (wireless zero configuration) Service

- Provides a generic set of configuration capabilities.
- Selecting "**Use Windows to configure my wireless network settings**" seizes control of the adapter from the vendor's client adapter utility.
- WZC Service enables one to:
    - View available networks
    - Manually specify and prioritize preferred networks.
    - Set authentication and association configuration.

## Client Adapter Utility and Driver Specific Configuration Settings

Configuration settings only accessible through the vendor's client adapter utility or the wireless adapter's properties typically include:
- Specifying the BSSID of preferred APs for manual load balancing or STA segregation.
- RTS/CTS and Fragmentation thresholds
- Transmit Power levels
- Power Save Mode
- Detailed status information
- Chip-set specific diagnostics
- Current and accumulated statistics communications statistics
- And a host of other adapter specific information.

## WZC Service & Client Adapter Utility Interaction

- Vendor client adapter utilities and the WZC Service often have unforeseen interactions.
- Configurations made through the wireless adapters properties setting are overridden by specific profiles
- Be cautious when you must toggle between the two forms of wireless client adapter configuration

## Scan for available networks

- A network monitor capture of the network discovery of the WZC Service and ACU is identical; it simply shows a flurry of probe requests on each channel.
- The WZC Service displays networks with:
  - Network Name (SSID)
  - WEP/WPA encryption type
  - Signal Strength in bars
- The Cisco ADU displays slightly different information.
  - The key icon specifies an encrypted network.
  - Signal Strength display is configurable "%" in dBm.
  - Most important, channel information is specified.
- *Only the Cisco ADU lists APs with the SSID suppressed in the beacon!*

## Frames types that may carry a SSID

- **Beacon**
  - configurable, but VLANs SSIDs are never advertised
- **Probe Request**
  - the hidden SSID is in the probe request of STAs preparing for association and periodic probe requests thereafter
- **Probe Response**
  - the SSID is never suppressed in a probe response frame
- **Association Request and Reassociation Request**
  - the target SSID always appears in Association Request and Reassociation Request frames

## Revealing the "Hidden" SSID

- Spoofing a Disassociation or Deauthentication frame from an associated STA forces it to automatically reassociate, exposing the "hidden" SSID.
- XP-based STAs continuously expose the hidden SSID with periodic probe requests!

## Channel Overlap & Captures

- If a network capture appliance is positioned too close to a STA's antenna it may capture probe request frames that are transmitted on overlapping channels
- Results in the impression that a STA is generating much more active probing traffic
    - Off channel frames have a lower signal strength

## Suppressing the SSID, a final Word?

- Doesn't enhance security
    - Only protects a BSS from programs such as NetStumbler which only actively probe with a null SSID
- Doesn't create significant additional probe request traffic
- However, it may increase support issues

## Ratio of Probe Requests to Responses

- The number of Probe Responses transmitted for each pair of probe requests is a function of:
    - Whether an AP is configured to response to a null SSID probe request
    - The design of overlapping and co-located BSAs
    - The number of APs in the ESS
- **How well the STA communicates its off-channel status and minimizes retransmissions of Probe Response frames**

## Null Data & the PwrMgmt Bit

- Power Mgmt, bit-5 of Frame Control Byte-1, is set to notify that a STA is:
    - Leaving AM (active mode) and entering PS (power save mode) or
    - Going off-channel to do active probing
- For either reason the AP buffers frames for the STA until it sends a frame with the PwrMgmt bit reset.
- The status of the PwrMgmt bit can be sent in any frame directed to the AP.
    - The Null Data frame is used to convey the status of the PwrMgmt bit when the STA has no other information to send.

| Number | Time | Destination | Source | Function |
|--------|------|-------------|--------|----------|
| [0-01]-1 | 00:00:10:529:065 | AP600-1 | Aironet-PCI | Null |

```
⊞ Physical Frame
⊟ IEEE 802.11 MAC Protocol
   ┝Function              Null
⊞ PLCP Header
⊟ Frame Control Byte 0
   ┝Protocol Level    [xxxxxx00]   0
   ┝Type              [xxxx10xx]   Data
   └Sub-Type          [0100xxxx]   Null
⊟ Frame Control Byte 1
   ┝Order             [0xxxxxxx]   off
   ┝WEP               [x0xxxxxx]   off
   ┝More Data         [xx0xxxxx]   off
   ┝Power Mgmt        [xxx1xxxx]   on
   ┝Retry             [xxxx0xxx]   off
   ┝More Fragments    [xxxxx0xx]   off
   ┝From DS           [xxxxxx0x]   off
   └To DS             [xxxxxxx1]   on
   ┝Duration ID       44
⊞ BSSID
⊞ Source Address
⊞ Destination Address
   ┝Fragment          [xxxxxxxx xxxx0000]   0
   └Sequence          [00001010 0000xxxx]   160
```

# Chapter 5: 802.11 Authentication & Association

## *802.11 Management Commands Analyzed*

- Authentication
- Association Request and Association Response
- Deauthentication and Disassociation
- Reassociation Request and Reassociation Response

## *802.11 Concepts*

- Station States 1-3 and Class 1, 2 & 3 frames
- Open and Shared Key Authentication
- Association
- MAC Address Filters relationship to Authentication and Association
- Reasons for Deauthentication and Disassociation
- WPA-PSK troubleshooting
- Orinoco's multicast implementation of the IAPP (inter-access point protocol)
- Reassociation and STA roaming

## STA States

802.11 specifies that a STA acquires access to the DSS through the process of authentication and association. ***EAP (extensible authentication protocol) security mechanisms such as 802.1x port-based security with RADIUS or simple WPA-PSK (pre-shared key) are applied after the STA has successfully authenticated and associated with the AP.***

A STA has three possible states:
- **State-1**: unauthenticated & unassociated
- **State-2**: authenticated & unassociated
- **State-3**: authenticated & associated

From a STA in State-1 the AP:
- Accepts Class 1 frames, i.e. frames intended to locate an AP and initiate authentication
- Rejects any frame with the To-DS Bit set – a STA's frames aren't processed by the DSS until it's associated.

From a STA in State-2 the AP:
- Accepts Class 1 & 2 frames
- Class 2 frames initiate association and deauthentication
- Continues to rejects frames with the To-DS bit set

From a STA in State-3 the AP:
- Accepts any 802.11 frame
- Accepts frames with the To-DS set

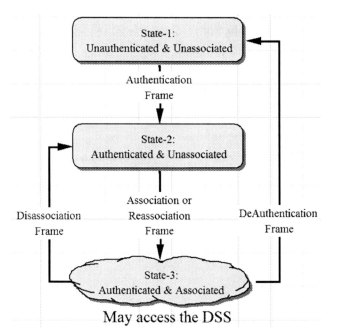

## Prohibiting Intra-BSS Traffic

Business-class APs support disabling intra-BSS communication. This excludes forwarding packets between STAs in the same BSS or ESS. ***In Cisco-speak this is called PSPF (Public Secure Packet Forwarding.)***

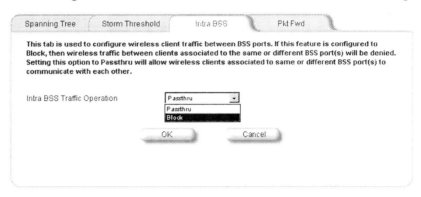

With the Orinoco AP600 intra-BSS traffic operation is configured under the bridge settings. ***Best practice is to block intra-BSS communication in a WLAN unless the network has peer-based resources*** – it's an easy way to improve security and performance

> **Troubleshooting Tip** If intra-BSS traffic is blocked you must run remote diagnostics, ping operations and XP remote desktop connections from a wired Ethernet node.

## Dedicating a Notebook as a Network Monitor

Promiscuous 802.11 network monitors are stealth devices; they usually don't authenticate or associate with an AP. To provide troubleshooting capabilities some network monitors can be configured to authenticate and associate to a specific SSID (wireless network) or BSSID (AP MAC address) while capturing the frames exchanged with the AP. Although this is a great convenience, it's always more reliable to troubleshoot by capturing traffic from a typical 802.11 STA. When the network monitor is also a wireless STA there are too many variables, including encryption technology limitations, driver incompatibilities, operating system bugs and potential packet loss. ***Keep it simple and reliable - dedicate a notebook computer as your 802.11 network monitor appliance.***

## Authentication

Traditional authentication is the process which verifies the identity of a security principal or the integrity of encrypted data. ***It's often said that 802.11 authentication is not authentication at all, but rather identification.*** When a STA presents an authentication request the AP simply links the STA's identity with its MAC address.

## Microsoft's Authentication Terminology

The WZC Service configures the 802.11 authentication type under the Association Tab. The 802.11 specification defines Open and Shared Key authentication. WPA and WPA-PSK are actually encryption, integrity checking and dynamic re-keying technologies that use Open authentication.

*The network properties, authentication tab doesn't configure 802.11 Authentication. It configures optional 802.1x/EAP authentication which is only applied after a STA reaches State-3.*

Open authentication provides the initial connection and 802.1x/EAP performs the subsequent, secure authentication.

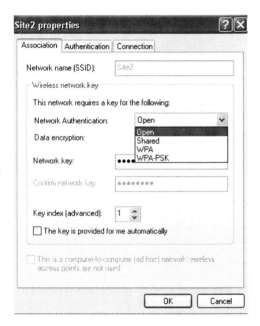

Cisco's approach to authentication terminology is a bit simpler. The ACU calls it "802.11 Authentication Mode" and offers three choices: Auto, Open and Shared. Encryption and keying schemes are configured in a separate "Security Options" page. *If any encryption method other than static WEP is chosen for the "Security Option," then the 802.11 Authentication Mode dialog box is grayed-out and inaccessible.*

Terminology tangles are frustrating. Both Microsoft and Cisco terminology are correct because WLAN authentication requires 802.11 Authentication but also supports optional security mechanisms share a common vocabulary. In this chapter we focus exclusively on 802.11 Authentication.

## 802.11 Authentication Schemes

- **Open** - null authenticator, doesn't authenticate anything.
- **Shared Key** – requires static WEP encryption. The STA must demonstrate that it possesses the shared WEP key. *Ironically, shared key authentication is a security disaster. Shared Key authentication renders WEP, which is already significantly flawed, virtually worthless.*
- **Auto** – The STA starts with open authentication, if rejected it automatically switches to shared authentication. Auto isn't supported by the WZC Service or all client adapter utilities.

## Open Authentication

In this example the BSS is using the long PLCP-preamble/header; you'll note that the duration field values are rather long. Load the PSP-SRV namespace, open the capture file DLinkOK, apply the Authentication filter and press **F5**. This capture records an AirLink client adapter's boot sequence. The first Authentication frame occurs at just over 59 seconds. Remove the filter by applying No Filter and press **F5**.

| Number | Time | Destination | Source | Function |
|---|---|---|---|---|
| [0-01]-109 | 00:00:59:938:292 | AP600-1 | AirLink | Authentication |
| [0-01]-110 | 00:00:59:938:608 | AirLink | | ACK |
| [0-01]-111 | 00:00:59:939:241 | AirLink | AP600-1 | Authentication |
| [0-01]-112 | 00:00:59:939:557 | AP600-1 | | ACK |

Go to frame 109 using the Go-to-Frame function by pressing **Ctrl-G.** *The authentication request and authentication response use the same frame* and support the two-frame Open Authentication or four-frame Shared Key Authentication sequences.

| Number | Time | Destination | Source | Protocol | Function |
|---|---|---|---|---|---|
| [0-01]-109 | 00:00:59:938:292 | AP600-1 | AirLink | IEEE 802.11 | Authentication |

### Frame-109: Authentication AirLink
requests authentication

Duration: 314-µs, the time required to send a 1-Mbps ACK frame with a long preamble. *Authentication frames must be acknowledged.*

Algorithm: 0, Open Authentication

Sequence Number: 1, the first frame in the two-step open authentication process

Status Code: 0, indicates success

```
⊕ Physical Frame
⊟ IEEE 802.11 MAC Protocol
   Function              Authentication
⊕ PLCP Header
⊟ Frame Control Byte 0
   Protocol Level    [xxxxxx00]  0
   Type              [xxxx00xx]  Management
   Sub-Type          [1011xxxx]  Authentication
⊕ Frame Control Byte 1
   Duration ID            314
⊕ Destination Address
⊕ Source Address
⊕ BSSID
   Fragment          [xxxxxxxx xxxx0000]  0
   Sequence          [01000111 0011xxxx]  1139
   Algorithm         0   Open
   Sequence Number   1
   Status Code       0   Reserved
```

### Frame-111: Authentication AP600-1's response
The source and destination addresses of frame-111 are the reverse of frame-109. We need only examine the last two fields in the response frame:

```
Algorithm         0   Open
Sequence Number   2
Status Code       0   Reserved
```

Sequence Number: 2, specifies a response to an authentication request.

Status Code: 0, indicates success. AirLink is now in State-2, authenticated and unassociated.

## Shared Key Authentication

Shared Key authentication is a simple, server-free attempt to secure 802.11 authentication. Open capture file **AA-SharedKey-OK** which illustrates the four-step Shared Key Authentication sequence between Aironet-PCI and Aironet-350AP.

| Number | Time | Destination | Source | Function |
|--------|------|-------------|--------|----------|
| [0-06]-6 | 00:00:06:149:464 | Aironet-350AP | Aironet-PCI | Authentication |
| [0-06]-7 | 00:00:06:149:760 | Aironet-PCI | | ACK |
| [0-06]-8 | 00:00:06:152:982 | Aironet-PCI | Aironet-350AP | Authentication |
| [0-06]-9 | 00:00:06:153:224 | Aironet-350AP | | ACK |
| [0-06]-10 | 00:00:06:155:173 | Aironet-350AP | Aironet-PCI | Authentication |
| [0-06]-11 | 00:00:06:155:476 | Aironet-PCI | | ACK |
| [0-06]-12 | 00:00:06:156:295 | Aironet-PCI | Aironet-350AP | Authentication |
| [0-06]-13 | 00:00:06:156:544 | Aironet-350AP | | ACK |
| [0-06]-14 | 00:00:06:157:849 | Aironet-350AP | Aironet-PCI | Association Request |
| [0-06]-15 | 00:00:06:158:149 | Aironet-PCI | | ACK |
| [0-01]-16 | 00:00:06:159:778 | Aironet-PCI | Aironet-350AP | Association Response |

1. <u>Frame-6</u>: **Sequence Number 1**.
   Aironet-PCI sends a frame requesting Shared Key authentication.

   ```
   Algorithm            1   Shared Key
   Sequence Number      1
   Status Code          0   Reserved
   ```

2. <u>Frame-8</u>: **Sequence Number 2**.
   The Challenge Text IE contains the 128 byte clear text challenge issued by Aironet-350AP.

   ```
   Algorithm            1   Shared Key
   Sequence Number      2
   Status Code          0   Reserved
   Information Element
      Identity             Challenge Text
      Length               128
   ```
   ```
   00   B0 00 02 01 00 40 96 A2 F4 34 00 09 B7 7E E9 AA
   16   00 09 B7 7E E9 AA 40 67 01 00 02 00 00 00 10 80
   32   9D 1C E1 23 97 7F 9B 53 33 55 F6 3B 63 C0 66 EE
   48   37 6F 3B B5 A7 66 5D 87 16 ED 25 50 CF 9F FD 81
   64   29 34 33 BA C4 AB 15 1B 35 C9 A4 21 4B B3 99 3D
   80   D5 FE 19 39 4C C4 31 23 6B 9E BB E2 38 30 E0 FB
   96   A1 37 18 FF A9 ED 66 5D 80 60 47 13 F9 4A 9F 51
   12   82 89 73 55 4D 69 59 61 D9 66 2C 63 B1 7F BB 7D
   ```

3. <u>Frame-10</u>: **Sequence Number 3**.
   The Challenge Text IE contains the 128 byte challenge text encrypted with Aironet-PCI's copy of the WEP key.

   ```
   Algorithm            1   Shared Key
   Sequence Number      3
   Status Code          0   Reserved
   Information Element
      Identity             Challenge Text
      Length               128
   ```
   ```
   00   B0 40 3A 01 00 09 B7 7E E9 AA 00 40 96 A2 F4 34
   16   00 09 B7 7E E9 AA 20 00 01 00 03 00 00 00 10 80
   32   9D 1C E1 23 97 7F 9B 53 33 55 F6 3B 63 C0 66 EE
   48   37 6F 3B B5 A7 66 5D 87 16 ED 25 50 CF 9F FD 81
   64   29 34 33 BA C4 AB 15 1B 35 C9 A4 21 4B B3 99 3D
   80   D5 FE 19 39 4C C4 31 23 6B 9E BB E2 38 30 E0 FB
   96   A1 37 18 FF A9 ED 66 5D 80 60 47 13 F9 4A 9F 51
   12   82 89 73 55 4D 69 59 61 D9 66 2C 63
   ```

4. <u>Frame-12</u>: **Sequence Number 4**.
   AP decrypts the STA's response and compares it to the original challenge. If they match, Status code 0 indicates success. Aironet-PCI is now in State-2, authenticated and unassociated

   ```
   Algorithm            1   Shared Key
   Sequence Number      4
   Status Code          0   Reserved
   ```

## Shared Key Authentication Weakens Security

"Known plain-text" is a common cryptographic attack. Obtaining the plain-text and encrypted challenges as illustrated in Frames 8 & 10 is the fast track to cracking the static WEP key. Follow this URL to a PDF that describes why WEP is so flawed http://www.drizzle.com/%7Eaboba/IEEE/rc4_ksaproc.pdf.

***If you must use static WEP don't configure shared key authentication.*** Better yet, use WPA-PSK as a more secure, yet equally convenient SOHO encryption scheme.

> **! Exam Alert**: The only place that you're likely to find shared-key authentication is on a certification exam. Remember the four step sequence, the concepts of "known plain text" attack and why shared key authentication should never be used. In fact, many new business-class APs don't support shared key authentication.

Let's examine two captures that illustrate failed authentication sequences. LinkFerret was configured with the static WEP key, so the data frames in the captures are in plaintext.

## Open Authentication with misconfigured pre-shared WEP Key

The WEP key can be manually or automatically configured:

- **Dynamic WEP** The key is provided by a RADIUS server with 802.1x port-based authentication. 802.1x also provides periodic dynamic rekeying.
- **Static WEP** Traditionally used in SOHOs. The WEP key must be manually entered into each client adapter's WLAN configuration profile. Because static WEP re-keying must be done manually it usually doesn't happen, and the network becomes a sitting duck for Open Source WEP cracking programs.

Remember: ***Only the 802.2 LLC header and data payload are encrypted, the 802.11 MAC-header is always sent in clear text.***

> **Troubleshooting Tip** Why isn't the MAC header encrypted? Virtual carrier is based on the value of the duration field, which requires that the MAC header be readable by all STAs in the BSA - this includes STAs in different BSSs that have overlapped BSAs, but have different static WEP keys. It becomes more complex with WPA because every STA has a unique pair-wise encryption key which is updated with every frame exchange.
>
> The good news is that the MAC header contains the majority of information required for effective troubleshooting and performance optimization and it's always readable by 802.11 network monitors.

**Scenario:** For this analysis remember these two facts about the Aironet-PCI STA.
- It's a DHCP client configured to receive an IP configuration from a DHCP server.
- It has been configured with the incorrect WEP key.

Open the capture file **AA-Open-WrongWEP** and ensure that No Filter is applied.

<u>Frames 7-13:</u> Illustrates a successful authentication and association.

| Number | Time | Destination | Source | Function |
|---|---|---|---|---|
| [0-06]-7 | 00:00:05:721:632 | Aironet-350AP | Aironet-PCI | Authentication |
| [0-06]-8 | 00:00:05:721:898 | Aironet-PCI | | ACK |
| [0-06]-9 | 00:00:05:722:600 | Aironet-PCI | Aironet-350AP | Authentication |
| [0-06]-10 | 00:00:05:722:859 | Aironet-350AP | | ACK |
| [0-06]-11 | 00:00:05:724:543 | Aironet-350AP | Aironet-PCI | Association Request |
| [0-06]-12 | 00:00:05:724:862 | Aironet-PCI | | ACK |
| [0-01]-13 | 00:00:05:726:524 | Aironet-PCI | Aironet-350AP | Association Response |

After frame 13 Aironet-PCI is in State-3, authenticated & associated and may transmit data frames to be processed by the DSS - so far, so good.

Apply the **Data-Data** filter and Press **F5**. Examine any data frame transmitted by Aironet-PCI. Even though LinkFerret has been configured with the correct WEP key, the network monitor flags every Aironet-PCI data frame as "undecryptable. "

| Number | Time | Destination | Source | Function |
|---|---|---|---|---|
| [0-06]-1 | 00:00:05:727:106 | Aironet-350AP | Aironet-PCI | Data (Undecryptable) |
| [0-06]-2 | 00:00:05:728:492 | Broadcast | Aironet-PCI | Data (Undecryptable) |

Apply the **Data-Null** filter and press **F5**. Examine any null-data frame transmitted by Aironet-PCI.

Null Data frames don't have an 802.2 LLC header or upper-layer payload field so they aren't encrypted. ***Note that the WEP bit in Frame Control Btye-1 is reset.***

This is an important distinction, because even with the incorrect WEP key a STA can send Null-Data frames to the AP.

Remove the filter by applying **No Filter** and press **F5**.

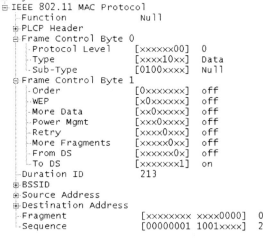

Let's use two of the built-in LinkFerret Display Filters to view the DHCP and ARP packets.

- In the LinkFerret menu choose: Filters, Display Filter.
- Click the "Disable All" tab
- Drag the "Address Resolution Protocol" and "Bootstrap Protocol" filter to the Enabled Protocols window
- Click OK and Press F5 to apply the filter.

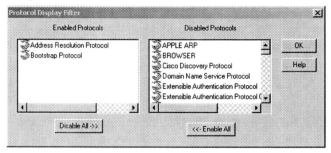

The LinkFerret display is empty, no ARP or DHCP were captured! Reconfigure the Display Filter to "Enable All" protocols and press **F5**.

Exceptional wireless client adapter utilities are one of the great overlooked troubleshooting resources. In this example Aironet-PCI is under control of the ACU, not the WZC Service.

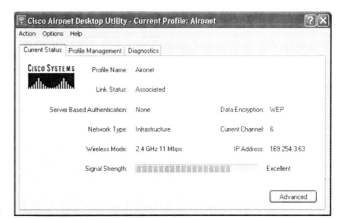

- Link Status: Associated
- Signal Strength: Excellent
- Data Encryption: WEP
- IP Address 169.254.3.63

*The dreaded APIPA*! (automatic private IP addressing) An address in network 169.254.x.y indicates that the DHCP client service timed-out and the system choose a random address in the 169.254.x.y network.

We can also quickly check the IP configuration of a Windows XP STA by right-clicking the client adapter's tray icon and choosing "Status." "**Limited or no connectively**" also indicates that DHCP failed. *The lack of IP configuration is a symptom, not a sign that the DHCP server is off-line*. Manually configuring a static IP configuration won't help.

> **Command Line Solution**: Command line hardheads (like myself) execute "*ipconfig /all*" to verify the IP configuration. But it doesn't provide wireless connection information fields!

**Conclusion:**
Open Authentication with a misconfigured static WEP key doesn't cause a STA to fail authentication or association. But the incorrectly encrypted data packets can't be exchanged with the AP.

DHCP is an upper-layer protocol. The absence of IP configuration means that the STA can't send or receive WEP encrypted data frames. An additional symptom is that every data frame sourced by the misconfigured STA and captured by LinkFerret is flagged as "Undecryptable" because the network monitor is configured with the correct WEP key.

When the STA is properly configured with the WEP key it should almost immediately receive an IP configuration and connect to the internal network.

## STA is configured for Shared Key in an Open Authentication Network

Here's an easy one. Although AirLink has the correct WEP key, it's configured for Shared Key authentication and AP600-1 is configured for Open authentication.

Open capture file **AA-SharedKey-OpenNet**, apply the **Authentication** filter and press **F5**.

| Number | Time | Destination | Source | Function |
|--------|------|-------------|--------|----------|
| [0-01]-1 | 00:00:12:498:385 | AP600-1 | AirLink | Authentication |
| [0-01]-2 | 00:00:12:499:219 | AirLink | AP600-1 | Authentication |
| [0-01]-3 | 00:00:12:500:230 | AP600-1 | AirLink | Authentication |
| [0-01]-4 | 00:00:12:501:042 | AirLink | AP600-1 | Authentication |

The filter reveals two sets of Authentication requests. In the first Authentication frame AirLink is requesting Shared Key Authentication.

```
Algorithm          1  Shared Key
Sequence Number    1
Status Code        0  Reserved
```

In the second Authentication frame AP600-1 responses

```
Algorithm          1  Shared Key
Sequence Number    2
Status Code        13 Specified authentication algorithm not supported
```

with Status Code 13, "Specified authentication algorithm not supported." Depending on the STA, this sequence repeats 2 to 4 times before the STA attempts to associate with another AP in the same ESS or another configured preferred network.

## *Association*

The Association process "plugs" a STA into the virtual WLAN, similar to plugging the cable of an Ethernet node into a switch port. After successful association the STA:

- has a 14-bit AID (association ID)
- may transmit frames with the To-DS Bit set that are processed by the DSS
- inform the AP when it's entering PS-mode so incoming packets are buffered

## Association Sequence

After authentication the STA sends an Association Request and the AP replies with an Association Response. Open capture file **DLink-OK**, apply **No Filter**, press **F5** and go-to (Ctrl-G) frame 109.

| Number | Time | Destination | Source | Function |
|--------|------|-------------|--------|----------|
| [0-01]-109 | 00:00:59:938:292 | AP600-1 | AirLink | Authentication |
| [0-01]-110 | 00:00:59:938:608 | AirLink | | ACK |
| [0-01]-111 | 00:00:59:939:241 | AirLink | AP600-1 | Authentication |
| [0-01]-112 | 00:00:59:939:557 | AP600-1 | | ACK |
| [0-01]-113 | 00:00:59:940:165 | AP600-1 | AirLink | Association Request |
| [0-01]-114 | 00:00:59:940:494 | AirLink | | ACK |
| [0-01]-115 | 00:00:59:941:199 | AirLink | AP600-1 | Association Response |
| [0-01]-116 | 00:00:59:941:520 | AP600-1 | | ACK |

Frames 113-116 illustrate a typical Association sequence.

### *Frame 113: Association Request*:

AirLink to AP600-1

```
Number       Time                   Destination  Source   Protocol     Function
[0-01]-113   00:00:59:940:165      AP600-1      AirLink  IEEE 802.11  Association Request
```

Duration = 314-µs, virtual carrier for AP600-1 to ACK this frame.

Capability Information
AirLink supports WEP (or WPA) and is associating with an infrastructure network, not an IBSS.

*Note that the short preamble bit is not set! If AirLink associates the entire BSS will fall-back to long preamble.* If AirLink can't be reconfigured to support short preamble then the client adapter should be replaced.

*If AP600-1 was configured for short preamble support only, AirLink's association request would be rejected.*

```
⊞ Physical Frame
⊟ IEEE 802.11 MAC Protocol
   ├ Function               Association Request
   ⊞ PLCP Header
   ⊟ Frame Control Byte 0
   │  ├ Protocol Level   [xxxxxx00]  0
   │  ├ Type             [xxxx00xx]  Management
   │  └ Sub-Type         [0000xxxx]  Association Request
   ⊞ Frame Control Byte 1
   ├ Duration ID            314
   ⊞ Destination Address
   ⊞ Source Address
   ⊞ BSSID
   ├ Fragment           [xxxxxxxx xxxx0000]  0
   ├ Sequence           [01000111 0100xxxx]  1140
   ⊟ Capability Information
   │  ├ Channel Agility  [0xxxxxxx xxxxxxxx]  Off
   │  ├ PBCC             [x0xxxxxx xxxxxxxx]  Off
   │  ├ Short Preamble   [xx0xxxxx xxxxxxxx]  Off
   │  ├ Privacy          [xxx1xxxx xxxxxxxx]  On
   │  ├ CF Poll Request  [xxxx0xxx xxxxxxxx]  Off
   │  ├ CF Pollable      [xxxxx0xx xxxxxxxx]  Off
   │  ├ IBSS             [xxxxxx0x xxxxxxxx]  Off
   │  ├ ESS              [xxxxxxx1 xxxxxxxx]  On
   │  └ Reserved         [xxxxxxxx 00000000]  0
   ├ Listen Interval        3
   ⊟ Information Element
   │  ├ Identity            SSID
   │  ├ Length              5
   │  └ SSID                Site2
   ⊟ Information Element
      ├ Identity            Supported Rates
      ├ Length              4
      ├ Rate               1.0 MB   [1xxxxxxx]  In Basic Rate Set
      ├ Rate               2.0 MB   [1xxxxxxx]  In Basic Rate Set
      ├ Rate               5.5 MB   [1xxxxxxx]  In Basic Rate Set
      └ Rate               11.0 MB  [1xxxxxxx]  In Basic Rate Set
```

Listen Interval field = 3
Applicable when the STA is in PS-mode, it specifies the maximum number of beacons that will pass until it wakes to check the beacon's TIM IE for buffered data. This AirLink client adapter is configured for medium sleep mode. A Cisco client adapter in Max PS-Mode has a listen interval of 10. Longer listen intervals require the AP to buffer greater amount of data. The AP may reject an association request if the listen interval is too large.

**SSID IE**
AirLink is associating with an AP in Site2. If AP600-1 is not configured for Site2 (either the primary SSID or a VLAN SSID) AirLink's association request will be rejected.

**Supported Rates IE**
The STA supports all four HR/DSSS rates. AirLink's association request can't be rejected for lack of basic bit-rate support.

```
Number       Time              Destination  Source   Protocol    Function
[0-01]-115  00:00:59:941:199   AirLink      AP600-1  IEEE 802.11 Association Response
```

**_Frame 115: Association Response_:**
AP600-1 to AirLink

<u>Duration</u> = 314-µs, virtual carrier for AirLink to ACK this frame with long preamble at 1-Mbps.

<u>Capability Information:</u>
Although the AP supports short preamble, the BSS must fall-back to long preamble – a big performance hit!

<u>Status Code</u> 0, a successful association

<u>Association ID:</u> 1
The AID is 14-bits. Bits 15 & 14 always set so AIDs start with 0xC001. Two byte values are stored in little endian format with the least significant byte first.

<u>Supported Rates IE</u>
AP600-1 is an 802.11g AP operating in mixed-mode. Since AirLink is an 802.11b STA the Supported Rates IE in the association response frame has the HR/DSSS rate set. *AP600-1 appears to AirLink as an 802.11b AP, because that's the only kind of AP that AirLink understands.*

For 802.11g STAs the ERP-OFDM rates through 36-Mbps appear in the association request and association response frames.

```
⊞ Physical Frame
⊟ IEEE 802.11 MAC Protocol
  ┊-Function             Association Response
  ⊞ PLCP Header
  ⊟ Frame Control Byte 0
    ┊-Protocol Level    [xxxxxx00]  0
    ┊-Type              [xxxx00xx]  Management
    ┊-Sub-Type          [0001xxxx]  Association Response
  ⊞ Frame Control Byte 1
    ┊ Duration ID        314
  ⊞ Destination Address
  ⊞ Source Address
  ⊞ BSSID
    ┊-Fragment          [xxxxxxxx xxxx0000]  0
    ┊-Sequence          [01011010 0010xxxx]  1442
  ⊟ Capability Information
    ┊-Channel Agility   [0xxxxxxx xxxxxxxx]  Off
    ┊-PBCC              [x0xxxxxx xxxxxxxx]  Off
    ┊-Short Preamble    [xx1xxxxx xxxxxxxx]  On
    ┊-Privacy           [xxx1xxxx xxxxxxxx]  On
    ┊-CF Poll Request   [xxxx0xxx xxxxxxxx]  Off
    ┊-CF Pollable       [xxxxx0xx xxxxxxxx]  Off
    ┊-IBSS              [xxxxxx0x xxxxxxxx]  Off
    ┊-ESS               [xxxxxxx1 xxxxxxxx]  On
    ┊-Reserved          [xxxxxxxx 00000000]  0
  ┊-Status Code          0
  ┊ Association ID       49153
  ⊟ Information Element
    ┊-Identity           Supported Rates
    ┊-Length             4
    ┊-Rate               1.0 MB   [1xxxxxxx]  In Basic Rate Set
    ┊-Rate               2.0 MB   [1xxxxxxx]  In Basic Rate Set
    ┊-Rate               5.5 MB   [1xxxxxxx]  In Basic Rate Set
    ┊-Rate               11.0 MB  [1xxxxxxx]  In Basic Rate Set
```

```
0000   10 00 3A 01 00 0D 88 E5 D3 2A 00 20 A6 4F 1F 94   ..:
0016   00 20 A6 4F 1F 94 20 5A 31 00 00 00 01 C0 01 04   ..
0032   82 84 8B 96                                        ...
```

📌 Association ID 2008 unique IDs 0xC001 - 0xC7D8. The maximum number of associated STAs is configurable at the AP

💡 AID 0xC000 is reserved to identify the presence of buffered broadcast/multicast traffic in the DTIM Beacon

💡 The AID is dynamically assigned by the AP during the association process

💡 Enables the AP to identify PS buffered data with the appropriate client station

✔ Also see <u>Pwr Mgmt</u> and <u>More Data</u> bits in Frame Control, Byte 1 and Chapter 7

## Status Codes: Why Authentication and Association Fails

We know that status code 0 specifies a successful operation. The following table lists the basic Status Codes returned with ***authentication, association response and reassociation response frames. Appendix-C*** lists the complete set of Status Codes.

| Status Code | Explanation |
| --- | --- |
| 0 | Successful |
| 1 | Unexpected failure |
| 2 – 9 | Reserved |
| 10 | Requested Capability Information Field not supported |
| 11 | Reassociation failure due to unknown reason |
| 12 | Association failure due to unknown reason |
| 13 | Specified authentication algorithm not supported |
| 14 | Authentication number out of sequence |
| 15 | Authentication handshake timeout (shared key or WPA-PSK) |
| 16 | Authentication time-out failure |
| 17 | Association failure due to AP buffer full |
| 18 | Association failure STA does not support basic rates |
| 19 | Association failure short preamble support required |
| 20 | Association failure STA does not support PBCC |
| 21 | Association failure STA does not support Channel Agility |
| 22 - 24 | Reserved |
| 25 | Association failure STA does not support Short Time Slot |
| 26 | Association failure STA does not support DSSS-OFDM |

We've seen an example of Status Code 13, "Specified authentication algorithm not supported." Failures 10, 18-21 shouldn't occur if the STA properly interprets the beacon and probe response frames. Take a few minutes to look through the reasons that an association may fall. Don't memorize the numerical status codes, the network monitor decodes the Status Code field into a meaningful text message.

***According to the IEEE 802.11 Handbook, many wireless client adapter drivers don't read the status code after a failed operation.*** Consequently they continue to repeat the operation that caused the initial failure. An 802.11 network monitor is the only direct means of identifying these driver failures.

## *The Short Preamble bit versus Barker Preamble Mode bit*

This section considers a subtle and puzzling issue, the relationship between the Short Preamble bit in the Capabilities Information field and the Barker Preamble Mode bit in the ERP IE.

Short Preamble Bit
- A subfield of Capability Information
- Transmitted by APs in beacon, probe response, association response and reassociation response frames
- Indicates the current preamble in-use by the BSS. Set indicates short preamble.
- ***The capability information field transmitted by STAs in association request and reassociation request frames is the STA's configuration, not the state of the BSS.***
- If a long preamble-only STA associates with the BSS, the short preamble bit is reset and all members of the BSS fall-back to long preamble.
- If an AP is configured for short preamble support only, any STA incapable of short preamble, as specified in the Capability Information field of the STA's association request, fails association with status code 19, "association failure, short preamble support required."

Barker Preamble Mode Bit
- A subfield of the ERP IE
- Transmitted by APs in beacon and probe response frames
- Specifies the type of DSSS preamble to use with the CTS-to-Self protection frame
- When set specifies long preamble

**What's wrong with the Picture?**
The Barker Preamble Mode bit seems redundant. Doesn't it perform the same function as the Short Preamble bit? Both bits specify which DSSS preamble to use with HR/DSSS PHY frames. So the bits will always be in agreement, they'll always specify the same DSSS preamble type, right?

```
⊕ Physical Frame
⊟ IEEE 802.11 MAC Protocol
    Function              Beacon
  ⊕ PLCP Header
  ⊕ Frame Control Byte 0
  ⊕ Frame Control Byte 1
    Duration ID           0
  ⊕ Destination Address
  ⊕ Source Address
  ⊕ BSSID
    Fragment        [xxxxxxxx xxxx0000]   0
    Sequence        [00011001 1100xxxx]   412
    Time Stamp      4017224173423165440
    Beacon Interval       100
  ⊟ Capability Information
      Channel Agility [0xxxxxxx xxxxxxxx]  Off
      PBCC            [x0xxxxxx xxxxxxxx]  Off
      Short Preamble  [xx1xxxxx xxxxxxxx]  On
      Privacy         [xxx1xxxx xxxxxxxx]  On
      CF Poll Request [xxxx0xxx xxxxxxxx]  Off
      CF Pollable     [xxxxx0xx xxxxxxxx]  Off
      IBSS            [xxxxxx0x xxxxxxxx]  Off
      ESS             [xxxxxxx1 xxxxxxxx]  On
      Reserved        [xxxxxxxx 00000000]  0
  ⊕ Information Element
  ⊕ Information Element
  ⊕ Information Element
  ⊕ Information Element
  ⊟ Information Element
      Identity            ERP
      Length              1
      Non-ERP Present [xxxx xxx1]  On
      Use Protection  [xxxx xx1x]  On
      Barker Preamble [xxxx x1xx]  On
```

Examine the beacon frame on the right. ***The Short Preamble bit is set specifying that short preamble is in use, i.e. only short preamble capable STAs are associated to the BSS. However, the Barker Preamble Mode bit in the ERP IE is also set, which specifies that CTS-to-Self frames must use long preamble!*** That sure seems like a contradiction.

Remember the PHY layer "clause" terminology relationships from Chapter 1:
- Clause 15 means DSSS rates
- Clause 18 means HR/DSSS rates
- Clause 19 means ERP-OFDM rates

Here's the IEEE's explanation of the Barker Preamble Mode bit (my emphasis added) straight from the 802.11g specification:

> "**ERP APs and ERP STA**s shall use **long preambles** when transmitting <u>Clause 15, Clause 18, and Clause 19 frames</u> after transmission or reception of an ERP Information Element with a **Barker_Preamble_Mode value of 1** in an MMPDU to or from the BSS that the **ERP AP or ERP STA** has joined or started, *regardless of the value of the short preamble capability bit from the same received or transmitted MMPDU that contained the ERP Information Element*. ERP APs and ERP STAs may additionally use long preambles when transmitting <u>Clause 15, Clause 18, and Clause 19 frames</u> at other times. ERP APs and ERP STAs may use **short preambles** when transmitting <u>Clause 15, Clause 18, and Clause 19</u> frames after transmission or reception of an ERP Information Element with a **Barker_Preamble_Mode value of 0** in an MMPDU to or from the BSS that the ERP AP or ERP STA has joined or started, *regardless of the value of the short preamble capability bit from the same received or transmitted MMPDU*. Non-ERP STAs and Non-ERP APs may also follow the rules given in this paragraph"

Those IEEE guys are real poets. The key statement is, "*regardless of the value of the short preamble capability bit from the same received or transmitted MMPDU that contained the ERP Information Element.*" That means while constructing a CTS-to-Self frame for protection purposes the Barker Preamble Mode bit setting is used, and the Short Preamble bit in Capability Information is ignored!

As the Phantom Protection Mini-Case study in Chapter 4 revealed, **CTS-to-Self protection is based on the concept of a physical BSA rather than a logical BSS**. When an AP receives an ERP IE "Use Protection" setting from other beacon or probe response frames, if the Barker Preamble Mode is set, specifying that DSSS long preamble is in use, then the AP not only sets its own "Use Protection" bit, but also sets the Barker Preamble Mode bit. **Thus the lowest common denominator CTS-to-Self setting for the entire BSA is achieved.** Now don't you feel enlightened?

## MAC Address Filtering, Authentication and Association

Most APs support MAC address filtering. SOHO-Class APs use static, manually maintained MAC filter tables. Business-Class APs use RADIUS servers and centrally maintained MAC filter tables. Usually the MAC filter table specifies a list of STAs that may "access the network." It's also possible to deny "access to the network" based on the MAC address list.

***Contrary to popular belief MAC filtering doesn't prevent a STA from authenticating and associating, rather the STA's traffic is blocked by the DSS not the radio card interface.*** The symptoms of a STA which is denied access to the distribution system due to MAC filtering are identical to a STA with a misconfigured pre-shared WEP Key. After authentication and association, the STA doesn't receive a valid IP configuration and its data frames are discarded by the DSS.

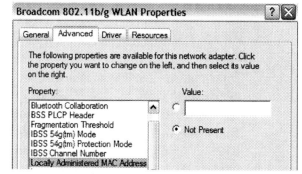

Manual 802.11 MAC filtering isn't worth the time and effort. Even worse it provides a false sense of security. An intruder with a promiscuous WLAN monitor only has to capture traffic and build a table of permitted MAC addresses. After a particular STA has shutdown or disassociated, an intruder running ***XP may spoof a valid MAC address by reconfiguring the client adapter in the adapter properties, advanced tab, Network Address or Locally Administered MAC Address field.***

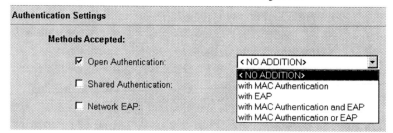

MAC filtering combined with RADIUS 802.1x EAP authentication creates an effective, centralized managed multiple-factor security policy.

## Disassociation and Deauthentication

Disassociation and deauthentication frames downgrade a STA's state. ***The Reason Code table specifies why a disassociation or deauthentication frame is generated.***

| Reason Code | Explanation |
| --- | --- |
| 0 | Reserved |
| 1 | Unspecified reason |
| 2 | Previous authentication is invalid |
| 3 | Deauthenticated because STA is leaving IBSS or ESS |
| 4 | Disassociated due to inactivity |
| 5 | Disassociated AP is unable to process currently connected STAs |
| 6 | State-2 frame received from non-associated STA |
| 7 | State-3 frame received from non-associated STA |
| 8 | Disassociated because sending STA is leaving the BSS |
| 9 | STA requesting association in not authenticated |
| All Others | See Appendix-D for the complete Reason Code table |

Rely on your network monitor to decode the Reason Code field and provide you with an appropriate text message. We'll analyze several deauthentication and disassociation frames and their reason codes in the next few sections.

## Disassociation

Disassociation returns a STA to State-2 (authenticated & unassociated). A disassociation frame and may be sent by an AP or a STA:

- An AP may disassociate a STA after a period of inactivity or if the AP's association buffer reaches maximum capacity.
- A STA may voluntarily disassociate with the BSS because of higher-level authentication or configuration issues, failures or conflicts. After the STA transmits the disassociation frame it usually probes for other APs in the ESS.

In this example AirLink sends AP600-1 a disassociation frame specifying Reason Code 8, "Disassociated because this STA is leaving the BSS." Essentially the STA is "unplugging" itself from the AP.

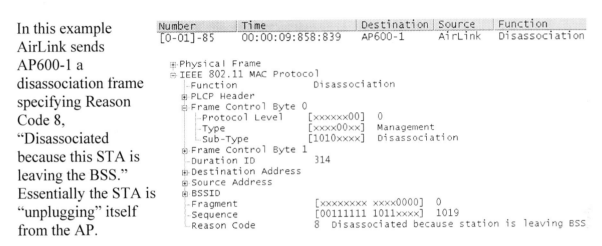

Reason Code 8 implies that the STA will attempt to associate with another AP in the ESS. However, it's important to understand that ***disassociation is not part of the standard roaming process***. Later in this chapter we'll see how a roaming STA reassociates with another AP in the ESS and is removed from the original AP's association table by direct AP-to-AP communications. When a STA sends a disassociation frame it's usually an indication of misconfiguration or incompatibility.

By actively probing the STA may find another AP in the ESS or attempt to reconnect to the original AP. ***Contrary to its State-2 status, the STA always initiates the next association sequence with an authentication request.***

## Deauthentication

Often confused with disassociation, deauthentication returns the STA to State-1, whereas Disassociation returns the STA to State-2, but that's a minor technical distinction. The key to troubleshooting disassociation and deauthentication issues is to focus on the reason code, which is only accessible in network monitor captures. Let's examine a common occurrence in a multi-ESS environment.

| Number | Time | Destination | Source | Function |
|---|---|---|---|---|
| [0-11]-1 | 00:00:06:486:291 | Belkin-AP | Aironet-PCI | Deauthentication |

```
⊞ Physical Frame
⊟ IEEE 802.11 MAC Protocol
   ┊ Function            Deauthentication
⊞ PLCP Header
⊟ Frame Control Byte 0
   ┊ Protocol Level    [xxxxxx00]  0
   ┊ Type              [xxxx00xx]  Management
   ┊ Sub-Type          [1100xxxx]  Deauthentication
⊞ Frame Control Byte 1
   ┊ Duration ID          314
⊞ Destination Address
⊞ Source Address
⊞ BSSID
   ┊ Fragment          [xxxxxxxx xxxx0000]  0
   ┊ Sequence          [00011101 0010xxxx]  466
   ┊ Reason Code          3  Deauthenticated because station is leaving IBSS or ESS
```

## Leaving the ESS

Consider an organization that has two ESSs: a fire-walled, secure, internal-only network and a second WLAN which provides Internet access with no in-bound services. When leaving an ESS to associate with an AP in another ESS a well-behaved STA sends a Deauthentication frame citing Reason Code 3, "Deauthenticated because the STA is leaving the IBSS or ESS."

## *Mini-Case Study: **WPA-PSK Configuration Part 1:***

WPA (Wi-Fi Protected Access) is a subset of the new IEEE 802.11i RSN (robust security network) specification. WPA uses dynamic keying, TKIP (temporal key integrity protocol) and several other features that address vulnerabilities with the original WEP standard. Standard WPA security requires the EAP/802.1x protocol and a RADIUS (remote access/authentication dial-in user services) server.

### *WPA-PSK*

A simplified version of WPA was created to provide secure pair-wise dynamically keyed encryption and data authentication in SOHO environments without a RADIUS server. WPA-PSK (WPA with a Pre-Shared Key) employs a passphrase. A passphrase (pre-shared key) is an alpha-numeric

| ☐ *WPA Station* | | |
|---|---|---|
| | Authentication Mode | 802.1x |
| | Cipher | TKIP |
| ☑ *WPA-PSK Station* | | |
| | Authentication Mode | PSK |
| | Cipher | TKIP |
| | PSK Passphrase | •••••••••••••• |
| ☐ *802.11i Station* | | |
| | Authentication Mode | 802.1x |
| | Cipher | AES |
| ☐ *802.11i-PSK Station* | | |
| | Authentication Mode | PSK |
| | Cipher | AES |
| | PSK Passphrase | ••••••••• |

string, employed after authentication and association, which secures the dynamic encryption key exchange between the AP and STA. ***The passphrase is never used to encrypt data frames!***

Earlier we considered how a misconfigured WEP STA authenticates and associates properly, but it doesn't receive an IP configuration or exchange encrypted data packets with the AP. Open capture file **AA-PwrBk-Wrong-PSK** in which a PowerBook is misconfigured with an incorrect passphrase attempts to associate with a Belkin SOHO-class AP. Ensure that the **PSP-SRV** namespace is loaded and **No Filter** is applied.

| Number | Time | Destination | Source | Function |
|---|---|---|---|---|
| [0-11]-28 | 00:00:02:566:876 | Belkin-AP | PwrBook-Airport | Authentication |
| [0-11]-29 | 00:00:02:567:134 | PwrBook-Airport | | ACK |
| [0-11]-30 | 00:00:02:567:781 | PwrBook-Airport | Belkin-AP | Authentication |
| [0-11]-31 | 00:00:02:568:107 | Belkin-AP | | ACK |
| [0-11]-32 | 00:00:02:569:136 | Belkin-AP | PwrBook-Airport | Association Request |
| [0-11]-33 | 00:00:02:569:375 | PwrBook-Airport | | ACK |
| [0-11]-34 | 00:00:02:570:338 | PwrBook-Airport | Belkin-AP | Association Response |
| [0-11]-35 | 00:00:02:570:653 | Belkin-AP | | ACK |
| [0-11]-36 | 00:00:02:571:606 | PwrBook-Airport | Belkin-AP | Key |
| [0-11]-37 | 00:00:02:571:806 | Belkin-AP | | ACK |
| [0-11]-38 | 00:00:02:573:366 | Belkin-AP | PwrBook-Airport | Key |
| [0-11]-39 | 00:00:02:573:555 | PwrBook-Airport | | ACK |
| [0-11]-40 | 00:00:03:569:041 | PwrBook-Airport | Belkin-AP | Key |
| [0-11]-41 | 00:00:03:569:236 | Belkin-AP | | ACK |
| [0-11]-42 | 00:00:03:570:125 | Belkin-AP | PwrBook-Airport | Key |
| [0-11]-43 | 00:00:03:570:308 | PwrBook-Airport | | ACK |
| [0-11]-44 | 00:00:04:569:325 | PwrBook-Airport | Belkin-AP | Key |
| [0-11]-45 | 00:00:04:569:512 | Belkin-AP | | ACK |
| [0-11]-46 | 00:00:04:570:391 | Belkin-AP | PwrBook-Airport | Key |
| [0-11]-47 | 00:00:04:570:594 | PwrBook-Airport | | ACK |
| [0-11]-48 | 00:00:05:569:646 | PwrBook-Airport | Belkin-AP | Key |
| [0-11]-49 | 00:00:05:569:857 | Belkin-AP | | ACK |
| [0-11]-50 | 00:00:05:570:716 | Belkin-AP | PwrBook-Airport | Key |
| [0-11]-51 | 00:00:05:570:899 | PwrBook-Airport | | ACK |
| [0-11]-52 | 00:00:05:572:743 | Belkin-AP | PwrBook-Airport | Key |
| [0-11]-53 | 00:00:05:572:935 | PwrBook-Airport | | ACK |
| [0-11]-54 | 00:00:06:570:505 | PwrBook-Airport | Belkin-AP | Deauthentication |

- <u>Frames 28 – 35</u> Successful open authentication and association sequence.
- <u>Frames 36 – 43</u> The 4-step key exchange sequence after successful completion the STA can send and receive encrypted data frames.
- <u>Frames 44 – 51</u> Repeats the failed key exchange.
- <u>Frame 54</u> Belkin-AP deauthenticates PwrBook-Airport

After failing a second key exchange sequence, the PwrBook is deauthenticated with Reason Code 15, "4-way handshake timeout."

| Number | Time | Destination | Source | Protocol | Function |
|---|---|---|---|---|---|
| [0-11]-36 | 00:00:02:571:606 | PwrBook-Airport | Belkin-AP | EAPOL | Key |

```
⊞ Physical Frame
⊞ IEEE 802.11 MAC Protocol
⊞ IEEE 802.2 Logical Link Control
⊟ IEEE Sub-Network Access Protocol
    Authority            000000    Xerox
    EtherType            888E      802.1x Authentication
⊟ Extensible Authentication Protocol Over LAN
    Version              1
    Type                 Key
    Length               119
    Descriptor Type      Unknown
```

| Number | Time | Destination | Source | Protocol | Function |
|---|---|---|---|---|---|
| [0-11]-54 | 00:00:06:570:505 | PwrBook-Airport | Belkin-AP | IEEE 802.11 | Deauthentication |

```
⊞ Physical Frame
⊟ IEEE 802.11 MAC Protocol
    Function                Deauthentication
  ⊞ PLCP Header
  ⊟ Frame Control Byte 0
      Protocol Level    [xxxxxx00]  0
      Type              [xxxx00xx]  Management
      Sub-Type          [1100xxxx]  Deauthenticatior
  ⊞ Frame Control Byte 1
    Duration ID             314
  ⊞ Destination Address
  ⊞ Source Address
  ⊞ BSSID
    Fragment          [xxxxxxxx xxxx0000]  0
    Sequence          [10001111 0111xxxx]  2295
    Reason Code         15 4-way handshake timeout
```

## *Mini-Case Study:* **WPA-PSK Configuration Part 2:**

Let's consider how consistent the previous behavior is with APs from different vendors. 802.11 devices behave in unexpected and inconsistent ways because so much of the specification is optional or open to interpretation.

Let's look at another WPA-PSK passphrase misconfiguration - this time with an all-Cisco cast: an Aironet-PCI client adapter and an Aironet-350 AP. Open capture file **AA-Airo-to-Airo-BadWPAKey**.

- Frames 8-15 illustrate the standard Authentication and Association process.
- Frames 16 – 66 illustrate the key exchange failures
- Frame 67 starts the Disassociation and Deauthentication process

| Number | Time | Destination | Source | Function |
|--------|------|-------------|--------|----------|
| [0-01]-67 | 00:00:10:242:548 | Aironet-PCI | Aironet-350AP | Disassociation |
| [0-01]-68 | 00:00:10:242:720 | Aironet-350AP | | ACK |
| [0-01]-69 | 00:00:10:243:083 | Aironet-PCI | Aironet-350AP | Deauthentication |
| [0-01]-70 | 00:00:10:243:660 | Aironet-PCI | Aironet-350AP | Deauthentication |
| [0-01]-71 | 00:00:10:244:359 | Aironet-PCI | Aironet-350AP | Deauthentication |
| [0-01]-72 | 00:00:10:245:007 | Aironet-PCI | Aironet-350AP | Deauthentication |
| [0-01]-73 | 00:00:10:245:840 | Aironet-PCI | Aironet-350AP | Deauthentication |
| [0-01]-74 | 00:00:10:246:018 | Aironet-350AP | | ACK |

Frame 67: Disassociation
Reason code 0 is reserved. Because both devices support Cisco 802.11 extensions it probably has a proprietary meaning.

| Number | Time | Destination | Source | Function |
|--------|------|-------------|--------|----------|
| [0-01]-67 | 00:00:10:242:548 | Aironet-PCI | Aironet-350AP | Disassociation |

```
⊞ Physical Frame
⊟ IEEE 802.11 MAC Protocol
   ├─Function              Disassociation
   ⊞-PLCP Header
   ⊞ Frame Control Byte 0
   ⊞ Frame Control Byte 1
   ├─Duration ID           162
   ⊞ Destination Address
   ⊞ Source Address
   ⊞ BSSID
   ├─Fragment       [xxxxxxxx xxxx0000]   0
   ├─Sequence       [00011101 1101xxxx]   477
   └─Reason Code          0  Reserved
```

Frame 68: ACK Aironet-PCI ACKs the disassociation frame.

Frame 69: Deauthentication
Why the one-two punch, with disassociation preceding deauthentication? Perhaps it's a Cisco specific function. *For those of you with LinkFerret running note that frames 70 -73 have the Retry bit set.* Aironet-350AP isn't being malicious; it just took four retries to receive an ACK!

Also note that reason code 2, "Previous authentication is no longer valid" is different than the previous example which specified reason code 15, a four-way handshake time-out.

| Number | Time | Destination | Source | Function |
|--------|------|-------------|--------|----------|
| [0-01]-69 | 00:00:10:243:083 | Aironet-PCI | Aironet-350AP | Deauthentication |

```
⊞ Physical Frame
⊟ IEEE 802.11 MAC Protocol
   ├─Function              Deauthentication
   ⊞-PLCP Header
   ⊞ Frame Control Byte 0
   ⊟ Frame Control Byte 1
      ├─Order          [0xxxxxxx]   off
      ├─WEP            [x0xxxxxx]   off
      ├─More Data      [xx0xxxxx]   off
      ├─Power Mgmt     [xxx0xxxx]   off
      ├─Retry          [xxxx0xxx]   off
      ├─More Fragments [xxxxx0xx]   off
      ├─From DS        [xxxxxx0x]   off
      └─To DS          [xxxxxxx0]   off
   ├─Duration ID           162
   ⊞ Destination Address
   ⊞ Source Address
   ⊞ BSSID
   ├─Fragment       [xxxxxxxx xxxx0000]   0
   ├─Sequence       [00011101 1110xxxx]   478
   └─Reason Code          2  Previous authentication no longer valid
```

## Troubleshooting Disassociation and Deauthentication Issues:

- Be flexible - different AP vendors implement procedures and errors codes with their own interpretation of the 802.11 standard.
- Develop a nose for the interaction between STAs and APS from different vendors. Use your intuition and avoid dogmatic diagnosis.
- Filter on disassociation and deauthentication frames and take your cue from the reason code.
- Learn to exploit the capabilities of the client adapter's configuration utility.

## Mini-Case Study: *STA Time-out*

It's natural to expect certain behaviors. When a computer with a wireless client adapter shuts-down or the computer enters standby mode I would expect that the system, being a good BSS citizen, notifies the AP of its departure by sending a deauthentication frame. When the STA's entry is removed from the association and bridging table the extraneous consumption of AP resources and BSA bandwidth is minimized. One of the dubious charms of 802.11 and computer operating systems in general are that they often exhibit unreasonable and inconsistent behavior.

**Scenario**:
- LinkFerret is configured with a disassociation and deauthentication capture filter.
- OS-X and Windows-XP STAs are associated to AP600-1.
- The PowerBook is gracefully shutdown, followed about one minute later by the PC
  - A graceful shutdown means that the system shutdown function was performed rather than simply powering down the system.
- Several minutes after shutdown both STAs are still listed in the AP's association table and no disassociation or deauthentication frames have been captured.
- We conclude, that although the systems were properly shutdown, neither system announced its departure to the AP.

Open capture file AP600-Deauth-Timeout. *The capture filter ensured that only disassociation and deauthentication frames were saved to the capture buffer.*

| Number | Time | Destination | Source | Function |
|--------|------|-------------|--------|----------|
| [O-01]-3 | 00:16:41:010:630 | PwrBook | AP600-1 | Deauthentication |
| [O-01]-4 | 00:16:41:011:120 | PwrBook | AP600-1 | Deauthentication |
| [O-01]-5 | 00:17:40:966:251 | Aironet-PCI | AP600-1 | Deauthentication |
| [O-01]-6 | 00:17:40:966:989 | Aironet-PCI | AP600-1 | Deauthentication |

Frames 1 & 2 have CRC errors, the capture yielded four valid frames.

- At 16:41 into the capture AP600-1 sent a deauthentication frame to PwrBook; it was retransmitted about 500µs later with the retry bit set.
- About one minute later AP600-1 sent a deauthentication frame to Aironet-PCI. It was retransmitted about 750µs later with the retry bit set.
- Both STAs are off-line, so the deauthentication frames are not acknowledged.

```
⊞ Physical Frame
⊟ IEEE 802.11 MAC Protocol
  ⊢ Function            Deauthentication
  ⊞ PLCP Header
  ⊟ Frame Control Byte 0
  ⊢ Protocol Level      [xxxxxx00]  0
  ⊢ Type                [xxxx00xx]  Management
  ⊢ Sub-Type            [1100xxxx]  Deauthentication
  ⊟ Frame Control Byte 1
  ⊢ Order               [0xxxxxxx]  off
  ⊢ WEP                 [x0xxxxxx]  off
  ⊢ More Data           [xx0xxxxx]  off
  ⊢ Power Mgmt          [xxx0xxxx]  off
  ⊢ Retry               [xxxx0xxx]  off
  ⊢ More Fragments      [xxxxx0xx]  off
  ⊢ From DS             [xxxxxx0x]  off
  ⊢ To DS               [xxxxxxx0]  off
  ⊢ Duration ID         314
  ⊞ Destination Address
  ⊞ Source Address
  ⊞ BSSID
  ⊢ Fragment            [xxxxxxxx xxxx0000]  0
  ⊢ Sequence            [01110000 0000xxxx]  1792
  ⊢ Reason Code         2  Previous authentication no longer valid
```

- All frames specify Reason Code 2, "Previous authentication is no longer valid."

To verify this behavior with a Cisco AP open the capture file **Airo-Deauth-Timeout** which repeats the previous scenario with an Aironet-350 AP. The only functional difference between the captures is the STA Timeout interval. The same reason code appears in all deauthentication frames in both captures.

## The Reassociation Frame & 802.11f IAPP

Before we discuss *"what"* a reassociation frame does, we must determine *"why"* reassociation is needed. An ESS is a group of BSSs that have a common SSID and DS backbone. Organizations deploy multiple APs to:

- Ensure WLAN accessibility in large or RF-unfriendly areas.
- Improve performance or capacity by co-locating up to three APs on non-overlapping channels.
- Provide redundancy and automatic failover.
- Provide seamless roaming through a building or an entire campus

Roaming enables mobile STAs to move seamlessly through the coverage area without losing frames or breaking logical sessions. The original 802.11 standard did not include roaming specifications. 802.11f defines the IAPP (inter-access point protocol) and was developed to provide vendor-independent roaming technology. ***Current implementations of IAPP are proprietary and do not provide true cross-vendor compatibility. The 802.11f specification is an IEEE trial document and probably won't be reaffirmed.*** It will continue to be supported in various proprietary implementations.

> **Technical Point**: Non-mobile STAs may "roam" if an AP goes off-line, a physical change occurs that affects RF coverage patterns, or narrow-band RFI results in high PER (packet error rates) and retries.

Let's examine Orinoco's multicast-based, RADIUS-free implementation of IAPP.

Business-Class APs and transparent bridges maintain two tables:
- Association Table of wireless STAs
- Bridge Learning Table specifying MAC addresses of nodes discovered on all interfaces. *Learning*

*tables are also called "forwarding tables" or in Cisco-speak, CAM (content addressable memory) tables.*

When a STA roams the association and learning tables in both the original AP and new AP must be updated. Orinoco's implementation of IAPP provides:
- A mechanism by which APs advertise their ESS affiliation and current status by transmitting multicast packets on the DS backbone.
- Fast update of association tables to ensure that the context for roaming STAs does not continue to consume resources on the original AP and to enforce 802.11's single STA association requirement.
- Fast update of bridge learning tables to minimize lost or redundant packets resulting from misdirection to original BSS.

## IAPP Announce Requests and Responses

| No. | Time | Source | Destination | Protocol | Info |
|-----|------|--------|-------------|----------|------|
| 55 | 46.808760 | 192.168.2.253 | 224.0.1.76 | IAPP | Announce Request(0) (version=1) |
| 57 | 48.807397 | 192.168.2.253 | 224.0.1.76 | IAPP | Announce Response(1) (version=1) |
| 66 | 62.091736 | 192.168.2.253 | 224.0.1.76 | IAPP | Announce Request(0) (version=1) |
| 68 | 64.090355 | 192.168.2.254 | 224.0.1.76 | IAPP | Announce Response(1) (version=1) |
| 548 | 168.721679 | 192.168.2.253 | 224.0.1.76 | IAPP | Announce Response(1) (version=1) |
| 617 | 184.004746 | 192.168.2.254 | 224.0.1.76 | IAPP | Announce Response(1) (version=1) |

These captures were performed with a tap on the ESS system backbone with Ethereal, an open source Ethernet monitor. Orinoco IAPP packets are transmitted to multicast group 224.0.1.76 on UDP port 2313.

The Announce Response from AP600-1 provides the information for APs in the ESS to update their ESS membership list:
- IP and MAC addresses of AP600-1
- IAPP capabilities,
- radio channel
- beacon interval
- ESS network name.

```
▷ Frame 68 (104 bytes on wire, 104 bytes captured)
▷ Ethernet II, Src: 00:20:a6:4b:6b:8e, Dst: 01:00:5e:00:01:4c
▷ Internet Protocol, Src Addr: 192.168.2.254 (192.168.2.254), Dst Addr: 224.0.1.76 (224.0.1.76)
▷ User Datagram Protocol, Src Port: 2313 (2313), Dst Port: 2313 (2313)
▽ Inter-Access-Point Protocol
    Version: 1
    Type: Announce Response(1)
  ▽ Protocol data units
      BSSID(1) Value: 00:20:a6:4f:1f:94
    ▽ Capabilities(4) Value: 66 (ForwardingWEP)
        .1..... Forwarding: Yes
        ..1.... WEP: Yes
      PHY Type(16) Value: Unknown
      Announce Interval(5) Value: 120 seconds
      Handover Timeout(6) Value: 512 Kus
    ▽ ELSA Authentication Info(129) Value:
        Unknown PDU Type(65) value:
      Regulatory Domain(17) Value: FCC (USA)
      Radio Channel(18) Value: 1
      Beacon Interval(19) Value: 100 Kus
      Network Name(0) Value: "Site2\000"
```

## The Reassociation Management Frame

A roaming STA doesn't simply associate with another AP in the ESS, it must reassociate. The Reassociation Request identifies the previous AP which enables the "new" AP to exchange IAPP information with the "old" AP. *The only difference between an Association Request and Reassociation Request is the Current AP field.*

Frame: Reassociation Request

A currently associated STA discovers another AP in the ESS with a "better" signal and initiates roaming.

**Addresses:**

Destination & BSSID: Aironet-PCI is requesting reassociation to AP600-1 which is considered to be the "new' AP

Current AP: AP600-2 is the "old" AP field. It specifies the BSSID of the AP to which the STA is currently associated.

```
| Number    | Time                | Destination | Source      | Function              |
| [0-01]-1  | 00:01:19:786:232    | AP600-1     | Aironet-PCI | Reassociation Request |
```

```
⊞ Physical Frame
⊟ IEEE 802.11 MAC Protocol
  ├ Function            Reassociation Request
  ⊞ PLCP Header
  ⊟ Frame Control Byte 0
  │ ├ Protocol Level    [xxxxxx00]  0
  │ ├ Type              [xxxx00xx]  Management
  │ └ Sub-Type          [0010xxxx]  Reassociation Request
  ⊞ Frame Control Byte 1
  ├ Duration ID         314
  ⊞ Destination Address
  ⊞ Source Address
  ⊟ BSSID
  │ ├ Hex Address       00-20-A6-4F-1F-94
  │ ├ Group Bit         [xxxxxxx0 xxxxxxxx xxxxxxxx xxxxxxxx xxxxxxxx]  off
  │ ├ Local Bit         [xxxxxx0x xxxxxxxx xxxxxxxx xxxxxxxx xxxxxxxx]  off
  │ ├ Logical Names     [[AP600-1]]
  │ └ Vendor Name       PROXIM
  ├ Fragment            [xxxxxxxx xxxx0000]  0
  ├ Sequence            [00010111 1110xxxx]  382
  ⊞ Capability Information
  ├ Listen Interval     1
  ⊟ Current AP
  │ ├ Hex Address       00-20-A6-4F-1F-79
  │ ├ Group Bit         [xxxxxxx0 xxxxxxxx xxxxxxxx xxxxxxxx xxxxxxxx]  off
  │ ├ Local Bit         [xxxxxx0x xxxxxxxx xxxxxxxx xxxxxxxx xxxxxxxx]  off
  │ ├ Logical Names     [[AP600-2]]
  │ └ Vendor Name       PROXIM
  ⊞ Information Element
  ⊞ Information Element
```

At this point AP600-2 is unaware that Aironet-PCI has initiated reassociation.

*If the reassociation is successful, the AP tables are updated when the "new" AP sends a Move Notify command and the "old" AP responses with a Move-Response.*

## *Mini-Case Study:* **Reassociation Link Integrity Failover**

In most computing environments the AP's primary function is to provide translational bridging services to an organization's internal Ethernet backbone. If the connection between the AP and default gateway fails, the STAs associated to the AP are cut-off from the production network. Link integrity checking forces an AP's radio interface to go off-link if a specified network connection fails. This in turn forces the associated STAs to move to another AP in the ESS. *Link integrity failover network design provides multiple co-located BSSs on non-overlapping channels*.

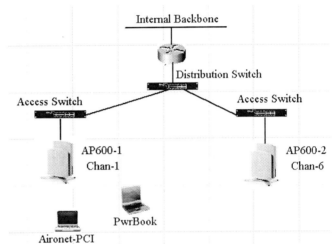

- Both APs are configured with link integrity checking. Every 500ms each AP's connection to the router is automatically verified. If the connection fails, the AP's radio interface is disabled. This forces the STAs to move to another AP in the ESS.
- Currently the STAs are associated to AP600-1. *They receive an adequate signal from AP600-2*.
- Aironet-PCI is an 802.11 a/b/g client running XP with a fair antenna.
- PwrBook is an 802.11b client running OS-X Tiger with an excellent antenna.
- Sadly, like almost all WLAN parameters in OS-X, PwrBook's roaming parameters aren't configurable. The Aironet-PCI roaming parameters are at Cisco defaults.

### Part-1: Breaking the router connection

The connection between AP600-1 and the router is broken and the radio interface is automatically disabled. Open capture file AP600-LnkInteg-Fail. LinkFerret is configured to Channel-6 to capture traffic as the two STAs move from AP600-1 to AP600-2. Apply the AssocReq&Res filter and press **F5**.

| Number | Time | Destination | Source | Function |
|---|---|---|---|---|
| [0-06]-1 | 00:00:09:800:652 | AP600-2 | PwrBook | Association Request |
| [0-06]-2 | 00:00:09:801:493 | PwrBook | AP600-2 | Association Response |
| [0-06]-3 | 00:00:11:303:837 | AP600-2 | Aironet-PCI | Association Request |
| [0-06]-4 | 00:00:11:305:087 | Aironet-PCI | AP600-2 | Association Response |

You may have anticipated that the STAs would roam from AP600-1 to AP600-2 by sending reassociation requests to AP600-2. But that's not the case. To understand why reassociation didn't happen, open capture file AP600-LnkInteg-Fail-AP1, apply No Filter and press **F5**.

| Number | Time | Destination | Source | Function |
|--------|------|-------------|--------|----------|
| [0-01]-1 | 00:00:06:374:779 | Broadcast | AP600-1-Ethernet | Request-192.168.2.1 |
| [0-01]-2 | 00:00:06:874:490 | Broadcast | AP600-1 | Disassociation |
| [0-01]-3 | 00:00:06:874:952 | Broadcast | AP600-1 | Deauthentication |
| [0-01]-4 | 00:00:06:907:241 | Broadcast | AP600-1 | Disassociation |
| [0-01]-5 | 00:00:06:907:730 | Broadcast | AP600-1 | Deauthentication |

| Number | Time | Destination | Source | Protocol | Function |
|--------|------|-------------|--------|----------|----------|
| [0-01]-1 | 00:00:06:374:779 | Broadcast | AP600-1-Ethernet | ARP | Request-192.168.2.1 |

This is a capture of channel 1 during the period when the connection to the router was broken. Frame-1 is the ***last ARP attempt*** on the router's IP address before AP600-1 starts to shutdown its radio interface.

| Number | Time | Destination | Source | Protocol | Function |
|--------|------|-------------|--------|----------|----------|
| [0-01]-2 | 00:00:06:874:490 | Broadcast | AP600-1 | IEEE 802.11 | Disassociation |

<u>Frames 2-5</u> show AP600-1 sending disassociation and deauthentication frames to the ***broadcast destination address***. This disassociates and deauthenticates all associated STAs.

The disassociation frame specifies Reason Code 8:

```
⊞ Physical Frame
⊟ IEEE 802.11 MAC Protocol
  ⊢ Function              Disassociation
  ⊞ PLCP Header
  ⊟ Frame Control Byte 0
    ⊢ Protocol Level    [xxxxxx00]  0
    ⊢ Type              [xxxx00xx]  Management
    ⊢ Sub-Type          [1010xxxx]  Disassociation
  ⊞ Frame Control Byte 1
    ⊢ Duration ID              0
  ⊞ Destination Address
  ⊞ Source Address
  ⊞ BSSID
    ⊢ Fragment          [xxxxxxxx xxxx0000]  0
    ⊢ Sequence          [10010000 1110xxxx]  2318
    ⊢ Reason Code       8 Disassociated because station is leaving BSS
```

"Disassociated because station is leaving BSS." In this context the "station" is actually the AP. The AP's radio interface is going off-line, so the AP (the station) is leaving the BSS.

| Number | Time | Destination | Source | Protocol | Function |
|--------|------|-------------|--------|----------|----------|
| [0-01]-3 | 00:00:06:874:952 | Broadcast | AP600-1 | IEEE 802.11 | Deauthentication |

The deauthentication frame specifies Reason Code 3: "Deauthenticated because station is leaving IBSS or ESS." This was transmitted to ensure that AP600-2 is aware that AP600-1 was leaving the ESS.

```
⊞ Physical Frame
⊟ IEEE 802.11 MAC Protocol
  ⊢ Function              Deauthentication
  ⊞ PLCP Header
  ⊞ Frame Control Byte 0
    ⊢ Protocol Level    [xxxxxx00]  0
    ⊢ Type              [xxxx00xx]  Management
    ⊢ Sub-Type          [1100xxxx]  Deauthentication
  ⊞ Frame Control Byte 1
    ⊢ Duration ID              0
  ⊞ Destination Address
  ⊞ Source Address
  ⊞ BSSID
    ⊢ Fragment          [xxxxxxxx xxxx0000]  0
    ⊢ Sequence          [10010000 1111xxxx]  2319
    ⊢ Reason Code       3 Deauthenticated because station is leaving IBSS or ESS
```

## Part-2: Reestablishing the router connection

Originally given the availability of AP600-1 and AP600-2 both STAs chose to associate with AP600-1. When they were evicted from AP600-1 the STAs happily associated with AP600-2. *What happens when AP600-1 comes back on-line?* Whether a STA continues to associate with AP600-2 or moves back to AP600-1 is a function of its roaming parameters. The roaming parameters are based on the RSSI and the quality of the signal received from each AP.

**General roaming considerations**:
- A STA misses a specified number of consecutive beacons from the concurrently associated AP
- The retry count is exceeded during frame retransmission
- Signal Strength and Transmit Rate fall below specified limits

As we learned in Chapter 4, a STA periodically goes off-channel to listen for beacons or transmit probe requests to update its AP availability table. Assume that the router connection has been reestablished. Open capture file AP600-LnkInteg-Restore, apply the ReassocReq&Res (the <u>Reassociation</u> request and response) filter and press **F5**.

| Number | Time | Destination | Source | Function |
|--------|------|-------------|--------|----------|
| [0-01]-1 | 00:01:19:786:232 | AP600-1 | Aironet-PCI | Reassociation Request |
| [0-01]-2 | 00:01:19:787:166 | Aironet-PCI | AP600-1 | Reassociation Response |

AP600-1 has enticed Aironet-PCI to reassociate, but PwrBook remained with AP600-2. This was probably due to different roaming thresholds, antennas and receiver sensitivity.

<u>Frame: Reassociation Request</u>

**Addresses**
<u>Source</u>: Aironet-PCI
<u>BSSID</u>: AP600-1

<u>Current AP</u>: AP600-2

After AP600-1 sends a Reassociation Response frame to Aironet-PCI, it sends an IAPP Move

```
⊞ Physical Frame
⊟ IEEE 802.11 MAC Protocol
   ⋯Function            Reassociation Request
   ⊞ PLCP Header
   ⊟ Frame Control Byte 0
   │  ⋯Protocol Level   [xxxxxx00]  0
   │  ⋯Type             [xxxx00xx]  Management
   │  ⋯Sub-Type         [0010xxxx]  Reassociation Request
   ⊞ Frame Control Byte 1
   ⋯Duration ID         314
   ⊞ Destination Address
   ⊞ Source Address
   ⊟ BSSID
   │  ⋯Hex Address      00-20-A6-4F-1F-94
   │  ⋯Group Bit        [xxxxxxx0 xxxxxxxx xxxxxxxx xxxxxxxx xxxxxxxx]  off
   │  ⋯Local Bit        [xxxxxx0x xxxxxxxx xxxxxxxx xxxxxxxx xxxxxxxx]  off
   │  ⋯Logical Names    [[AP600-1]]
   │  ⋯Vendor Name      PROXIM
   ⋯Fragment            [xxxxxxxx xxxx0000]  0
   ⋯Sequence            [00010111 1110xxxx]  382
   ⊞ Capability Information
   ⋯Listen Interval     1
   ⊟ Current AP
   │  ⋯Hex Address      00-20-A6-4F-1F-79
   │  ⋯Group Bit        [xxxxxxx0 xxxxxxxx xxxxxxxx xxxxxxxx xxxxxxxx]  off
   │  ⋯Local Bit        [xxxxxx0x xxxxxxxx xxxxxxxx xxxxxxxx xxxxxxxx]  off
   │  ⋯Logical Names    [[AP600-2]]
   │  ⋯Vendor Name      PROXIM
   ⊞ Information Element
   ⊞ Information Element
```

Notify command to AP600-2 on the Ethernet DS backbone and AP600-2 responses with a Move-Response. Thus the seamless roaming of Aironet-PCI is accomplished.

## Cisco Roaming Parameters

The Aironet a/b/g roaming parameters are accessed in adapter properties, advanced tab:

- **BSS Aging Interval**: (Default 120 seconds) length of time that the STA keeps an AP in its list of available APs after it loses contact with the device.
- **Scan Valid Interval**: (Default 60 seconds) time before the STA scans for a better AP after reaching the roaming threshold or missing beacons.

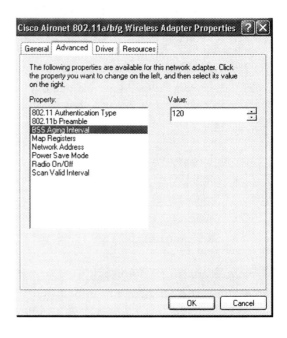

## BroadCom-b/g Integrated Wireless Roaming Parameters

- The BroadCom parameters are a bit more intuitive. The "roaming decision" can be based on maintaining the best performance or hanging onto the greatest distance. The appropriate value is based on the architecture of your ESS and BSA overlap.

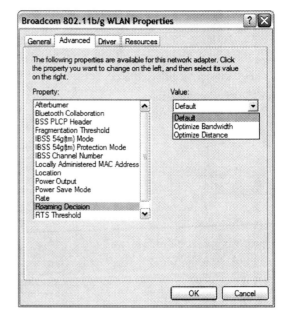

# Chapter 5 Review

Subsequent to initiating authentication a STA discovers an AP in the preferred ESS using a combination of passive and active scanning techniques as detailed in Chapter 4. Either from a beacon frame or probe response the STA:

1. Synchronizes its internal clock with the AP's timestamp.
2. Through Capability Information learns if the AP supports WEP (privacy) and short preamble.
3. Through Supported Rates and Extended Rates IEs determines the mandatory rates in the basic rate set and optional supported rates.
4. Through the DS Parameter Set IE determines the channel on which the AP is configured. This is required because the 2.4-GHz 11-Channel overlap makes it difficult for a STA to precisely determine the AP's channel as demonstrated in Chapter 2.
5. Through the ERP IE on an AP supporting b/g mixed mode determines if any non-ERP STAs are associated to the BSS, whether it should use CTS-to-Self protection for the BSA and which DSSS preamble must be used for the CTS-to-Self frame.
6. Through the WPA IE determines what the type of WPA encryption, the method of negotiating pair-wise and broadcast keys.
7. From a beacon frame reads the TIM IE to determine the DTIM period

Only if all of the parameters discovered in the AP's beacon/probe response are acceptable, should the STA initiate authentication. Nevertheless, the Capability and Supported Rate sets are double and triple checked during the association request and response frames.

- Like all management frames, the authentication and association frames are not processed by the distribution system, the To/From DS bits = 0.
- Although each management frame has three MAC addresses, two of the addresses are always the MAC address of the AP's radio card. Either the source or destination address and the BSSID address are the AP's radio card MAC address. This apparent redundancy was explained in Chapter 3; the first address in the MAC header is always the next node to process the frame. Thus a management frame sent to the AP will have the AP's MAC address as the destination address and also as the BSSID.
- Management frames are MAC entities only – they don't carry an upper-layer payload; they are never encrypted and the WEP (privacy) bit is always reset.
- An exception to the previous statement (and one you'll see on exams) is Sequence Number 3 of Shared Key Authentication which specifies WEP encryption to indicate that the Challenge Text of Sequence Number 2 is encrypted as the Challenge Response.
- Authentication defines a 2 or 4 frame sequence, each identified with a Sequence Number field.
- Authentication and Association frames have a Status Code field. The table in this chapter lists the most common status codes. Appendix-C is a complete list of status codes, it contains several QoS (quality of service, 802.11e) and RSN (robust security network, 802.11i) status codes which are supported in the new generation of access points and client adapters.

- The Reason Code field specifies why a Disassociation or Deauthentication frame was generated. The IEEE warns that,

> *"Algorithms that fail to take the reason code into account are very likely to perform exactly the same action that caused the disassociation or deauthentication frame to be delivered with the reason code in the first place, receiving the same reason code"* IEEE 802.11 Handbook, 2nd Edition

This is a common reason for adapters flapping between associated and unassociated states as illustrated in the *Flapping D-Link Adapter Case Study*. A well-written driver responds to the reason code by creating a log entry or generating a user-level error message. Alas, few drivers are well-written. Currently the only efficient way to troubleshoot these failures is with a promiscuous WLAN monitor.

- The complete set of reason codes appears in Appendix-C. As with the Status Codes it contains several QoS and RSN Reason Codes.

## Authentication: Open, Sequence Number 1

Not really authentication, but rather identification of a STA's MAC address. This is the only 802.11 management frame that is used as both a request and a response frame.

**Duration** = 314-μs, long enough for SIFS + ACK at 1-Mbps with long preamble.

**Algorithm** 0 = Open Authentication
**Sequence Number** 1 = STA's request
**Status Code** 0 = so far, so good

```
⊞ Physical Frame
⊟ IEEE 802.11 MAC Protocol
   ⋅ Function              Authentication
   ⊞ PLCP Header
   ⊟ Frame Control Byte 0
      ⋅ Protocol Level     [xxxxxx00]  0
      ⋅ Type               [xxxx00xx]  Management
      ⋅ Sub-Type           [1011xxxx]  Authentication
   ⊟ Frame Control Byte 1
      ⋅ Order              [0xxxxxxx]  off
      ⋅ WEP                [x0xxxxxx]  off
      ⋅ More Data          [xx0xxxxx]  off
      ⋅ Power Mgmt         [xxx0xxxx]  off
      ⋅ Retry              [xxxx0xxx]  off
      ⋅ More Fragments     [xxxxx0xx]  off
      ⋅ From DS            [xxxxxx0x]  off
      ⋅ To DS              [xxxxxxx0]  off
   ⋅ Duration ID           314
   ⊟ Destination Address
      ⋅ Hex Address        00-09-B7-7E-E9-AA
      ⋅ Group Bit          [xxxxxxx0 xxxxxxxx xxxxxxxx xxxxxxxx xxxxxxxx]  off
      ⋅ Local Bit          [xxxxxx0x xxxxxxxx xxxxxxxx xxxxxxxx xxxxxxxx]  off
      ⋅ Logical Names      [[Aironet-350AP]]
      ⋅ Vendor Name        Cisco Systems
   ⊞ Source Address
      ⋅ Hex Address        00-40-96-A2-F4-34
      ⋅ Group Bit          [xxxxxxx0 xxxxxxxx xxxxxxxx xxxxxxxx xxxxxxxx]  off
      ⋅ Local Bit          [xxxxxx0x xxxxxxxx xxxxxxxx xxxxxxxx xxxxxxxx]  off
      ⋅ Logical Names      [[Aironet-PCI]]
      ⋅ Vendor Name        Aironet Wireless Communication
   ⊟ BSSID
      ⋅ Hex Address        00-09-B7-7E-E9-AA
      ⋅ Group Bit          [xxxxxxx0 xxxxxxxx xxxxxxxx xxxxxxxx xxxxxxxx]  off
      ⋅ Local Bit          [xxxxxx0x xxxxxxxx xxxxxxxx xxxxxxxx xxxxxxxx]  off
      ⋅ Logical Names      [[Aironet-350AP]]
      ⋅ Vendor Name        Cisco Systems
   ⋅ Fragment              [xxxxxxxx xxxx0000]  0
   ⋅ Sequence              [00000000 0001xxxx]  1
   ⋅ Algorithm             0  Open
   ⋅ Sequence Number       1
   ⋅ Status Code           0  Reserved
```

## Authentication: Open, Sequence Number 2 (last three fields)

**Sequence Number** 2 = AP's response
**Status Code** 0 = Success, the STA is authenticated and in State-2, authenticated and unassociated. It will immediately proceed to the association sequence.

```
   ⋅ Algorithm             0  Open
   ⋅ Sequence Number       2
   ⋅ Status Code           0  Reserved
```

## Authentication: Shared Key, Sequence Number 1

Shared Key makes the WEP key even more vulnerable – don't use it! Many new business-class APs have dropped support for shared key authentication.

**Duration** = 314-µs, long enough for a SIFS + ACK at 1-Mbps and long preamble.

**Algorithm** 1 = Shared Key Authentication
**Sequence** 1 = 1 of 4 frames
**Status Code** 0 = so far, so good

```
⊞ Physical Frame
⊟ IEEE 802.11 MAC Protocol
    Function              Authentication
  ⊞ PLCP Header
  ⊟ Frame Control Byte 0
      Protocol Level    [xxxxxx00]  0
      Type              [xxxx00xx]  Management
      Sub-Type          [1011xxxx]  Authentication
  ⊟ Frame Control Byte 1
      Order             [0xxxxxxx]  off
      WEP               [x0xxxxxx]  off
      More Data         [xx0xxxxx]  off
      Power Mgnt        [xxx0xxxx]  off
      Retry             [xxxx0xxx]  off
      More Fragments    [xxxxx0xx]  off
      From DS           [xxxxxx0x]  off
      To DS             [xxxxxxx0]  off
    Duration ID          314
  ⊞ Destination Address
  ⊞ Source Address
  ⊞ BSSID
    Fragment             [xxxxxxxx xxxx0000]  0
    Sequence             [00000000 0001xxxx]  1
    Algorithm            1  Shared Key
    Sequence Number      1
    Status Code          0  Reserved
```

## Authentication: Shared Key, Sequence Number 2 (last four fields)

**Sequence** 2 = 2 of 4 frames
**Status Code** 0 = so far, so good
**IE 16 (0x10) Challenge Text** – the only conventional IE that appears outside of a beacon or probe response frame. It contains a 128-byte challenge in clear text; an intruder captures this challenge text and the Sequence 3 encrypted response to crack the WEP key!

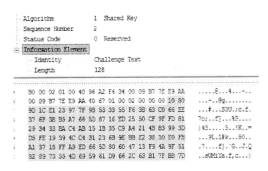

## Authentication: Shared Key, Sequence Number 3 (last four fields)

**WEP** (privacy) bit is set in Frame Control Byte-1
**Sequence** 3 = 3 of 4 frames
**Status Code** 0 = so far, so good
**IE 16** (0x10) 128-byte encrypted response

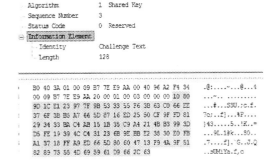

## Authentication: Shared Key, Sequence Number 4 (last three fields)

**Sequence** 4 = four of four frames
**Status Code** 0 = Success
The STA is in State-2, authenticated and unassociated.
It will immediately proceed to the association sequence.

```
  Algorithm           1  Shared Key
  Sequence Number     4
  Status Code         0  Reserved
```

## Failure Example: AP configured for Shared Key, STA for Open – Failure (last three fields)

```
Algorithm          0  Open
Sequence Number    2
Status Code        13 Specified authentication algorithm not supported
```

**Status Code** 13 = the STA is configured to support open authentication.

## Association Request

In this example an 802.11g STA is associating to an 802.11b AP

**Duration = 314-μs**. the virtual carrier required for a SIFS + ACK transmitted at 1-Mbs and long preamble.

**Capability Information**: This STA supports short preamble and privacy.

**Listen Interval = 1** Listen Intervals of STAs range from 1 – 200, depending on the PS-mode configuration. The association request may be rejected if the listen interval is so long that the AP can't commit sufficient buffer resources.

**SSID IE** = Aironet-350AP, the ESS to which the STA is associating.

**Supported Rates IE** = The STA responses with standard HS-DSSS rates with are not in its basic rate set. The 802.11g STA established the type of modulation and rates

```
Physical Frame
IEEE 802.11 MAC Protocol
  Function              Association Request
  PLCP Header
  Frame Control Byte 0
    Protocol Level   [xxxxxx00]  0
    Type             [xxxx00xx]  Management
    Sub-Type         [0000xxxx]  Association Request
  Frame Control Byte 1
    Order            [0xxxxxxx]  off
    WEP              [x0xxxxxx]  off
    More Data        [xx0xxxxx]  off
    Power Mgmt       [xxx0xxxx]  off
    Retry            [xxxx0xxx]  off
    More Fragments   [xxxxx0xx]  off
    From DS          [xxxxxx0x]  off
    To DS            [xxxxxxx0]  off
  Duration ID          314
  Destination Address
    Hex Address      00-09-B7-7E-E9-AA
    Group Bit        [xxxxxxx0 xxxxxxxx xxxxxxxx xxxxxxxx xxxxxxxx]  off
    Local Bit        [xxxxxx0x xxxxxxxx xxxxxxxx xxxxxxxx xxxxxxxx]  off
    Logical Names    [[Aironet-350AP]]
    Vendor Name      Cisco Systems
  Source Address
    Hex Address      00-40-96-A2-F4-34
    Group Bit        [xxxxxxx0 xxxxxxxx xxxxxxxx xxxxxxxx xxxxxxxx]  off
    Local Bit        [xxxxxx0x xxxxxxxx xxxxxxxx xxxxxxxx xxxxxxxx]  off
    Logical Names    [[Aironet-PCI]]
    Vendor Name      Aironet Wireless Communication
  BSSID
    Hex Address      00-09-B7-7E-E9-AA
    Group Bit        [xxxxxxx0 xxxxxxxx xxxxxxxx xxxxxxxx xxxxxxxx]  off
    Local Bit        [xxxxxx0x xxxxxxxx xxxxxxxx xxxxxxxx xxxxxxxx]  off
    Logical Names    [[Aironet-350AP]]
    Vendor Name      Cisco Systems
  Fragment             [xxxxxxxx xxxx0000]  0
  Sequence             [00000000 0010xxxx]  2
  Capability Information
    Channel Agility  [0xxxxxxx xxxxxxxx]  Off
    PBCC             [x0xxxxxx xxxxxxxx]  Off
    Short Preamble   [xx1xxxxx xxxxxxxx]  On
    Privacy          [xxx1xxxx xxxxxxxx]  On
    CF Poll Request  [xxxx0xxx xxxxxxxx]  Off
    CF Pollable      [xxxxx0xx xxxxxxxx]  Off
    IBSS             [xxxxxx0x xxxxxxxx]  Off
    ESS              [xxxxxxx1 xxxxxxxx]  On
    Reserved         [xxxxxxxx 00000000]  0
  Listen Interval      1
  Information Element
    Identity         SSID
    Length           13
    SSID             Aironet-350AP
  Information Element
    Identity         Supported Rates
    Length           4
    Rate             1.0 MB   [0xxxxxxx]  Not in Basic Rate Set
    Rate             2.0 MB   [0xxxxxxx]  Not in Basic Rate Set
    Rate             5.5 MB   [0xxxxxxx]  Not in Basic Rate Set
    Rate             11.0 MB  [0xxxxxxx]  Not in Basic Rate Set
  Information Element
    Identity         Unknown
    Length           30
```

supported on the 802.11b AP through a beacon or probe response. This is reflected in the capabilities and supported rates fields.

**Information Element Unknown** – Both the AP and STA support Cisco extensions. LinkFerret currently does not decode proprietary IEs.

**Reassociation Request** is identical to an association request with the addition of the Current AP field.

```
Current AP
  Hex Address      00-20-A6-4F-1F-79
  Group Bit        [xxxxxxx0 xxxxxxxx
  Local Bit        [xxxxxx0x xxxxxxxx
  Logical Names    [[AP600-2]]
  Vendor Name      Proxim,
```

## Association Response

**Duration** = 162-μs. Virtual carrier length for a SIFS + ACK at 5.5-Mbps with short preamble. The AP received the supported rates information from the STA's association request and bumped up the link speed to 5.5-Mbps.

**Capability Information**: identical to the STAs capability information field in the association request.

**Status Code** = 0 indicates a successful association

**Association ID** = 49,175 (0xc001) the first AID. This is the only STA associated to the AP.

**Supported Rates IE**
The AP requires 1- and 2-Mbps support, and optionally supports 5.5- and 11-Mbps. Association

```
⊞ Physical Frame
⊟ IEEE 802.11 MAC Protocol
   ·· Function              Association Response
⊞ PLCP Header
⊟ Frame Control Byte 0
   ·· Protocol Level    [xxxxxx00]   0
   ·· Type              [xxxx00xx]   Management
   ·· Sub-Type          [0001xxxx]   Association Response
⊟ Frame Control Byte 1
   ·· Order             [0xxxxxxx]   off
   ·· WEP               [x0xxxxxx]   off
   ·· More Data         [xx0xxxxx]   off
   ·· Power Mgmt        [xxx0xxxx]   off
   ·· Retry             [xxxx0xxx]   off
   ·· More Fragments    [xxxxx0xx]   off
   ·· From DS           [xxxxxx0x]   off
   ·· To DS             [xxxxxxx0]   off
   ·· Duration ID          162
⊟ Destination Address
   ·· Hex Address          00-40-96-A2-F4-34
   ·· Group Bit         [xxxxxxx0 xxxxxxxx xxxxxxxx xxxxxxxx xxxxxxxx]   off
   ·· Local Bit         [xxxxxx0x xxxxxxxx xxxxxxxx xxxxxxxx xxxxxxxx]   off
   ·· Vendor Name          Aironet Wireless Communication
⊟ Source Address
   ·· Hex Address          00-09-B7-7E-E9-AA
   ·· Group Bit         [xxxxxxx0 xxxxxxxx xxxxxxxx xxxxxxxx xxxxxxxx]   off
   ·· Local Bit         [xxxxxx0x xxxxxxxx xxxxxxxx xxxxxxxx xxxxxxxx]   off
   ·· Vendor Name          Cisco Systems
⊟ BSSID
   ·· Hex Address          00-09-B7-7E-E9-AA
   ·· Group Bit         [xxxxxxx0 xxxxxxxx xxxxxxxx xxxxxxxx xxxxxxxx]   off
   ·· Local Bit         [xxxxxx0x xxxxxxxx xxxxxxxx xxxxxxxx xxxxxxxx]   off
   ·· Vendor Name          Cisco Systems
   ·· Fragment           [xxxxxxxx xxxx0000]  0
   ·· Sequence           [00001110 1110xxxx]  238
⊟ Capability Information
   ·· Channel Agility   [0xxxxxxx xxxxxxxx]   off
   ·· PBCC              [x0xxxxxx xxxxxxxx]   off
   ·· Short Preamble    [xx1xxxxx xxxxxxxx]   On
   ·· Privacy           [xxx1xxxx xxxxxxxx]   On
   ·· CF Poll Request   [xxxx0xxx xxxxxxxx]   off
   ·· CF Pollable       [xxxxx0xx xxxxxxxx]   off
   ·· IBSS              [xxxxxx0x xxxxxxxx]   off
   ·· ESS               [xxxxxxx1 xxxxxxxx]   On
   ·· Reserved          [xxxxxxxx 00000000]  0
   ·· Status Code          0
   ·· Association ID       49175
⊟ Information Element
   ·· Identity             Supported Rates
   ·· Length               4
   ·· Rate               1.0 MB   [1xxxxxxx]   In Basic Rate Set
   ·· Rate               2.0 MB   [1xxxxxxx]   In Basic Rate Set
   ·· Rate               5.5 MB   [0xxxxxxx]   Not in Basic Rate Set
   ·· Rate              11.0 MB   [0xxxxxxx]   Not in Basic Rate Set
```

fails if a STA doesn't support every basic rate set with Status Code 18, "*Association denied, requesting STA doesn't support all of the data rates in the BSSBasicRateSet parameter.*"

## A word about the MAC MIB (management information base)

Occasionally in technical literature you'll see terms, such as BSSBasicRateSet or dot11OperationalRateSet, where several acronyms and words are concatenated without spaces. The MAC MIB (management information base) defines every 802.11 (dot11) operating parameter on a STA or AP. In routine administration and troubleshooting we use standard terms such as "basic rate set" instead of the more technically precise "BSSBasicRateSet." The most common application of MAC MIB terms is when configuring a business-class AP from a telnet or SSH command line. The CLI (command line interface) provides access to dozens of obscure configuration settings that are not supported through the menu-driven web browser interface. Beware of the motivations of people and books that casually toss around MAC MIB terminology when standard "dot11 techno-speak" is adequate; who are they trying to impress?

## Reassociation Response

Reassociation response is identical to an association response except that it follows a reassociation request. Employing Cisco's proprietary WDS (wireless domain services) or a vendor-specific version of IAPP, the new AP communicates with the AP specified in the current AP field of the reassociation request to ensure:

- that the STA is dropped from the original AP's association and learn tables
- frames for the STA are forward to the new AP

## Deauthentication

Deauthentication may be unilaterally issued by either an AP or STA.

**Duration** = 314-μs, the virtual carrier for a SIFS + ACK at the lowest basic rate of 1-Mbps and long preamble. Often deauthentication frames are sent by an AP after the STA has departed. If you see a flurry deauthentication frames without subsequent ACKs, check the retry bit to verify that the frames are retransmissions.

```
⊞ Physical Frame
⊟ IEEE 802.11 MAC Protocol
   ┊ Function              Deauthentication
  ⊞ PLCP Header
  ⊟ Frame Control Byte 0
   ┊ ┊ Protocol Level     [xxxxxx00]  0
   ┊ ┊ Type               [xxxx00xx]  Management
   ┊ └ Sub-Type           [1100xxxx]  Deauthentication
  ⊟ Frame Control Byte 1
   ┊ ┊ Order              [0xxxxxxx]  off
   ┊ ┊ WEP                [x0xxxxxx]  off
   ┊ ┊ More Data          [xx0xxxxx]  off
   ┊ ┊ Power Mgmt         [xxx0xxxx]  off
   ┊ ┊ Retry              [xxxx0xxx]  off
   ┊ ┊ More Fragments     [xxxxx0xx]  off
   ┊ ┊ From DS            [xxxxxx0x]  off
   ┊ └ To DS              [xxxxxxx0]  off
   ┊ Duration ID          314
  ⊟ Destination Address
   ┊ ┊ Hex Address        00-11-50-0E-BC-53
   ┊ ┊ Group Bit          [xxxxxxx0 xxxxxxxx xxxxxxxx xxxxxxxx xxxxxxxx]  off
   ┊ ┊ Local Bit          [xxxxxx0x xxxxxxxx xxxxxxxx xxxxxxxx xxxxxxxx]  off
   ┊ ┊ Logical Names      [[Belkin-AP]]
   ┊ └ Vendor Name        Belkin
  ⊟ Source Address
   ┊ ┊ Hex Address        00-40-96-A2-F4-34
   ┊ ┊ Group Bit          [xxxxxxx0 xxxxxxxx xxxxxxxx xxxxxxxx xxxxxxxx]  off
   ┊ ┊ Local Bit          [xxxxxx0x xxxxxxxx xxxxxxxx xxxxxxxx xxxxxxxx]  off
   ┊ ┊ Logical Names      [[Aironet-PCI]]
   ┊ └ Vendor Name        Aironet Wireless Communication
  ⊟ BSSID
   ┊ ┊ Hex Address        00-11-50-0E-BC-53
   ┊ ┊ Group Bit          [xxxxxxx0 xxxxxxxx xxxxxxxx xxxxxxxx xxxxxxxx]  off
   ┊ ┊ Local Bit          [xxxxxx0x xxxxxxxx xxxxxxxx xxxxxxxx xxxxxxxx]  off
   ┊ ┊ Logical Names      [[Belkin-AP]]
   ┊ └ Vendor Name        Belkin
   ┊ Fragment             [xxxxxxxx xxxx0000]  0
   ┊ Sequence             [00011101 0010xxxx]  466
   └ Reason Code          3  Deauthenticated because station is leaving IBSS or ESS
```

## Reason Code

Although the drivers might ignore it, you should always verify that the reason code for the deauthentication is reasonable. In this example the STA is leaving the EWG ESS to join another ESS, so the reason code makes sense. There's nothing in this frame detail that directly specifies that the STA is being deauthenticated from EWG. But it does specify the BSSID and you should know your WLAN architecture well enough to know which SSIDs are supported on a particular AP. Also remember this limitation - since you are capturing network traffic on a single channel, you will not capture the authentication and association sequence between the STA and its new AP because that occurs on a different channel.

## Disassociation

Like the deauthentication frame, the disassociation frame can be sent by a STA or AP.

**Duration** = 0
**Destination Address** = broadcast
This frame is disassociating every STA from the AP600-1. Since it is broadcast, the duration value of 0 indicates that the frame is not acknowledged.

As we discussed in painful detail in Chapter 3, only broadcast frames with the To DS Bit = 1 are acknowledged. Broadcast frames with the To DS Bit = 0 are never acknowledged because they aren't processed by the DS.

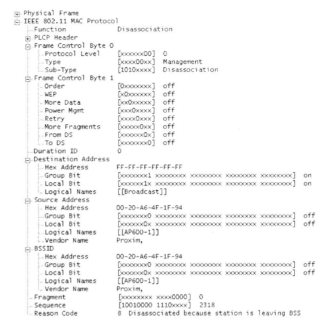

A disassociation frame sent to a unicast address should be acknowledged. The duration value is set to reserve the virtual carrier for a SIFS + ACK at the low basic rate.

## Reason Code

Considering that this frame was transmitted by an AP evicting all of its associated STAs, Reason Code 8, "disassociated because the station is leaving the BSS" may not appear to be enlightening. But given the context of the broadcast destination address and the AP source address, you can imagine that an event transpired that caused the AP to reboot or otherwise disable its radio card.

In this example, the AP was configured for link integrity checking with the default gateway. When that link was lost the AP could no longer provide a practical service to its associated clients so they were disassociated and the AP shut-down the BSS. A properly designed network would never configure link integrity checking without ensuring that the BSA was covered with overlapped BSAs from other APs in the same ESS.

# Chapter 6: 802.11 Fragmentation and RTS/CTS

## *802.11 Commands Analyzed:*
- RTS and CTS control frames

## *802.11 Concepts:*
- 802.11 maximum MSDU size
- 802.11 plain text and encryption overhead
- Acceptable packet error rate
- RFI and Fragmentation
- IP Fragmentation versus 802.11 Fragmentation
- Fragmentation: Myth, Fact, Overhead, Applications and Frame Analysis
- Frame Control Byte-1, More Fragments Bit
- Sequence/Fragments Field
- RTS/CTS medium reservation: Myth, Fact, Overhead, Applications and Frame Analysis
- Hidden Terminal issue
- Overlapped BSAs issue

## *Perspective*

Fragmentation and RTS threshold configuration is supported by almost all 802.11b wireless client adapter utilities. However, most 802.11bg wireless client adapter utilities no longer support fragmentation and RTS threshold configuration. Setting these parameters has always been more art than science and one can argue that most administrators did more damage than good by incorrectly implementing fragmentation and RTS. Learning the concepts in this chapter and studying the capture files, however impractical these techniques may be in modern wireless networks, still provides extremely important insight into understanding the limitations of 802.11 communications in non-ideal operating environments.

## *802.11 Overhead and Maximum Payload*

Open up the IEEE 802.11 Handbook or any wireless text and you'll discover that the maximum size of an unencrypted MSDU is 2,304 bytes - that's over 50% larger than the maximum Ethernet MSDU of 1,500. Understanding the relationship between 802.11 and Ethernet maximum frame sizes is a key factor in performing network optimization.

In order to find the true maximum size of an 802.11 frame we must ensure that Ethernet frame translation doesn't occur. To that end we'll execute a ping between STAs in the same BSS without involving the frame translation and bridging functions of the DSS. The command Ping –n 2 –l 1850 192.168.2.223 transmits two ICMP Echo Requests with a data length of 1,850 bytes.

Open the capture file Ping-1850 and PSP-SRV namespace, ensure that **No Filter** is applied and press **F5**, the press **Ctrl-g** and go-to frame-18.

```
Number      Time                Destination      Source         Function
[0-01]-18   00:00:03:459:863    iMac-Air2        Aironet-PCI    Echo Request
[0-01]-19   00:00:03:459:868    Aironet-PCI                     ACK
[0-01]-20   00:00:03:460:644    iMac-Air2        Aironet-PCI    Unknown Message [97]
[0-01]-21   00:00:03:460:723    Aironet-PCI                     ACK
[0-06]-22   00:00:03:464:082    iMac-Air2        Aironet-PCI    Echo Request
[0-06]-23   00:00:03:464:085    Aironet-350AP                   ACK
[0-06]-24   00:00:03:464:722    iMac-Air2        Aironet-PCI    Unknown Message [97]
[0-06]-25   00:00:03:464:894    Aironet-350AP                   ACK
[0-06]-26   00:00:03:467:775    Aironet-PCI      iMac-Air2      Echo Reply
[0-06]-27   00:00:03:467:779    iMac-Air2                       ACK
[0-06]-28   00:00:03:468:962    Aironet-PCI      iMac-Air2      Unknown Message [97]
[0-06]-29   00:00:03:469:154    iMac-Air2                       ACK
[0-01]-30   00:00:03:471:196    Aironet-PCI      iMac-Air2      Echo Reply
[0-01]-31   00:00:03:471:199    Aironet-350AP                   ACK
[0-01]-32   00:00:03:471:700    Aironet-PCI      iMac-Air2      Unknown Message [97]
[0-01]-33   00:00:03:471:804    Aironet-350AP                   ACK
```

Frames 18 – 25 are associated with the Each Echo Request and Frames 26 – 33 are associated with the Echo Reply. *That's twice as many frames as the second example in* ***Chapter 3***.

```
Number      Time                Destination      Source         Function
[0-01]-18   00:00:03:459:863    iMac-Air2        Aironet-PCI    Echo Request
```

Frame-18 Echo Request
**Physical Frame:** Frame Size 1,532 bytes
That's puzzling because the ping specified 1,850 bytes of data and that doesn't include several protocol headers. *What about the fabled 2,304 byte MSDU size of 802.11?* Virtually all APs have an Ethernet translational bridging interface. Regardless of the 802.11 specification, the largest unencrypted frame that you're likely to capture is 1,532 bytes.

```
Physical Frame
  Status                 No Errors
  Interface Number       0
  Frame Number           18
  Frame size             1532
  Bytes Captured         1532
  Frame Media Type       IEEE 802.11
  Frame Captured         June  8, 200
  Frame Captured         June  8, 200
  Trace Delta            00:00:03:459
  Packet Delta           00:00:01:040
  Channel                1
  Speed                  0MBS
  Signal                 81
  Quality                0
IEEE 802.11 MAC Protocol
IEEE 802.2 Logical Link Control
IEEE Sub-Network Access Protocol
Internet Protocol
Internet Control Message Protocol
```

To calculate the maximum MSDU, we have to determine Mac-Header overhead. Expand all of the fields in frame-18.

**802.11 MAC-Header**
An 802.11 Data frame with three addresses has 24-bytes of MAC Header overhead. *In the rare case of a data frame traversing a WDS the MAC-header has four addresses and a total of 30-bytes.*

| Frame Control: | 2 bytes |
|---|---|
| Duration/ID: | 2 bytes |
| Addresses: (3 @ 6-bytes) | 18 bytes |
| Fragment/Sequence: | 2 bytes |
| **Total:** | **24 bytes** |

**MSDU (802.2 LLC + Payload):** 1,532 bytes – 24-bytes = 1,508 bytes
Subtract the 3 byte 802.2 LLC Header and the 5 byte SNAP Header from the 1,508 byte MSDU and the *802.11 Data frame and Ethernet frame both have the same maximum MSDU payload of 1,500 bytes. Now isn't that convenient!*

**Fragmentation and OSI Layers**: IP fragmentation and L2 802.11 fragmentation are different technologies that address different issues. Since IP fragmentation is independent of the network's L1/L2 implementation it functions identically in Ethernet and 802.11 frames.

A MSDU which exceeds the MTU must be fragmented. Payload fragmentation is a function of L3 and the IP protocol.

The More Fragments Bit in the Fragmentation Information subfield is set, indicating that the frame is fragmented. The Offset field assists the receiver in fragment reassembly. The first fragment has an offset of zero. *IP fragmentation size is a function of the maximum MSDU, it's not configurable.*

```
⊟ Internet Protocol
   ├ Header Version        4            [0100 xxxx]
   ├ Header Length         20 bytes     [xxxx 0101]
   ├ Type of Service       0
   ├ Datagram Length       1500
   ├ Differentiator        364
  ⊟ Fragmentation Information
   │ ├ More Fragments      on      xx1x xxxx xxxx xxxx
   │ ├ Don't Fragment      off     x0xx xxxx xxxx xxxx
   │ └ Offset              0       xxx0 0000 0000 0000
   ├ Time To Live          128
   ├ Protocol              Internet Control Message Protocol
   ├ Header Checksum       0x8ca7
   ├ Source Address        192.168.2.222
   └ Destination Address   192.168.2.223
```

| Number | Time | Destination | Source | Function |
|---|---|---|---|---|
| [0-01]-20 | 00:00:03:460:644 | iMac-Air2 | Aironet-PCI | Unknown Message [97] |

Frame 20: Unknown Message
*Every field except for the ICMP Header is duplicated in every fragment.* That's why LinkFerret flags this frame as an "Unknown Message". Totaling all of the headers in the two fragments yields:

```
⊟ Physical Frame
   ├ Status              No Errors
   ├ Interface Number    0
   ├ Frame Number        20
   ├ Frame size          430
   ├ Bytes Captured      430
   ├ Frame Media Type    IEEE 802.11
   ├ Frame Captured      June  8, 2005
   ├ Frame Captured      June  8, 2005
   ├ Trace Delta         00:00:03:460:6
   ├ Packet Delta        00:00:00:000:7
   ├ Channel             1
   ├ Speed               0MBS
   ├ Signal              81
   └ Quality             0
```

| MAC Header: | 2 x 24 = 48 bytes |
|---|---|
| 802.2 LLC/SNAP | 2 x 8 = 16 bytes |
| IP Header | 2 x 20 = 40 bytes |
| ICMP Header | 1 x 8 = 8 bytes Header |
| **Total Header Size** | 112 bytes |

*The two data fragment frames total 1,962 bytes (1,532 bytes + 430 bytes). Subtracting the overhead from the total byte count yields: 1,962 – 112 = 1,850 bytes, the specified ping data!*

Frame 20: IP Field
Expand the IP field in frame 20. The More Fragments Bit is reset indicating that this is the last fragment. The Offset of 185 instructs the receiver where to append the data from this fragment with data from the first fragment. Because IP datagrams may be received out of order, this guarantees that the original frame will be correctly reassembled.

```
⊟ Internet Protocol
   ├ Header Version        4            [0100 xxxx]
   ├ Header Length         20 bytes     [xxxx 0101]
   ├ Type of Service       0
   ├ Datagram Length       398
   ├ Differentiator        364
  ⊟ Fragmentation Information
   │ ├ More Fragments      off     xx0x xxxx xxxx xxxx
   │ ├ Don't Fragment      off     x0xx xxxx xxxx xxxx
   │ └ Offset              185     xxx0 0000 1011 1001
   ├ Time To Live          128
   ├ Protocol              Internet Control Message Protocol
   ├ Header Checksum       0xb03c
   ├ Source Address        192.168.2.222
   └ Destination Address   192.168.2.223
```

An IP fragmentation offset represents a specified number of 8-byte "fragmentation blocks." An offset of 185 translates to 1,480 bytes. That's the size of the ICMP field and data in the first fragment. IP glues the second ICMP field fragment to the first ICMP field fragment at 1,480 bytes, thus recreating an ICMP data field of 1,850 bytes.

Now let's determine why it takes eight frames to transmit one Echo Request.

| Number | Time | Destination | Source | Function |
|--------|------|-------------|--------|----------|
| [0-01]-18 | 00:00:03:459:863 | iMac-Air2 | Aironet-PCI | Echo Request |
| [0-01]-19 | 00:00:03:459:868 | Aironet-PCI | | ACK |
| [0-01]-20 | 00:00:03:460:644 | iMac-Air2 | Aironet-PCI | Unknown Message [97] |
| [0-01]-21 | 00:00:03:460:723 | Aironet-PCI | | ACK |
| [0-06]-22 | 00:00:03:464:082 | iMac-Air2 | Aironet-PCI | Echo Request |
| [0-06]-23 | 00:00:03:464:085 | Aironet-350AP | | ACK |
| [0-06]-24 | 00:00:03:464:722 | iMac-Air2 | Aironet-PCI | Unknown Message [97] |
| [0-06]-25 | 00:00:03:464:894 | Aironet-350AP | | ACK |
| [0-06]-26 | 00:00:03:467:775 | Aironet-PCI | iMac-Air2 | Echo Reply |
| [0-06]-27 | 00:00:03:467:779 | iMac-Air2 | | ACK |
| [0-06]-28 | 00:00:03:468:962 | Aironet-PCI | iMac-Air2 | Unknown Message [97] |
| [0-06]-29 | 00:00:03:469:154 | iMac-Air2 | | ACK |
| [0-01]-30 | 00:00:03:471:196 | Aironet-PCI | iMac-Air2 | Echo Reply |
| [0-01]-31 | 00:00:03:471:199 | Aironet-350AP | | ACK |
| [0-01]-32 | 00:00:03:471:700 | Aironet-PCI | iMac-Air2 | Unknown Message [97] |
| [0-01]-33 | 00:00:03:471:804 | Aironet-350AP | | ACK |

**Frames 18 – 21**: The IP driver on Aironet-PCI divides the Echo Request into two fragments and transmits them to Aironet-350-AP.

**Frames 22 – 25**: Aironet-350AP retransmits the fragments to iMac-Air2.

**Frames 26 – 33**: Repeats the process with the Echo Reply.

The AP must wait to receive all fragments (two in this example) before relaying them to iMac-Air2. Verify the state of the To/From DS bits in frames 18-25 to ensure that you understand how the IP fragments are being processed by the AP's DSS.

## *Acceptable Error Rate*

Assuming that there aren't overlapping BSAs or significant RFI, what's an acceptable packet error rate in a production 802.11 network? That's impossible to precisely quantify because corrupted packets result from many installation-specific factors:

1. What's the BSS Mode: 802.11b-only, 802.11g-only or mixed?
2. If mixed mode, is CTS-to-Self protection implemented?
3. What are the BSS basic rates? Lower rates accommodate greater distances and automatic rate fallback, but also produce higher error rates.
4. Does the BSA cell size and shape accommodate all of the supported STAs?
5. What are the transmit power settings on the AP and STAs?
6. If an AP has an omni-directional antenna, is it physically positioned in the center of the network?
7. If an AP has semi-directional antenna, does the main lobe cover all STAs?
8. Is multipath an issue? Are there physical obstacles or RF reflective surfaces in the area? If so, do the STA's client adapters support antenna diversity and is it enabled?

9. What's the ratio of fixed STAs to mobile STAs? Error rates in an ESS that supports roaming are a function of how well the BSA coverage areas overlap.
10. Antenna issues are the most common reason that individual STAs experience high error rates. Typical issues are:
    - PC-Card stub antennas on the opposite side of the notebook computer from the AP or blocked by the user's hand when operating a mouse
    - Built-in notebook antenna with a loose internal connector - watch those tiny MC connectors that tend to pop-off
    - PCI 2.2-dBi rubber duckies obscured at the back of the system unit placed on the floor and behind a metal desk
11. ***Central to remainder of the chapter are fragmentation and RTS thresholds - what is the packet size distribution as viewed in Link Ferret's Packet Size tab in the Statistics Window?***

The proactive approach to optimization is to perform weekly and monthly network monitor baseline captures. ***Determining "what's changed" is much more illuminating than determining "what currently is."*** Included in the baseline captures should be large file transfers which enable end-to-end data throughput to be quantified.

***The error rate in a mixed-mode BSS with 20 non-mobile STAs with visible antennas and a mix of email, http and file server access is typically 10% to 15%. Because error rates, like the back-off timer CW, increase at an exponential rate WLAN throughput can degrade quickly.***

**Troubleshooting Tip:** User satisfaction is based on network throughput which is much more difficult to measure than error rate. Maximum theoretical throughput is reduced by the accumulated latencies of the server, routers, switches and the WLAN. A low error rate doesn't always indicate high-throughput. In a busy, yet well-behaved BSS, the error rate may be low even if the AP and STAs wait long periods to transmit.

## RFI (Radio Frequency Interference)

When CSMA/CA is properly functioning and CTS-to-Self protection is implemented, RFI and high BSA bandwidth utilization are the most common causes of high error rates. High bandwidth utilization is addressed by making more efficient usage of the bandwidth or creating more bandwidth:
- Upgrade all STAs to 802.11g and define high basic rates.
- Create more BSAs by load balancing co-located APs configured on non-overlapping channels.

The only objective method of detecting and measuring RFI is to employ a 2.4-GHz receiver/spectrum analyzer such as Berkeley Varitronics System's YellowJacket. Don't guess whether RFI is an issue: measure it, isolate it, remove it or compensate for it.

Multipath interference is more difficult to detect. Offices are jammed with partitions, file cabinets, metallic blinds, reflective ceiling tiles and metallic light fixtures which reflect RF energy and provide multiple out-of-phase signal paths (that's why it's called multipath) between the transmitter and receivers. Antenna diversity is the most common way to compensate for multipath. ***ERP-OFDM is much more resistant to multipath signal corruption than HR/DSSS***. Another tactic is to reposition the access point, perform a capture and compare error rates with the previous capture.

## 802.11 Frame Fragmentation – The Double-Edged Sword

At the beginning of the chapter we determined that the largest unencrypted 802.11 frame is 1,532 bytes. ***802.11 has a configurable frame fragmentation mechanism to addresses large data frame corruption in a high RFI environment***. This is the reasoning behind L2 fragmentation:

1. Noisy RFI environment produce high errors rates
2. Larger frames require longer the transmission times. The longer the transmission time, the greater the probability of frame corruption.
3. The retransmission of large frames consumes significant bandwidth and is more likely to result in additional frame corruption.
4. Theoretically, ***when large frames are fragmented and transmitted as multiple fragments there is less probably of corruption, and if corruption does occur, the retransmission of smaller fragments consumes less bandwidth***.
5. On the other hand, 802.11 fragmentation adds overhead. ***Each fragment requires a separate SIFS + PLCP-Preamble/Header + MAC Header + FCS***.

> **Terminology Alert** 802.11 Fragmentation fragments the original MSDU into multiple MSDUs. Each fragmented MSDU is then encapsulated in its own MPDU. Thus each fragment has the same L2 overhead as a non-fragmented data frame.

The bottom line: If the bandwidth saved by reducing the number of retransmissions is greater than the bandwidth consumed by the fragmentation overhead, then BSA throughput is increased.

The 802.11 fragment threshold is configurable and the upper-layer protocol headers are not duplicated as occurs in L3 fragmentation. However, it's very difficult to know when to implement fragmentation and determine the most efficient fragmentation threshold.

### Client Adapter Fragmentation Threshold Configuration

As noted at the beginning of the chapter, most 802.11g APs and wireless client adapter utilities no longer support fragmentation or RTS threshold configuration. This table lists seven popular client adapters and their fragmentation and RTS support.

| Client Adapter Fragmentation and RTS Threshold Configuration | | |
|---|---|---|
| **Client Adapter** | **Vendor Utility** | **Driver Properties Advanced Tab** |
| Aironet-350 (802.11b) | Yes | No |
| Aironet-abg | No | No |
| BroadCom mini-PCI | No | Yes |
| DLink DWL-G120 (USB) | No | No |
| NetGear WG511 | No | No |
| Proxim/Orinoco Gold-abg | No | No |
| Proxim/Orinoco Gold- bg | No | No |

## 802.11 MAC-Header Fragmentation Support Fields

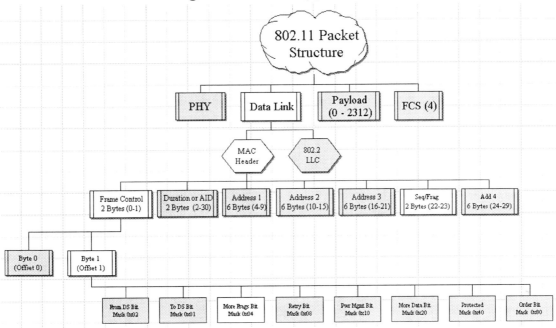

**More Fragments Bit:** Frame Control Byte-1, Bit-2

Set to specify that at least one more fragment remains to be transmitted. The More Fragments Bit is reset for frames that are not fragmented or the last frame is a fragment sequence.

**Sequence/Fragment Field**:

- ***Data and Management frames have a Seq/Frag field.***
- The fragment subfield is 4-bits and supports a maximum of 16-fragments/frame.
- ***Control frames don't have a Seq/Frag field so they can't be fragmented.*** That's OK because control frames (14 or 20 bytes) are much too short for fragmentation.
- Management frames have a Seq/Frag field but, like Control frames they are much too short for practical fragmentation. The largest management frame is the beacon. The number of IEs in beacon frames continues to grow but currently the largest

802.11g beacon frame with WPA/RSN IEs and several proprietary IEs is less than 195-bytes. Much too small for practical fragmentation.

- ***802.11 fragmentation is associated with large data frames and high RFI***
- Most APs and client adapters that support fragmentation have a default fragmentation threshold of 2,346. Any fragmentation threshold over 1,532 bytes essentially disables L2 fragmentation in an unencrypted BSS.
- The lowest configurable fragmentation threshold is typically 256 bytes.
- As we'll see in the fragmentation analysis, the lowest practical fragmentation threshold is approximately 550 bytes in a BSS employing TKIP encryption. This ensures that maximum sized frames are fragmented into three approximately equal sized fragments, and that strategy optimizes the fragmentation overhead.

## Fragmented Frame Filter

A fragmented frame can be identified in two ways:

- The More Fragments bit is set
- The More Fragments bit is reset, but the fragment number is non-zero, which identifies the last fragment

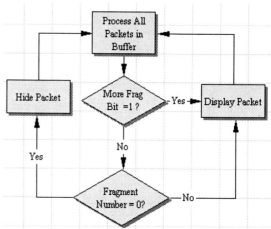

This filter will be written to also include ACKs. That enables us to visually recognize retries without having to apply a Retry filter.

The filter could have been written as a one statement with two tests: ***If More Fragments bit = 0 and Fragment Number = 0, then exclude the frame.*** Most people find that the two test method is more intuitive. As a simple LinkFerret filter creation exercise, rewrite this filter with one statement and two tests.

---

**Troubleshooting Tip** It's routine to create simple filters on-the-fly. A well-conceived filter reveals frames that would otherwise be lost in the clutter. ***An essential component of mastering frame analysis is learning how to view a capture.***

---

## More Fragments Bit test:

- Offset: 1 - test frame control byte-1
- Mask: 0x04 (0000 0100) – only test bit-2, ignore all of the other bits
- Value: 0x04 (0000 0100) - include the frame if the More Fragments Bit is set.

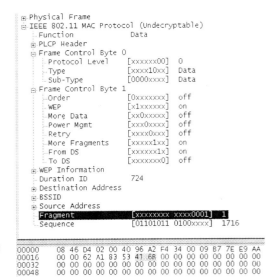

## Testing on the Fragment Number

The fragment number subfield is trickier than it first appears. The 16-bit Seq/Frag field is stored in little-endian with the least significant byte first. The Fragment subfield is in bits 0-3. Notice the highlighted double-byte that contains the fragment number. Although it is the least significant byte, it appears first in the hex decode window. ***Little Endian format makes the offset for the fragment subfield byte 22, instead of byte 23!***

## Fragment Number Test

- Offset: 22
- Mask: 0x0f (0000 1111) least significant 4-bits
- Value 0x00 (0000 0000) fragment number 0
- Test Type: Not Equal - test for a non-zero fragment number

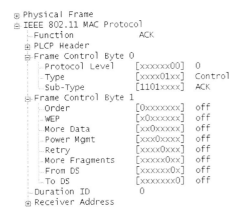

## ACK Control Frame Test:

- Offset: 0 (test frame control, byte-0)
- Mask: 0xfc (1111 1100), bits 2-3 are the frame type, bits 4-7 the sub-type
- Value: 0xd4 (1101 01xx), the ACK Control frame

We'll call the filter **Fragmented Frames** and use it later in the chapter. The following screenshots show the More Fragments, Fragment Number and ACK frame tests.

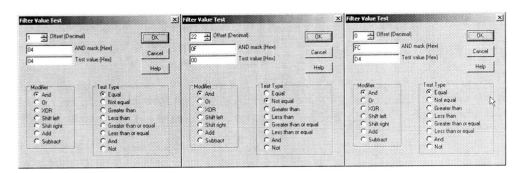

## Why and Where to implement Fragmentation

Configuring 802.11 fragmentation is a best guess scenario. If you don't have the time or patience for multiple iterations of setting the fragmentation threshold and testing throughput, don't fragment – you're more than likely to diminish performance than improve it.

> **! *Exam Alert***: A frame is fragmented when the size of the MPDU exceeds the specified fragmentation threshold.

Encryption adds several fields to the MPDU. The maximum size of a MPDU depends on the type of encryption employed in the BSS.

| Payload + 802.2 LLC + SNAP | 1,508-bytes | | |
|---|---|---|---|
| Mac Header | 24-bytes | | |
| Encryption | None | WEP 8-bytes | TKIP (WPA) 20-bytes |
| Total | 1,532-bytes | 1,540-bytes | 1,552-bytes |

## The Cisco and Orinoco View of Fragmentation

From the Cisco Aironet-1100 AP Manual:

*"The fragmentation threshold determines the size at which packets are fragmented (sent as several pieces instead of as one block). Use a low setting in areas where communication is poor or where there is a great deal of radio interference."*

The vague advice to "**use a low setting**" where communications "**is poor**" or "**there is a great deal of RFI**" just about summarizes the collective wisdom regarding fragmentation.

The following is from the Orinoco AP-600 manual, but *it only applies to APs with 802.11b radios. Orinoco 802.11g capable radios do not support fragmentation*.

*"**Interference Robustness:** Enable this option if other electrical devices in the 2.4 GHz frequency band (such as a microwave oven or a cordless phone) may be interfering with the wireless signal. The AP will automatically fragment large packets into multiple smaller packets when interference is detected to increase the likelihood that the messages will be received in the presence of interference. The receiving radio reassembles the original packet once all fragments have been received. This feature is available only if you are using an Orinoco Classic Gold card. This option is disabled by default."*

That was a more interesting, automated and proprietary approach to enabling fragmentation, it enabled the AP determine the fragmentation threshold and when to enable it.

According to both Cisco and Orinoco the "why" to implement fragmentation is to **compensate for packet corruption due to the presence of RFI.** That's consistent with the IEEE's description of why L2 fragmentation was included in the 802.11 standard. With ERP-OFDM's greater resistant to RFI corruption the need to implement fragmentation is becoming less relevant.

In an environment consisting of a standard mix of authentication, file, print, web, mail and database servers over 70% of the collective WLAN traffic are client requests for server-based resources. **Opening a server-based document produces large data packets which the AP must transmit into the BSA. This consumes significant bandwidth and, in the presence of RFI, results in a greater probability of frame corruption.**

Most service requests, including authentication, employ data frames that are well under any reasonable fragmentation threshold. **A STA transmits large data frames when saving a file, printing a document or a sending email with attachments.**

**LinkFerret Fact:** Since network monitors can't decrypt WPA traffic the Top Senders/Receivers Statistic Windows can't track frames by IP address. In production networks servers are located on different subnets than the wireless network so the Top Sender will always be the MAC address of the default gateway.

## Using Network Statistics to Determine the Fragmentation Threshold

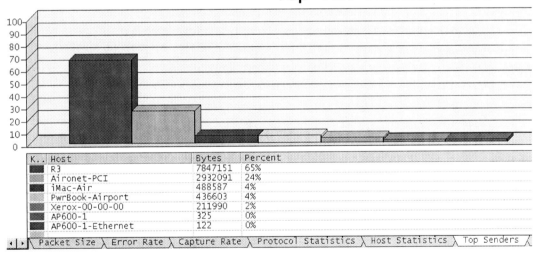

The Top Ten Transmitters statistic is based on the accumulated number of bytes transmitted. Traffic is tracked by the frame's source MAC address. In this example R3, the default gateway, is the source of 65% of the BSA traffic. Frames transmitted by R3 and bound for STAs in the BSS are translated by the AP's bridging function from Ethernet to 802.11 and forwarded out the radio interface. **Regardless of which nodes are most affected by the RFI, the fragmentation threshold is usually configured at the AP first.**

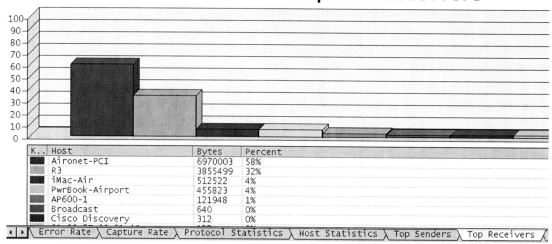

The Top Ten Receivers traffic is tracked by the frame's destination MAC address. In this example Aironet-PCI is the top receiver of BSA traffic receiving 58% of the frames.

***Traffic to R3, the default gateway, is the accumulated traffic destined for servers on remote subnets***. If the BSS employs dynamically keyed encryption (non-WEP), the AP's Ethernet interface must be taped to quantify individual server traffic statistics.

## The Packet Size Distribution Statistic

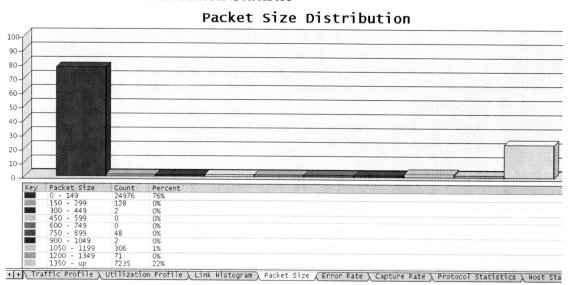

The Packet Size Distribution displays the percentage of frames based on size. The majority of 802.11 frames are small control and management frames. In this capture several file transfers occurred and a large server-based PDF document was opened. ***Although only 22% of the frames were over 1,350 bytes they represent over 97% of the BSA bandwidth consumed.***

# Maximum MPDU with TKIP Encryption

For the following fragmentation calculations assume:

- A noisy RFI environment
- The analysis of corrupted frames versus packet size has concluded that the maximum frame size should be less than 600 bytes.
- The network is using WPA with TKIP encryption.

| Mac Header | 24-bytes |
|---|---|
| 802.2 LLC | 3-bytes |
| SNAP Header | 5-bytes |
| L3 – L7 Payload | 1,500 bytes |
| TKIP | 20-bytes |
| Total | 1,552-bytes |

```
⊟ Physical Frame
    Status              Frame Error [WEP Error]
    Interface Number    0
    Frame Number        1339
    Frame size          1552
    Bytes Captured      1552
    Frame Media Type    IEEE 802.11
    Frame Captured      June 12, 2005  20:18:48:ŧ
    Frame Captured      June 12, 2005  13:18:48:ŧ
    Trace Delta         00:00:07:547:615
    Packet Delta        00:00:00:007:536
    Channel             1
    Speed               0MBS
    Signal              69
    Quality             0
⊟ IEEE 802.11 MAC Protocol (Undecryptable)
    Function            Data
  ⊞ PLCP Header
  ⊞ Frame Control Byte 0
  ⊞ Frame Control Byte 1
  ⊞ WEP Information
    Duration ID         127
  ⊞ Destination Address
  ⊞ BSSID
  ⊞ Source Address
    Fragment            [xxxxxxxx xxxx0000]   0
    Sequence            [00100011 0010xxxx]   562
```

When a TKIP encrypted frame is fragmented, *each fragment has*:

- 24-byte MAC Header
- Data segment with a maximum size of the fragmentation threshold, minus the MAC Header and encryption overhead.
- 20-byte TKIP encryption overhead **(that's not entirely true as revealed at the end of this section.)**

The 802.2 LLC and SNAP headers are appended to the data field - 1,508 bytes divided by 3 fragments is just over 503 bytes. *Considering the MAC Header and TKIP encryption overhead, let's set the AP fragmentation threshold at 550 bytes. This maximizes the efficiently of large server file read operations.*

*File server write operations are addressed by configuring the fragmentation threshold on appropriate STAs.* In the previous example Aironet-PCI was the second biggest transmitter. If Aironet-PCI has a high PER that we suspect is due to RFI corruption, the fragmentation threshold may be set as an attempt to reduce the PER.

The fragmentation threshold setting range is 256 to 2,346 bytes. With WPA encryption, any fragmentation threshold greater than 1,552 bytes effectively disables fragmentation. *For this capture the Aironet-350 AP is configured with a fragmentation threshold of 550 bytes as specified in the previous paragraph.*

| Beacon Period: | 100 | (20-4000 Kusec) |
|---|---|---|
| Max. Data Retries: | 64 | (1-128) |
| Fragmentation Threshold: | 550 | (256-2346) |

## Fragmented Frame Capture Analysis

The main data activity in the capture is Aironet-PCI opening a document stored on the file server D1DC2S2 which resides on same IP subnet. Each data frame in the brief decode window is flagged as Undecryptable because TKIP encryption is employed.

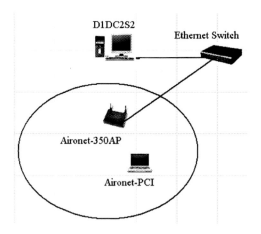

Open the capture file **Fragment-550**, apply the **Fragmented Frames** filter and press **F5**. Press **Ctrl-G** and go to Frame 280.

| Number | Time | Destination | Source | Protocol | Function |
|---|---|---|---|---|---|
| [0-01]-280 | 00:00:27:148:223 | Aironet-PCI | D1DC2S2 | IEEE 802.11 | Data (Undecryptable) |
| [0-01]-281 | 00:00:27:148:352 | Aironet-350AP | | IEEE 802.11 | ACK |
| [0-01]-282 | 00:00:27:148:874 | Aironet-PCI | D1DC2S2 | IEEE 802.11 | Data (Undecryptable) Fragment 1 |
| [0-01]-283 | 00:00:27:148:947 | Aironet-350AP | | IEEE 802.11 | ACK |
| [0-01]-284 | 00:00:27:149:476 | Aironet-PCI | D1DC2S2 | IEEE 802.11 | Data (Undecryptable) Fragment 2 |
| [0-01]-285 | 00:00:27:149:564 | Aironet-350AP | | IEEE 802.11 | ACK |
| [0-01]-286 | 00:00:27:150:291 | Aironet-PCI | D1DC2S2 | IEEE 802.11 | Data (Undecryptable) |

Transmitting a 1,552-byte MPDU with a fragmentation threshold of 550-bytes requires three 802.11 data frame fragments. In the following analysis the frame size of each fragment and the duration values are the key elements in understanding 802.11 fragmentation.

| Number | Time | Destination | Source | Function |
|--------|------|-------------|--------|----------|
| [0-01]-280 | 00:00:27:148:223 | Aironet-PCI | D1DC2S2 | Data (Undecryptable) |

### Frame 280: Data fragment 0

Status: Frame Error [WEP Error] the WEP bit is set, but can't be verified because the TKIP MIC (message integrity check) is encrypted with the MSDU.

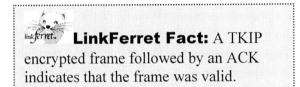 **LinkFerret Fact:** A TKIP encrypted frame followed by an ACK indicates that the frame was valid.

Frame Size: 550 bytes, the fragmentation threshold. This includes the MAC Header, payload and 20 bytes of TKIP encryption fields.

To/From DS = 0,1: The frame is sourced by the DSS, so the AP fragmentation threshold is applied.

More Fragments: Set, more fragments are to follow.

```
⊟ Physical Frame
  ┊ Status                Frame Error [WEP Error]
  ┊ Interface Number      0
  ┊ Frame Number          280
  ┊ Frame size            550
  ┊ Bytes Captured        64
  ┊ Frame Media Type      IEEE 802.11
  ┊ Frame Captured        June  6, 2005  18:17:31:2
  ┊ Frame Captured        June  6, 2005  11:17:31:2
  ┊ Trace Delta           00:00:27:148:223
  ┊ Packet Delta          00:00:00:005:287
  ┊ Channel               1
  ┊ Speed                 0MBS
  ┊ Signal                80
  ┊ Quality               0
⊟ IEEE 802.11 MAC Protocol (Undecryptable)
  ┊ Function              Data
  ⊞ PLCP Header
  ⊞ Frame Control Byte 0
  ⊟ Frame Control Byte 1
    ┊ Order               [0xxxxxxx]  off
    ┊ WEP                 [x1xxxxxx]  on
    ┊ More Data           [xx0xxxxx]  off
    ┊ Power Mgmt          [xxx0xxxx]  off
    ┊ Retry               [xxxx0xxx]  off
    ┊ More Fragments      [xxxxx1xx]  on
    ┊ From DS             [xxxxxx1x]  on
    ┊ To DS               [xxxxxxx0]  off
  ⊞ WEP Information
  ┊ Duration ID           742
  ⊞ Destination Address
  ⊞ BSSID
  ⊞ Source Address
  ┊ Fragment      [xxxxxxxx xxxx0000]   0
  ┊ Sequence      [01101010 1100xxxx]   1708
```

Fragment Number: 0 - the first fragment
Sequence Number: 1708 - all fragments will have this sequence number.

Duration: 742-µs – normally the duration value of a data frame accommodates a SIFS + ACK. *At 11-Mbps with a short PLCP-preamble/header that's 117-µs.* Data fragments are sent in a sequential burst without the transmitting node contending for media access. Because this isn't the last frame, its duration value also protects the next data fragment and its subsequent ACK. The duration value of all but the last data fragment has the general format: **{SIFS + ACK} + {SIFS + Next Fragment} + {SIFS + ACK}**

*If the data fragment isn't ACKed, the EIFS recovery mechanism is implemented and the transmitter must contend for the medium before sending the remaining fragments.*

| Number | Time | Destination | Source | Function |
|--------|------|-------------|--------|----------|
| [0-01]-281 | 00:00:27:148:352 | Aironet-350AP | | ACK |

### Frame 281: ACK for fragment 0

Duration: 626-µs
An ACK usually has a duration value of zero; in this case the ACK must protect fragment 1 and its subsequent ACK:
**{SIFS + Fragment1} + {SIFS + ACK} =**
742-µs - 117-µs = 625-µs

```
⊞ Physical Frame
⊟ IEEE 802.11 MAC Protocol
  ┊ Function              ACK
  ⊞ PLCP Header
  ⊞ Frame Control Byte 0
  ⊞ Frame Control Byte 1
  ┊ Duration ID           626
  ⊞ Receiver Address
```

***Some of our calculations are 1-µs shorter than the captured duration field value. The IEEE states that duration values are always rounded up to the nearest microsecond.***

| Number | Time | Destination | Source | Function |
|--------|------|-------------|--------|----------|
| [0-01]-282 | 00:00:27:148:874 | Aironet-PCI | D1DC2S2 | Data (Undecryptable) Fragment 1 |

## *Frame 282:*
## *Data Fragment 1 (the second fragment)*

Frame Size: 550-bytes, the fragmentation threshold. The first two fragments total 1,100-bytes.

More Fragments: Set, more fragments are to follow.

Fragment Number: 1 - the second fragment
Sequence Number: 1708 – the same as frame 280

Duration: 724-µs protects the ACK, the next (and last) fragment and its subsequent ACK. The last fragment is only 524 bytes, so this duration value is 18-µs shorter than the duration value in fragment 0.

```
⊟ Physical Frame
   ├ Status                Frame Error [WEP Error]
   ├ Interface Number      0
   ├ Frame Number          282
   ├ Frame size            550
   ├ Bytes Captured        64
   ├ Frame Media Type      IEEE 802.11
   ├ Frame Captured        June  6, 2005  18:17:31:23
   ├ Frame Captured        June  6, 2005  11:17:31:23
   ├ Trace Delta           00:00:27:148:874
   ├ Packet Delta          00:00:00:000:522
   ├ Channel               1
   ├ Speed                 0MBS
   ├ Signal                80
   └ Quality               0
⊟ IEEE 802.11 MAC Protocol (Undecryptable)
   ├ Function              Data
   ⊞ PLCP Header
   ⊞ Frame Control Byte 0
   ⊟ Frame Control Byte 1
      ├ Order          [0xxxxxxx]  off
      ├ WEP            [x1xxxxxx]  on
      ├ More Data      [xx0xxxxx]  off
      ├ Power Mgmt     [xxx0xxxx]  off
      ├ Retry          [xxxx0xxx]  off
      ├ More Fragments [xxxxx1xx]  on
      ├ From DS        [xxxxxx1x]  on
      └ To DS          [xxxxxxx0]  off
   ⊞ WEP Information
   ├ Duration ID           724
   ⊞ Destination Address
   ⊞ BSSID
   ⊞ Source Address
   ├ Fragment       [xxxxxxxx xxxx0001]  1
   └ Sequence       [01101010 1100xxxx]  1708
```

## *Frame 283:*
## *ACK for Data Fragment 1*

| Number | Time | Destination | Source | Function |
|--------|------|-------------|--------|----------|
| [0-01]-283 | 00:00:27:148:947 | Aironet-350AP | | ACK |

Duration/ID: 608-µs - virtual carrier for the last fragment and subsequent ACK: **724-µs - 116-µs = 608-µs**

```
⊞ Physical Frame
⊟ IEEE 802.11 MAC Protocol
   ├ Function              ACK
   ⊞ PLCP Header
   ⊞ Frame Control Byte 0
   ⊞ Frame Control Byte 1
   ├ Duration ID           608
   ⊞ Receiver Address
```

| Number | Time | Destination | Source | Function |
|---|---|---|---|---|
| [0-01]-284 | 00:00:27:149:476 | Aironet-PCI | D1DC2S2 | Data (Undecryptable) Fragment 2 |

### *Frame 284:*
### *Data Fragment 2 (the last fragment)*

Frame Size: 524-bytes. Total size of all fragments **550 + 500 + 524 = 1,624 bytes.**

More Fragments: Reset, this is the last fragment.

Fragment Number: 2 - the last fragment
Sequence Number: 1708 – the same as the previous two fragments

Duration: 117-µs, just like a standard data frame. It only needs to protect a SIFS + ACK.

```
⊟ Physical Frame
   ⌐Status               Frame Error [WEP Error]
   ⌐Interface Number     0
   ⌐Frame Number         284
   ⌐Frame size           524
   ⌐Bytes Captured       64
   ⌐Frame Media Type     IEEE 802.11
   ⌐Frame Captured       June  6, 2005  18:17:31:2⊣
   ⌐Frame Captured       June  6, 2005  11:17:31:2⊣
   ⌐Trace Delta          00:00:27:149:476
   ⌐Packet Delta         00:00:00:000:528
   ⌐Channel              1
   ⌐Speed                0MBS
   ⌐Signal               80
   ⌐Quality              0
⊟ IEEE 802.11 MAC Protocol (Undecryptable)
   ⌐Function             Data
   ⊞ PLCP Header
   ⊞ Frame Control Byte 0
   ⊟ Frame Control Byte 1
      ⌐Order         [0xxxxxxx]   off
      ⌐WEP           [x1xxxxxx]   on
      ⌐More Data     [xx0xxxxx]   off
      ⌐Power Mgmt    [xxx0xxxx]   off
      ⌐Retry         [xxxx0xxx]   off
      ⌐More Fragments [xxxxx0xx]  off
      ⌐From DS       [xxxxxx1x]   on
      ⌐To DS         [xxxxxxx0]   off
   ⊞ WEP Information
   ⌐Duration ID          117
   ⊞ Destination Address
   ⊞ BSSID
   ⊞ Source Address
   ⌐Fragment      [xxxxxxxx xxxx0010]   2
   ⌐Sequence      [01101010 1100xxxx]   1708
```

### *Frame 285:*
### *ACK for Data Fragment 2*

| Number | Time | Destination | Source | Function |
|---|---|---|---|---|
| [0-01]-285 | 00:00:27:149:564 | Aironet-350AP | | ACK |

Duration: 0, releasing the virtual carrier for the BSA. STAs waiting to transmit may now enter the back-off timer loop

```
⊞ Physical Frame
⊟ IEEE 802.11 MAC Protocol
   ⌐Function             ACK
   ⊞ PLCP Header
   ⊞ Frame Control Byte 0
   ⊞ Frame Control Byte 1
   ⌐Duration ID          0
   ⊞ Receiver Address
```

## Fragmentation Burst Summary

Fragments are sent in sequential bursts to compensate for reduced data frame fragmentation performance. If a fragment is not ACKed, EIFS error recovery occurs and the transmitter must contend for the medium before transmitting the remaining fragments.

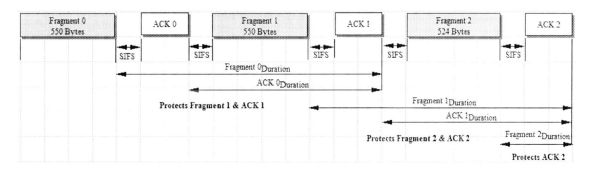

> **Troubleshooting Tip** After implementing fragmentation if the data fragments themselves have a high error rate, then either the fragmentation threshold is set too high or RFI isn't an issue! Create a new network monitor baseline capture and verify the presence of RFI with your spectrum analyzer. Perhaps your original diagnosis was wrong!

## Fragmentation Overhead Wrap-Up

Those of you with eagle eyes may have noticed a slight discrepancy in the total number of bytes contained in the three fragments. We expected:

1,508 bytes (Data + 802.2 LLC + SNAP)
72 bytes of MAC Header (24 x 3)
60 bytes of TKIP support (20 x 3)
**Total 1,640 bytes**

*However, the three data fragments only total 1,624 bytes – we're 16 bytes short*. The explanation is that every TKIP field is not repeated in every fragment. *The MIC (message integrity check) protects the original unfragmented MSDU from modification. It's calculated once and then appended to the payload and encrypted with the 802.2 LLC, SNAP header and Data.* The TKIP IV/KeyID, Extended IV and ICV fields are recalculated and included with every fragment.

| MAC Header | IV/KeyID | Extended IV | 802.2 LLC & Snap | PSDU | MIC | ICV |
|---|---|---|---|---|---|---|
| 24 bytes | 4 bytes | 4 bytes | 8 bytes | 1500 bytes | 8 bytes | 4 bytes |

That means the TKIP overhead is 20 bytes for the first fragment, but only 12 bytes for subsequent fragments. In a three fragment burst that explains the missing 16 bytes!

> *Don't Get Obsessed*: Although useful while learning new concepts, in normal practice we don't calculate every duration value or account for every byte in a capture. However, having the ability to verify suspicious time intervals and dig through captures to reveal unnoticed discrepancies may often be a key in determining the underlying fault.

## *RTS/CTS Medium Reservation Protocol*

You're very familiar with the ERP IE "Use Protection" bit and the CTS-to-Self frame. We now examine the complete RTS/CTS mechanism. *Like 802.11 fragmentation threshold configuration, RTS threshold configuration support has been dropped from most 802.11g client adapter utilities.* However, it is still supported on most APs.

## The "Hidden Node" Scenario

The "hidden node" (a.k.a. "hidden terminal") issue appears on every wireless certification exam. Most networks have some level of hidden node corruption, but it typically only affects the throughput of a few STAs. Only in extreme cases does hidden node corruption significantly impact the entire BSA. Consider the following scenario:

1. STA-D is located in a office with a wall separating it from the rest of the BSS
2. The RSSI on STA-D is marginal
3. Common sense suggests a simple solution, move the AP closer to the wall.
4. After repositioning the AP every STA can reliably communicate with the AP and access network resources.

## Problem solved, right?

It may seem counter-intuitive, but the ability to access resources on the internal network from every STA doesn't mean that all is well because it doesn't consider performance issues. ***At the beginning of the book***

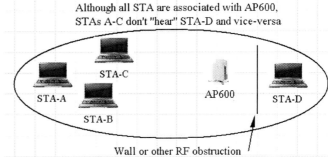

Although all STA are associated with AP600, STAs A-C don't "hear" STA-D and vice-versa

Wall or other RF obstruction

***we established that CSMA/CA functionality depends on *every* STA reliably receiving *every* transmission in the BSA.***

When STAs don't receive all transmissions the BSA:
- **Worst Case**: both physical sense and virtual carrier fails. STA-D doesn't detect the carrier from STAs A-C. Both physical carrier and virtual carrier (NAV timer) fail. STA-D will simultaneously transmit with STAs A-C and the AP receives corrupted frames.
- **Moderate Case:** physical CS functions, but virtual carrier fails. STA-D detects the carrier from STAs A-D, but the signal-to-noise ratio is so low that every frame is corrupted and STA-D doesn't properly set its NAV timer and spending a great deal of time in EIFS error recovery mode as described in Chapter 2.

The converse is also true for STAs A-C not responding to transmissions from STA-D. STA-D transmits regardless of the state of STAs A-C and STAs A-C transmit regardless of the state of STA-D. All things equal including antenna gain/orientation and receiver sensitivity, ***hidden node is a relative condition that usually exists between two or more STAs!***

## Hidden Node Reality Check

As long as a particular STA's transmissions are received by every other STA in the BSA, that node's throughput won't be directly affected by the hidden issue. However, if several hidden nodes are simultaneously transmitting, the collisions and subsequent retransmissions increase the overall BSA load factor and all nodes spend more time in EIFS error recovery mode and have to defer longer before transmitting.

The reduction of a BSA's throughput is directly proportional to the number of simultaneous transmissions generated by STAs that do not "hear" each other. It's only a statistical probability that hidden nodes will simultaneously transmit. All moderate to large BSAs have hidden nodes, it's the nature of the beast. The common components of offices produce hidden nodes, but typically they only represent a small percentage of STAs and produce minimal impact on the aggregate BSA throughput.

**Troubleshooting Tip:** Don't troubleshoot non-existent problems! Only go hidden node hunting when a STA's PER increases and periodic baseline *captures show chronic retries transmitted by distant or physically obscured STAs within a short time interval*.

## Verifying the Hidden Node Issue

*In the example on the previous page the definitive question is, "does STA-D receive the transmissions from STAs A-C?"* Assume that STA-D and the network monitor notebook computer have comparable antennas and receiver sensitivity.

1. Start a continuous ping between the most distant STA (STA-A in this case) and the AP
2. Place the network monitor in the office near STA-D
3. Configure the appropriate channel, start the capture
4. *A hidden node condition exists if you receive Echo Responses from the AP, but not Echo Requests from STA-A*.
5. If you receive Echo Responses from the AP and several corrupted frames instead of Echo Request frames, the carrier is being sensed but the RSSI is low.

Let's examine a hidden node scenario that could disastrously impact the BSA throughput.
- Running a baseline capture with LinkFerret you determine that the PER is above 25%.
- Your 2.4-GHz spectrum analyzer doesn't detect any RFI.
- You're aware of a potential hidden node issue because the AP is not in the center of the BSA and a wall (or any RF barrier) separates the two main groups of STAs.

**Facts**:
- All STAs successfully associate with AP600.
- STAs A-E receive each other's transmissions.
- STAs F-H receive each other's transmissions.

Are hidden nodes and the subsequent failure of virtual and/or physical carrier the cause of the PER?

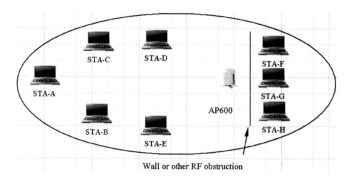

Wall or other RF obstruction

Let's assume that all of the client adapters have the same types of antennas, receiver sensitivity and transmit power. Place the network monitor in the room with STAs F-H and perform the Echo Request test starting with STA-A which is the furthest node from AP600. If the network monitor captures Echo Requests, then hidden node is not an issue.

Here are the results:

| Execute Echo Request | Receive with Network Monitor | Hidden Node? |
|---|---|---|
| STA-A | No | Yes |
| STA-B | Yes | No |
| STA-C | No | Yes |
| STA-D | Yes | No |
| STA-E | Yes | No |

***STAs A & C don't receive the transmissions of STAs F, G & H and vice-versa.***

## Solving (i.e. fixing) Hidden Node

STAs inability to receive all transmissions in the BSS is the issue, *moving the AP has no affect on hidden node, but it might impact the ability of some STAs to associate with the BSS!* Solutions to the hidden node issue illustrated in the example are:
- Tear down the wall (or at least punch some big holes in it.)
- Create another BSS on a non-overlapping channel. If the STAs don't share the same BSA, they don't have to (nor will they) receive each other's transmissions.

## Compensating for Hidden Node – RTS/CTS Medium Reservation

It's always best to fix a problem, but sometimes that's not practical or within budget. *RTS/CTS medium reservation compensates for hidden node at the price of additional overhead.* That sounds a lot like the fragmentation issues that we just examined. *If the throughput gained is greater than the RTS/CTS overhead then the effort is a success.*

As the Fragmentation and RTS Threshold Configuration table on page 183 illustrated, RTS threshold configuration is not supported on many new 802.11g client adapters. To the best of my knowledge Apple AirPort cards have never supported 802.11 fragmentation or RTS threshold configuration. As illustrated in this graphic the BroadCom mini-PCI and several others still support fragmentation and RTS threshold configuration which is accessed in the advanced tab of the adapter's properties.

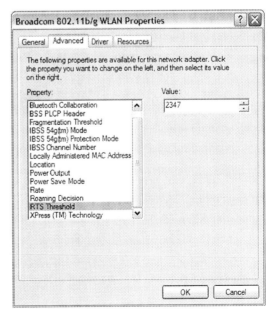

## CTS-to-Self Doesn't Address Hidden Node

A STA transmits a CTS-to-Self frame with HR/DSSS modulation to reserve the medium for the length of time specified in the duration field. ***This doesn't address the hidden node issue, because, by definition, hidden nodes don't receive the CTS-to-Self transmission.***

## RTS/CTS and Hidden Node

In order to associate with an AP a STA must be able to reliability receive transmissions from the AP. ***The one property that all members of a BSS have in common is their ability to receive transmissions from the AP***. If a hidden node could simply ask the AP to send a CTS frame with the appropriate duration value, then the entire BSS is guaranteed to receive the CTS frame and set their NAV timers. ***RTS/CTS compensates for both the physical and virtual carrier sense failure of hidden nodes***.

For the sake of the following example assume that the frame sequence:
**{SIFS + CTS} + {SIFS + Data frame} + {SIFS + ACK}** requires 626-μs.

***The RTS/CTS, data frame and subsequent ACK process is called a four-way handshake.***

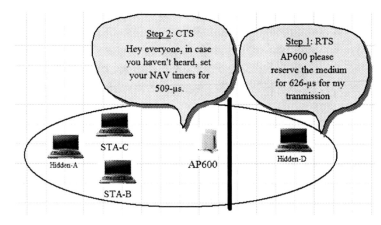

1. Hidden-D transmits a RTS frame to AP600 with a duration value of 626-μs. ***All the STAs except Hidden-A receive the RTS frame and set their NAV timers.***
2. AP600 responds with a CTS frame with a duration value of 626-μs - 117-μs or 509-μs. ***The STAs that didn't receive transmissions from Hidden-D (Hidden-A in this example) receive the CTS frame and set their NAV timers.*** Now every STA in the BSA is counting down the same medium reservation value, a duration that protects one data frame and subsequent ACK.
3. After receiving the CTS, Hidden-D transmits a data frame
4. After receiving the data frame, the AP transmits an ACK with a duration value of 0 and virtual carrier releases the medium is for contention.

> **Technical Point:** A STA sets its NAV timer to the duration field value in the last valid received frame only if the duration value in that frame is greater than the current value of the STA's NAV timer. STAs that receive both the RTS and CTS frames first set their NAV timer to the RTS duration value, and then to the CTS duration value. ***Hidden nodes don't receive the RTS frame. They set their NAV timers to the value of the duration field in the CTS frame***. Nonetheless, at that point all nodes in the BSA are counting down the same virtual carrier value in their NAV timers.

# RTS Threshold Configuration

The fragmentation threshold is configured with the idea that larger frames are more likely to be corrupted by RFI and retransmissions of large frames consume more bandwidth. It's calculated at a value that represented a trade-off between the fragmentation overhead and increased BSA bandwidth that results from a reduction in the PER.

The RTS threshold is set in a similar manner. *Instead of compensating for RFI, RTS threshold reduces the collisions that would occur when multiple hidden nodes simultaneously transmit.* What factors are used to set the RTS threshold to reduce hidden node collisions?

- How many nodes are hidden? The possibility of collisions is proportional to the number of hidden nodes.
- What is the transmit bit rate of the hidden nodes? Slower bit rates take longer transmission times, which increase the probability of collisions.
- How much traffic is each hidden node transmitting?
- The current phase of the moon
- And of course, the big one, *what's the average size packet corrupted because of hidden node collisions?*

Luckily, like the fragmentation issue, network monitor capture statistics can help you gather the information required to confront those vague and perplexing questions.

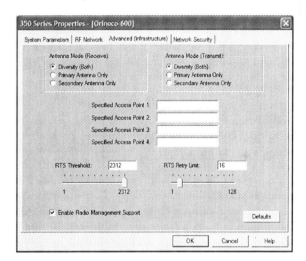

## *Cisco 350 (802.11b) RTS Threshold Configuration*

**RTS Threshold**: When the MPDU size exceeds the RTS Threshold the data frame transmission is preceded with a RTS medium reservation request and only transmitted after the reception of a CTS frame.

**RTS Retry Limit**: The number of times a RTS frame is retransmitted without the reception of CTS before the operation is terminated.

## *RTS/CTS Capture File Configuration*

AirLink is configured for a RTS threshold of 500 bytes. In the capture AirLink saves a large graphics file to server D1DC2S2 in the Ethernet network. Every AirLink MPDU that exceeds 500 bytes is preceded by a RTS frame. A CTS frame must be received from Aironet-350AP before transmitting the data frame.

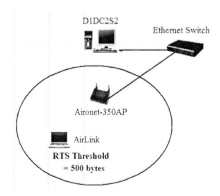

## RTS/CTS Capture Analysis

Open capture file AirLink-RTS-CTS.500, apply the RTS-CTS filter and press **F5**. You'll see 19 pairs of RTS/CTS frames. *The fact that the RTS/CTS frames are nicely paired is a good sign. However since each frame is only 20 and 14 bytes respectively, the odds of them being corrupted is very small.* Nonetheless, it's a good exercise to ensure that each RTS has a timely CTS response. Remove the filter by applying **No Filter** and press **F5**. Use **Ctrl-G** and go to frame 178, the first RTS frame.

| Number | Time | Destination | Source | Protocol | Function |
|---|---|---|---|---|---|
| [0-01]-178 | 00:00:04:812:086 | Aironet-350AP | AirLink | IEEE 802.11 | RTS |
| [0-01]-179 | 00:00:04:812:240 | AirLink | | IEEE 802.11 | CTS |
| [0-01]-180 | 00:00:04:813:691 | D1DC2S2 | AirLink | SMB | Write and X Request |
| [0-01]-181 | 00:00:04:813:695 | AirLink | | IEEE 802.11 | ACK |
| [0-01]-182 | 00:00:04:813:905 | Aironet-350AP | AirLink | IEEE 802.11 | RTS |
| [0-01]-183 | 00:00:04:814:039 | AirLink | | IEEE 802.11 | CTS |
| [0-01]-184 | 00:00:04:815:298 | D1DC2S2 | AirLink | NBSS | Session Message |
| [0-01]-185 | 00:00:04:815:301 | AirLink | | IEEE 802.11 | ACK |
| [0-01]-186 | 00:00:04:815:540 | Aironet-350AP | AirLink | IEEE 802.11 | RTS |
| [0-01]-187 | 00:00:04:815:684 | AirLink | | IEEE 802.11 | CTS |
| [0-01]-188 | 00:00:04:816:939 | D1DC2S2 | AirLink | NBSS | Data |
| [0-01]-189 | 00:00:04:816:941 | AirLink | | IEEE 802.11 | ACK |

### *Frame 178: Step 1: RTS*

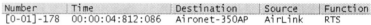

| Number | Time | Destination | Source | Function |
|---|---|---|---|---|
| [0-01]-178 | 00:00:04:812:086 | Aironet-350AP | AirLink | RTS |

To/From DS = 0,0 RTS is a control frame and control frames aren't processed by the DSS.

Duration = 1,458-μs. This is the duration to complete the remaining three frames of the four-way handshake.

**{SIFS + CTS} +**
**{SIFS + Data Frame} +**
**{SIFS + ACK}**

**Addresses:**
Receiver: Aironet-350AP, RTS frames are addressed to the BSSID.
Transmitter: AirLink. AirLink is configured with a 500 byte RTS threshold.

```
⊞ Physical Frame
⊟ IEEE 802.11 MAC Protocol
   ─Function              RTS
   ⊞ PLCP Header
   ⊟ Frame Control Byte 0
      ─Protocol Level    [xxxxxx00]  0
      ─Type              [xxxx01xx]  Control
      ─Sub-Type          [1011xxxx]  RTS
   ⊟ Frame Control Byte 1
      ─Order             [0xxxxxxx]  off
      ─WEP               [x0xxxxxx]  off
      ─More Data         [xx0xxxxx]  off
      ─Power Mgmt        [xxx0xxxx]  off
      ─Retry             [xxxx0xxx]  off
      ─More Fragments    [xxxxx0xx]  off
      ─From DS           [xxxxxx0x]  off
      ─To DS             [xxxxxxx0]  off
   ─Duration ID          1458
   ⊟ Receiver Address
      ─Hex Address       00-09-B7-7E-E9-AA
      ─Group Bit         [xxxxxxx0 xxxxxxxx x
      ─Local Bit         [xxxxx0x xxxxxxxx x
      ─Logical Names     [[Aironet-350AP]]
      ─Vendor Name       Cisco Systems
   ⊟ Transmitter Address
      ─Hex Address       00-0D-88-E5-D3-2A
      ─Group Bit         [xxxxxxx0 xxxxxxxx x
      ─Local Bit         [xxxxx0x xxxxxxxx x
      ─Logical Names     [[AirLink]]
      ─Vendor Name       D-link
```

### Frame 179: Step2: CTS

This is AirLink's acknowledgement that the AP received the RTS and has reserved the medium for the data transmissin and subsequent ACK.

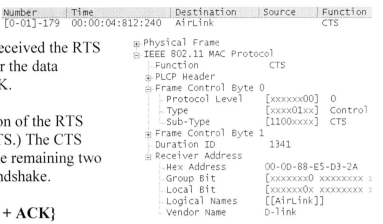

Duration = 1,341-µs, the duration of the RTS frame minus 117-µs (SIFS + CTS.) The CTS frame duration value protects the remaining two components of the four-way handshake.

**{SIFS + Data Frame} + {SIFS + ACK}**

All STAs, including hidden nodes, set their NAV timers to the value of 1,341-µs.

If the CTS frame isn't received within the CTS Timeout interval, AirLink re-contends for transmit access and retransmits the RTS frame as specified by the RTS Retry Limit value. *Unlike a missing ACK, a missing CTS frame doesn't cause the BSA to enter EIFS recovery mode.*

```
Number      | Time              | Destination | Source  | Function
[0-01]-180  00:00:00:001:451    D1DC2S2       AirLink   Write and X Request
```

### Frame 180: Step 3: Data

After receiving the CTS, AirLink may transmit the data frame.

Frame Size: 1,532 bytes exceeds the 500 byte CTS threshold configured on AirLink.

Duration: 117-µs, the time required to protect the subsequent ACK:
**{SIFS + ACK}**

```
⊟ Physical Frame
   ─Status                No Errors
   ─Interface Number      0
   ─Frame Number          180
   ─Frame size            1532
   ─Bytes Captured        1532
   ─Frame Media Type      IEEE 802.11
   ─Frame Captured        June 10, 2005  15:42:21:54
   ─Frame Captured        June 10, 2005  08:42:21:54
   ─Trace Delta           00:00:04:813:691
   ─Packet Delta          00:00:00:001:451
   ─Channel               1
   ─Speed                 0MBS
   ─Signal                83
   ─Quality               0
⊟ IEEE 802.11 MAC Protocol
   ─Function              Data
   ⊞ PLCP Header
   ⊞ Frame Control Byte 0
   ⊞ Frame Control Byte 1
   ─Duration ID           117
   ⊞ BSSID
   ⊞ Source Address
   ⊞ Destination Address
   ─Fragment              [xxxxxxxx xxxx0000]   0
   ─Sequence              [10111101 1001xxxx]   3033
⊞ IEEE 802.2 Logical Link Control
⊞ IEEE Sub-Network Access Protocol
⊞ Internet Protocol
⊞ Transmission Control Protocol
⊞ NetBios Session Service Protocol
⊞ Server Message Block Protocol
```

### *Frame 181: Step 4: ACK*

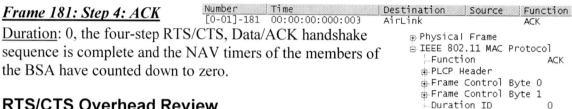

Duration: 0, the four-step RTS/CTS, Data/ACK handshake sequence is complete and the NAV timers of the members of the BSA have counted down to zero.

## RTS/CTS Overhead Review

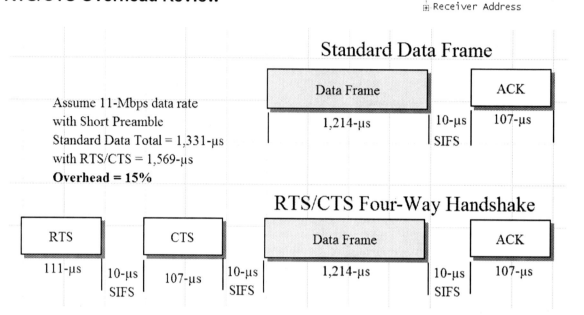

Exceeding the RTS threshold adds an overhead of {RTS + SIFS} + {CTS + SIFS} transmitted at the STA's current PHY layer and bit rate. In the previous example AirLink was using a short preamble and a bit rate of 11-Mbps. *The RTS/CTS overhead of 15% was calculated with a data frame of 1,532 bytes. As the size of the data fame goes down, the relative overhead goes up. Using the same parameters a data frame of 500 bytes has a 31% RTS/CTS overhead – that's double the overhead!* Setting too low of a fragmentation threshold will dramatically reduce the throughput of the specific node and also put a larger load on the overall BSA bandwidth.

---

**Troubleshooting Tip** Low basic rates enable a STA to reduce transmission speed in response to packet errors. If RFI or hidden node is an issue, lowering the bit rate requires longer transmission times and results in more corruption! *Keep your basic rates high and limit the size of your BSAs!*

---

**! Exam Alert 1**: Associate 802.11 frame fragmentation with large frames and RFI corruption and RTS/CTS with frame corruption due to hidden nodes.

---

**! Exam Alert 2**: A RTS frame is transmitted when a MPDU exceeds the transmitter's configured RTS threshold. A CTS frame is transmitted as a response to receiving a RTS frame.

---

## Network Monitor Timestamps

It's useful to have a captured frame time reference. LinkFerret Preferences provides four timestamp formats:

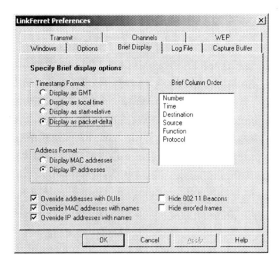

1. **GMT**: Regional independent timestamp
2. **Local time**: For performance baselines, it's important to know when peak loads occur. Also used for troubleshooting transient conditions. If you know when an anomalous event occurs, you have a better chance of determining its origin.
3. **Start-Relative**: the clock starts ticking when the capture starts.
4. *Packet-Delta*: the time interval between the reception of the preceding packet and the current packet. Unfortunately, the accuracy of this time is not consistent. According to the LinkFerret developers:

> ***"The timestamp is applied by the driver relatively early in the processing, however the driver doesn't see the packet until it has been completely captured and stored in system memory"***

| Number | Time | Destination | Source | Function |
|---|---|---|---|---|
| [0-01]-178 | 00:00:00:013:476 | Aironet-350AP | AirLink | RTS |
| [0-01]-179 | 00:00:00:000:153 | AirLink | | CTS |
| [0-01]-180 | 00:00:00:001:451 | D1DC2S2 | AirLink | Write and X Request |
| [0-01]-181 | 00:00:00:000:003 | AirLink | | ACK |
| [0-01]-182 | 00:00:00:000:210 | Aironet-350AP | AirLink | RTS |
| [0-01]-183 | 00:00:00:000:134 | AirLink | | CTS |
| [0-01]-184 | 00:00:00:001:259 | D1DC2S2 | AirLink | Session Message |
| [0-01]-185 | 00:00:00:000:003 | AirLink | | ACK |
| [0-01]-186 | 00:00:00:000:238 | Aironet-350AP | AirLink | RTS |
| [0-01]-187 | 00:00:00:000:144 | AirLink | | CTS |
| [0-01]-188 | 00:00:00:001:254 | D1DC2S2 | AirLink | Data |
| [0-01]-189 | 00:00:00:000:002 | AirLink | | ACK |
| [0-01]-190 | 00:00:00:000:234 | Aironet-350AP | AirLink | RTS |
| [0-01]-191 | 00:00:00:000:129 | AirLink | | CTS |
| [0-01]-192 | 00:00:00:001:263 | D1DC2S2 | AirLink | Session Message |
| [0-01]-193 | 00:00:00:000:003 | AirLink | | ACK |
| [0-01]-194 | 00:00:00:000:241 | Aironet-350AP | AirLink | RTS |
| [0-01]-195 | 00:00:00:000:127 | AirLink | | CTS |
| [0-01]-196 | 00:00:00:001:258 | D1DC2S2 | AirLink | Data |
| [0-01]-197 | 00:00:00:000:002 | AirLink | | ACK |
| [0-01]-198 | 00:00:00:000:587 | Aironet-350AP | AirLink | RTS |
| [0-01]-199 | 00:00:00:000:155 | AirLink | | CTS |
| [0-01]-200 | 00:00:00:001:392 | D1DC2S2 | AirLink | Data |
| [0-01]-201 | 00:00:00:000:002 | AirLink | | ACK |

The duration field value of every CTS frame in the capture is 1,341-µs and the subsequent data frame has 1,532 bytes. One would assume that the packet-delta time would be the same because every frame consists of a SIFS + 1,532 byte MPDU.

The recorded packet deltas of the data frames are 1,451-, 1,259-, 1,254-, 1,263-, 1,258- and 1,392-µs. The combined latency of the driver, client adapter and system memory contribute to this issue. For example, the latency of writing the packet to memory varies according to the number of bytes captured, which is configurable from 64 bytes to the entire frame.

Packet-delta times are extremely useful and revealing, but they aren't consistent or exact – don't use them for performing precise calculations.

## RTS/CTS Other Issues

### TMT (Too Much Traffic)

Consider a BSS that has TMT. In the absence of hidden nodes, all STA are receiving every frame's duration value and properly setting their NAV timers. When a shortage of bandwidth is the issue RTS/CTS doesn't increase throughput because the collisions and low throughput are a function of the exponentially increasing CW of the back-off timer and the EIF recovery mode periods. In fact, the overhead of RTS/CTS only adds fuel to the fire. The only solution is adding bandwidth with faster APs and STAs, or load balancing across multiple BSSs on non-overlapping BSAs.

## STA on an Overlapped BSA

Thought experiments are useful, they force us to probe the depth of our understanding. In light of the new generation of client adapters one has to ask the obvious question, ***"Why is RTS/CTS supported on most new APs, but not new client adapters?"*** So far we've established that the only issue addressed by RTS/CTS is hidden-node. So why is the RTS threshold configurable on an AP when, by definition, an AP can't be a hidden node?

Consider two overlapped BSAs with the APs configured on the same channel. Regardless of which BSS STA-A is associated with, it receives transmissions from both BSAs. All things are equal, STA-A only half of the normal bandwidth because it senses physical and virtual carrier from both BSSs and receives all traffic from both overlapped BSAs. It may be a great location for a network monitor, but the user at STA-A might not be satisfied with the network response.

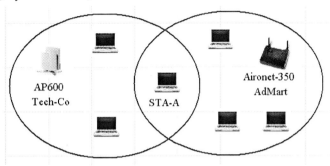

## Overlapped APs

Consider two organizations that are located in physically adjacent office suites. Each has an AP configured on the same or overlapping channel. Assume that both APs have omni-directional antennas and are configured for the maximum transmit power of 100-mW.

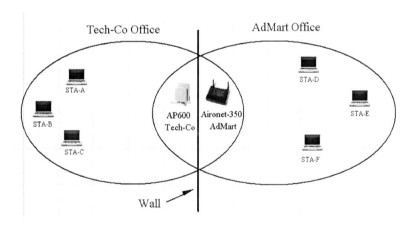

- STAs A-C are associated with AP600 and the Tech-Co BSS.
- STAs D-F are associated with Aironet-350 and the AdMart BSS.

All of the STAs receive physical carrier sense and set their NAV timers on transmissions from:

- Other STAs in the same BSS
- The AP to which they are associated
- The AP to which they are not associated

The last point deserves clarification. Since both APs reside in both BSAs, STAs in both BSSs receives transmissions from both APs and set their NAV timers. The same is true for physical carrier. In this sense the APs are also sharing the BSA bandwidth because each AP sets its NAV timer based on the other AP's transmissions. The throughput in both BSSs is probably marginal because each BSS only has a subset of the bandwidth of the BSA.

What would happen if RTS/CTS were configured on all of the STAs in both BSS? Talk about compounding a disaster! *If every STA sent a RTS for every large data frame, the AP's CTS response would cause every STA in both BSAs set their NAV timers, consuming the entire bandwidth of both BSAs!*

Obviously this isn't a valid application of RTS/CTS!

## Overlapped STAs and RTS/CTS

In desperation to determine why RTS threshold would ever be configured on an AP, let's consider another scenario.

- The APs are configured on the same channel
- They are located on opposite sides of the BSAs
- STAs B-C and E-F receive transmissions from both APs.
- When the APs simultaneously transmit, the RF energy collides in the overlapped portion of the BSAs, corrupting the data.

*Configuring RTS at a reasonable threshold on both APs helps compensate for the overlap.*

- When AP600 sends a frame larger than the RTS threshold, it precedes the transmission with a RTS. All STAs in the BSA, including STAs E-F set their NAV timers.
- The same is true from when Aironet-350 sends a frame larger than the RTS threshold.
- When the destination STA is B-C or E-F the responding CTS is received by all STAs in both BSAs.

This is an incomplete solution because:
- RTS/CTS transmissions between AP600 and STA-A do not set the NAV timers for STA-D or Aironet-350 and their transmission may corrupt the signal in the overlapped portion of the BSAs.
- And the same is true of transmissions between Aironet-350 and STA-D

**Troubleshooting Tip** One of the functions of a formal site survey performed prior to the installation of a WLAN is to establish the BSA's physical boundaries. By nature WLANs support chaotic and physically dynamic environments. The results of the original site survey often have little resemblance to current operating conditions. It's very important that you know the characteristics of your client adapters: antenna location, directionality and gain, receiver sensitivity and transmit power. If frames from multiple BSSs (on the same or adjacent channels) occur in the same capture, you have discovered an overlapped BSA.

Do overlapped BSAs always indicate an area of significant corruption and performance degradation? Absolutely not! In fact, some AP functionality such as WDS (wireless distribution system) that use a single radio interface require that APs are configured on the same channel in 20% overlapped BSAs. *Know where your BSAs overlap, they are definitely "areas of interest."*

I've co-located two APs on the same shelf, configured on the same channel for 20-mW transmit power with six STAs associated to each AP and the throughput was only minimally degraded. On the other hand, the new generation of multi-channel bonding "bad neighbor" APs based on "Super-G" technology are gluttonous monsters that devour hideous amounts of bandwidth and destroy the BSA for all other APs on every ISM channels. See the BroadCom document #204120 for the gruesome details.

Short of putting up RF absorbing panels or building a chicken-wire fence, there are two simple ways to address the issue of overlapped BSAs:

- Eliminate them by reconfiguring one of the APs to a less-overlapping channel
- Physically move STAs out of the overlapped areas

If this isn't possible and both organizations agree, the cell size can be reduced by:

- Reducing the transmit power on both APs. If the transmissions of the STAs continue to overlap, the NAV timers and physical CCA will be partially affective in reducing collisions.
- Reposition the antennas on the APs or use low-gain or semi-directional antennas.
- Reduce the transmit power on the STAs so that the AP can reliably receive the STA's transmissions, but STAs in the other BSS can't.

Once again, the network monitor is the go-to tool to perform these tests and adjustments.

# Chapter 6 Review

## Performance Overhead Issues

Regardless of the frame type (management, control or data) every 802.11 frame a PLCP-Preamble/Header and 32-bit FCS. The following must be considered to calculate the length of time required to transmit the frame:

- What are the current bit rates supported between the STA and AP?
  - o Frames such as Beacon and CTS that must be received by every member of the BSS are transmitted at the highest basic rate supported by all of the STAs.
  - o Other frames are transmitted at the highest rate supported between the AP and STA. This rate is automatically shifted depending on the current conditions and frame error rate.
- Which PLCP Preamble/Header is currently in use:
  - o Long Preamble DSS
  - o Short Preamble DSS
  - o ERP native preamble
- In a native 802.11g BSS which slot time is in use:
  - o Standard slots time (20-µs)
  - o Short slot time (9-µs)
- Note:
  - o SIFS is always 10-µs
  - o FCS is 4-bytes

## Theoretical maximum 802.11 MSDU

Unencrypted maximum MSDU is 2,305 bytes, which includes 802.2 LLC and SNAP Headers, and upper-layer payload.

## Practical Maximum 802.11 MSDU Breakdown:

802.11 MAC Header
- Frame Control: 2 bytes
- Duration/ID: 2 bytes
- 3 Addresses: 18 bytes
- Fragment/Sequence: 2 bytes
- Total: 24-bytes

MSDU (Payload)
- 1,532 – 24 = 1,508 bytes

802.2 LLC/SNAP Overhead
- 802.2 LLC header: 3 bytes
- SNAP Header: 5 bytes

MSDU, upper-layer payload = 1,508 – 8 = 1,500 bytes, the same as Ethernet!

## Encrypted Frame Overhead and Maximum MPDU Size

| | | | |
|---|---|---|---|
| Payload + 802.2 LLC + SNAP | 1,508-bytes | | |
| Mac Header | 24-bytes | | |
| Encryption | None | WEP 8-bytes | TKIP (WPA) 20-bytes |
| Total | 1,532-bytes | 1,540-bytes | 1,552-bytes |

The encryption fields are removed before the 802.11 frame is processed by the distribution system. Therefore, the encryption overhead is never passed onto the Ethernet network. So the Ethernet MSDU size of 1,500 bytes is maintained.

## IP Fragmentation

- Data-link layer technology independent, occurs at layer-3
- Ensures that the IP datagram doesn't exceed the data-link layer's MTU
- Not configurable, a function of the Ethernet MTU
- Upper-layer protocol headers are duplicated in each frame

## Frame Errors result from many factors:

- What is the BSS Mode: 802.11b, 802.11g or mixed mode?
- Is CTS-to-Self protection implemented?
- What are the BSS Basic Rates? Lower rates accommodate greater distances, but result in higher error rates: lower bit rates require greater transmission times and are more likely to be corrupted by RFI or hidden node transmissions.
- Does the BSA cell size and shape accommodate the supported STAs?
- What are the transmit power settings on the AP and STAs?
- Does an AP with an omni-directional antenna reside in the middle of the STAs?
- Does the main lobe of an AP with a semi-directional antenna cover all STAs?
- Is multipath an issue? Are there physical obstacles or RF reflective surfaces in the cell? If so, do the STA's client adapters support antenna diversity?
- What the ratio is of fixed to mobile STAs? Error rates in an ESS that supports roaming are a function of how well the BSA coverage areas overlap.
- Antenna issues are the most common reason that individual STAs may experience high error rates: PC-Card Stubs, built-in notebook antennas, PCI 2.2-dBi rubber duckies obscured at the back of the system unit on the floor and behind a metal desk?

## TMT (too much traffic)

High BSA bandwidth utilization errors (TMT) are addressed by:
- Use the bandwidth more efficiently
  - Define high basic rates - many frames such as beacons and CTS-to-Self are transmitted at the lowest basic rates.
  - Upgrade all STAs to 802.11g – only support short preamble and short slot times!
- Create more bandwidth:

   o Creating more BSAs with load balanced, co-located APs on non-overlapping channels

## Detecting and Quantifying RFI

- Employ a 2.4-GHz receiver/spectrum analyzer to detect and measure RFI
- Don't guess whether RFI is an issue:
   o measure it
   o isolate it
   o remove it or
   o compensate for it by setting the fragmentation thresholds

## Multipath Corruption

- Offices are jammed with RF reflective objects that provide multiple paths for RF energy to propagate to a receiver.
- When multiple, out-of-phase signals are received, the signal quality is degraded and packet corruption may occur.
   o it is usually impractical to remove all of the causes of multipath
- Compensate for multipath:
   o Antenna diversity (standard test question)
   o Upgrade to 802.11g
      ▪ ERP-OFDM is more resistant to multipath than DSSS

## 802.11 Frame Fragmentation Review

- Noisy RFI environment have high errors rates
   o Fragmentation addresses the issue of frame corruption due to RFI!
   o Large frames are corrupted at a higher rates
   o Retransmission consumes significant bandwidth and is more likely to result in additional corruption.
- Rational:
   o If large frames are fragmented, there will be less packet corruption and retransmissions will consume less bandwidth.
- Overhead:
   o Each additional fragmentation requires a duplicate
      ▪ **SIFS + PLCP-Preamble + PLCP-Header + MAC Header + FCS**
- Evaluation:
   o If the bandwidth saved by reducing the number of retransmissions is greater than the bandwidth consumed by fragmentation overhead then BSA throughput is increased.
- Fragmentation Support:
   o Many new 802.11g APs don't support fragmentation
   o Fragmentation configuration has been omitted from most 802.11g client adapter utilities.
- Fragment Threshold Configuration
   o Frame is fragmented when the MPDU size > fragment threshold
   o Fragmentation range: 256 to 2,346 bytes

- 2,346 bytes is the default
  - threshold greater than 1,532 effectively disables fragmentation of clear text
  - Configured in a STA's:
    - Utility program
    - Driver Properties, Advanced tab
- Consider fragmentation as a solution if:
  - 2.4-GHz spectrum analyzer/receiver reveals significant RFI
  - Network Monitor Packet Error Rate is greater than 20%
- Network Monitor Statistics used to determine how/where to configuration fragmentation threshold
  - Top Ten Receivers
  - Top Ten Transmitters
  - Packet Size Distribution

## Fragment Bursting and Duration values

- All fragments of a data frame are sent in a continuous burst
  - If an acknowledgement is not received for a data fragment, the transmitter must re-contend for the medium before transmitting a retry frame
- In all but the last data fragment burst, the duration value is the same as a RTS frame: SIFS + ACK + SIFS + Next Data Fragment
  - This ensures that all fragments are transmitted in a continuous burst without observing CSMA/CA access control
  - The final data fragment has a standard duration value: SIFS + ACK
  - Unlike a normal ACK which has a duration value of zero, in all but the last ACK in a fragment burst performs like a CTS frame
  - provides virtual carrier for the next data fragment
  - $ACK_{Duration} = Frag0_{Duration} - (SIFS + ACK) = SIFS + Frag1_{Duration}$

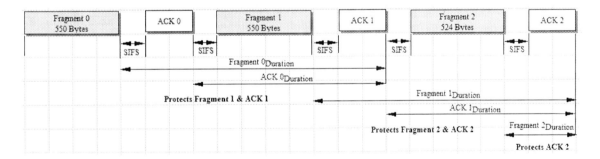

## Sequence/Fragmentation Field Summary

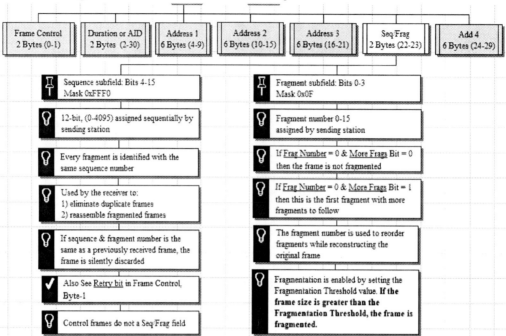

## Hidden Node (Hidden Terminal) Issues

### CSMA/CA is predicated on all nodes reliably receiving all transmissions in the BSA

- All associated STAs reliably receive transmissions from the AP
- STA-D and STAs A-C do not receive each other's transmissions!
- From STAs A-C's perspective, STA-D is a "hidden terminal" or "hidden node"
- The complement is also true, from STA-A's perspective STAs A-C are hidden nodes!

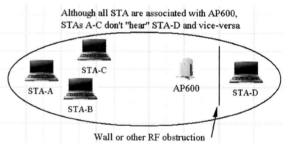

### Hidden Nodes affect on the BSA

- <u>Worst Case</u> - Physical and Virtual carrier both fail!
- <u>Moderate Case</u> - Virtual carrier fails and NAV timers are not set

### Verifying Hidden Node

- Place the network monitor near STA-D
- From STA-A ping the AP
- A hidden node condition exists if:
    - o STA-A Echo Requests from are <u>not captured</u>
    - o Capturing Echo Responses from

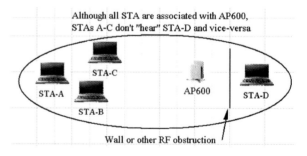

the AP and intertwined with corrupted frames instead of Echo Request frames, the carrier is being sensed but the RSSI is low which indicates the moderate hidden node condition.

## Fixing Hidden Node

- Remember: Moving the AP has no affect!
- Remove obstructions so all STAs will hear all transmissions
- Shrink The BSA by moving the most distant STAs (or those identified as "hidden" closer to the AP (this is rarely practical!)
- Create another BSA on a non-overlapping channel.

## Compensating for Hidden Node

- Configure the <u>RTS threshold</u> on the <u>STAs</u> which are hidden
    - o RTS/CTS configuration is not supported on many of the new 802.11g client adapter utilities
    - o Like fragmentation, if improperly set will reduce BSA throughput instead of increasing it!

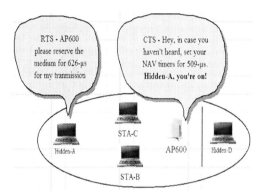

## RTS/CTS Medium Reservation is not CTS-to-Self!

- CTS-to-Self transmits a single frame with DSSS modulation to reserve the medium for subsequent OFDM frame
- Doesn't address hidden node because, by definition, the hidden nodes don't receive the CTS-to-Self transmission

## 802.11 Fragmentation versus RTS/CTS Medium Reservation

- Implemented for entirely different reasons!
    - o Fragmentation addresses large data frames that are corrupted by RFI
        - Diagnosed with network monitor statistics
    - o RTS/CTS addresses the hidden node issue
        - Also diagnosed with network monitor statistics, but verified by capturing both sides of an ICMP Echo (Ping) operation
- Common features:
    - o Both Fragmentation and RTS are "triggered" when the MPDU size on the transmitter exceeds the specified threshold
    - o Both add overhead which may be greater than the bandwidth saved

## RTS Configuration Settings

- *RTS Threshold:* The MPDU size that forces the STA to precede a transmission with a RTS frame and wait for the subsequent CTS
- *RTS Retry Limit:* The number of times a RTS frame is retransmitted (without reception of a CTS) before the STA terminates the transmit operation.

## Configuring the RTS Threshold

- After the hidden nodes have been identified with the ping test, run a standard baseline capture
- Filter on retries and the MAC addresses of hidden nodes
- If the retries are within the same time interval, you may infer that the original collisions were due to hidden node
- Note the average size of the retry data frames
- Set the RTS thresholds on the hidden STAs
- Run another baseline capture and determine whether the BSA throughput increased or decreased?

| Number | Time | Destination | Source | Function |
|---|---|---|---|---|
| [0-01]-178 | 00:00:04:812:086 | Aironet-350AP | AirLink | RTS |

## RTS Frame Details

- Size: 16-bytes + 4-byte FCS
- **To/From DS = 0,0**
  - o control frames are not processed by the DS
- **Duration = 1,458-μs.**
  - o protects the entire four-step data transfer
  - o **SIFS + CTS + SIFS + Data Frame + SIFS + ACK**
- **Receiver:** When a STA transmits a RTS frame the receiver is always the AP
- **Transmitter:** The STA which has been determined to be a hidden node

```
⊞ Physical Frame
⊟ IEEE 802.11 MAC Protocol
    Function              RTS
  ⊞ PLCP Header
  ⊟ Frame Control Byte 0
      Protocol Level    [xxxxxx00]   0
      Type              [xxxx01xx]   Control
      Sub-Type          [1011xxxx]   RTS
  ⊟ Frame Control Byte 1
      Order             [0xxxxxxx]   off
      WEP               [x0xxxxxx]   off
      More Data         [xx0xxxxx]   off
      Power Mgmt        [xxx0xxxx]   off
      Retry             [xxxx0xxx]   off
      More Fragments    [xxxxx0xx]   off
      From DS           [xxxxxx0x]   off
      To DS             [xxxxxxx0]   off
    Duration ID           1458
  ⊟ Receiver Address
      Hex Address       00-09-B7-7E-E9-AA
      Group Bit         [xxxxxxx0 xxxxxxxx x
      Local Bit         [xxxxxx0x xxxxxxxx x
      Logical Names     [[Aironet-350AP]]
      Vendor Name       Cisco Systems
  ⊟ Transmitter Address
      Hex Address       00-0D-88-E5-D3-2A
      Group Bit         [xxxxxxx0 xxxxxxxx x
      Local Bit         [xxxxxx0x xxxxxxxx x
      Logical Names     [[AirLink]]
      Vendor Name       D-link
```

## CTS Frame Details

| Number | Time | Destination | Source | Function |
|---|---|---|---|---|
| [0-01]-179 | 00:00:04:812:240 | AirLink | | CTS |

- Size: 10-bytes + 4-byte FCS
- Identical to a CTS-to-Self frame, except that it is transmitted by an AP
  - Every STA in the BSA receives the CTS
- Hidden nodes set their NAV timers to the value of:
  - **SIFS + Data Frame + SIFS + ACK**
- Other STAs have already set their NAV timers to the RTS duration value of:
  - **SIFS + CTS + SIFS + Data Frame + SIFS + ACK**
- Every STA in the BSA is now synchronized to the same virtual carrier duration.
- The STA may now transmit the data frame

```
⊕ Physical Frame
⊟ IEEE 802.11 MAC Protocol
   Function              CTS
  ⊕ PLCP Header
  ⊟ Frame Control Byte 0
     Protocol Level    [xxxxxx00]  0
     Type              [xxxx01xx]  Control
     Sub-Type          [1100xxxx]  CTS
  ⊕ Frame Control Byte 1
   Duration ID           1341
  ⊟ Receiver Address
     Hex Address         00-0D-88-E5-D3-2A
     Group Bit         [xxxxxxx0 xxxxxxxx ⋯
     Local Bit         [xxxxxx0x xxxxxxxx ⋯
     Logical Names     [[AirLink]]
     Vendor Name         D-link
```

## RTS/CTS Frame Protection

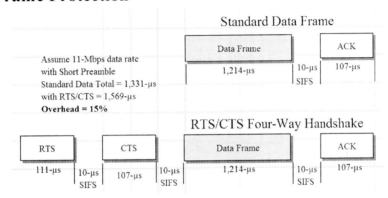

## RTS/CTS Duration Values

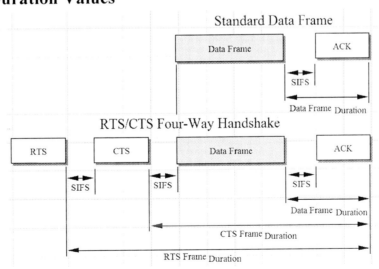

## RTS/CTS and Overlapped BSAs

- The BSAs are overlapped
- STAs reside in the overlapped areas, but the APs don't
- Configuring RTS threshold on the APs ensures that all of the STAs in the overlapped area will correctly set their NAV timers

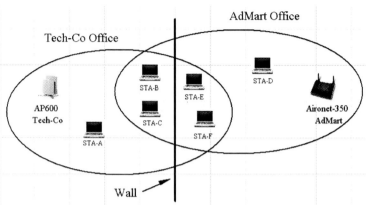

# Chapter 7: Performance Issues and PS-Mode

## *802.11 Management Commands Analyzed*:

- PS-Poll Control Frame
- Null-Data Frame

## *802.11 Concepts*:

- 802.11 maximum bit rate calculations based on data called in a TCP segment
- Wireless Client Adapter Power Management
- Beacon TIM IE
- Frame Control Byte-1: PwrMgmt, More Data and Order bits
- Broadcast/Multicast DTIM Period & DTIM Count
- Bitmap Control and Partial Virtual Bitmap fields
- Setting Client Adapter PS configuration
- Broadcast and Multicast Latency Issues

## *802.11 Performance Calculations*

There's nothing guaranteed to glaze over a reader's eyes quicker than several pages of performance calculations. But performance optimization is based on expectations, and you must understand the theoretical maximum throughput of the various 802.11 implementations before you can evaluation and tune your WLAN. Users don't care about overhead, they care about throughput. The following calculations assume that user data is transported in TCP/IP packets and the contending node waits only one DIFS interval before transmitting. The analysis ignores CSMA/CA contention times, the back-off timer loop and retransmissions resulting from collisions, RFI or multipath.

## Maximum Throughput versus Access Point Bandwidth Utilization

The calculations in this chapter address the maximum theoretical throughput for a single STA, not the aggregate BSS. This graphic shows *Network Observer's* ***Wireless Access Point Load Monitor***. It indicates the selected AP's percentage of utilization. In the

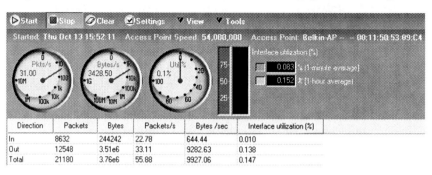

graphic the Access Point Speed is configured as 54-Mbps. *Imagine the situation when the Wireless Access Point Load Monitor specifies that the AP is operating at less than 25% utilization, but we discover that the BSA bandwidth is saturated!* This could easily happen in a typical 802.11bg mixed-mode BSS with several 802.11b STAs and a few physically distant 802.11g STAs that are communicating at 24-Mbps. Although the AP might appear to be barely breaking a sweat and that there's plenty of network capacity for future expansion, in reality the bandwidth is already maxed out. *It's extremely important to differentiate access point utilization from BSA utilization; BSA utilization is the single most important load factor assessment.*

Once you've completed the performance calculations in this chapter you'll be able to tune the ***Wireless Access Point Load Monitor*** by reconfiguring it to reflect the concept of "air time" instead of "bit-rate." That's accomplished by integrating the information from *Network Observer's* ***Network Summary*** statistic. The ***Percentage of Packets by Wireless Data Rate*** is the key to understanding how the bandwidth is being consumed. Notice in this mixed-mode BSS that although the 802.11b STAs are all connected at 11-Mbps a significant percentage of the control and management frames are transmitted at the DSSS basic rate. The same is true for the 802.11g STAs; although the data frames are transmitted at 54-Mbps, much of the 802.11g management and control traffic is exchanged at 24-Mbps.

| Network Details | Value | Packets | %Packets |
|---|---|---|---|
| Network Type | Wireless | | |
| Network Speed | 54 Mbit/s | | |
| Total bytes | 20.8e6 | | |
| Total packets | 110075 | | |
| Broadcasts | 18276 | | |
| Multicasts | 444 | | |
| Retries | 1971 | | |
| Error Packets | 0 | | |
| Size Distribution | | | |
| <=64 | | 37198 | 33.793 |
| 65-127 | | 28014 | 25.450 |
| 128-255 | | 449 | 0.408 |
| 256-511 | | 11594 | 10.533 |
| 512-1023 | | 461 | 0.419 |
| 1024-1518 | | 227 | 0.206 |
| >1518 | | 7858 | 7.139 |
| Errors | | | |
| Wireless Data Rates | | | |
| Pkts at 1 Mbps | | 20126 | 18.284 |
| Pkts at 2 Mbps | | 255 | 0.232 |
| Pkts at 5.5 Mbps | | 370 | 0.336 |
| Pkts at 6 Mbps | | 0 | 0.000 |
| Pkts at 9 Mbps | | 0 | 0.000 |
| Pkts at 11 Mbps | | 19373 | 17.600 |
| Pkts at 12 Mbps | | 69 | 0.063 |
| Pkts at 18 Mbps | | 97 | 0.088 |
| Pkts at 24 Mbps | | 22518 | 20.457 |
| Pkts at 36 Mbps | | 409 | 0.372 |
| Pkts at 48 Mbps | | 718 | 0.652 |
| Pkts at 54 Mbps | | 21866 | 19.865 |
| Pkts at 72 Mbps | | 0 | 0.000 |
| Pkts at 96 Mbps | | 0 | 0.000 |
| Pkts at 108 Mbps | | 0 | 0.000 |

All things equal, a freeway with cars averaging 100-Mph has twice the throughput as a freeway where cars average 50-Mph. The BSA is much more akin to a typical freeway in which vehicles travel at a variety of incompatible speeds while attempting to harmoniously share the roadway. ***To accurately determine BSA bandwidth reserve you must calculate the AP load factor as a function of frame size versus bit rate.*** That's why we're going to devote the next seven pages to tedious, but extremely useful calculations.

## General Performance Issues

- Every frame has a PLCP-preamble and PLCP-header
    - o The preamble length is independent of the PSDU bit rate
    - o The DSSS short preamble is 96-μs, 50% of the length of a long preamble
    - o The ERP-OFDM native preamble is 20-μs plus a 6-μs signal extension, or about 25% of a short preamble.
- Every frame has a 4-byte FCS
    - o Transmitted at the PSDU bit rate
- Unicast data frames and broadcast data frames To-DS=1 are ACKed by the receiver
    - o **{SIFS + PLCP-preamble/header + ACK + FCS}**
    - o Every frame has the potential to be corrupted.
    - o UnAcked frames result in a retransmission and also restrict the BSA throughput with an EIFS recovery interval.
- Encryption overhead is ignored in the following calculations because it comprises less than 1% of the PPDU.
    - o However, the encryption/decryption process consumes significant AP CPU resources. A typical business class AP configured with WPA EAP authentication and TKIP (128-bit) encryption may only support 80% of the STAs as a non-encrypted BSS! AES (160-bit) encryption imposes a much greater CPU load.

## Maximum Theoretical Throughputs

We'll examine maximum theoretical throughput in the following BSS configurations:
1. 802.11b with long preamble
2. 802.11b with short preamble
3. 802.11g ERP-OFDM native mode with short time slot
4. 802.11g mixed mode BSS with CTS-to-Self protection

The test frame is a maximum sized TCP data frame. As frame size decreases, the percentage of overhead increases and data throughput decreases. That's why implementation of 802.11 fragmentation and RTS/CTS thresholds is such a double-edged sword.

## The Basic TCP Frame

| MAC-Header | 802.2 LLC SNAP | IP Header | TCP Header | TCP Data |
|---|---|---|---|---|
| 24-bytes | 8-bytes | 20-bytes | 20-bytes | 1,460-bytes |

As we determined in the last chapter, the maximum size unencrypted 802.11 MPDU is 1,532-bytes. This screen shot of an Orinoco AP shows that the maximum packet size (MSDU) of the wireless interface is 1,500 bytes.

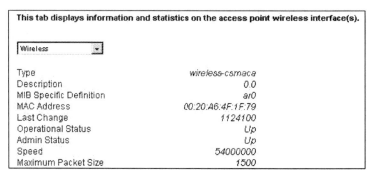

Assuming a MSDU of 1,500 bytes we calculate the maximum theoretical throughput by determining the overhead associated with each data frame. The TCP (L4), IP (L3), 802.2 LLC and MAC (L2) headers total 72 bytes. An unencrypted 1,532 byte 802.11 frame carries 1,460 bytes of data.

## Adding the PLCP and Error Checking Components

| PLCP-Preamble & Header | MAC-Header | 802.2 LLC SNAP | IP Header | TCP Header | TCP Data | FCS |
|---|---|---|---|---|---|---|
| | 24-bytes | 8-bytes | 20-bytes | 20-bytes | 1,460-bytes | 4-bytes |

We can't forget the PLCP-preamble/header and FCS fields. Although not explicitly displayed by a network monitor, they add significant overhead to every 802.11 frame. The PLCP-Preamble/Header rate is independent of the PSDU rate as specified in the signal field of the PLCP-header.

- PLCP-Preamble/Header:
  - o Long Barker 192-µs
  - o Short Barker 96-µs
  - o ERP-OFDM 20-µs and 6-µs Signal Extension
- FCS is a 4-byte field transmitted at the PSDU bit rate

## All Unicast Data Frames and Broadcast Data Frames with To-DS=1 Frames Require an ACK

| PLCP- Preamble & Header | A C K | FCS |
|---|---|---|
| | 10- bytes | 4-bytes |

The data frame must be acknowledged. The 802.11 ACK frame adds another element to the data frame overhead. The SIFS preceding the ACK will be included in the calculations.

## TCP L4 Acknowledgement

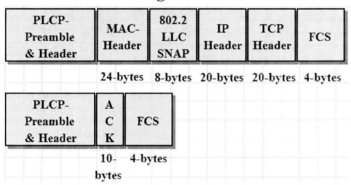

| PLCP- Preamble & Header | MAC- Header | 802.2 LLC SNAP | IP Header | TCP Header | FCS |
|---|---|---|---|---|---|
| | 24-bytes | 8-bytes | 20-bytes | 20-bytes | 4-bytes |

| PLCP- Preamble & Header | A C K | FCS |
|---|---|---|
| | 10- bytes | 4-bytes |

TCP is a connection-oriented reliable data delivery service: the receiver acknowledges the reception of a valid TCP data segment. ***The TCP ACK is an L4 function and isn't related to the L2 802.11 ACK frame***. The receiver's sliding window allows one TCP ACK to acknowledge the reception of multiple TCP segments. ***This analysis assumes a one-to-one relationship between the reception of a valid TCP data segment and a TCP ACK. In a production network the ratio of TCP data segments to each TCP ACK may be as high as 4:1.***

## Assembling the IFS, PLCP components and Frames

### *TCP Data Frame and 802.11 ACK*

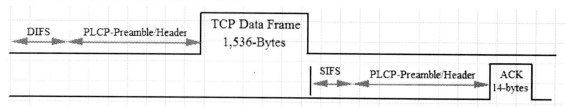

**DIFS + Preamble/Header + TCP Data + SIFS + Preamble/Header + ACK**

- DIFS = SIFS + (2 * slot time)
- PLCP-Preamble/Header
- TCP data frame = 1,536-bytes transmitted at the PSDU bit-rate: 1,532-byte unencrypted frame plus 4-byte FCS.
- SIFS = 10-µs
- PLCP-Preamble/Header
- ACK frame = 14-bytes transmitted at the data frame's bit-rate: 10-byte ACK frame plus 4-byte FCS.

### *TCP ACK Frame and 802.11 ACK*

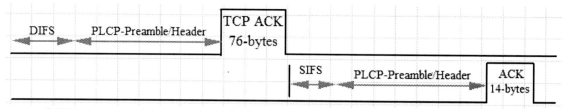

**DIFS + Preamble/Header + TCP ACK + SIFS + Preamble/Header + ACK**

- DIFS = SIFS + (2 * slot time)
- PLCP-Preamble/Header
- TCP ACK frame = 76-bytes at the PSDU bit-rate
- SIFS = 10-µs
- PLCP-Preamble/Header
- ACK frame = 14-bytes at the TCP ACK frame's bit-rate

## Maximum Throughput for a node in an 802.11b BSS

11-Mbps (megabits/sec) divided by 8 bits/byte yields a data rate of 1.375 megabytes/sec. Long preamble is a performance killer. Let's assume a short preamble.

- Data Rate = 1.375 megabytes/sec
- SIFS = 10-µs
- Slot time = 20-µs
- DIFS = 50-µs

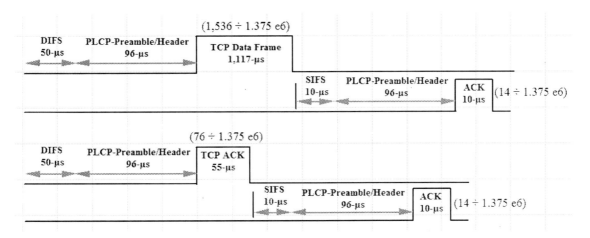

*Total Time to transfer 1,460 data bytes is 1,696-µs = 860,849 bytes/sec or 6.8-Mbps, approximately 60% of 11-Mbps.*

### Long Preamble

Substituting the short PLCP-preamble/header value in each of the four occurrences with a long preamble value of 192-µs yields a throughput of 5.6-Mbps, *about a 20% reduction!*

## Maximum Throughput for a node in an ERP Native Mode BSS

This calculation is for a native ERP-OFDM BSS, assuming the maximum IEEE supported rate of 54-Mbps and short slot time.

- Data Rate = 6.75 megabytes/sec
- SIFS = 10-μs
- Slot time = 9-μs
- DIFS = 28-μs
- ERP-Preamble/Header = 20-μs
- PLCP-Signal Extension = 6-μs ( provides the frame's end delimiter)

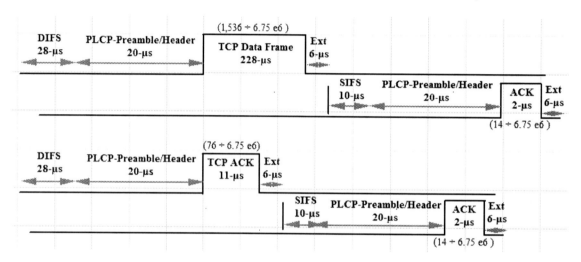

*Total Time to transfer 1,460 data bytes is 423-μs = 3.45 megabytes/sec or 27.6-Mbps, approximately 52% of 54-Mbps.*

## Maximum Throughput for a mixed-mode BSS with Protection

The mixed mode BSS is the norm for many business environments. A perennial design issue is, "what's the best solution that accommodates 802.11g & g STAs?"
- Mixed mode BSS with protection disabled
  - high ratio of 802.11g to 802.11b STAs
- Mixed mode BSS with protection enabled
  - high ratio of 802.11b to 802.11g STAs
- Separate BSSs for 802.11b and 802.11g
  - Difficult to provide concurrent seamless roaming for both technologies

> **AP Protection Configuration** At the time of this writing Cisco and Orinoco APs don't support disabling 802.11bg mixed-mode protection. Some 3COM business-class APs support several mixed mode protection configuration settings.

## 802.11 mixed mode specifications

- Data Rates
    - DS/DSSS: 11-Mbps or 1.375 megabytes/sec
    - ERP-OFDM: 54-Mbps or 6.75 megabytes/sec
- SIFS = 10-µs
- Slot time = 20-µs (short slot time isn't supported in mixed mode)
- DIFS = 50-µs
- PLCP Components:
    - HS/DSSS: short preamble/header 96-µs
    - ERP-OFDM: native preamble/header 20-µs
    - ERP-OFDM signal extension 6-µs

> **CTS-to-Self**: To ensure that all HR/DSSS STAs set their NAV timers the CTS-to-Self is transmitted at a rate supported by all of the currently associated 802.11b STAs. This analysis assumes that 11-Mbps is the only HS/DSSS basic rate supported.

The CTS frame is the same size number of bytes as the ACK frame. The duration of the PLCP components in each frame time estimate are taken from the previous diagrams:

- **CTS:** HS/DSSS @ 11-Mbps = 106-µs
- **TCP Data** (1,532 bytes): ERP-OFDM @ 54-Mpbs = 254-µs
- **TCP ACK** (76 bytes): ERP-OFDM @ 54-Mpbs = 37-µs
- **ACK:** ERP-OFDM @ 54-Mpbs = 28-µs

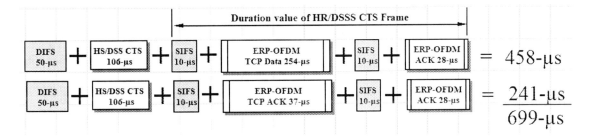

*Total Time to transfer 1,460 data bytes is 699-µs or 2.1 megabytes/sec = 16.7-Mbps, approximately 31% of 54-Mbps. CTS-to-Self imposes 21% overhead on native mode ERP-OFDM transmissions!*

## PS (Power Save) Operation

Power save operation is one of the least understood and most complex aspects of 802.11 because it involves many frame control bits and several frame types. In most BSSs it has a minor impact on BSA throughput. *PS-mode configuration is a trade-off between the power savings of individual STA's and the maximum latency tolerated by multicast applications and broadcast timeouts.* Throughput the book we've seen that an 802.11 network monitor is the only objective means of determining the current health of the BSS and this is especially true when it comes to the analysis of PS-mode issues.

### Computer Stand-By vs. Wireless Client Adapter PS-Mode

Don't confuse 802.11 PS-mode with a computer's stand-by mode. A computer enters stand-by mode (aka sleep mode) after a specified number of minutes of inactivity. The

contents of RAM are retained but all computational tasks are suspended. A computer reenters active mode when operator input occurs, pressing a key or moving the mouse. Most operating systems also support wake-on-Ethernet.

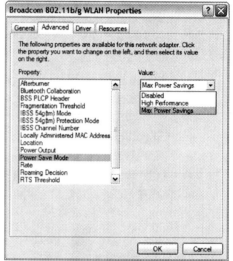

802.11 PS-mode is best described as the wireless client adapter taking lots of very short "cat naps." The IEEE uses the term "dozing." The wireless client adapter isn't awakened by outside events. It wakes itself periodically to read a beacon frame to determine if it has buffered data at the AP.

Typically there are three wireless client adapter PS mode configuration levels:

- **Disabled** the adapter never enters PS-mode.
- **High Performance** Trade-off between power savings and performance.
- **Max Power Savings** The adapter takes deeper and more frequent cat naps at the expense of performance.

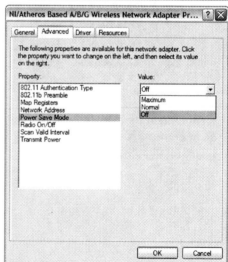

Frames bound for PS-mode STAs are buffered by the AP. This includes unicast frames for each PS-mode STA and all broadcast/multicast frames for the entire BSS - *a single PS-mode STA increases incoming broad/multicast reception latency for the entire BSS!*

*The STA's internal timer continues to run in PS-mode. This enables the STA to wake just before a TBTT to check the TIM IE for buffered traffic.*

## Going Off Channel

A STA whose receiver is disabled or tuned to another channel can't receive frames from its current BSS. The STA informs the AP before going off-channel by sending a frame with the Frame Control Byte-1, PwrMgmt bit set. STAs go off-channel for two reasons.

- **Enter PS-mode** to extend battery life. Dozing is the ultimate off-channel state; the receiver is disabled, effectively tuned to "no channel."
- **Scanning for APs on other channels**.
    - Passive scanning is slow; it consumes over 1.25 TUs per channel. However, it's efficient because it doesn't transmit or load the BSA.
    - Active scanning is fast; it consumes power transmitting probe requests and adds a minor amount of traffic to the BSA.
    - Windows XP STAs typically perform an active scan every 60 seconds or when the RSSI falls below a specified threshold. *For most 802.11g wireless client adapters the active scanning interval and conditions are not directly configurable.*

Note: We have seen several examples of configuring roaming parameters which does indirectly affect active scanning activity.

The most consistent location to configure PS-Mode is in the advanced tab of the wireless client adapter's properties. If the setting doesn't appear there, try the vendor's client adapter configuration utility.

## PS-Mode Components

802.11 power management employs more fields and frames than any other operation. PS-Mode also impacts certain basic BSS functions. The affects of XP's aggressive active probing creates many probe requests and consequent probe responses. Depending on the number of co-located BSSs in the BSA, active probing may produce a significant number of retransmitted probe response frames. Recognizing this as normal behavior enables you to focus on relevant optimization and troubleshooting issues.

## Beacon's TIM IE

- The DTIM (Delivery Traffic Indication Map) Count and Period fields are associated with broad/multicast traffic buffering.
- The Bitmap Control field has two subfields. One bit specifies the presence of buffered broad/multicast traffic and the other seven bits specify the offset into the variable length Partial Virtual Bitmap field associated with unicast buffered frames.
- LinkFerret doesn't decode the partial virtual bitmap field, so we'll dig it out directly from the Hex Decode window in our analysis.
- *A STA operating in AM (active mode) doesn't process the TIM IE*

| Information Element | |
| --- | --- |
| Identity | TIM |
| Length | 4 |
| DTIM Count | 1 |
| DTIM Period | 2 |
| Bitmap Control | 0 |

## Frame Control Byte-1

- **PwrMgmt bit** Set indicates that the STA is entering (or remaining in) PS mode and is not available for communication. Reset specifies that the STA is entering (or remaining in) AM. The PwrMgmt bit appears in every frame, but the common frames types used to toggle the STA's power management state are Null-data, PS-Poll and Probe Request.

```
⊕ Physical Frame
⊕ IEEE 802.11 MAC Protocol
    Function           Null
  ⊕ PLCP Header
  ⊕ Frame Control Byte 0
  ⊕ Frame Control Byte 1
      Order          [0xxxxxxx]   off
      WEP            [x0xxxxxx]   off
      More Data      [xx0xxxxx]   off
      Power Mgmt     [xxx1xxxx]   on
      Retry          [xxxx0xxx]   off
      More Fragments [xxxxx0xx]   off
      From DS        [xxxxxx0x]   off
      To DS          [xxxxxxx1]   on
    Duration ID        44
  ⊕ BSSID
  ⊕ Source Address
  ⊕ Destination Address
    Fragment       [xxxxxxxx xxxx0000]   0
    Sequence       [00100110 0110xxxx]   614
```

- **More Data bit** is associated with the AP's delivery of buffered traffic. Set indicates that the AP has additional buffered data. Reset specifies that the AP's buffer has been emptied.
- **Order bit** Set indicates that the data frame uses an upper-layer protocol which requires "strictly ordered service." *Frames with the Order bit set are never buffered by the AP.* The use of the order bit is uncommon. 802.11e QoS is used to ensure the delivery of time critical data in a WLAN.

## Null-Data frame

- Transmitted by a STA to toggle its power state when it has no other information to communicate. At the end of Chapter 4 we analyzed the **PwrMgmt-NullData** capture file after applying the **Data-Null** filter. The state of the PwrMgmt bit toggled with each Null-Data frame as the STA flipped between AM and PS-mode.

## PS-Poll Control frame

- Used by PS-Mode STA to request the delivery of unicast buffered data
- Transmitted by a STA when its buffered data indicator bit in the TIM IE Partial Virtual Bitmap field is set.
- The AP may respond with an ACK before transmitting the data frame, or it may immediately transmit a single data frame without a preceding ACK. We'll examine several captures that explore this concept.
- If the More Data bit in the received data frame is set, the AP has additional buffered data and the STA transmits a subsequent PS-Poll frame.

## Duration/ID field

- In the PS-Poll frame the duration/ID field specifies the STA's AID
- The duration value of a PS-Poll frame is implied to be a $SIFS + ACK$ interval at the current bit-rate and preamble.

## Association Request, Listen Interval Field

- Specifies the maximum number of beacons before the PS-mode STA wakes to read the TIM IE.
- The AP maintains a STA's buffered unicast frames for a minimum of one Listen Interval.
- Listen Interval doesn't specify how often the STA actually checks the beacon, just the maximum case.
- Longer Listen Intervals place greater demands on AP buffer resources
- These two examples show Listen Intervals of 3 and 256.

```
⊕ Physical Frame
⊟ IEEE 802.11 MAC Protocol
    Function              Association Request
  ⊕ PLCP Header
  ⊕ Frame Control Byte 0
  ⊕ Frame Control Byte 1
    Duration ID           314
  ⊕ Destination Address
  ⊕ Source Address
  ⊕ BSSID
    Fragment              [xxxxxxxx xxxx0000]   0
    Sequence              [10100110 0101xxxx]   2661
  ⊕ Capability Information
    Listen Interval       3
  ⊕ Information Element
  ⊕ Information Element
```

```
⊟ 🔧 Association Request
  ⊕ 📄 Capability Information    ESS Privacy 'Short Preamble'
    📄 Listen Interval          256
  ⊕ 📄 SSID                     Airo350Site1
  ⊕ 📄 Supported Rates          1.0, 2.0, 5.5, 11.0 Mbps
  ⊕ 📄 Vendor Specific
  ⊕ 📄 Vendor Specific
  ⊕ 📄 RSN Information Element
```

## Broadcast/Multicast Traffic Buffering

DTIM Count and DTIM Period are associated with buffering broad/multicast traffic.

- **DTIM Count** is decremented with each beacon until it equals zero, which identifies A DTIM beacon. *After the DTIM beacon, DTIM Count is initialized to DTIM Period - 1*. (See the next capture analysis for details.)

```
⊟ Information Element
    Identity        TIM
    Length          4
    DTIM Count      0
    DTIM Period     1
    Bitmap Control  0
```

- **DTIM Period** is configured at the AP. It specifies how often a DTIM beacon occurs. *When the DTIM Period is 1 (as in this example) every beacon is a DTIM beacon and the DTIM Count is always zero.*

---

**TIM Terminology Tangles** Documentation and whitepapers specify two types of beacons, the standard Beacon and the DTIM Beacon. *The DTIM Beacon Interval is the Beacon Interval multiplied by the DTIM Period*. When the Beacon Interval is 100-TUs and the DTIM Period is 5, the DTIM Beacon Interval is 500-TUs. *Broad/Multicast traffic forwarding to the BSS is delayed by a maximum of one DTIM Beacon Interval*. Some manuals call the DTIM Beacon the "Data Beacon."

Many whitepapers define the DTIM field as the "Deferred Traffic Indicator Map." In the IEEE documentation it's consistently called the "Delivery Traffic Indication Map." *"Deferred traffic indicator map" may be a more accurate interpretation of DTIM, but technically it's not the official IEEE term. Beware of this on exams*.

*The IEEE defines two types of TIMs*, the standard TIM in which the DTIM Count is non-zero and the DTIM which has a DTIM count of zero. In most documentation "DTIM beacon" is used rather than "DTIM IE."

---

These issues must be considered when broad/multicast frames are buffered at the AP.
- How much latency can broadcast frames tolerate?
- How much latency can multicast applications tolerate?
- Which broad/multicast frames are buffered and when are they buffered?
- Is each broad/multicast frame transmitted twice? Once for the AM STAs and again after the DTIM Beacon for the PS STAs?
- How much traffic does this add to the BSA?

Every STA has a ReceiveDTIMs parameter. ***When ReceiveDTIMs is set the STA wakes to receive every DTIM beacon***. ReceiveDTIMs is always set on a STA that's a member of a multicast host group. ***The wireless client adapter's driver determines if a PS-mode STA checks every DTIM beacon just for the presence of buffered broadcast frames***. For performance calculations assume that ReceiveDTIMs is set on every STA.

Most broadcast frames announce a network-wide service and don't expect a reply. The ARP (address resolution protocol) Request is an exception. It has a MAC broadcast destination address and is used to determine the MAC address associated with the specified IP (protocol)

```
⊟ Address Resolution Protocol
   Hardware Type          Ethernet (10Mb)
   Protocol Type          0800  IP
   Hardware Addr Size     6
   Protocol Addr Size     4
   ARP Function           Address Resolution Request
   Sender HW Address      00-0A-E6-96-47-C5
   Sender Prot Address    172.16.0.2
   Target HW Address      00-00-00-00-00-00
   Target Prot Address    172.16.0.14
```

address. In this example the STA with IP address 172.16.0.14 should respond to the ARP request.

The most common source of incoming BSS ARP requests is the subnet's default gateway. Cisco routers tolerate over 500-ms of ARP request reply latency or greater than a DTIM Period of 5 at the default beacon interval. Longer DTIM Periods may cause ARP request to fail, forcing the router to discard unicast TCP/UDP packets. ***If you suspect that an application is failing because of ARP request failures, the WLAN network monitor is the most direct and efficient means to test the supposition.***

If you're employing multicast applications, determine the maximum latency of each application and configure the DTIM Period accordingly.

## Broadcast/Multicast Buffering Flowchart

The IEEE 802.11 specification is fairly cogent concerning when broad/multicast frames are buffered by the AP:

> "***If any STA in its BSS is in PS mode***, *the AP shall buffer all broadcast and multicast MSDUs and deliver them to all STAs immediately following the next Beacon frame containing a delivery TIM (DTIM) transmission.*"

# Broadcast/Multicast Frame Received

Points A and B describe what occurs when the frame is received at the AP's Ethernet or Radio interface. If the conditions specify that the frame should be buffered, then the processing of both cases is identical starting at Point C.

A) <u>AP's Ethernet interface.</u> If at least one STA is in PS-Mode, the AP buffers the broad/multicast frame at point C in the flow chart. Otherwise the frame is immediately forwarded to the AP's radio interface with From-DS=1.

B) <u>AP's Radio interface with To-DS=1</u> Frame is immediately processed by the DSS and forwarded to the AP's Ethernet interface. If at least one STA is in PS-mode, the AP buffers the broad/multicast frame at point C in the flow chart
   1. control/management frames have To-DS=0; they are never buffered at the AP
   2. buffered broad/multicast frames sourced by a STA are transmitted twice: by the STA with To-DS=1 and by the AP with From DS=1 after the DTIM Beacon

C) Buffer the broad/multicast frame and set bit-0 of the TIM IE's Bitmap Control Field to indicate the presence of buffered broad/multicast traffic.

D) Wait for the next DTIM beacon.

E) The More Data bit in Frame Control Byte-1 is set to indicate additional buffered broad/multicast frames are to follow. PS-mode STAs with ReceiveDTIMs set stay awake until the More Data bit is reset in a received buffered data frame.

F) More Data bit is reset and the last frame is transmitted. Bit-0 in the TIM IE's Bitmap Control field is reset.

## DTIM Beacon and Buffered Broadcast Capture Analysis

In this example we'll analyze the buffered broadcast traffic that occurs when a computer on the Ethernet Pings a computer in the BSS. IAS1(RADIUS) pings AirLink, a STA associated to AP600-2.

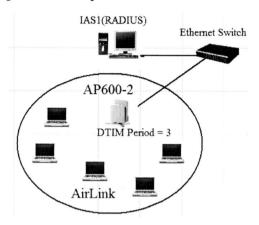

- AP600-2 is configured with a DTIM Period of 3
- AirLink is configured for maximum PS-mode and has the IP address 172.16.0.14

***Ensure that beacons are not suppressed by clearing the "Hide 802.11 Beacons" checkbox in LinkFerret Preferences, Brief Display Tab.***

Open capture file Ethernet-DTIM-TIM, apply the Beacon filter, load the PSP-SRV namespace, and press **F5**. The filter produces 76 beacon frames. Go to frame 2.

Frame 2: DTIM Beacon, DTIM Count = 0
AP600-2 is configured with a DTIM Period of 3.

```
⊟ Information Element
   Identity        TIM
   Length          4
   DTIM Count      0
   DTIM Period     3
   Bitmap Control  0
```

Frame 3: Beacon following the DTIM Beacon, DTIM Count =2
Following a DTIM beacon the DTIM Count is initialized to the DTIM Period - 1.

```
⊟ Information Element
   Identity        TIM
   Length          4
   DTIM Count      2
   DTIM Period     3
   Bitmap Control  0
```

Frame 4: Second Beacon following the DTIM Beacon, DTIM Count = 1. The next beacon is a DTIM beacon.

```
⊟ Information Element
   Identity        TIM
   Length          4
   DTIM Count      1
   DTIM Period     3
   Bitmap Control  0
```

Frame 5: DTIM Beacon
The DTIM Count = 0. This is a DTIM beacon. ***This is a typical exam trick question.*** Many people confuse when the DTIM Beacon occurs - remember three things:

```
⊟ Information Element
   Identity        TIM
   Length          4
   DTIM Count      0
   DTIM Period     3
   Bitmap Control  0
```

- the DTIM Count is initialized to the DTIM Period – 1
- The DTIM Count is decremented with each beacon
- After the DTIM Beacon, the DTIM Count is reinitialized to the DTIM Period – 1.

Apply No Filter, press **F5** and go to frame-33.

| Number | Time | Destination | Source | Protocol | Function |
|--------|------|-------------|--------|----------|----------|
| [0-01]-33 | 00:00:03:274:952 | Broadcast | AP600-2 | IEEE 802.11 | Beacon |
| [0-01]-34 | 00:00:03:275:544 | Broadcast | IAS1(RADIUS) | ARP | Request-172.16.0.14 |
| [0-01]-35 | 00:00:03:275:950 | IAS1(RADIUS) | AirLink | ARP | Response-172.16.0.14 |
| [0-01]-36 | 00:00:03:276:162 | AirLink | | IEEE 802.11 | ACK |
| [0-01]-37 | 00:00:03:377:353 | Broadcast | AP600-2 | IEEE 802.11 | Beacon |
| [0-01]-38 | 00:00:03:378:074 | AP600-2 | AirLink | IEEE 802.11 | PS-Poll |
| [0-01]-39 | 00:00:03:378:387 | AirLink | | IEEE 802.11 | ACK |
| [0-01]-40 | 00:00:03:378:734 | AirLink | IAS1(RADIUS) | ICMP | Echo Request |
| [0-01]-41 | 00:00:03:378:951 | AP600-2 | | IEEE 802.11 | ACK |
| [0-01]-42 | 00:00:03:379:426 | IAS1(RADIUS) | AirLink | ICMP | Echo Reply |

| Number | Time | Destination | Source | Protocol | Function |
|--------|------|-------------|--------|----------|----------|
| [0-01]-33 | 00:00:03:274:952 | Broadcast | AP600-2 | IEEE 802.11 | Beacon |

### Frame 33: DTIM Beacon

TIM IE

**DTIM Count 0** specifies that this is a DTIM beacon
**DTIM Period 3**, every third beacon is a DTIM beacon
**Bitmap Control** 0x01 (0000 0001) bit-0 is set specifying the presence of buffered broad/multicast frames.

```
⊕ Physical Frame
⊜ IEEE 802.11 MAC Protocol
    Function              Beacon
  ⊕ PLCP Header
  ⊕ Frame Control Byte 0
  ⊕ Frame Control Byte 1
    Duration ID          0
  ⊕ Destination Address
  ⊕ Source Address
  ⊕ BSSID
    Fragment             [xxxxx]
    Sequence             [11010(
    Time Stamp           396320(
    Beacon Interval      100
  ⊕ Capability Information
  ⊕ Information Element
  ⊕ Information Element
  ⊕ Information Element
  ⊜ Information Element
      Identity           TIM
      Length             4
      DTIM Count         0
      DTIM Period        3
      Bitmap Control     1
  ⊕ Information Element
─────────────────────────────────
'0064    03 01 00 2A 01 07 32 04
```

| Number | Time | Destination | Source | Protocol | Function |
|--------|------|-------------|--------|----------|----------|
| [0-01]-34 | 00:00:03:275:544 | Broadcast | IAS1(RADIUS) ARP | | Request-172.16.0.14 |

### Frame 34 Buffered ARP Broadcast
*How do we know that this is a buffered broadcast frame?*

1. The previous frame was a DTIM Beacon
2. Bitmap Control, bit-0 was set
3. This is the first data frame transmitted by the AP following the DTIM beacon

*The maximum latency in this example is the DTIM Period multiplied by the Beacon interval or 300-TUs.*

More Data = 0 indicates that this is the last buffered broad/multicast transmission for this DTIM Beacon.

```
⊕ Physical Frame
⊜ IEEE 802.11 MAC Protocol
    Function              Data
  ⊕ PLCP Header
  ⊕ Frame Control Byte 0
  ⊜ Frame Control Byte 1
      Order       [0xxxxxxx]  off
      WEP         [x1xxxxxx]  on
      More Data   [xx0xxxxx]  off
      Power Mgmt  [xxx0xxxx]  off
      Retry       [xxxx0xxx]  off
      More Fragments [xxxxx0xx] off
      From DS     [xxxxxx1x]  on
      To DS       [xxxxxxx0]  off
  ⊕ WEP Information
    Duration ID          0
  ⊕ Destination Address
  ⊕ BSSID
  ⊕ Source Address
    Fragment    [xxxxxxx xxxx0000]  0
    Sequence    [11010001 0000xxxx] 3344
  ⊕ IEEE 802.2 Logical Link Control
  ⊕ IEEE Sub-Network Access Protocol
  ⊕ Address Resolution Protocol
```

Frames 35 – 42 illustrate the remaining frame exchange for an Ethernet to 802.11 Ping.

*AirLink's IP address is the target of the ARP. Can we assume that the AP buffered the ARP broadcast because of the PS-mode state of AirLink? Absolutely not!* Without tracking the power management state of every STA all we know is that at least one STA was in PS-mode when the AP received the broadcast frame on its Ethernet interface.

## Mini-Case Study: The Duplicate ARP Request, Revisited

This mini-case study illustrates an intra-BSS Ping in which both the source and destination of the ping reside in the same BSS. ***The central issue in this case study is, "are broadcasts that originate in the BSS also buffered and retransmitted by the AP?"*** If the broadcast isn't buffered than it will be missed by STAs in PS-mode. On the other hand, if it's buffered by the AP and transmitted after a DTIM beacon then the broadcast frame is duplicated, transmitted once by the original STA and then retransmitted by the AP.

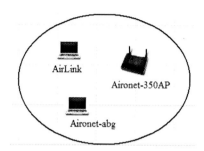

Open capture file **IntraBSS-DTIM-TIM**, ensure that **No Filter** is applied and the PSP-SRV namespace is loaded. Let's focus on frames 26 through 33. Frame 26 is the original ARP broadcast transmitted by Aironet-abg and it appears again at Frame 32 about 396-ms later.

| Number | Time | Destination | Source | Protocol | Function |
|---|---|---|---|---|---|
| [0-01]-26 | 00:00:02:538:754 | Broadcast | Aironet-abg | ARP | Request-172.16.0.14 |
| [0-01]-27 | 00:00:02:539:056 | Aironet-abg | | IEEE 802.11 | ACK |
| [0-01]-28 | 00:00:02:627:108 | Broadcast | Aironet-350AP | IEEE 802.11 | Beacon |
| [0-01]-29 | 00:00:02:729:511 | Broadcast | Aironet-350AP | IEEE 802.11 | Beacon |
| [0-01]-30 | 00:00:02:831:914 | Broadcast | Aironet-350AP | IEEE 802.11 | Beacon |
| [0-01]-31 | 00:00:02:934:317 | Broadcast | Aironet-350AP | IEEE 802.11 | Beacon |
| [0-01]-32 | 00:00:02:934:697 | Broadcast | Aironet-abg | ARP | Request-172.16.0.14 |
| [0-01]-33 | 00:00:02:935:318 | Aironet-abg | AirLink | ARP | Response-172.16.0.14 |

| Number | Time | Destination | Source | Protocol | Function |
|---|---|---|---|---|---|
| [0-01]-26 | 00:00:02:538:754 | Broadcast | Aironet-abg | ARP | Request-172.16.0.14 |

### Frame 26: ARP Broadcast

<u>To:DS = 1, From DS = 0</u> This frame will be processed by the DSS

**Addresses**:
<u>Source</u> Aironet-abg
<u>Destination</u> Broadcast

<u>Target Protocol Address</u> 172.16.0.14, the IP address of AirLink. If AirLink is in AM, we'd expect to see an ARP Response frame after a maximum delay of 25-ms.

```
 Physical Frame
 IEEE 802.11 MAC Protocol
   Function              Data
   PLCP Header
   Frame Control Byte 0
   Frame Control Byte 1
     Order             [0xxxxxxx]  off
     WEP               [x1xxxxxx]  on
     More Data         [xx0xxxxx]  off
     Power Mgmt        [xxx0xxxx]  off
     Retry             [xxxx0xxx]  off
     More Fragments    [xxxxx0xx]  off
     From DS           [xxxxxx0x]  off
     To DS             [xxxxxxx1]  on
   WEP Information
   Duration ID           314
   BSSID
   Source Address
   Destination Address
   Fragment          [xxxxxxxx xxxx0000]  0
   Sequence          [11101101 1011xxxx]  3803
 IEEE 802.2 Logical Link Control
 IEEE Sub-Network Access Protocol
 Address Resolution Protocol
   Hardware Type         Ethernet (10Mb)
   Protocol Type         0800  IP
   Hardware Addr Size    6
   Protocol Addr Size    4
   ARP Function          Address Resolution Request
   Sender HW Address     00-40-96-A6-9C-3E
   Sender Prot Address   172.16.0.11
   Target HW Address     00-00-00-00-00-00
   Target Prot Address   172.16.0.14
```

## *Frame 27: ACK*

Broadcast frames with the To-DS bit set are ACKed by the AP and processed by the DSS.

| Number | Time | Destination | Source | Protocol | Function |
|--------|------|-------------|--------|----------|----------|
| [0-01]-28 | 00:00:02:627:108 | Broadcast | Aironet-350AP | IEEE 802.11 | Beacon |

## *Frame 28: Beacon*

### **TIM IE**

<u>DTIM Count 3</u> The next two beacons are standard beacons and the third beacon is the DTIM beacon.

<u>DTIM Period 5</u> Assuming the default beacon interval of 100-TUs, the AP broadcasts a DTIM Beacon every 500-TUs. That is the worst case buffered broad/multicast latency.

<u>Bitmap Control 0x01</u> bit-0 is set which indicates that the AP has buffered broad/multicast traffic which will be transmitted after the next DTIM beacon.

```
⊕ Physical Frame
⊖ IEEE 802.11 MAC Protocol
    Function                    Beacon
  ⊕ PLCP Header
  ⊕ Frame Control Byte 0
  ⊕ Frame Control Byte 1
    Duration ID                 0
  ⊕ Destination Address
  ⊕ Source Address
  ⊕ BSSID
    Fragment                    [xxxxx:
    Sequence                    [00100:
    Time Stamp                  106785<
    Beacon Interval             100
  ⊕ Capability Information
  ⊕ Information Element
  ⊕ Information Element
  ⊕ Information Element
  ⊖ Information Element
      Identity                  TIM
      Length                    4
      DTIM Count                3
      DTIM Period               5
      Bitmap Control            1
```

Let's jump forward to Frame 31 which should be, according to this frame's DTIM count value, a DTIM beacon.

| Number | Time | Destination | Source | Protocol | Function |
|--------|------|-------------|--------|----------|----------|
| [0-01]-31 | 00:00:02:934:317 | Broadcast | Aironet-350AP | IEEE 802.11 | Beacon |

## *Frame 31: DTIM Beacon*

### **DTIM IE**

<u>DTIM Count 0</u> indicates that this is a DTIM beacon.

<u>Bitmap Control</u> bit-0 remains set until the buffered broad/multicast buffer has been emptied. In the rare event that this doesn't occur before the next TBTT, the bit stays set and the buffered broad/multicast traffic will continue to be processed after the next DTIM beacon.

```
⊖ IEEE 802.11 MAC Protocol
    Function                    Beacon
  ⊕ PLCP Header
  ⊕ Frame Control Byte 0
  ⊕ Frame Control Byte 1
    Duration ID                 0
  ⊕ Destination Address
  ⊕ Source Address
  ⊕ BSSID
    Fragment                    [xxxxx:
    Sequence                    [00100:
    Time Stamp                  104534:
    Beacon Interval             100
  ⊕ Capability Information
  ⊕ Information Element
  ⊕ Information Element
  ⊕ Information Element
  ⊖ Information Element
      Identity                  TIM
      Length                    4
      DTIM Count                0
      DTIM Period               5
      Bitmap Control            1
```

| Number | Time | Destination | Source | Protocol | Function |
|--------|------|-------------|--------|----------|----------|
| [0-01]-32 | 00:00:02:934:697 | Broadcast | Aironet-abg | ARP | Request-172.16.0.14 |

```
⊕ Physical Frame
⊟ IEEE 802.11 MAC Protocol
  ˙Function              Data
  ⊕ PLCP Header
  ⊕ Frame Control Byte 0
  ⊟ Frame Control Byte 1
    ˙Order              [0xxxxxxx]   off
    ˙WEP                [x1xxxxxx]   on
    ˙More Data          [xx0xxxxx]   off
    ˙Power Mgmt         [xxx0xxxx]   off
    ˙Retry              [xxxx0xxx]   off
    ˙More Fragments     [xxxxx0xx]   off
    ˙From DS            [xxxxxx1x]   on
    ˙To DS              [xxxxxxx0]   off
  ⊕ WEP Information
  ˙Duration ID            0
  ⊕ Destination Address
  ⊕ BSSID
  ⊟ Source Address
    ˙Fragment           [xxxxxxxx xxxx0000]   0
    ˙Sequence           [00100100 0101xxxx]   581
⊕ IEEE 802.2 Logical Link Control
⊕ IEEE Sub-Network Access Protocol
⊟ Address Resolution Protocol
  ˙Hardware Type         Ethernet (10Mb)
  ˙Protocol Type         0800  IP
  ˙Hardware Addr Size    6
  ˙Protocol Addr Size    4
  ˙ARP Function          Address Resolution Request
  ˙Sender HW Address     00-40-96-A6-9C-3E
  ˙Sender Prot Address   172.16.0.11
  ˙Target HW Address     00-00-00-00-00-00
  ˙Target Prot Address   172.16.0.14
```

### Frame 32: Buffered ARP Broadcast

To-DS =0, From DS=1
The only difference between the two ARP broadcasts is that the first was directed to the DSS and the second is sourced by the DSS.

***Of course, the internal order of the three addresses also specifies that the AP was the source of the second ARP broadcast.***

The DS backbone only receives the first ARP broadcast. The second ARP broadcast is only transmitted to the BSS, not to the DS backbone. That makes sense because the intent of the second ARP broadcast is to ensure that PS-mode STAs in the BSS have the opportunity to receive the broadcast frame.

| Number | Time | Destination | Source | Protocol | Function |
|--------|------|-------------|--------|----------|----------|
| [0-01]-33 | 00:00:02:935:318 | Aironet-abg | AirLink | ARP | Response-172.16.0.14 |

```
⊕ Physical Frame
⊟ IEEE 802.11 MAC Protocol
  ˙Function              Data
  ⊕ PLCP Header
  ⊕ Frame Control Byte 0
  ⊟ Frame Control Byte 1
    ˙Order              [0xxxxxxx]   off
    ˙WEP                [x1xxxxxx]   on
    ˙More Data          [xx0xxxxx]   off
    ˙Power Mgmt         [xxx1xxxx]   on
    ˙Retry              [xxxx0xxx]   off
    ˙More Fragments     [xxxxx0xx]   off
    ˙From DS            [xxxxxx0x]   off
    ˙To DS              [xxxxxxx1]   on
  ⊕ WEP Information
  ˙Duration ID            117
  ⊕ BSSID
  ⊕ Source Address
  ⊕ Destination Address
  ˙Fragment             [xxxxxxxx xxxx0000]   0
  ˙Sequence             [10010101 0010xxxx]   2386
⊕ IEEE 802.2 Logical Link Control
⊕ IEEE Sub-Network Access Protocol
⊟ Address Resolution Protocol
  ˙Hardware Type         Ethernet (10Mb)
  ˙Protocol Type         0800  IP
  ˙Hardware Addr Size    6
  ˙Protocol Addr Size    4
  ˙ARP Function          Address Resolution Response
  ˙Sender HW Address     00-0D-88-E5-D3-2A
  ˙Sender Prot Address   172.16.0.14
  ˙Target HW Address     00-40-96-A6-9C-3E
  ˙Target Prot Address   172.16.0.11
```

### Frame 33 ARP Response
AirLink's ReceiveDTIMs parameter was set, because AirLink woke to receive the buffered broadcast transmission.

PwrMgmt bit is set.
This response indicates a STA that is configured for maximum power save mode. The AP reads the PwrMgmt bit in every frame and sets the STA power management status accordingly.

***Although it may seem like a contradiction, AirLink is responding to the ARP request but staying in PS-mode.*** The AP continues to buffer all broad/unicast frames and unicast frames directed to AirLink.

## Configuring the DTIM Period

Modern multimedia applications such as LAN TV, collaborative computing, and desktop conferencing communicate using IP multicasting which provides one-to-many transmission. This saves a significant amount of network bandwidth compared to traditional one-to-one network applications. The Multicast IP address is mapped by the subnet's router to a MAC multicast addresses. For a quick overview of multicast technology see the 20 page Cisco whitepaper, *"Multicast Deployment Made Easy."*

Routers constrain broadcasts to the local broadcast domain. With backbone router support IP multicast is scaleable to an entire enterprise. IP multicast enables a server to transmit one frame that is delivered to all members of the IP multicast host group as described in RFC 1112. Host group members can be located anywhere on the IP network. The membership of a host group is dynamic, and specific to the multicast application. Individual nodes may independently join or leave a group.

- If extended battery life isn't an issue, disable PS-mode on every STA in the BSS and set the AP's DTM Period to 1. *Note that even if a STA is configured never to enter PS-mode, it still toggles its power management state prior to off-channel scanning, setting the DTIM Period is always an important precaution.*
- Remember that WZC Service-based STAs actively probe every 60 seconds. As a prelude to scanning off-channel the STA sends either a probe request or a null-data frame with the PwrMgmt bit set.
  - I've read several articles which claim that active scanning can be suppressed in STAs controlled by the WZC service, but the articles never document the mechanism and neither does Microsoft TechNet or MSDN. If you find it, please drop me a line!
- If extended battery life of the STAs that support multicast applications is an issue, you have a quandary. You must determine the maximum tolerated latency for all of the multicast applications in use and set the DTIM Period as a compromise between battery-life and multicast application performance.

### *Setting the DTIM*

The DTIM is configured at the AP. It's usually in the radio interface settings. Typical default values are from 1 to 5. These configuration screen shots are from an Orinoco and Cisco Aironet AP.

| Physical Interface Type | 802.11g (OFDM / DSSS 2.4 GHz) |
| MAC Address | 00:20:A6:4F:1F:79 |
| Regulatory Domain | USA (FCC) |
| Network Name (SSID) | AP600Site1 |
| Enable Auto Channel Select | ☐ |
| Frequency Channel | 1 - 2.412 GHz |
| Transmit Rate | Auto Fallback |
| DTIM Period (1-255 ) | 1 |
| RTS/CTS Medium Reservation (2347=off) | 2347 |
| Enable Closed System | ☐ |
| Wireless Service Status | Resume |

| Beacon Period: | 100 | (20-4000 Kusec) | Data Beacon Rate (DTIM): | 3 | (1-100) |
|---|---|---|---|---|---|
| Max. Data Retries: | 64 | (1-128) | RTS Max. Retries: | 64 | (1-128) |
| Fragmentation Threshold: | 2346 | (256-2346) | RTS Threshold: | 2312 | (0-2347) |

## The TIM IE's Partial Virtual Bitmap

Let's move on to PS-mode buffered unicast traffic. The AP buffers:

- data frames bridged from the DS backbone and destined for a PS-mode STA
- data frames sourced by a STA in the BSS and destined for a PS-mode STA in the same BSS
- unicast management frames, such as a probe response, which are sourced by the AP and destined for a PS-mode STA

***"Why would a PS-mode STA ever receive a unicast frame"?*** One second of server latency response provides a STA with a great opportunity to enter PS-mode and conserve battery power. Unsolicited frames such as those sourced by network management software, and application and antivirus update pushes are occasions when a dozing STA might receive an unsolicited unicast frame. Many of these updates would be more efficient as multicast applications, but it all depends on the distribution mechanism.

Theoretically an AP can support a maximum of 2007 associated STAs, where each associated STA has a unique AID in the range of 0xC001 (1) through 0xC7D7 (2007).

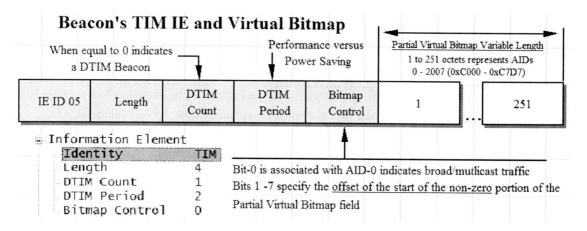

**Bitmap Control** has two separate subfields:
- Bit-0 indicates the presence of broad/multicast traffic
- Bits 1-7 specify the offset of the first non-zero octet in the Partial Virtual Bitmap field.

**Partial Virtual Bitmap**

The Partial Virtual Bitmap field is an array which consists of a maximum of 2,008 bits (251 octets x 8 bits) where each bit represents one AID. ***The first bit, bit-0 is not used because individual STAs start with AID-1 (0xC001.)*** This field is a "partial virtual bitmap" because ***the entire 2,008 bits aren't transmitted with every beacon. Only that portion of the virtual bitmap that contains bits which are set, indicating STAs with buffered unicast traffic, is transmitted.***

- Seven bits can represent $2^7$ or 128 numbers. That's a problem because the virtual bitmap field is 251 octets long. To compensate bits 1-7 of the Bitmap Control field represents the number of *the first non-zero octet in the Partial Virtual Bitmap field divided by 2*, which always makes the starting octet an even number.

- *The end of the partial virtual bitmap field is determined by the TIM IE length field*.
- The default TIM Length field value is 4, which includes one byte each for the DTIM Count, DTIM Period, Bitmap Control and Partial Virtual Bitmap.
- The Partial Virtual Bitmap is a variable length field between 1 and 251 bytes.
- When the partial virtual bitmap field has a non-zero bit, *the TIM IE length field is (End – Start) + 4*. Where "end" represents the last octet and "start" represents the first octet as defined in B-1 through B7 of the Bitmap Control field.

---

**! Exam Alert** Partial Virtual Bitmap field calculations make most people a bit queasy. Don't be concerned with the details. Know the definition and function of each TIM IE field and you'll be fine.

---

Unfortunately, LinkFerret doesn't decode the partial virtual bitmap field. However it's easy to see in the hex view. Select the Bitmap Control field, in the detail view and the byte(s) to the right of the selected byte in the hex view are the partial virtual bitmap values. In this case the partial virtual bitmap field is one byte long and has a value of 0x04. Remember the Reading Bit Positions section back in Chapter 2. *Start counting with the number zero from the least significant bit*. This TIM indicates that the STA with AID-2 (0000 0100) has buffered unicast data at the AP.

```
⊟ Information Element
    ·Identity          TIM
    ·· Length           4
    ·DTIM Count         2
    ·DTIM Period        3
    ·Bitmap Control     0
⊟ Information Element
    ·Identity          ERP
...................................
)00      80 00 00 00 FF FF FF
)16      00 20 A6 4F 1F 79 A0
)32      64 00 31 00 00 0A 41
)48      01 08 82 84 8B 96 0C
)64      03 00 04 2A 01 07 32
```

## The PS-Poll Control Frame

The AP is prompted to transmit buffered unicast frames in two ways:
- When a STA switches to AM the AP immediately transmits all of its unicast buffered data and management frames.
  - Any frame that the STA transmits with the PwrMgmt bit reset indicates that it is operating in AM.
- A PS mode STA may stay in PS-mode and retrieve buffered data by sending a PS-Poll control frame to the AP with the PwrMgmt bit set.

The Listen Interval parameter is usually a fixed value, specific to a vendor's driver implementation driver and independent of the STA's PS-mode configuration. An activity aging algorithm running on the STA determines how often it wakes to receive a beacon. If the bit associated with the STA's AID is set in the Partial Virtual Bitmap, then the process of retrieving the buffered data is initiated by the STA, either by switching to AM or staying in PS-mode and transmitting a PS-Poll frame.

*For a STA to successfully change power management modes the transmitted frame with the appropriate PwrMgmt bit setting and must be ACKed by the AP. That ensures the STA and AP agree on the STA's current power management state.*

## Multiple STAs with Concurrent Buffered Unicast Frames

A collision between the PS-Poll frames of two STAs retrieving buffered data is likely to happen when more than one bit is set in the partial virtual bitmap. When that occurs each STA enters the collision avoidance loop by generating a random delay in the range of its CW before transmitting the PS-Poll frame.

## Frame Type: PS-Poll Control

The PS-mode STA must send one PS-Poll frame for each buffered frame it retrieves from the AP. The state of the More Data bit in the subsequent data frame indicates whether the AP has additional buffered unicast frames.

<u>To/From DS = 0,0</u> Control frames aren't processed by the DSS

<u>PwrMgmt bit is set</u> The STA is staying in PS-mode as indicated by the state of the PwrMgmt bit. After the STA reads the buffered data, the AP continues to buffer new unicast frames.

<u>Duration/ID</u> The PS-Poll frame is the only frame without an explicit duration value. All STAs receiving a PS-Poll frame set their NAV timers to ***SIFS + ACK*** at the current bit rate and PLCP-preamble type. In this example the STA has AID 3 (0xC003).

<u>Addresses</u>
**BSSID** MAC address of the AP to which the STA is associated
**Transmitter** MAC address of the STA

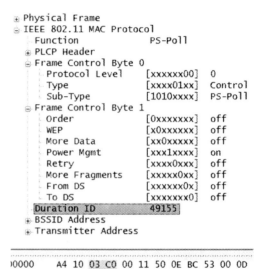

```
⊞ Physical Frame
⊟ IEEE 802.11 MAC Protocol
   Function              PS-Poll
 ⊞ PLCP Header
 ⊟ Frame Control Byte 0
     Protocol Level    [xxxxxx00]  0
     Type              [xxxx01xx]  Control
     Sub-Type          [1010xxxx]  PS-Poll
 ⊟ Frame Control Byte 1
     Order             [0xxxxxxx]  off
     WEP               [x0xxxxxx]  off
     More Data         [xx0xxxxx]  off
     Power Mgmt        [xxx1xxxx]  on
     Retry             [xxxx0xxx]  off
     More Fragments    [xxxxx0xx]  off
     From DS           [xxxxxx0x]  off
     To DS             [xxxxxxx0]  off
   Duration ID              49155
 ⊞ BSSID Address
 ⊞ Transmitter Address
─────────────────────────────────
)0000    A4 10 03 C0 00 11 50 0E BC 53 00 0D
```

## *Why ACK Instead of Transmitting the Data Frame?*

Most books and whitepapers describe the same buffered data retrieval sequence:
1) STA sends PS-Poll frame
2) AP sends Data frame
3) STA ACKs Data frame
4) If the data frame has More Data bit set, STA sends another PS-Poll frame.

Go visit your favorite business-class AP and crank up your network monitor. The odds are good that that the AP replies to a PS-Poll frame with an ACK instead of a data frame.
- Because the duration value of a PS-Poll frame is implied as a ***SIFS + ACK*** it's safer for an AP to respond with an ACK, and then follow with the buffered data frame. ***Especially in a mixed mode system, the CTS-to-Self preceding the data frame ensures that the entire transmission is protected with virtual carrier!***
- If a beacon is also a DTIM beacon buffered broad/multicast frames are transmitted first to satisfy PS-mode STAs with ReceiveDTIMs set. If a STA sneaks in a PS-Poll frame before the AP empties the broad/multicast frame buffer, the ACK

acknowledges the PS-Poll frame and the AP continues to empty its broad/multicast buffer before delivering unicast buffered frames.

## Unicast Buffered Data Analysis

Let's continue analyzing the capture file from the rebroadcast ARP section. Open capture file IntraBSS-DTIM-TIM, ensure that No Filter is applied and PSP-SRV namespace is loaded. Focus on frames 39 – 47.

| Number | Time | Destination | Source | Protocol | Function |
|--------|------|-------------|--------|----------|----------|
| [0-01]-37 | 00:00:02:938:482 | AirLink | Aironet-abg | ICMP | Echo Request |
| [0-01]-38 | 00:00:02:938:780 | Aironet-abg | | IEEE 802.11 | ACK |
| [0-01]-39 | 00:00:03:036:729 | Broadcast | Aironet-350AP | IEEE 802.11 | Beacon |
| [0-01]-40 | 00:00:03:037:218 | Aironet-350AP | AirLink | IEEE 802.11 | PS-Poll |
| [0-01]-41 | 00:00:03:037:452 | AirLink | | IEEE 802.11 | ACK |
| [0-01]-42 | 00:00:03:037:814 | AirLink | Aironet-abg | ICMP | Echo Request |
| [0-01]-43 | 00:00:03:037:947 | Aironet-350AP | | IEEE 802.11 | ACK |
| [0-01]-44 | 00:00:03:038:287 | Aironet-abg | AirLink | ICMP | Echo Reply |
| [0-01]-45 | 00:00:03:038:437 | AirLink | | IEEE 802.11 | ACK |
| [0-01]-46 | 00:00:03:039:123 | Aironet-abg | AirLink | ICMP | Echo Reply |
| [0-01]-47 | 00:00:03:039:271 | Aironet-350AP | | IEEE 802.11 | ACK |
| [0-01]-48 | 00:00:03:139:124 | Broadcast | Aironet-350AP | IEEE 802.11 | Beacon |

### Frames 37 & 38: Echo Request and ACK

Aironet-abg sends an Echo Request to destination STA AirLink. The data frame is received and ACKed by the AP. We'll verify this after we inspect the next Beacon frame, but AirLink is in PS-mode so the AP must buffer the unicast Echo Request relay frame, until AirLink sends a PS-Poll frame or changes it power management state to AM.

### Frame 39: Beacon

| Number | Time | Destination | Source | Protocol | Function |
|--------|------|-------------|--------|----------|----------|
| [0-01]-39 | 00:00:03:036:729 | Broadcast | Aironet-350AP | IEEE 802.11 | Beacon |

**TIM IE**

Length = 10 means that the Partial Virtual Bitmap field is 7 bytes long.

Bitmap Control

- **Bit-0 = 0** indicating no buffered broad/multicast traffic.
- **Bits 1 – 7 = 0** specifies that the offset into the partial virtual bitmap control field is zero.

Partial Virtual Bitmap Control

As mentioned earlier this field isn't decoded by LinkFerret. Because we know that it follows the Bitmap Control field and is seven bytes long it can be inspected directly in the Hex Decode window. The seven bytes were manually highlighted for this example. A 7 byte partial virtual bitmap with an offset of 0 represents AIDS 0 – 55.

```
⊕ Physical Frame
⊟ IEEE 802.11 MAC Protocol
    Function              Beacon
  ⊕ PLCP Header
  ⊕ Frame Control Byte 0
  ⊕ Frame Control Byte 1
    Duration ID           0
  ⊕ Destination Address
  ⊕ Source Address
  ⊕ BSSID
    Fragment      [xxxxxxxx xxxx0000]  0
    Sequence      [00100100 1001xxxx]  585
    Time Stamp           1013819064398643200
    Beacon Interval      100
  ⊕ Capability Information
  ⊕ Information Element
  ⊕ Information Element
  ⊕ Information Element
  ⊟ Information Element
      Identity           TIM
      Length             10
      DTIM Count         4
      DTIM Period        5
      Bitmap Control     0
  ⊟ Information Element
```

```
'0000  80 00 00 00 FF FF FF FF FF FF 00 09 B7 7E E9 AA
'0016  00 09 B7 7E E9 AA 90 24 0E 11 CF 11 50 00 00 00
'0032  64 00 31 00 00 0C 41 69 72 6F 33 35 30 53 69 74
'0048  65 31 01 04 02 04 8B 96 03 01 01 05 0A 04 05 00
'0064  00 00 00 00 00 00 20 85 1E 00 00 86 12 07 00 FF
'0080  03 11 00 41 69 72 6F 33 35 30 2D 31 00 00 00 00
'0096  00 00 00 02 00 00 22 96 06 00 40 96 00 07 00 DD
```

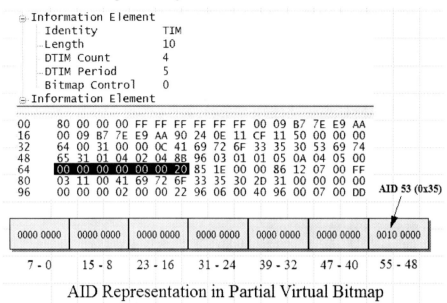

AID Representation in Partial Virtual Bitmap

The partial virtual bitmap in frame 39 indicates that the STA with AID 53 (0x35) has buffered unicast data. Take a moment to get a sense of how the octets and the individual bits are represented in the partial virtual bitmap field.

| Number | Time | Destination | Source | Protocol | Function |
|---|---|---|---|---|---|
| [0-01]-40 | 00:00:03:037:218 | Aironet-350AP | AirLink | IEEE 802.11 | PS-Poll |

Frame 40: PS-Poll
AirLink polls Aironet-350AP for buffered data.

PwrMgmt bit is set; AirLink is staying in PS-Mode

Duration/ID AirLink's AID is 0xC035 ($53_{10}$) as we determined from the TIM IE's partial virtual bitmap in the previous frame.

Remember the cause and affect here: *AirLink transmits a PS-Poll frame because the virtual bitmap in the preceding frame specified that unicast data was buffered for the STA with AID 0xC035.*

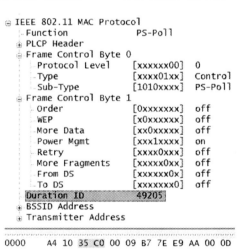

If AirLink didn't wake to receive the beacon in frame 39, the AP's buffer aging function guarantees to retain the data for a minimum of AirLink's Listen Interval.

| Number | Time | Destination | Source | Protocol | Function |
|---|---|---|---|---|---|
| [0-01]-41 | 00:00:03:037:452 | AirLink | | IEEE 802.11 | ACK |

## Frame 41 ACK

We've determined that the AP may respond to a PS-Poll frame with buffered data or an ACK. However, the data frame isn't fully protected with virtual carrier because the PS-Poll frame only has an implied duration of ***SIFS + ACK***. To fully protect the buffered data frame the AP responds with an ACK and then sends a subsequent data frame.

| Number | Time | Destination | Source | Protocol | Function |
|---|---|---|---|---|---|
| [0-01]-42 | 00:00:03:037:814 | AirLink | Aironet-abg | ICMP | Echo Request |

## Frame 42 Echo Request

This is the buffered Echo Request frame.

More Data is reset which indicates that this is the last unicast buffered frame for AirLink. If More Data was set, AirLink would respond with another PS-Poll frame.

If AirLink changes its power management state to AM, then any remaining buffered unicast data would be automatically delivered without being prompted by PS-Poll frames.

```
⊕ Physical Frame
⊟ IEEE 802.11 MAC Protocol
    Function            Data
  ⊕ PLCP Header
  ⊕ Frame Control Byte 0
  ⊟ Frame Control Byte 1
      Order           [0xxxxxxx]   off
      WEP             [x1xxxxxx]   on
      More Data       [xx0xxxxx]   off
      Power Mgmt      [xxx0xxxx]   off
      Retry           [xxxx0xxx]   off
      More Fragments  [xxxxx0xx]   off
      From DS         [xxxxxx1x]   on
      To DS           [xxxxxxx0]   off
  ⊕ WEP Information
    Duration ID       117
  ⊕ Destination Address
  ⊕ BSSID
  ⊕ Source Address
    Fragment          [xxxxxxxx xxxx0000]   0
    Sequence          [00100100 1100xxxx]   588
⊕ IEEE 802.2 Logical Link Control
⊕ IEEE Sub-Network Access Protocol
⊕ Internet Protocol
⊕ Internet Control Message Protocol
```

| Number | Time | Destination | Source | Protocol | Function |
|---|---|---|---|---|---|
| [0-01]-43 | 00:00:03:037:947 | Aironet-350AP | | IEEE 802.11 | ACK |

## Frame 43 ACK

AirLink ACKs the reception of buffered data frame and ***Aironet-350AP may now delete the frame from its buffer***.

PwrMgmt bit is set. Every frame carries the power management state of the STA. This ACK communicates to the AP that AirLink is remaining in PS-mode; broad/multicast frames will be buffered until the next DTIM beacon and unicast frames buffered until AirLink enters AM or transmits a PS-Poll frame.

```
⊕ Physical Frame
⊟ IEEE 802.11 MAC Protocol
    Function            ACK
  ⊕ PLCP Header
  ⊕ Frame Control Byte 0
  ⊟ Frame Control Byte 1
      Order           [0xxxxxxx]   off
      WEP             [x0xxxxxx]   off
      More Data       [xx0xxxxx]   off
      Power Mgmt      [xxx1xxxx]   on
      Retry           [xxxx0xxx]   off
      More Fragments  [xxxxx0xx]   off
      From DS         [xxxxxx0x]   off
      To DS           [xxxxxxx0]   off
    Duration ID       0
  ⊟ Receiver Address
      Hex Address     00-09-B7-7E-E9-AA
      Group Bit       [xxxxxxx0 xxxxxxxx]
      Local Bit       [xxxxxx0x xxxxxxxx]
      Logical Names   [[Aironet-350AP]]
      Vendor Name     Cisco Systems
```

Frames 44 – 47 show that the Echo Request is successfully completed. Note that AirLink's Echo Reply (frame 44) has the PwrMgmt bit set. This is the behavior of a STA that's configured for maximum power savings.

| Number | Time | Destination | Source | Protocol | Function |
|--------|------|-------------|--------|----------|----------|
| [0-01]-48 | 00:00:03:139:124 | Broadcast | Aironet-350AP | IEEE 802.11 | Beacon |

**Frame 48 Beacon**

```
⊞ Physical Frame
⊟ IEEE 802.11 MAC Protocol
    Function                  Beacon
  ⊞ PLCP Header
  ⊞ Frame Control Byte 0
  ⊞ Frame Control Byte 1
    Duration ID               0
  ⊞ Destination Address
  ⊞ Source Address
  ⊞ BSSID
    Fragment                  [xxxxxxxx xxxx0000]   0
    Sequence                  [00100100 1011xxxx]   587
    Time Stamp                1054352560556605440
    Beacon Interval           100
  ⊞ Capability Information
  ⊞ Information Element
  ⊞ Information Element
  ⊞ Information Element
  ⊟ Information Element
      Identity                TIM
      Length                  4
      DTIM Count              3
      DTIM Period             5
      Bitmap Control          0
```

**TIM IE**

Length 4, the default length of the TIM IE

Bitmap Control 0x00 specifies no buffered multi/broadcast frames and the default partial virtual bitmap offset of 0.

Partial Virtual Bitmap 0x00 indicates that no unicast frames are buffered.

This is consistent with the activity that we've seen in frames 26 – 48 of this capture.

```
)0000    80 00 00 00 FF FF FF FF FF FF 00 09 B7 7E E9 AA
)0016    00 09 B7 7E E9 AA B0 24 0E A1 D0 11 50 00 00 00
)0032    64 00 31 00 00 0C 41 69 72 6F 33 35 30 53 69 74
)0048    65 31 01 04 02 04 8B 96 03 01 01 05 04 03 05 00
)0064    00 85 1E 00 00 86 12 07 00 FF 03 11 00 41 69 72
```

## The Last Analysis

Frame analysis is the great revealer. Viewed through the lens of hash reality, frame flow challenges most sterile descriptions found in books and whitepapers. This isn't arrogant posturing or finger pointing, but rather a warning that dogma ends the moment you press the start capture button on your network monitor. ***Interpreting captures must be accomplished within the structure of theory but tempered with flexibility, creativity and experience.*** Often the frame interaction in your captures will be at odds with everything you read and think that you know.

A prime example of this contradiction is the null data frame. Here's a quote from the *IEEE 802.11 Handbook: A Designer's Companion*:

> ***"The <u>sole purpose</u> for this frame is to carry the power management bit in the Frame Control field to the AP when a STA changes to a low power operating state."***

The obvious mistake is that a STA not only uses a null-data frame to toggle its power state from AM to PS, but also from PS to AM as was demonstrated with the PwrMgmt-NullData capture file back in Chapter 4. Forgive me, that's the kind of picky trivial sniping that's usually reserved for certification exams. What I'm looking for here is an omission of substance, something in that statement that might confuse the heck out of the rookie frame chaser. I'll state the issue as a question:

> ***"When does an access point transmit a null-data frame?"***

According to the IEEE (and every book and article I've ever read) the answer to that question is a resounding, never!

The players in the following capture are R4000-BC an 802.11g STA and Belkin-AP2, an 802.11bg access point operating in mixed mode. To make it interesting the BSS has associated 802.11b STAs that only support long preamble. The beacon's ERP IE specifies that CTS-to-Self protection is implemented with long Barker Preamble. From a performance perspective that's about as ugly as it gets. Remember that the long PCLP-preamble and PLCP-header are transmitted at 1-Mbps.

```
⊟ Information Element
  ┊ Identity          ERP
  ┊ Length            1
  ┊ Non-ERP Present   [xxxx xxx1] On
  ┊ Use Protection    [xxxx xx1x] On
  ┊ Barker Preamble   [xxxx x1xx] On
```

But why is long barker preamble required? An examination of the beacon's Capability Information field shows that one or more long preamble-only STAs are associated to the BSS. It turns out that we have a couple Apple PowerBooks that only support the original

```
⊟ Capability Information
  ┊ Channel Agility  [0xxxxxxx xxxxxxxx]  Off
  ┊ PBCC             [x0xxxxxx xxxxxxxx]  Off
  ┊ Short Preamble   [xx0xxxxx xxxxxxxx]  Off
  ┊ Privacy          [xxx1xxxx xxxxxxxx]  On
  ┊ CF Poll Request  [xxxx0xxx xxxxxxxx]  Off
  ┊ CF Pollable      [xxxxx0xx xxxxxxxx]  Off
  ┊ IBSS             [xxxxxx0x xxxxxxxx]  Off
  ┊ ESS              [xxxxxxx1 xxxxxxxx]  On
  ┊ Reserved         [xxxxxxxx 00000000]  0
```

Apple Airport 802.11b PC-Card, which in-turn only supports long preamble. There aren't any viable third-party wireless client adapters for those notebook computers, so we're stuck with a huge performance penalty – Thanks Steve, stick with the iPods.

Open capture file **AP-Null-Data**, select the **Data-Null** filter and press **F5**. The filter produces 151 Null Data frames, but the interesting observation is (you guessed it) that, contrary to the IEEE description, the null-data frames were transmitted by an AP.

| Number | Time | Destination | Source | Protocol | Function |
|---|---|---|---|---|---|
| [0-11]-1 | 00:00:00:081:941 | R4000-BC | Belkin-AP2 | IEEE 802.11 | Null |

Examining a specific Null-data frame doesn't provide any insight because the Null-Data frame is null, other than the MAC-header it doesn't carry any information. Remove the filter by selecting **No Filter**, press **F5** and go to (Ctrl-G) frame 48.

| Number | Time | Destination | Source | Protocol | Function |
|---|---|---|---|---|---|
| [0-11]-48 | 00:00:00:688:473 | Broadcast | Belkin-AP2 | IEEE 802.11 | Beacon |
| [0-11]-49 | 00:00:00:689:023 | Belkin-AP2 | R4000-BC | IEEE 802.11 | PS-Poll |
| [0-11]-50 | 00:00:00:689:331 | R4000-BC | | IEEE 802.11 | ACK |
| [0-11]-51 | 00:00:00:690:007 | Belkin-AP2 | | IEEE 802.11 | CTS |
| [0-11]-52 | 00:00:00:690:220 | R4000-BC | Belkin-Gateway | UDP | Datagram |
| [0-11]-53 | 00:00:00:690:223 | Belkin-AP2 | | IEEE 802.11 | ACK |
| [0-11]-54 | 00:00:00:690:509 | Belkin-AP2 | R4000-BC | IEEE 802.11 | PS-Poll |
| [0-11]-55 | 00:00:00:690:834 | R4000-BC | | IEEE 802.11 | ACK |
| [0-11]-56 | 00:00:00:691:250 | Belkin-AP2 | | IEEE 802.11 | CTS |
| [0-11]-57 | 00:00:00:691:480 | R4000-BC | Belkin-Gateway | UDP | Datagram |
| [0-11]-58 | 00:00:00:691:483 | Belkin-AP2 | | IEEE 802.11 | ACK |
| [0-11]-59 | 00:00:00:691:787 | Belkin-AP2 | R4000-BC | IEEE 802.11 | PS-Poll |
| [0-11]-60 | 00:00:00:692:096 | R4000-BC | | IEEE 802.11 | ACK |
| [0-11]-61 | 00:00:00:692:563 | Belkin-AP2 | | IEEE 802.11 | CTS |
| [0-11]-62 | 00:00:00:692:833 | R4000-BC | Belkin-Gateway | UDP | Datagram |
| [0-11]-63 | 00:00:00:692:836 | Belkin-AP2 | | IEEE 802.11 | ACK |
| [0-11]-64 | 00:00:00:693:133 | Belkin-AP2 | R4000-BC | IEEE 802.11 | PS-Poll |
| [0-11]-65 | 00:00:00:693:403 | R4000-BC | | IEEE 802.11 | ACK |
| [0-11]-66 | 00:00:00:693:952 | Belkin-AP2 | | IEEE 802.11 | CTS |
| [0-11]-67 | 00:00:00:694:083 | R4000-BC | Belkin-AP2 | IEEE 802.11 | Null |
| [0-11]-68 | 00:00:00:694:218 | Belkin-AP2 | | IEEE 802.11 | ACK |

<u>Frames 48 – 68</u> This block of frames starts with a Beacon and is followed by a total of four PS-Poll frames transmitted by R4000-BC.

First 5 Frame PS-Poll Block

| [0-11]-49 | 00:00:00:689:023 | Belkin-AP2 | R4000-BC | IEEE 802.11 | PS-Poll |
|---|---|---|---|---|---|
| [0-11]-50 | 00:00:00:689:331 | R4000-BC | | IEEE 802.11 | ACK |
| [0-11]-51 | 00:00:00:690:007 | Belkin-AP2 | | IEEE 802.11 | CTS |
| [0-11]-52 | 00:00:00:690:220 | R4000-BC | Belkin-Gateway | UDP | Datagram |
| [0-11]-53 | 00:00:00:690:223 | Belkin-AP2 | | IEEE 802.11 | ACK |

**Performance Issue**: The Beacon, PS-Poll frame and ACK to the PS-Poll are all transmitted at 1-Mbps. As we determined at the beginning of the analysis we're stuck with long preamble.

| Speed | 1MBS |
|---|---|
| Signal | 78 |
| Quality | 0 |

However, by reconfiguring the AP to only support 5.5- and 11-Mbps basic rates we can guarantee that the PSDU of beacons, PS-Poll and ACKs are transmitted at a minimum of 5.5-Mbps.

The AP sets virtual carrier in frame-51 with a CTS-to-Self frame. What's the transmission rate of the CTS-to-Self frame? Seeing the previous three frames you might assume that is was also transmitted at 1-Mbps but an examination of the physical field shows that it was transmitted at 11-Mbps. The currently associated 802.11b STAs all support an 11-Mbps connection, so that's the lowest common denominator. Why isn't the PS-Poll frame transmitted at 11-Mbps? The PS-Poll was sourced by a STA, and the STA has no knowledge of the lowest common connection rate, so it defaults to the lowest basic rate and the AP must, in turn, transmits the ACK at the lowest basic rate. As stated in the previous paragraph, the only solution to this mess is to crank up the basic rates supported by the AP and get rid of our PowerBooks.

| Speed | 11MBS |
| Signal | 78 |
| Quality | 0 |

| Number | Time | Destination | Source | Protocol | Function |
|--------|------|-------------|--------|----------|----------|
| [0-11]-52 | 00:00:00:690:220 | R4000-BC | Belkin-Gateway | UDP | Datagram |

### Frame 52 – buffered Data Frame

The data frame is transmitted with ERP-OFDM at 54-Mbps and protected by the preceding CTS-to-Self frame.

| Speed | 54MBS |
| Signal | 78 |
| Quality | 0 |

More Data bit is set which indicates that the AP has additional buffered unicast frames for R4000-BC. The STA must transmit additional PS-Poll frame(s) or enter AM to receive the remaining buffered frames.

Duration 44-µs - this frame and the subsequent ACK is protected by the preceding DSSS CTS-to-Self frame.

```
⊞ Physical Frame
⊟ IEEE 802.11 MAC Protocol
   Function              Data
  ⊞ PLCP Header
  ⊞ Frame Control Byte 0
  ⊟ Frame Control Byte 1
     Order           [0xxxxxxx]   off
     WEP             [x1xxxxxx]   on
     More Data       [xx1xxxxx]   on
     Power Mgmt      [xxx0xxxx]   off
     Retry           [xxxx0xxx]   off
     More Fragments  [xxxxx0xx]   off
     From DS         [xxxxxx1x]   on
     To DS           [xxxxxxx0]   off
  ⊞ WEP Information
   Duration ID           44
```

### Frame 53 – ACK

transmitted at 24-Mbps. It's common for the ACK to be transmitted at a low ERP basic rate. Remember, every ERP-OFDM STA must receive this ACK or they will enter the EIFS recovery mode.

Frames 54 – 58 and 59 - 63 are identical to the first five frame block. Note that the More Data bit in frame 57 is still set, indicating that the AP has additional buffered data.

```
⊞ Frame Control Byte 1
   Order           [0xxxxxxx]   off
   WEP             [x1xxxxxx]   on
   More Data       [xx1xxxxx]   on
   Power Mgmt      [xxx0xxxx]   off
   Retry           [xxxx0xxx]   off
   More Fragments  [xxxxx0xx]   off
   From DS         [xxxxxx1x]   on
   To DS           [xxxxxxx0]   off
```

<u>Frames 64 – 68</u> is the last PS-Poll frame block.

| Number | Time | Destination | Source | Protocol | Function |
|--------|------|-------------|--------|----------|----------|
| [0-11]-64 | 00:00:00:693:133 | Belkin-AP2 | R4000-BC | IEEE 802.11 | PS-Poll |
| [0-11]-65 | 00:00:00:693:403 | R4000-BC | | IEEE 802.11 | ACK |
| [0-11]-66 | 00:00:00:693:952 | Belkin-AP2 | | IEEE 802.11 | CTS |
| [0-11]-67 | 00:00:00:694:083 | R4000-BC | Belkin-AP2 | IEEE 802.11 | Null |
| [0-11]-68 | 00:00:00:694:218 | Belkin-AP2 | | IEEE 802.11 | ACK |

**We expect frame 67 to be a standard data frame but instead it's a Null-Data frame!** This AP always sets the More Data bit when transmitting multiple buffered data frames. When a STA's buffered unicast data has all been transmitted, the final data frame is a null-data frame with the More Data bit reset. On the reception of the subsequent ACK the AP resets the bit in the partial virtual bitmap associated with R4000-BC's AID.

| Frame Control Byte 1 | | |
|---|---|---|
| Order | [0xxxxxxx] | off |
| WEP | [x0xxxxxx] | off |
| More Data | [xx0xxxxx] | off |
| Power Mgmt | [xxx0xxxx] | off |
| Retry | [xxxx0xxx] | off |
| More Fragments | [xxxxx0xx] | off |
| From DS | [xxxxxx1x] | on |
| To DS | [xxxxxxx0] | off |

I've seen this behavior in access points from several vendors. But what does it all prove? The IEEE often emphasizes that 802.11 is very much a standard whose implementation specifics are open to interpretation. A network monitor reveals all. As you're exposed to APs and wireless client adapters from many vendors you will observe inconsistent and often inexplicable behavior. You've now developed the skill set to tackle standard troubleshooting and performance optimization. The next step is to perform your own live captures in your test or production network, and develop a baseline analysis to determine its current operational state.

In closing, I am reminded of the sage words of Eddy Merckx, the legendary cyclist, who when asked how one becomes a "world-class bicyclist" responded with true Belgian understatement, "Ride a lot." And thus will you become a world-class frame chaser.

Byron W. Putman
November, 2005 Palm Springs, CA

## Chapter 7 Review

### Maximum Theoretical Throughputs

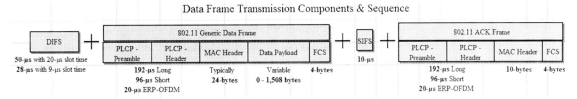

Data Frame Transmission Components & Sequence

### Maximum Throughput for a node in an 802.11b BSS

- Total Time to transfer 1,460 data bytes is 1,696-μs = 860,849 bytes/sec or 6.8-Mbps, *approximately 60% of 11-Mbps.*

### Maximum Throughput for a node in an ERP Native Mode BSS

- Total Time to transfer 1,460 data bytes is 423-μs = 3.45 megabytes/sec or 27.6-Mbps, *approximately 52% of 54-Mbps.*

### Maximum Throughput for a mixed mode BSS with Protection

- Total Time to transfer 1,460 data bytes is 699-μs or 2.1 megabytes/sec = 16.7-Mbps, *approximately 31% of 54-Mbps. CTS-to-Self imposes 21% overhead on native mode ERP-OFDM transmissions*!

### PS (Power Save) Operation

- Usually set in adapter properties, advanced tab
- Three levels: Disabled, High Performance or Max Power Savings

### PS-Mode Components

- Beacon TIME IE
  - o DTIM Count, DTM Period, Bitmap Control and Partial Virtual Bitmap
- Frame Control Byte-1
  - o PwrMgmt bit, More Data bit, Order bit
- Null-Data Frame
  - o Communicates power state when there's no other information to communicate.
- PS-Poll Frame
  - o Requests one frame of unicast buffered data
- Duration/ID field
  - o In PS-Poll frame specifies AID
- Association Request, Listen Interval field
  - o Specifies the maximum number of beacons that may occur between the STA checking for buffered unicast frames

## Establishing PS-Mode Parameters

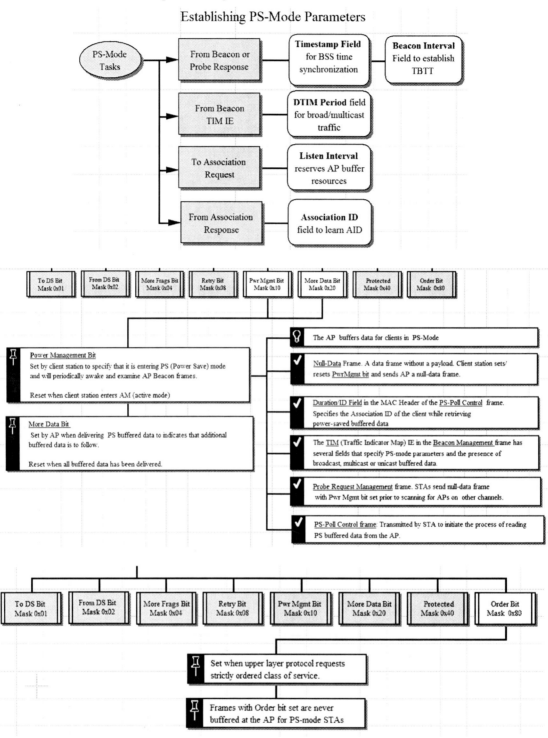

## Off-Channel Scanning

STAs with power management disabled use PS-mode when going off-channel to actively scan.

- XP typically scans every 60 seconds
- Probe Requests are have a broadcast address with To-DS =0, they are not ACKed
- Probe Responses have a unicast address and they should be ACKed
- Often STAs do not stay on-channel long enough to receive a probe response resulting in many probe response retries.
- Most 802.11g client adapters scanning parameters can't be configured

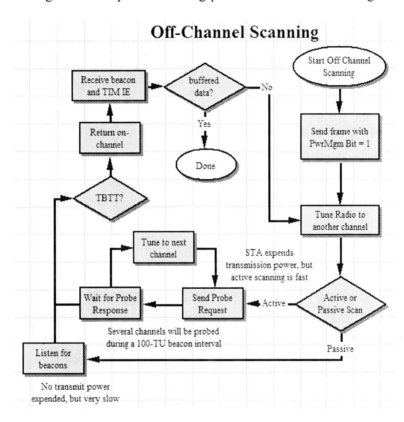

## TIM IE and Buffered Broad/Multicast Frames

DTIM Count and DTIM Period are associated with buffering broad/multicast traffic.

- **DTIM Count** is decremented with each beacon, when zero identifies A DTIM beacon.
- **DTIM Period** is configured at the AP. It specifies how often a DTIM beacon occurs.
- **Bitmap Control**, bit-0 specifies the presence of buffered broad/multicast data.
- *If any STA is in PS-mode, the AP buffers broad/multicast frames until the next DTIM Beacon.*

```
⊟ Information Element
    Identity         TIM
    Length           4
    DTIM Count       0
    DTIM Period      1
    Bitmap Control   0
```

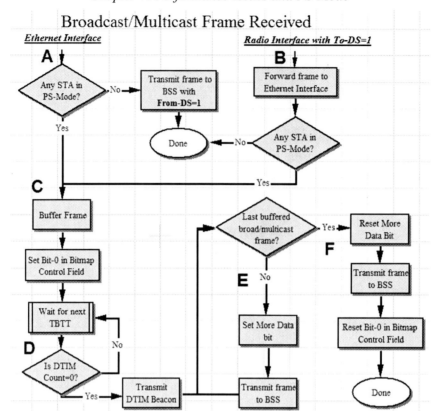

Broadcast/Multicast Frame Received

## The TIM IE's Partial Virtual Bitmap

The AP buffers unicast:
- data frames bridged from the DS backbone and destined for a PS-mode STA
- data frames sourced by a STA in the BSS and destined for a PS-mode STA in the same BSS
- unicast management frames, such as a probe response, which are sourced by the AP and destined for a PS-mode STA

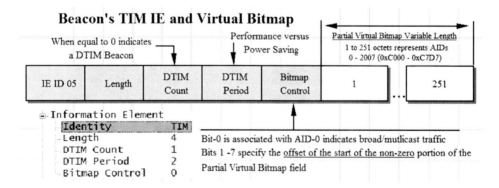

Beacon's TIM IE and Virtual Bitmap

# Appendix A: Example Frame Type Detail Captures

## Association Request

```
⊞ Physical Frame
⊟ IEEE 802.11 MAC Protocol
    Function          Association Request
  ⊞ PLCP Header
  ⊟ Frame Control Byte 0
    Protocol Level    [xxxxxx00]   0
    Type              [xxxx00xx]   Management
    Sub-Type          [0000xxxx]   Association Request
  ⊟ Frame Control Byte 1
    Order             [0xxxxxxx]   off
    WEP               [x0xxxxxx]   off
    More Data         [xx0xxxxx]   off
    Power Mgmt        [xxx0xxxx]   off
    Retry             [xxxx0xxx]   off
    More Fragments    [xxxxx0xx]   off
    From DS           [xxxxxx0x]   off
    To DS             [xxxxxxx0]   off
    Duration ID       314
  ⊟ Destination Address
    Hex Address       00-09-B7-7E-E9-AA
    Group Bit         [xxxxxxx0 xxxxxxxx xxxxxxxx xxxxxxxx xxxxxxxx]   off
    Local Bit         [xxxxxx0x xxxxxxxx xxxxxxxx xxxxxxxx xxxxxxxx]   off
    Logical Names     [[Aironet-350AP]]
    Vendor Name       Cisco Systems
  ⊟ Source Address
    Hex Address       00-40-96-A2-F4-34
    Group Bit         [xxxxxxx0 xxxxxxxx xxxxxxxx xxxxxxxx xxxxxxxx]   off
    Local Bit         [xxxxxx0x xxxxxxxx xxxxxxxx xxxxxxxx xxxxxxxx]   off
    Logical Names     [[Aironet-PCI]]
    Vendor Name       Aironet Wireless Communication
  ⊟ BSSID
    Hex Address       00-09-B7-7E-E9-AA
    Group Bit         [xxxxxxx0 xxxxxxxx xxxxxxxx xxxxxxxx xxxxxxxx]   off
    Local Bit         [xxxxxx0x xxxxxxxx xxxxxxxx xxxxxxxx xxxxxxxx]   off
    Logical Names     [[Aironet-350AP]]
    Vendor Name       Cisco Systems
    Fragment          [xxxxxxxx xxxx0000]   0
    Sequence          [00000000 0010xxxx]   2
  ⊟ Capability Information
    Channel Agility   [0xxxxxxx xxxxxxxx]   Off
    PBCC              [x0xxxxxx xxxxxxxx]   Off
    Short Preamble    [xx1xxxxx xxxxxxxx]   On
    Privacy           [xxx1xxxx xxxxxxxx]   On
    CF Poll Request   [xxxx0xxx xxxxxxxx]   Off
    CF Pollable       [xxxxx0xx xxxxxxxx]   Off
    IBSS              [xxxxxx0x xxxxxxxx]   Off
    ESS               [xxxxxxx1 xxxxxxxx]   On
    Reserved          [xxxxxxxx 00000000]   0
    Listen Interval   1
  ⊟ Information Element
    Identity          SSID
    Length            13
    SSID              Aironet-350AP
  ⊟ Information Element
    Identity          Supported Rates
    Length            4
    Rate              1.0 MB    [0xxxxxxx]   Not in Basic Rate Set
    Rate              2.0 MB    [0xxxxxxx]   Not in Basic Rate Set
    Rate              5.5 MB    [0xxxxxxx]   Not in Basic Rate Set
    Rate              11.0 MB   [0xxxxxxx]   Not in Basic Rate Set
  ⊟ Information Element
    Identity          Unknown
    Length            30
```

## Association Response

```
⊞ Physical Frame
⊟ IEEE 802.11 MAC Protocol
    Function            Association Response
 ⊞ PLCP Header
 ⊟ Frame Control Byte 0
     Protocol Level    [xxxxxx00]  0
     Type              [xxxx00xx]  Management
     Sub-Type          [0001xxxx]  Association Response
 ⊟ Frame Control Byte 1
     Order             [0xxxxxxx]  off
     WEP               [x0xxxxxx]  off
     More Data         [xx0xxxxx]  off
     Power Mgmt        [xxx0xxxx]  off
     Retry             [xxxx0xxx]  off
     More Fragments    [xxxxx0xx]  off
     From DS           [xxxxxx0x]  off
     To DS             [xxxxxxx0]  off
    Duration ID        162
 ⊟ Destination Address
     Hex Address       00-40-96-A2-F4-34
     Group Bit         [xxxxxxx0 xxxxxxxx xxxxxxxx xxxxxxxx xxxxxxxx]  off
     Local Bit         [xxxxxx0x xxxxxxxx xxxxxxxx xxxxxxxx xxxxxxxx]  off
     Vendor Name       Aironet Wireless Communication
 ⊟ Source Address
     Hex Address       00-09-B7-7E-E9-AA
     Group Bit         [xxxxxxx0 xxxxxxxx xxxxxxxx xxxxxxxx xxxxxxxx]  off
     Local Bit         [xxxxxx0x xxxxxxxx xxxxxxxx xxxxxxxx xxxxxxxx]  off
     Vendor Name       Cisco Systems
 ⊟ BSSID
     Hex Address       00-09-B7-7E-E9-AA
     Group Bit         [xxxxxxx0 xxxxxxxx xxxxxxxx xxxxxxxx xxxxxxxx]  off
     Local Bit         [xxxxxx0x xxxxxxxx xxxxxxxx xxxxxxxx xxxxxxxx]  off
     Vendor Name       Cisco Systems
    Fragment           [xxxxxxxx xxxx0000]  0
    Sequence           [00001110 1110xxxx]  238
 ⊟ Capability Information
     Channel Agility   [0xxxxxxx xxxxxxxx]  Off
     PBCC              [x0xxxxxx xxxxxxxx]  Off
     Short Preamble    [xx1xxxxx xxxxxxxx]  On
     Privacy           [xxx1xxxx xxxxxxxx]  On
     CF Poll Request   [xxxx0xxx xxxxxxxx]  off
     CF Pollable       [xxxxx0xx xxxxxxxx]  off
     IBSS              [xxxxxx0x xxxxxxxx]  off
     ESS               [xxxxxxx1 xxxxxxxx]  On
     Reserved          [xxxxxxxx 00000000]  0
    Status Code        0
    Association ID     49175
 ⊟ Information Element
     Identity          Supported Rates
     Length            4
     Rate              1.0 MB   [1xxxxxxx]  In Basic Rate Set
     Rate              2.0 MB   [1xxxxxxx]  In Basic Rate Set
     Rate              5.5 MB   [0xxxxxxx]  Not in Basic Rate Set
     Rate              11.0 MB  [0xxxxxxx]  Not in Basic Rate Set
```

## *Reassociation Request*

Identical with an association request with the addition of the Current AP field

```
⊞ Pnysical Frame
⊟ IEEE 802.11 MAC Protocol
    ┈ Function              Reassociation Request
    ⊞ PLCP Header
    ⊟ Frame Control Byte 0
    │   ┈ Protocol Level    [xxxxxx00]  0
    │   ┈ Type              [xxxx00xx]  Management
    │   ┈ Sub-Type          [0010xxxx]  Reassociation Request
    ⊟ Frame Control Byte 1
    │   ┈ Order             [0xxxxxxx]  off
    │   ┈ WEP               [x0xxxxxx]  off
    │   ┈ More Data         [xx0xxxxx]  off
    │   ┈ Power Mgmt        [xxx0xxxx]  off
    │   ┈ Retry             [xxxx0xxx]  off
    │   ┈ More Fragments    [xxxxx0xx]  off
    │   ┈ From DS           [xxxxxx0x]  off
    │   ┈ To DS             [xxxxxxx0]  off
    ┈ Duration ID           258
    ⊟ Destination Address
    │   ┈ Hex Address       00-20-A6-4F-1F-94
    │   ┈ Group Bit         [xxxxxxx0 xxxxxxxx xxxxxxxx xxxxxxxx xxxxxxxx]  off
    │   ┈ Local Bit         [xxxxxx0x xxxxxxxx xxxxxxxx xxxxxxxx xxxxxxxx]  off
    │   ┈ Logical Names     [[AP600-1]]
    │   ┈ Vendor Name       Proxim,
    ⊟ Source Address
    │   ┈ Hex Address       00-30-65-2B-48-1C
    │   ┈ Group Bit         [xxxxxxx0 xxxxxxxx xxxxxxxx xxxxxxxx xxxxxxxx]  off
    │   ┈ Local Bit         [xxxxxx0x xxxxxxxx xxxxxxxx xxxxxxxx xxxxxxxx]  off
    │   ┈ Logical Names     [[PwrBook-Airport]]
    │   ┈ Vendor Name       Apple Computer,
    ⊟ BSSID
    │   ┈ Hex Address       00-20-A6-4F-1F-94
    │   ┈ Group Bit         [xxxxxxx0 xxxxxxxx xxxxxxxx xxxxxxxx xxxxxxxx]  off
    │   ┈ Local Bit         [xxxxxx0x xxxxxxxx xxxxxxxx xxxxxxxx xxxxxxxx]  off
    │   ┈ Logical Names     [[AP600-1]]
    │   ┈ Vendor Name       Proxim,
    ┈ Fragment              [xxxxxxxx xxxx0000]  0
    ┈ Sequence              [01100011 1011xxxx]  1595
    ⊟ Capability Information
    │   ┈ Channel Agility   [0xxxxxxx xxxxxxxx]  Off
    │   ┈ PBCC              [x0xxxxxx xxxxxxxx]  Off
    │   ┈ Short Preamble    [xx0xxxxx xxxxxxxx]  Off
    │   ┈ Privacy           [xxx1xxxx xxxxxxxx]  On
    │   ┈ CF Poll Request   [xxxx0xxx xxxxxxxx]  Off
    │   ┈ CF Pollable       [xxxxx0xx xxxxxxxx]  Off
    │   ┈ IBSS              [xxxxxx0x xxxxxxxx]  Off
    │   ┈ ESS               [xxxxxxx1 xxxxxxxx]  On
    │   ┈ Reserved          [xxxxxxxx 00000000]  0
    ┈ Listen Interval       1
    ⊟ Current AP
    │   ┈ Hex Address       00-20-A6-4F-1F-79
    │   ┈ Group Bit         [xxxxxxx0 xxxxxxxx xxxxxxxx xxxxxxxx xxxxxxxx]  off
    │   ┈ Local Bit         [xxxxxx0x xxxxxxxx xxxxxxxx xxxxxxxx xxxxxxxx]  off
    │   ┈ Logical Names     [[AP600-2]]
    │   ┈ Vendor Name       Proxim,
    ⊟ Information Element
    │   ┈ Identity          SSID
    │   ┈ Length            5
    │   ┈ SSID              Site2
    ⊟ Information Element
    │   ┈ Identity          Supported Rates
    │   ┈ Length            4
    │   ┈ Rate              1.0 MB   [0xxxxxxx]  Not in Basic Rate Set
    │   ┈ Rate              2.0 MB   [0xxxxxxx]  Not in Basic Rate Set
    │   ┈ Rate              5.5 MB   [0xxxxxxx]  Not in Basic Rate Set
    │   ┈ Rate              11.0 MB  [0xxxxxxx]  Not in Basic Rate Set
```

## Reassociation Response

Identical to association response except that it follows a reassociation request

```
⊞ Physical Frame
⊟ IEEE 802.11 MAC Protocol
    ··· Function              Reassociation Response
  ⊞ PLCP Header
  ⊟ Frame Control Byte 0
    ··· Protocol Level       [xxxxxx00]  0
    ··· Type                 [xxxx00xx]  Management
    ··· Sub-Type             [0011xxxx]  Reassociation Response
  ⊟ Frame Control Byte 1
    ··· Order                [0xxxxxxx]  off
    ··· WEP                  [x0xxxxxx]  off
    ··· More Data            [xx0xxxxx]  off
    ··· Power Mgmt           [xxx0xxxx]  off
    ··· Retry                [xxxx0xxx]  off
    ··· More Fragments       [xxxxx0xx]  off
    ··· From DS              [xxxxxx0x]  off
    ··· To DS                [xxxxxxx0]  off
    ··· Duration ID          314
  ⊟ Destination Address
    ··· Hex Address          00-30-65-2B-48-1C
    ··· Group Bit            [xxxxxxx0 xxxxxxxx xxxxxxxx xxxxxxxx xxxxxxxx]  off
    ··· Local Bit            [xxxxxx0x xxxxxxxx xxxxxxxx xxxxxxxx xxxxxxxx]  off
    ··· Logical Names        [[PwrBook-Airport]]
    ··· Vendor Name          Apple Computer,
  ⊟ Source Address
    ··· Hex Address          00-20-A6-4F-1F-79
    ··· Group Bit            [xxxxxxx0 xxxxxxxx xxxxxxxx xxxxxxxx xxxxxxxx]  off
    ··· Local Bit            [xxxxxx0x xxxxxxxx xxxxxxxx xxxxxxxx xxxxxxxx]  off
    ··· Logical Names        [[AP600-2]]
    ··· Vendor Name          Proxim,
  ⊟ BSSID
    ··· Hex Address          00-20-A6-4F-1F-79
    ··· Group Bit            [xxxxxxx0 xxxxxxxx xxxxxxxx xxxxxxxx xxxxxxxx]  off
    ··· Local Bit            [xxxxxx0x xxxxxxxx xxxxxxxx xxxxxxxx xxxxxxxx]  off
    ··· Logical Names        [[AP600-2]]
    ··· Vendor Name          Proxim,
    ··· Fragment             [xxxxxxxx xxxx0000]  0
    ··· Sequence             [00110110 0001xxxx]  865
  ⊟ Capability Information
    ··· Channel Agility      [0xxxxxxx xxxxxxxx]  Off
    ··· PBCC                 [x0xxxxxx xxxxxxxx]  Off
    ··· Short Preamble       [xx1xxxxx xxxxxxxx]  On
    ··· Privacy              [xxx1xxxx xxxxxxxx]  On
    ··· CF Poll Request      [xxxx0xxx xxxxxxxx]  Off
    ··· CF Pollable          [xxxxx0xx xxxxxxxx]  Off
    ··· IBSS                 [xxxxxx0x xxxxxxxx]  Off
    ··· ESS                  [xxxxxxx1 xxxxxxxx]  On
    ··· Reserved             [xxxxxxxx 00000000]  0
    ··· Status Code          0
    ··· Association ID        49154
  ⊟ Information Element
    ··· Identity             Supported Rates
    ··· Length               4
    ··· Rate                 1.0 MB    [1xxxxxxx]  In Basic Rate Set
    ··· Rate                 2.0 MB    [1xxxxxxx]  In Basic Rate Set
    ··· Rate                 5.5 MB    [1xxxxxxx]  In Basic Rate Set
    ··· Rate                 11.0 MB   [1xxxxxxx]  In Basic Rate Set
```

# *Probe Request with SSID*

```
⊞ Physical Frame
⊟ IEEE 802.11 MAC Protocol
    Function              Probe Request
  ⊞ PLCP Header
  ⊟ Frame Control Byte 0
      Protocol Level      [xxxxxx00]  0
      Type                [xxxx00xx]  Management
      Sub-Type            [0100xxxx]  Probe Request
  ⊟ Frame Control Byte 1
      Order               [0xxxxxxx]  off
      WEP                 [x0xxxxxx]  off
      More Data           [xx0xxxxx]  off
      Power Mgmt          [xxx0xxxx]  off
      Retry               [xxxx0xxx]  off
      More Fragments      [xxxxx0xx]  off
      From DS             [xxxxxx0x]  off
      To DS               [xxxxxxx0]  off
    Duration ID           0
  ⊟ Destination Address
      Hex Address         FF-FF-FF-FF-FF-FF
      Group Bit           [xxxxxxx1 xxxxxxxx xxxxxxxx xxxxxxxx xxxxxxxx]  on
      Local Bit           [xxxxxx1x xxxxxxxx xxxxxxxx xxxxxxxx xxxxxxxx]  on
      Logical Names       [[Broadcast]]
  ⊟ Source Address
      Hex Address         00-40-96-A2-F4-34
      Group Bit           [xxxxxxx0 xxxxxxxx xxxxxxxx xxxxxxxx xxxxxxxx]  off
      Local Bit           [xxxxxx0x xxxxxxxx xxxxxxxx xxxxxxxx xxxxxxxx]  off
      Logical Names       [[Aironet-PCI]]
      Vendor Name         Aironet Wireless Communication
  ⊟ BSSID
      Hex Address         FF-FF-FF-FF-FF-FF
      Group Bit           [xxxxxxx1 xxxxxxxx xxxxxxxx xxxxxxxx xxxxxxxx]  on
      Local Bit           [xxxxxx1x xxxxxxxx xxxxxxxx xxxxxxxx xxxxxxxx]  on
      Logical Names       [[Broadcast]]
    Fragment              [xxxxxxxx xxxx0000]  0
    Sequence              [00010000 1001xxxx]  265
  ⊟ Information Element
      Identity            SSID
      Length              5
      SSID                Site2
  ⊟ Information Element
      Identity            Supported Rates
      Length              8
      Rate                1.0 MB    [0xxxxxxx]  Not in Basic Rate Set
      Rate                2.0 MB    [0xxxxxxx]  Not in Basic Rate Set
      Rate                5.5 MB    [0xxxxxxx]  Not in Basic Rate Set
      Rate                11.0 MB   [0xxxxxxx]  Not in Basic Rate Set
      Rate                6.0 MB    [0xxxxxxx]  Not in Basic Rate Set
      Rate                12.0 MB   [0xxxxxxx]  Not in Basic Rate Set
      Rate                24.0 MB   [0xxxxxxx]  Not in Basic Rate Set
      Rate                36.0 MB   [0xxxxxxx]  Not in Basic Rate Set
```

# *Null Probe Request – SSID Information Element*

```
⊟ Information Element
    Identity        SSID
    Length          0
    SSID
```

# *Probe Response 802.11bg Access Point*

```
⊞ Physical Frame
⊟ IEEE 802.11 MAC Protocol
   ┊ Function          Probe Response
   ⊞ PLCP Header
   ⊟ Frame Control Byte 0
   ┊  ┊ Protocol Level   [xxxxxx00]  0
   ┊  ┊ Type             [xxxx00xx]  Management
   ┊  └ Sub-Type         [0101xxxx]  Probe Response
   ⊟ Frame Control Byte 1
   ┊  ┊ Order            [0xxxxxxx]  off
   ┊  ┊ WEP              [x0xxxxxx]  off
   ┊  ┊ More Data        [xx0xxxxx]  off
   ┊  ┊ Power Mgmt       [xxx0xxxx]  off
   ┊  ┊ Retry            [xxxx0xxx]  off
   ┊  ┊ More Fragments   [xxxxx0xx]  off
   ┊  ┊ From DS          [xxxxxx0x]  off
   ┊  └ To DS            [xxxxxxx0]  off
   ┊ Duration ID       314
   ⊟ Destination Address
   ┊  ┊ Hex Address      00-40-96-A2-F4-34
   ┊  ┊ Group Bit        [xxxxxxx0 xxxxxxxx xxxxxxxx xxxxxxxx xxxxxxxx]  off
   ┊  ┊ Local Bit        [xxxxxx0x xxxxxxxx xxxxxxxx xxxxxxxx xxxxxxxx]  off
   ┊  ┊ Logical Names    [[Aironet-PCI]]
   ┊  └ Vendor Name      Aironet Wireless Communication
   ⊟ Source Address
   ┊  ┊ Hex Address      00-20-A6-4F-1F-94
   ┊  ┊ Group Bit        [xxxxxxx0 xxxxxxxx xxxxxxxx xxxxxxxx xxxxxxxx]  off
   ┊  ┊ Local Bit        [xxxxxx0x xxxxxxxx xxxxxxxx xxxxxxxx xxxxxxxx]  off
   ┊  ┊ Logical Names    [[AP600-1]]
   ┊  └ Vendor Name      Proxim,
   ⊟ BSSID
   ┊  ┊ Hex Address      00-20-A6-4F-1F-94
   ┊  ┊ Group Bit        [xxxxxxx0 xxxxxxxx xxxxxxxx xxxxxxxx xxxxxxxx]  off
   ┊  ┊ Local Bit        [xxxxxx0x xxxxxxxx xxxxxxxx xxxxxxxx xxxxxxxx]  off
   ┊  ┊ Logical Names    [[AP600-1]]
   ┊  └ Vendor Name      Proxim,
   ┊ Fragment          [xxxxxxxx xxxx0000]  0
   ┊ Sequence          [01000010 1111xxxx]  1071
   ┊ Time Stamp        8946850475991367680
   ┊ Beacon Interval   100
   ⊟ Capability Information
   ┊  ┊ Channel Agility  [0xxxxxxx xxxxxxxx]  Off
   ┊  ┊ PBCC             [x0xxxxxx xxxxxxxx]  Off
   ┊  ┊ Short Preamble   [xx1xxxxx xxxxxxxx]  On
   ┊  ┊ Privacy          [xxx1xxxx xxxxxxxx]  On
   ┊  ┊ CF Poll Request  [xxxx0xxx xxxxxxxx]  Off
   ┊  ┊ CF Pollable      [xxxxx0xx xxxxxxxx]  Off
   ┊  ┊ IBSS             [xxxxxx0x xxxxxxxx]  Off
   ┊  ┊ ESS              [xxxxxxx1 xxxxxxxx]  On
   ┊  └ Reserved         [xxxxxxxx 00000100]  4
   ⊟ Information Element
   ┊  ┊ Identity         SSID
   ┊  ┊ Length           5
   ┊  └ SSID             Site2
   ⊟ Information Element
   ┊  ┊ Identity         Supported Rates
   ┊  ┊ Length           8
   ┊  ┊ Rate             1.0 MB   [1xxxxxxx]  In Basic Rate Set
   ┊  ┊ Rate             2.0 MB   [1xxxxxxx]  In Basic Rate Set
   ┊  ┊ Rate             5.5 MB   [1xxxxxxx]  In Basic Rate Set
   ┊  ┊ Rate             11.0 MB  [1xxxxxxx]  In Basic Rate Set
   ┊  ┊ Rate             6.0 MB   [0xxxxxxx]  Not in Basic Rate Set
   ┊  ┊ Rate             12.0 MB  [0xxxxxxx]  Not in Basic Rate Set
   ┊  ┊ Rate             24.0 MB  [0xxxxxxx]  Not in Basic Rate Set
   ┊  └ Rate             36.0 MB  [0xxxxxxx]  Not in Basic Rate Set
   ⊟ Information Element
   ┊  ┊ Identity         DS Parameter Set
   ┊  ┊ Length           1
   ┊  └ Current Channel  1
   ⊟ Information Element
   ┊  ┊ Identity         ERP
   ┊  ┊ Length           1
   ┊  ┊ Non-ERP Present  [xxxx xxx0]  Off
   ┊  ┊ Use Protection   [xxxx xx0x]  Off
   ┊  └ Barker Preamble  [xxxx x0xx]  Off
   ⊟ Information Element
   ┊  ┊ Identity         Extended Rates
   ┊  ┊ Length           4
   ┊  ┊ Rate             9.0 MB   [0xxxxxxx]  Not in Basic Rate Set
   ┊  ┊ Rate             18.0 MB  [0xxxxxxx]  Not in Basic Rate Set
   ┊  └ Rate             48.0 MB  [0xxxxxxx]  Not in Basic Rate Set
```

# *Probe Response Cisco Aironet-350 802.11b Access Point*

```
⊞ Physical Frame
⊟ IEEE 802.11 MAC Protocol
   ⋯ Function              Probe Response
   ⊞ PLCP Header
   ⊟ Frame Control Byte 0
   │  ⋯ Protocol Level     [xxxxxx00]  0
   │  ⋯ Type               [xxxx00xx]  Management
   │  ⋯ Sub-Type           [0101xxxx]  Probe Response
   ⊟ Frame Control Byte 1
   │  ⋯ Order              [0xxxxxxx]  off
   │  ⋯ WEP                [x0xxxxxx]  off
   │  ⋯ More Data          [xx0xxxxx]  off
   │  ⋯ Power Mgmt         [xxx0xxxx]  off
   │  ⋯ Retry              [xxxx0xxx]  off
   │  ⋯ More Fragments     [xxxxx0xx]  off
   │  ⋯ From DS            [xxxxxx0x]  off
   │  ⋯ To DS              [xxxxxxx0]  off
   ⋯ Duration ID           314
   ⊟ Destination Address
   │  ⋯ Hex Address        00-0D-88-E5-D3-2A
   │  ⋯ Group Bit          [xxxxxxx0 xxxxxxxx xxxxxxxx xxxxxxxx xxxxxxxx]  off
   │  ⋯ Local Bit          [xxxxxx0x xxxxxxxx xxxxxxxx xxxxxxxx xxxxxxxx]  off
   │  ⋯ Logical Names      [[AirLink]]
   │  ⋯ Vendor Name        D-link
   ⊟ Source Address
   │  ⋯ Hex Address        00-09-B7-7E-E9-AA
   │  ⋯ Group Bit          [xxxxxxx0 xxxxxxxx xxxxxxxx xxxxxxxx xxxxxxxx]  off
   │  ⋯ Local Bit          [xxxxxx0x xxxxxxxx xxxxxxxx xxxxxxxx xxxxxxxx]  off
   │  ⋯ Logical Names      [[Aironet-350AP]]
   │  ⋯ Vendor Name        Cisco Systems
   ⊟ BSSID
   │  ⋯ Hex Address        00-09-B7-7E-E9-AA
   │  ⋯ Group Bit          [xxxxxxx0 xxxxxxxx xxxxxxxx xxxxxxxx xxxxxxxx]  off
   │  ⋯ Local Bit          [xxxxxx0x xxxxxxxx xxxxxxxx xxxxxxxx xxxxxxxx]  off
   │  ⋯ Logical Names      [[Aironet-350AP]]
   │  ⋯ Vendor Name        Cisco Systems
   ⋯ Fragment              [xxxxxxxx xxxx0000]  0
   ⋯ Sequence              [01011011 0000xxxx]  1456
   ⋯ Time Stamp            7620694032028532736
   ⋯ Beacon Interval       100
   ⊟ Capability Information
   │  ⋯ Channel Agility     [0xxxxxxx xxxxxxxx]  Off
   │  ⋯ PBCC                [x0xxxxxx xxxxxxxx]  Off
   │  ⋯ Short Preamble      [xx1xxxxx xxxxxxxx]  On
   │  ⋯ Privacy             [xxx1xxxx xxxxxxxx]  On
   │  ⋯ CF Poll Request     [xxxx0xxx xxxxxxxx]  Off
   │  ⋯ CF Pollable         [xxxxx0xx xxxxxxxx]  Off
   │  ⋯ IBSS                [xxxxxx0x xxxxxxxx]  Off
   │  ⋯ ESS                 [xxxxxxx1 xxxxxxxx]  On
   │  ⋯ Reserved            [xxxxxxxx 00000000]  0
   ⊟ Information Element
   │  ⋯ Identity            SSID
   │  ⋯ Length              13
   │  ⋯ SSID                Aironet-350AP
   ⊟ Information Element
   │  ⋯ Identity            Supported Rates
   │  ⋯ Length              4
   │  ⋯ Rate                1.0 MB   [1xxxxxxx]  In Basic Rate Set
   │  ⋯ Rate                2.0 MB   [1xxxxxxx]  In Basic Rate Set
   │  ⋯ Rate                5.5 MB   [0xxxxxxx]  Not in Basic Rate Set
   │  ⋯ Rate                11.0 MB  [0xxxxxxx]  Not in Basic Rate Set
   ⊟ Information Element
   │  ⋯ Identity            DS Parameter Set
   │  ⋯ Length              1
   │  ⋯ Current Channel     6
   ⊟ Information Element
   │  ⋯ Identity            Unknown
   │  ⋯ Length              30
   ⊟ Information Element
   │  ⋯ Identity            Unknown
   │  ⋯ Length              6
   ⊟ Information Element
   │  ⋯ Identity            Vendor-Specific
   │  ⋯ Length              6
   │  ⋯ OUI                 Aironet Wireless Communication
   ⊟ Information Element
   │  ⋯ Identity            Vendor-Specific
   │  ⋯ Length              22
   │  ⋯ OUI                 Aironet Wireless Communication
```

## *Beacon 802.11g-only with WPA IE, Part-1*
### Control bytes through Capability Info
Note:The only difference between a beacon and probe response frame is the TIM IE

```
⊞ Physical Frame
⊟ IEEE 802.11 MAC Protocol
   ┈ Function            Beacon
   ⊞ PLCP Header
   ⊟ Frame Control Byte 0
      ┈ Protocol Level   [xxxxxx00]  0
      ┈ Type             [xxxx00xx]  Management
      ┈ Sub-Type         [1000xxxx]  Beacon
   ⊟ Frame Control Byte 1
      ┈ Order            [0xxxxxxx]  off
      ┈ WEP              [x0xxxxxx]  off
      ┈ More Data        [xx0xxxxx]  off
      ┈ Power Mgmt       [xxx0xxxx]  off
      ┈ Retry            [xxxx0xxx]  off
      ┈ More Fragments   [xxxxx0xx]  off
      ┈ From DS          [xxxxxx0x]  off
      ┈ To DS            [xxxxxxx0]  off
   ┈ Duration ID         0
   ⊟ Destination Address
      ┈ Hex Address      FF-FF-FF-FF-FF-FF
      ┈ Group Bit        [xxxxxxx1 xxxxxxxx xxxxxxxx xxxxxxxx xxxxxxxx]  on
      ┈ Local Bit        [xxxxxx1x xxxxxxxx xxxxxxxx xxxxxxxx xxxxxxxx]  on
      ┈ Logical Names    [[Broadcast]]
   ⊟ Source Address
      ┈ Hex Address      00-20-A6-4F-1F-94
      ┈ Group Bit        [xxxxxxx0 xxxxxxxx xxxxxxxx xxxxxxxx xxxxxxxx]  off
      ┈ Local Bit        [xxxxxx0x xxxxxxxx xxxxxxxx xxxxxxxx xxxxxxxx]  off
      ┈ Logical Names    [[AP600-1]]
      ┈ Vendor Name      Proxim,
   ⊟ BSSID
      ┈ Hex Address      00-20-A6-4F-1F-94
      ┈ Group Bit        [xxxxxxx0 xxxxxxxx xxxxxxxx xxxxxxxx xxxxxxxx]  off
      ┈ Local Bit        [xxxxxx0x xxxxxxxx xxxxxxxx xxxxxxxx xxxxxxxx]  off
      ┈ Logical Names    [[AP600-1]]
      ┈ Vendor Name      Proxim,
   ┈ Fragment           [xxxxxxxx xxxx0000]  0
   ┈ Sequence           [00010000 1000xxxx]  264
   ┈ Time Stamp         4030890995582238720
   ┈ Beacon Interval    100
   ⊟ Capability Information
      ┈ Channel Agility  [0xxxxxxx xxxxxxxx]  Off
      ┈ PBCC             [x0xxxxxx xxxxxxxx]  Off
      ┈ Short Preamble   [xx1xxxxx xxxxxxxx]  On
      ┈ Privacy          [xxx1xxxx xxxxxxxx]  On
      ┈ CF Poll Request  [xxxx0xxx xxxxxxxx]  Off
      ┈ CF Pollable      [xxxxx0xx xxxxxxxx]  Off
      ┈ IBSS             [xxxxxx0x xxxxxxxx]  Off
      ┈ ESS              [xxxxxxx1 xxxxxxxx]  On
      ┈ Reserved         [xxxxxxxx 00000100]  4
```

## *Beacon 802.11g-only with WPA IE, Part-2*
### SSID IE through WPA IE

```
Information Element
    Identity          SSID
    Length            5
    SSID              Site2
Information Element
    Identity          Supported Rates
    Length            8
    Rate              6.0 MB    [1xxxxxxx]   In Basic Rate Set
    Rate              12.0 MB   [1xxxxxxx]   In Basic Rate Set
    Rate              24.0 MB   [1xxxxxxx]   In Basic Rate Set
    Rate              36.0 MB   [0xxxxxxx]   Not in Basic Rate Set
    Rate              9.0 MB    [0xxxxxxx]   Not in Basic Rate Set
    Rate              18.0 MB   [0xxxxxxx]   Not in Basic Rate Set
    Rate              48.0 MB   [0xxxxxxx]   Not in Basic Rate Set
    Rate              54.0 MB   [0xxxxxxx]   Not in Basic Rate Set
Information Element
    Identity          DS Parameter Set
    Length            1
    Current Channel   1
Information Element
    Identity          TIM
    Length            4
    DTIM Count        0
    DTIM Period       1
    Bitmap Control    0
Information Element
    Identity          ERP
    Length            1
    Non-ERP Present   [xxxx xxx0]  Off
    Use Protection    [xxxx xx0x]  Off
    Barker Preamble   [xxxx x0xx]  Off
Information Element
    Identity          Vendor-Specific
    Length            22
    OUI               Microsoft
    Type              1
    Version           1
    Group Key Cipher Suite
        OUI           Microsoft
        Type          TKIP
    Pairwise Count    1
    Pairwise Key Cipher Suite
        OUI           Microsoft
        Type          TKIP
    Auth Count        1
    Authenticated Key Management Suite
        OUI           Microsoft
        Type          TKIP
```

## Authentication: Open, Sequence Number 1

```
⊞ Physical Frame
⊟ IEEE 802.11 MAC Protocol
   ⋯ Function              Authentication
   ⊞ PLCP Header
   ⊟ Frame Control Byte 0
      ⋯ Protocol Level     [xxxxxx00]   0
      ⋯ Type               [xxxx00xx]   Management
      ⋯ Sub-Type           [1011xxxx]   Authentication
   ⊟ Frame Control Byte 1
      ⋯ Order              [0xxxxxxx]   off
      ⋯ WEP                [x0xxxxxx]   off
      ⋯ More Data          [xx0xxxxx]   off
      ⋯ Power Mgmt         [xxx0xxxx]   off
      ⋯ Retry              [xxxx0xxx]   off
      ⋯ More Fragments     [xxxxx0xx]   off
      ⋯ From DS            [xxxxxx0x]   off
      ⋯ To DS              [xxxxxxx0]   off
   ⋯ Duration ID           314
   ⊟ Destination Address
      ⋯ Hex Address        00-09-B7-7E-E9-AA
      ⋯ Group Bit          [xxxxxxx0 xxxxxxxx xxxxxxxx xxxxxxxx xxxxxxxx]   off
      ⋯ Local Bit          [xxxxxx0x xxxxxxxx xxxxxxxx xxxxxxxx xxxxxxxx]   off
      ⋯ Logical Names      [[Aironet-350AP]]
      ⋯ Vendor Name        Cisco Systems
   ⊟ Source Address
      ⋯ Hex Address        00-40-96-A2-F4-34
      ⋯ Group Bit          [xxxxxxx0 xxxxxxxx xxxxxxxx xxxxxxxx xxxxxxxx]   off
      ⋯ Local Bit          [xxxxxx0x xxxxxxxx xxxxxxxx xxxxxxxx xxxxxxxx]   off
      ⋯ Logical Names      [[Aironet-PCI]]
      ⋯ Vendor Name        Aironet Wireless Communication
   ⊟ BSSID
      ⋯ Hex Address        00-09-B7-7E-E9-AA
      ⋯ Group Bit          [xxxxxxx0 xxxxxxxx xxxxxxxx xxxxxxxx xxxxxxxx]   off
      ⋯ Local Bit          [xxxxxx0x xxxxxxxx xxxxxxxx xxxxxxxx xxxxxxxx]   off
      ⋯ Logical Names      [[Aironet-350AP]]
      ⋯ Vendor Name        Cisco Systems
   ⋯ Fragment              [xxxxxxxx xxxx0000]   0
   ⋯ Sequence              [00000000 0001xxxx]   1
   ⋯ Algorithm             0   Open
   ⋯ Sequence Number       1
   ⋯ Status Code           0   Reserved
```

## Authentication: Open, Sequence Number 2 (fragment)

```
⋯ Algorithm             0   Open
⋯ Sequence Number       2
⋯ Status Code           0   Reserved
```

## *Authentication: Shared Key*

### Sequence Number 1

Shared Key makes WEP even more vulnerable – don't use either!

```
⊕ Physical Frame
⊟ IEEE 802.11 MAC Protocol
    Function            Authentication
  ⊕ PLCP Header
  ⊟ Frame Control Byte 0
      Protocol Level    [xxxxxx00]  0
      Type              [xxxx00xx]  Management
      Sub-Type          [1011xxxx]  Authentication
  ⊟ Frame Control Byte 1
      Order             [0xxxxxxx]  off
      WEP               [x0xxxxxx]  off
      More Data         [xx0xxxxx]  off
      Power Mgmt        [xxx0xxxx]  off
      Retry             [xxxx0xxx]  off
      More Fragments    [xxxxx0xx]  off
      From DS           [xxxxxx0x]  off
      To DS             [xxxxxxx0]  off
    Duration ID         314
  ⊕ Destination Address
  ⊕ Source Address
  ⊕ BSSID
    Fragment            [xxxxxxxx xxxx0000]  0
    Sequence            [00000000 0001xxxx]  1
    Algorithm           1  Shared Key
    Sequence Number     1
    Status Code         0  Reserved
```

### Sequence Number 2 (Last 4 fields)

```
  Algorithm            1  Shared Key
  Sequence Number      2
  Status Code          0  Reserved
⊟ Information Element
    Identity             Challenge Text
    Length               128
```

```
B0 00 02 01 00 40 96 A2 F4 34 00 09 B7 7E E9 AA    .....@...4...~..
00 09 B7 7E E9 AA 40 67 01 00 02 00 00 00 10 80    ...~..@g........
9D 1C E1 23 97 7F 9B 53 33 55 F6 3B 63 C0 66 EE    ...#...S3U.;c.f.
37 6F 3B B5 A7 66 5D 87 16 ED 25 50 CF 9F FD 81    7o;..f]...%P....
29 34 33 BA C4 AB 15 1B 35 C9 A4 21 4B B3 99 3D    )43.....5..!K..=
D5 FE 19 39 4C C4 31 23 6B 9E BB E2 38 30 E0 FB    ...9L.1#k...80..
A1 37 18 FF A9 ED 66 5D 80 60 47 13 F9 4A 9F 51    .7....f].`G..J.Q
82 89 73 55 4D 69 59 61 D9 66 2C 63 B1 7F BB 7D    ..sUMiYa.f,c...}
```

### Sequence Number 3 (last 4 fields)

```
  Algorithm            1  Shared Key
  Sequence Number      3
  Status Code          0  Reserved
⊟ Information Element
    Identity             Challenge Text
    Length               128
```

```
B0 40 3A 01 00 09 B7 7E E9 AA 00 40 96 A2 F4 34    .@:....~...@...4
00 09 B7 7E E9 AA 20 00 01 00 03 00 00 00 10 80    ...~... ........
9D 1C E1 23 97 7F 9B 53 33 55 F6 3B 63 C0 66 EE    ...#...S3U.;c.f.
37 6F 3B B5 A7 66 5D 87 16 ED 25 50 CF 9F FD 81    7o;..f]...%P....
29 34 33 BA C4 AB 15 1B 35 C9 A4 21 4B B3 99 3D    )43.....5..!K..=
D5 FE 19 39 4C C4 31 23 6B 9E BB E2 38 30 E0 FB    ...9L.1#k...80..
A1 37 18 FF A9 ED 66 5D 80 60 47 13 F9 4A 9F 51    .7....f].`G..J.Q
82 89 73 55 4D 69 59 61 D9 66 2C 63             ..sUMiYa.f,c
```

### Sequence Number 4 (Last 3 fields)

```
  Algorithm            1  Shared Key
  Sequence Number      4
  Status Code          0  Reserved
```

## AP configured for Shared Key, STA for Open - Failure

```
Algorithm              0  Open
Sequence Number        2
Status Code           13 Specified authentication algorithm not supported
```

## Deauthentication

```
Physical Frame
IEEE 802.11 MAC Protocol
   Function            Deauthentication
   PLCP Header
   Frame Control Byte 0
      Protocol Level   [xxxxxx00]  0
      Type             [xxxx00xx]  Management
      Sub-Type         [1100xxxx]  Deauthentication
   Frame Control Byte 1
      Order            [0xxxxxxx]  off
      WEP              [x0xxxxxx]  off
      More Data        [xx0xxxxx]  off
      Power Mgmt       [xxx0xxxx]  off
      Retry            [xxxx0xxx]  off
      More Fragments   [xxxxx0xx]  off
      From DS          [xxxxxx0x]  off
      To DS            [xxxxxxx0]  off
   Duration ID         314
   Destination Address
      Hex Address      00-11-50-0E-BC-53
      Group Bit        [xxxxxxx0 xxxxxxxx xxxxxxxx xxxxxxxx xxxxxxxx]  off
      Local Bit        [xxxxxx0x xxxxxxxx xxxxxxxx xxxxxxxx xxxxxxxx]  off
      Logical Names    [[Belkin-AP]]
      Vendor Name      Belkin
   Source Address
      Hex Address      00-40-96-A2-F4-34
      Group Bit        [xxxxxxx0 xxxxxxxx xxxxxxxx xxxxxxxx xxxxxxxx]  off
      Local Bit        [xxxxxx0x xxxxxxxx xxxxxxxx xxxxxxxx xxxxxxxx]  off
      Logical Names    [[Aironet-PCI]]
      Vendor Name      Aironet Wireless Communication
   BSSID
      Hex Address      00-11-50-0E-BC-53
      Group Bit        [xxxxxxx0 xxxxxxxx xxxxxxxx xxxxxxxx xxxxxxxx]  off
      Local Bit        [xxxxxx0x xxxxxxxx xxxxxxxx xxxxxxxx xxxxxxxx]  off
      Logical Names    [[Belkin-AP]]
      Vendor Name      Belkin
   Fragment            [xxxxxxxx xxxx0000]  0
   Sequence            [00011101 0010xxxx]  466
   Reason Code         3  Deauthenticated because station is leaving IBSS or ESS
```

## Disassociation

```
⊞ Physical Frame
⊟ IEEE 802.11 MAC Protocol
    ⋯Function              Disassociation
  ⊞ PLCP Header
  ⊟ Frame Control Byte 0
    ⋯Protocol Level     [xxxxxx00]  0
    ⋯Type               [xxxx00xx]  Management
    ⋯Sub-Type           [1010xxxx]  Disassociation
  ⊟ Frame Control Byte 1
    ⋯Order              [0xxxxxxx]  off
    ⋯WEP                [x0xxxxxx]  off
    ⋯More Data          [xx0xxxxx]  off
    ⋯Power Mgmt         [xxx0xxxx]  off
    ⋯Retry              [xxxx0xxx]  off
    ⋯More Fragments     [xxxxx0xx]  off
    ⋯From DS            [xxxxxx0x]  off
    ⋯To DS              [xxxxxxx0]  off
    ⋯Duration ID        0
  ⊟ Destination Address
    ⋯Hex Address        FF-FF-FF-FF-FF-FF
    ⋯Group Bit          [xxxxxxx1 xxxxxxxx xxxxxxxx xxxxxxxx xxxxxxxx]  on
    ⋯Local Bit          [xxxxxx1x xxxxxxxx xxxxxxxx xxxxxxxx xxxxxxxx]  on
    ⋯Logical Names      [[Broadcast]]
  ⊟ Source Address
    ⋯Hex Address        00-20-A6-4F-1F-94
    ⋯Group Bit          [xxxxxxx0 xxxxxxxx xxxxxxxx xxxxxxxx xxxxxxxx]  off
    ⋯Local Bit          [xxxxxx0x xxxxxxxx xxxxxxxx xxxxxxxx xxxxxxxx]  off
    ⋯Logical Names      [[AP600-1]]
    ⋯Vendor Name        Proxim,
  ⊟ BSSID
    ⋯Hex Address        00-20-A6-4F-1F-94
    ⋯Group Bit          [xxxxxxx0 xxxxxxxx xxxxxxxx xxxxxxxx xxxxxxxx]  off
    ⋯Local Bit          [xxxxxx0x xxxxxxxx xxxxxxxx xxxxxxxx xxxxxxxx]  off
    ⋯Logical Names      [[AP600-1]]
    ⋯Vendor Name        Proxim,
    ⋯Fragment           [xxxxxxxx xxxx0000]  0
    ⋯Sequence           [10010000 1110xxxx]  2318
    ⋯Reason Code        8  Disassociated because station is leaving BSS
```

## *PS-Poll*

- Duration/ID value is the STA's association ID-3, 0xc003 (49,155)
- Implied duration of SIS +ACK
- STA AIDs start with 0xC001

```
⊞ Physical Frame
⊟ IEEE 802.11 MAC Protocol
   ┈ Function          PS-Poll
 ⊞ PLCP Header
 ⊟ Frame Control Byte 0
   ┈ Protocol Level    [xxxxxx00]  0
   ┈ Type              [xxxx01xx]  Control
   ┈ Sub-Type          [1010xxxx]  PS-Poll
 ⊟ Frame Control Byte 1
   ┈ Order             [0xxxxxxx]  off
   ┈ WEP               [x0xxxxxx]  off
   ┈ More Data         [xx0xxxxx]  off
   ┈ Power Mgmt        [xxx1xxxx]  on
   ┈ Retry             [xxxx0xxx]  off
   ┈ More Fragments    [xxxxx0xx]  off
   ┈ From DS           [xxxxxx0x]  off
   ┈ To DS             [xxxxxxx0]  off
   ┈ Duration ID       49155
 ⊟ BSSID Address
   ┈ Hex Address       00-11-50-0E-BC-53
   ┈ Group Bit         [xxxxxxx0 xxxxxxxx xxxxxxxx xxxxxxxx xxxxxxxx]  off
   ┈ Local Bit         [xxxxxx0x xxxxxxxx xxxxxxxx xxxxxxxx xxxxxxxx]  off
   ┈ Logical Names     [[Belkin-AP]]
   ┈ Vendor Name       Belkin
 ⊟ Transmitter Address
   ┈ Hex Address       00-0D-88-E5-D3-2A
   ┈ Group Bit         [xxxxxxx0 xxxxxxxx xxxxxxxx xxxxxxxx xxxxxxxx]  off
   ┈ Local Bit         [xxxxxx0x xxxxxxxx xxxxxxxx xxxxxxxx xxxxxxxx]  off
   ┈ Logical Names     [[AirLink]]
   ┈ Vendor Name       D-link
```

```
0000    A4 10 03 C0 00 11 50 0E BC 53 00 0D 88 E5 D3 2A    ......P..S.....*
```

# RTS

- Duration =SIS +CTS +SIS +time to transmit data +SIS +ACK
- Compensates for hidden-node and BSA overlap issues

```
+- Physical Frame
+- IEEE 802.11 MAC Protocol
    |--- Function           RTS
    +- PLCP Header
    +- Frame Control Byte 0
    |    |--- Protocol Level   [xxxxxx00]   0
    |    |--- Type            [xxxx01xx]   Control
    |    |--- Sub-Type        [1011xxxx]   RTS
    +- Frame Control Byte 1
    |    |--- Order          [0xxxxxxx]   off
    |    |--- WEP            [x0xxxxxx]   off
    |    |--- More Data       [xx0xxxxx]   off
    |    |--- Power Mgmt      [xxx0xxxx]   off
    |    |--- Retry          [xxxx0xxx]   off
    |    |--- More Fragments   [xxxxx0xx]   off
    |    |--- From DS         [xxxxxx0x]   off
    |    |--- To DS          [xxxxxxx0]   off
    |--- Duration ID          1458
    +- Receiver Address
    |    |--- Hex Address      00-09-B7-7E-E9-AA
    |    |--- Group Bit        [xxxxxxx0 xxxxxxxx xxxxxxxx xxxxxxxx xxxxxxxx]   off
    |    |--- Local Bit        [xxxxxx0x xxxxxxxx xxxxxxxx xxxxxxxx xxxxxxxx]   off
    |    |--- Logical Names     [[Aironet-350AP]]
    |    |--- Vendor Name      Cisco Systems
    +- Transmitter Address
        |--- Hex Address      00-0D-88-E5-D3-2A
        |--- Group Bit        [xxxxxxx0 xxxxxxxx xxxxxxxx xxxxxxxx xxxxxxxx]   off
        |--- Local Bit        [xxxxxx0x xxxxxxxx xxxxxxxx xxxxxxxx xxxxxxxx]   off
        |--- Logical Names     [[AirLink]]
        |--- Vendor Name      D-link
```

## *CTS*

CTS and CTS-to-Self frames are identical except:

- CTS is sent in response to receiving a RTS frame
- CTS duration field is $RTS_{duration} - (SIFS + CTS)$
- CTS-to-Self is transmitted by ERP-OFDM STA in response to 'Use Protection' bit set in ERP IE
- CTS-to-Self is transmitted with DSSS modulation at the lowest basic rate with duration field set to SIFS + the ERP-OFDM frame length + SIFS + ACK
- CTS-to-Self is followed by an ERP-OFDM transmission and ACK

```
⊞ Physical Frame
⊟ IEEE 802.11 MAC Protocol
   ┊── Function              CTS
   ⊞ PLCP Header
   ⊟ Frame Control Byte 0
   ┊   ┊── Protocol Level    [xxxxxx00]  0
   ┊   ┊── Type              [xxxx01xx]  Control
   ┊   ┊── Sub-Type          [1100xxxx]  CTS
   ⊟ Frame Control Byte 1
   ┊   ┊── Order             [0xxxxxxx]  off
   ┊   ┊── WEP               [x0xxxxxx]  off
   ┊   ┊── More Data         [xx0xxxxx]  off
   ┊   ┊── Power Mgmt        [xxx0xxxx]  off
   ┊   ┊── Retry             [xxxx0xxx]  off
   ┊   ┊── More Fragments    [xxxxx0xx]  off
   ┊   ┊── From DS           [xxxxxx0x]  off
   ┊   ┊── To DS             [xxxxxxx0]  off
   ┊── Duration ID           1341
   ⊟ Receiver Address
       ┊── Hex Address       00-0D-88-E5-D3-2A
       ┊── Group Bit         [xxxxxxx0 xxxxxxxx xxxxxxxx xxxxxxxx xxxxxxxx]  off
       ┊── Local Bit         [xxxxxx0x xxxxxxxx xxxxxxxx xxxxxxxx xxxxxxxx]  off
       ┊── Logical Names     [[AirLink]]
       ┊── Vendor Name       D-link
```

## *Data*

```
⊞ Physical Frame
⊟ IEEE 802.11 MAC Protocol
    Function          Data
  ⊞ PLCP Header
  ⊟ Frame Control Byte 0
      Protocol Level   [xxxxxx00]  0
      Type             [xxxx10xx]  Data
      Sub-Type         [0000xxxx]  Data
  ⊟ Frame Control Byte 1
      Order            [0xxxxxxx]  off
      WEP              [x0xxxxxx]  off
      More Data        [xx0xxxxx]  off
      Power Mgmt       [xxx0xxxx]  off
      Retry            [xxxx0xxx]  off
      More Fragments   [xxxxx0xx]  off
      From DS          [xxxxxx0x]  off
      To DS            [xxxxxxx1]  on
    Duration ID        162
  ⊟ BSSID
      Hex Address      00-09-B7-7E-E9-AA
      Group Bit        [xxxxxxx0 xxxxxxxx xxxxxxxx xxxxxxxx xxxxxxxx]  off
      Local Bit        [xxxxxx0x xxxxxxxx xxxxxxxx xxxxxxxx xxxxxxxx]  off
      Logical Names    [[Aironet-350AP]]
      Vendor Name      Cisco Systems
  ⊟ Source Address
      Hex Address      00-40-96-A2-F4-34
      Group Bit        [xxxxxxx0 xxxxxxxx xxxxxxxx xxxxxxxx xxxxxxxx]  off
      Local Bit        [xxxxxx0x xxxxxxxx xxxxxxxx xxxxxxxx xxxxxxxx]  off
      Logical Names    [[Aironet-PCI]]
      Vendor Name      Aironet Wireless Communication
  ⊟ Destination Address
      Hex Address      00-00-62-A1-83-53
      Group Bit        [xxxxxxx0 xxxxxxxx xxxxxxxx xxxxxxxx xxxxxxxx]  off
      Local Bit        [xxxxxx0x xxxxxxxx xxxxxxxx xxxxxxxx xxxxxxxx]  off
      Logical Names    [[D1DC2S2]]
      Vendor Name      Bull Hn Information Systems
    Fragment           [xxxxxxxx xxxx0000]  0
    Sequence           [01000001 1100xxxx]  1052
⊞ IEEE 802.2 Logical Link Control
⊞ IEEE Sub-Network Access Protocol
⊞ Internet Protocol
⊞ User Datagram Protocol
```

## Data Fragment with more fragments to follow

- fragmentation threshold is set at transmitter
- fragmentation may compensate for large frame data corruption due to RF

```
⊞ Physical Frame
⊟ IEEE 802.11 MAC Protocol
    Function          Data
  ⊞ PLCP Header
  ⊟ Frame Control Byte 0
      Protocol Level   [xxxxxx00]  0
      Type             [xxxx10xx]  Data
      Sub-Type         [0000xxxx]  Data
  ⊟ Frame Control Byte 1
      Order            [0xxxxxxx]  off
      WEP              [x1xxxxxx]  on
      More Data        [xx0xxxxx]  off
      Power Mgmt       [xxx0xxxx]  off
      Retry            [xxxx0xxx]  off
      More Fragments   [xxxxx1xx]  on
      From DS          [xxxxxx1x]  on
      To DS            [xxxxxxx0]  off
  ⊞ WEP Information
    Duration ID        523
  ⊞ Destination Address
  ⊞ BSSID
  ⊞ Source Address
    Fragment           [xxxxxxxx xxxx0010]  2
    Sequence           [00100011 0001xxxx]  561
```

## *ACK: standard*

```
⊞ Physical Frame
⊟ IEEE 802.11 MAC Protocol
    Function            ACK
  ⊞ PLCP Header
  ⊟ Frame Control Byte 0
      Protocol Level    [xxxxxx00]  0
      Type              [xxxx01xx]  Control
      Sub-Type          [1101xxxx]  ACK
  ⊟ Frame Control Byte 1
      Order             [0xxxxxxx]  off
      WEP               [x0xxxxxx]  off
      More Data         [xx0xxxxx]  off
      Power Mgmt        [xxx0xxxx]  off
      Retry             [xxxx0xxx]  off
      More Fragments    [xxxxx0xx]  off
      From DS           [xxxxxx0x]  off
      To DS             [xxxxxxx0]  off
    Duration ID         0
  ⊟ Receiver Address
      Hex Address       00-40-96-A2-F4-34
      Group Bit         [xxxxxxx0 xxxxxxxx xxxxxxxx xxxxxxxx xxxxxxxx]  off
      Local Bit         [xxxxxx0x xxxxxxxx xxxxxxxx xxxxxxxx xxxxxxxx]  off
      Logical Names     [[Aironet-PCI]]
      Vendor Name       Aironet Wireless Communication
```

## *ACK: in fragmentation burst*

Duration value protects next data fragment

```
⊞ Physical Frame
⊟ IEEE 802.11 MAC Protocol
    Function            ACK
  ⊞ PLCP Header
  ⊟ Frame Control Byte 0
      Protocol Level    [xxxxxx00]  0
      Type              [xxxx01xx]  Control
      Sub-Type          [1101xxxx]  ACK
  ⊟ Frame Control Byte 1
      Order             [0xxxxxxx]  off
      WEP               [x0xxxxxx]  off
      More Data         [xx0xxxxx]  off
      Power Mgmt        [xxx0xxxx]  off
      Retry             [xxxx0xxx]  off
      More Fragments    [xxxxx0xx]  off
      From DS           [xxxxxx0x]  off
      To DS             [xxxxxxx0]  off
    Duration ID         448
  ⊟ Receiver Address
      Hex Address       00-09-B7-7E-E9-AA
      Group Bit         [xxxxxxx0 xxxxxxxx xxxxxxxx xxxxxxxx xxxxxxxx]  off
      Local Bit         [xxxxxx0x xxxxxxxx xxxxxxxx xxxxxxxx xxxxxxxx]  off
      Logical Names     [[Aironet-350AP]]
      Vendor Name       Cisco Systems
```

## Null Data

Communicates the PwrMgmt bit state. Following this frame the STA enters PS-mode and all unicast frames destined for the STA are buffered at the AP. A second Null-data frame with PwrMgmt bit reset indicates that STA has entered AM (active mode.)

```
⊞ Physical Frame
⊟ IEEE 802.11 MAC Protocol
   ⋯ Function              Null
   ⊞ PLCP Header
   ⊟ Frame Control Byte 0
      ⋯ Protocol Level     [xxxxxx00]  0
      ⋯ Type               [xxxx10xx]  Data
      ⋯ Sub-Type           [0100xxxx]  Null
   ⊟ Frame Control Byte 1
      ⋯ Order              [0xxxxxxx]  off
      ⋯ WEP                [x0xxxxxx]  off
      ⋯ More Data          [xx0xxxxx]  off
      ⋯ Power Mgmt         [xxx1xxxx]  on
      ⋯ Retry              [xxxx0xxx]  off
      ⋯ More Fragments     [xxxxx0xx]  off
      ⋯ From DS            [xxxxxx0x]  off
      ⋯ To DS              [xxxxxxx1]  on
   ⋯ Duration ID           117
   ⊟ BSSID
      ⋯ Hex Address        00-09-B7-7E-E9-AA
      ⋯ Group Bit          [xxxxxxx0 xxxxxxxx xxxxxxxx xxxxxxxx xxxxxxxx]  off
      ⋯ Local Bit          [xxxxxx0x xxxxxxxx xxxxxxxx xxxxxxxx xxxxxxxx]  off
      ⋯ Logical Names      [[Aironet-350AP]]
      ⋯ Vendor Name        Cisco Systems
   ⊞ Source Address
   ⊞ Destination Address
   ⋯ Fragment              [xxxxxxxx xxxx0000]  0
   ⋯ Sequence              [10001100 0110xxxx]  2246
```

# Appendix B: Reason Codes

The Reason Codes field specifies the why an unsolicited disassociation or deauthentication frame is transmitted. Drivers that don't examine the reason code tend to repeat the action that originally caused the disassociation or deauthentication frame to occur. The driver should either modify its logic based on the reason code or provide a user dialog to address the issue. The reason code can be directly observed in a network monitor capture.

| Reason Code | Meaning |
| --- | --- |
| 0 | Reserved |
| 1 | Unspecified Reason |
| 2 | Previous authentication is no longer valid |
| 3 | Deauthenticated because sending STA is leaving the ESS |
| 4 | Disassociated due to inactivity |
| 5 | Disassociated because AP is unable to handle all currently associated STAs |
| 6 | Class 2 frame received from nonauthenticated STA |
| 7 | Class 3 frame received from nonassociated STA |
| 8 | Disassociated because sending STA is leaving BSS |
| 9 | STA requesting (re)association is not authenticated with responding STA |
| 10 | Disassociated because the information in the Power Capability IE is unacceptable |
| 11 | Disassociated because the information in the Supported Channels IE is unacceptable |
| 12 | Reserved |
| 13 | Invalid IE |
| 14 | MIC (message integrity check) field failure |
| 15 | 4-Way Handshake timeout |
| 16 | Group key update timeout |
| 17 | IE in 4-Way Handshake is different form (Re)Association Req, Probe Res or Beacon |
| 18 | Group cipher is not valid |
| 19 | Pairwise cipher is not valid |
| 20 | AKMP is not valid |
| 21 | Unsupported RSN IE version |
| 22 | Invalid RSN IE capabilities |
| 23 | 802.1x authentication failed |
| 24 | Cipher suite is rejected per security policy |
| 25 – 31 | Reserved |
| 32 | Disassociated for unspecified, QoS related reason |
| 33 | Disassociated because QAP (QoS AP) lacks sufficient bandwidth for this QSTA (QoS STA) |
| 34 | Disassociated because of excessive number of frames that need to be acknowledged, but are not acknowledged for AP transmissions and/or poor channel conditions |

| 35 | Disassociated because QSTA is transmitting outside the limits of its TXOPs |
|---|---|
| 36 | Requested from peer QSTA as the QSTA is leaving the QBSS (QoS BSS) |
| 37 | Requested from peer QSTA as it does not want to use the mechanism |
| 38 | Request from peer QSTA as the QSTA received frames using the mechanism for which a set up is required |
| 39 | Requested from peer QSTA due to time out |
| 40 – 44 | Reserved |
| 45 | Peer QSTA does not support the requested cipher suite |

# Appendix C: Status Codes

Status Code field is 16-bits and indicates the status of the request operation. Zero specifies success; a non-zero value indicates a failure. Status code errors appear in authentication or association/reassociation response frames.

| Status Code | Meaning |
|---|---|
| 0 | Successful |
| 1 | Unspecified failure |
| 2 - 9 | Reserved |
| 10 | Cannot support all request capabilities in the Capability IE |
| 11 | Reassociation denied due to inability to confirm the association |
| 12 | Association denied due to reason outside the scope of the standard |
| 13 | Responding STA does not support the specified authentication algorithm |
| 14 | Received an authentication frame with authentication transaction sequence number out of expected sequence |
| 15 | Authentication rejected because of challenge failure |
| 16 | Authentication rejected due to timeout waiting for next frame in sequence |
| 17 | Association denied because AP is unable to handle additional associated STAs |
| 18 | Association denied because requesting STA does not support all of the data rates in the basic rate set |
| 19 | Association denied because requesting STA does not support the short preamble option |
| 20 | Association denied because requesting STA does not support the PBCC modulation option |
| 21 | Association denied because requesting STA does not support the channel agility option |
| 22 | Association denied because spectrum management capability is required |
| 23 | Association denied because the information in the power capability IE is unacceptable |
| 24 | Association request rejected because the information in the support channels IE is unacceptable |
| 25 | Association denied because requesting STA does not support the short slot time option |
| 26 | Association denied because requesting STA does not support the DSSS-OFDM option |
| 27 – 31 | Reserved |
| 32 | Unspecified QoS-related failure |
| 33 | Association denied because QAP has insufficient bandwidth to handle another QSTA |
| 34 | Association denied due to excessive frame loss rates and/or poor conditions on current operating channel |
| 35 | Association with QBSS denied because requesting STA does not support the |

| | QoS facility |
|---|---|
| 36 | Reserved |
| 37 | Request declined |
| 38 | Request not successful because one or more parameters have invalid values |
| 39 | TS not created because the request cannot be honored - a suggested TSPEC is provided so that the initiating QSTA may attempt to set another TS with the suggested changes to the TSPEC |
| 40 | Invalid IE |
| 41 | Group cipher not valid |
| 42 | Pairwise cipher not valid |
| 43 | AKMP not valid |
| 44 | Unsupported RSN IE version |
| 45 | Invalid RSN IE capabilities |
| 46 | Cipher suite rejected per security policy |
| 47 | TS not created – the HC may be capable of creating a TS in response to a request after the time indicated in the TS Delay IE |
| 48 | Direct link not allowed in the BSS by policy |
| 49 | Destination STA not present within this QBSS |
| 50 | Destination STA not a QSTA |
| 51 - above | Reserved |

# Appendix D: Information Elements

Information elements enable beacon and probe response frames to be expanded to support new standard and proprietary information. Network monitors do not decode all proprietary IEs.

| Status Code | Meaning |
|---|---|
| 0 | SSID |
| 1 | Supported rates |
| 2 | FH parameter set |
| 3 | DS parameter set |
| 4 | CF parameter set |
| 5 | TIM |
| 6 | IBSS parameter set |
| 7 | Country |
| 8 | Hopping pattern parameters |
| 9 | Hopping pattern table |
| 10 | Request |
| 11 | QBSS load |
| 12 | EDCA parameter set |
| 13 | TSPEC (traffic specification) |
| 14 | Traffic classification |
| 15 | Schedule |
| 16 | Challenge text |
| 17-31 | Reserved for challenge text extension |
| 32 | Power constraint |
| 33 | Power capability |
| 34 | TPC request |
| 35 | TPC report |
| 36 | Supported channels |
| 37 | Channel switch announcement |
| 38 | Measurement request |
| 39 | Measurement report |
| 40 | Quiet |
| 41 | IBSS DFS |
| 42 | ERP Information |
| 43 | TS delay |
| 44 | TCLAS processing |
| 45 | Reserved |
| 46 | QoS Capability |
| 47 | Reserved |
| 48 | RSN |

| | |
|---|---|
| 49 | Reserved |
| 50 | Extended supported rates |
| 51-220 | Reserved |
| 221 | Vendor specific (WPA/RSN) |
| 222-255 | Reserved |

# Index

Printed in the United States
206274BV00011B/9-10/A

9 781425 907358